THEATER OF STATE

Theater of State

PARLIAMENT AND POLITICAL CULTURE

IN EARLY STUART ENGLAND

Chris R. Kyle

STANFORD UNIVERSITY PRESS

Stanford, California

Stanford University Press
Stanford, California
© 2012 by the Board of Trustees of the
Leland Stanford Junior University
All rights reserved

Library of Congress Cataloging-in-Publication Data

Kyle, Chris R., author.
  Theater of state : Parliament and political culture in early Stuart
England / Chris R. Kyle.
    pages cm.
  Includes bibliographical references and index.
  ISBN 978-0-8047-5288-6(cloth : alk. paper)
    1. Great Britain. Parliament—History—17th century. 2. Political
culture—Great Britain—History—17th century. 3. Political
oratory—Great Britain—History—17th century. 4. Communication
in politics—Great Britain—History—17th century. 5. Great
Britain—Politics and government—1603–1649. I. Title.

JN534.K95   2012

306.20941'09032—dc22   2011032091

Printed in the United States of America
on acid-free, archival-quality paper

Typeset at Stanford University Press in 10/13.5 Galliard

For Dympna

Contents

Acknowledgments

In the process of writing a book one of the most enjoyable tasks is working out the acknowledgments. It means that the book is nearly finished (at least, I don't know anyone who writes the acknowledgments first) and provides the author with the opportunity to bestow a modest form of immortality on friends, colleagues, and libraries.

Theater of State started as an idea in Auckland, was planned in London, San Marino, and Washington, DC, and finally built and opened in Syracuse. Perhaps not an unusual geographical spread in distance but most likely a unique one. In all these cities and many others, countless scholars have generously shared references and ideas, and provided encouragement. The Folger Shakespeare Library has been a welcome second home throughout these years and a generous benefactor as well, through a long-term Mellon Fellowship. My thanks are due to all the Reading Room staff, especially Betsy Walsh and Georgiana Ziegler, the fellowships administrator Carol Brobeck, the curator of manuscripts, Heather Wolfe, and the director, Gail Kern Paster. In San Marino, the Henry E. Huntington Library not only provided a short-term fellowship but also proved a delightful oasis of intellectual lunchtime conversation and postprandial strolling in the gardens; thanks in particular to my fellow walkers, the late David Underdown, with whom I probably shared more conversation about cricket than early modern England, and Norman Jones, who, bemused by cricket, was forced to discuss seventeenth-century Parliaments. It would be facetious to list all the archives and their staff who have contributed to this project, but it would also be remiss not to acknowledge those at the Parliamentary Archives (HLRO), the Guildhall Library, Duke Humfrey's Library in the

Bodleian, and the British Library Manuscripts Room for their unfailing assistance over the years. And to all those libraries and archives that allow digital photography, thanks from a grateful scholar for making life easier and helping to preserve the record of the past. I would also like to thank Valerie Cromwell, Paul Seaward, and Andrew Thrush at the History of Parliament Trust for access to unpublished material from the 1604–29 section. My colleagues, too, at Syracuse University have provided a stimulating and intellectual environment in which to work, while the office staff (Patti Blincoe, Fran Bockus, and Patti Bohrer) have always made it a pleasure to walk in the door. Samantha Herrick, Norman Kutcher, and Dennis Romano, in particular, have all read sections or all of the manuscript and proffered many helpful suggestions as well as their friendship. I am also grateful to the deans of the Maxwell School of Citizenship and Public Affairs, and the College of Arts and Sciences for allowing me to take leave during this project.

My debt to others working in the field of early modern history is clear from the footnotes and bibliography, and I have benefited greatly from their advice and ideas: Susan Amussen, Ian Archer, Alastair Bellany, Linda Clark, Pauline Croft, Richard Cust, David Dean, Barbara Donagan, Paul Hammer, Tim Harris, David Hayton, Simon Healy, Sean Kelsey, Peter Lake, Patrick Little, Michael Mendle, Markku Peltonen, Stephen Roberts, the late Conrad Russell, David Scott, David Smith, Laura Stewart, Andrew Thrush, and Rachel Weil deserve special thanks. I have been fortunate as well to be drawn into the orbit of Renaissance literature, and this book has been changed for the better through the conversations and perspective of Fran Dolan, Jean Howard, Rebecca Lemon, Zachary Lesser, Laurie Maguire, Pat Parker, Bill Sherman, Peter Stallybrass, and Garrett Sullivan. I am especially grateful to those who have read much of the manuscript, commented on papers, and done it all with a generosity of sharing their intellect and friendship. Tom Cogswell and David Cressy served as enlightened readers for Stanford University Press, and I am very grateful for their astute comments. Lori Anne Ferrell over many years has been a wonderfully encouraging friend, and her suggestions have vastly improved the book. Paul Hunneyball was kind enough to contribute his considerable map-making skills and read many pages of the typescript. To all the above I owe a great intellectual debt.

If books are not completed in intellectual isolation, then neither are they started or finished without the encouragement and support of friends (largely) outside the world of early modern history and literature. To Alyson, Annette, Rich, Paul and Catherine, Mark and Sara, Mark and Cristina, Eric and Nancy, Dieter and Daniela, Deborah and David, Bob and Deb, Jolynn and Mike, Ethan and Amy, Carol and Andrew, David and Deirdre, and my welcoming father-in-law, the late Eamonn Callaghan, and wonderful sister-in-law, Margaret Newcombe—thanks to you all. During the final stages of this book, two people, without whom it would never have been started let alone finished, passed away. In memoriam: a great historian, friend, and bon vivant, my PhD supervisor Michael Graves. Sadly, too, my mother, Alison Rae Kyle, did not live to see the final product. She was a wonderful, kind person who is deeply missed. But both in friendship and intellectually the biggest debt I owe is to Jason Peacey, who has read the entire manuscript (many times), spent countless hours in coffee bars, restaurants, record offices, conferences, and most frequently at 'The Jack,' listening to my ideas ranging from the improbable to the unprovable, all with unfailing generosity, patience, and a willingness to buy the next round.

This book is dedicated my brilliant wife, Dympna Callaghan, whose intellectual energy, gentle critiques, and positive influence are felt on every page. From our first meeting at the Huntington (thanks, Rachel) she has patiently endured my archival visits, wielded a red pen through every page I have written, and learned more about the three reading procedure for legislation than any person should ever have to know.

Introduction

In 1628 John Selden claimed that the 'secret' counsels of Parliament were being laid on bookstalls.[1] Shortly thereafter, Charles I dispensed entirely with the 'counsel,' vowing to govern without Parliament and ushering in the period of 'personal rule.' This book tells the story of the expansion and creation of new public spheres in and around Parliament in the early Stuart period. My analysis focuses on two closely interconnected narratives, the changing nature of communication and discourse within the parliamentary chambers themselves, and the interaction of Parliament with the wider world of political dialogue and the dissemination of information. The aim of this book is to examine the political and social culture of Parliament, concentrating on the rapidly changing practices of Parliament in the 1620s in print culture, rhetorical strategy, and lobbying as Parliament moved toward the center stage of politics, becoming a 'theater of state' and the 'point of contact' for a national audience.[2]

John Hooker drew attention to the physical resemblance between Parliament and the theater in 1572 when he remarked that the interior structure of the Lower House was 'like a theatre.'[3] With the advent of public, political debate and exchange, Parliament became the preeminent institution of the 'public sphere' and as it did so, its intrinsically theatrical dynamics, vividly illustrated in the 1620s, came to comport more fully with the theater than with any other early modern venue, institution, or practice. As a place of staged rhetorical performance in an auditorium as vigorous and dynamic as any playhouse, Parliament was understood by its members and by early moderns more generally to be an institution whose structures and practices were closely analogous to those of the theater. However, Parliament was theatrical not only in terms of its increasingly important relationship to the public it served and represented. Parliament was preeminently a place of performance, and the late Elizabethan and early Stuart period is characterized by a growing awareness of this 'audience' outside the walls of the chambers. What follows, then, is an exploration of the intersection of oral and manuscript transmission with the printed, political, and theatrical cultures of sixteenth- and early-seventeenth-century parliamentary history.

Parliament was displayed, perused, and sold as printed matter. This study contextualizes the 'writings of Parliament' in which the material product of Parliaments, its texts—official and unofficial; printed and manuscript—were viewed as part of a growing consciousness of politics and interaction with Parliament among an increasingly broad section of the populace. The project thus engages with and forms a part of the recent emphasis on early modern political and material culture, especially the concept of a post-Reformation public sphere and the notion of 'popularity.'[4] I look to move parliamentary history in a new direction away from the traditional emphasizes that have long dominated the field—relations between the Crown and Parliament; introspective studies of procedure; and empiricist grand narratives—toward an understanding of how the public perceived Parliament and how peers and MPs viewed their responsibilities toward the public and also as part of the political elite.

While this study engages with the recent intellectual approaches to early Stuart political culture,[5] typified by Tom Cogswell, Richard Cust, and Alastair Bellany, it draws as well on material approaches first identified by 'old-school' historians such as Wallace Notestein on printed parliamentary material and Sir J. E. Neale on the ethos of the Commons chamber.[6] In melding high political culture with the daily activities of Parliament, the chapters that follow point toward a new interpretation of Parliament in the 1620s,[7] one which in many ways foreshadows the developments in propaganda, print, petitioning, and rhetorical strategies that have hitherto been thought to demarcate Parliament in the early 1640s from its 1620s predecessors.[8] This is not to state that we can find in the earlier period the sophisticated use of propaganda, petitioning, and mass media that marks out the key developments in strategy and procedure in the Long Parliament. But it is to suggest that many of these elements were present in embryonic form by the time Charles I dissolved Parliament in 1629. I argue that the break with the past in 1640 was not so radical or emphatic as traditional scholarship has suggested. Thus my study calls into question the traditional periodization of early modern Parliaments in which the early Stuart Parliaments have been lumped together largely as the more irascible stepchildren of their Elizabethan predecessors. I argue instead that the 1620s witnessed a sharp break from those beforehand in management, procedure, and political culture,[9] and in doing so I place Parliament in the post-Reformation public sphere identified by Peter Lake and Steven Pincus.[10] Their reconfiguration of political pressure, who brings it to bear and how, is located in the center, within the enclosed groups of elites seeking to pressure the Elizabethan and early Stuart monarchy. Like Lake and Pincus, however, I find that the emergence of this public sphere is not a linear progression but something that ebbs and flows around a series of political and religious flashpoints. They cite, for example, the Marprelate controversy of the late 1580s and the attacks on George Villiers, Duke of Buckingham, in early Caroline England. But it was in the 1620s, as they note, that 'the heady mixture of international confessional conflict, domestic religious dispute, royal marriage, war and the rise to power of a classic evil counselor combined to create a sustained pitch of public political discourse equal to that achieved in the 1590s.'[11] *Theater of State* examines this 'sustained political discourse' and how it impacted most heavily on Parliament where print, for the first time, competed with scribal documents, where new management techniques were required to promote legislation and grievances, and where the words of MPs and peers recorded verbatim were circulated throughout England.

This book, then, fills one of the major lacunae in parliamentary history—namely, that gap between the much studied and center-orientated public spheres of Elizabethan politics and that of the 'transitional moment' of the British Civil Wars. This history, therefore, starts within the chambers, examining parliamentary discourse, procedures, and committees. The next section of this narrative progresses to Parliament's communication with all that lay beyond it, and finally, the third phase of this narrative addresses the ways in which the nation penetrated the boundaries of Parliament by means of petitions, lobbying, and the physical presence of nonparliamentary persons at the very threshold of the Commons and Lords. This is a history then that moves from the inside out, and back again, charting the flow and exchange of information across a much more porous and permeable boundary than previous histories of Parliament have hitherto allowed. The flow of discursive information across the material structure of St. Stephen's

Chapel grew exponentially as the 1620s progressed. It must be emphasized, however, that this multidirectional movement of information, far from being smooth and harmonious, is often characterized by stops and starts, moments of almost violent intrusion of the public world upon Parliament's institutional structures, and by the fits and starts of political contest and engagement.

Chapter One examines the communicative strategies within the Houses where success or failure was determined by how MPs and peers navigated the minefields of eloquence and rhetoric. Nowhere was the porous nature of Parliament activity more evident than in the ways reputations were made and lost on the center stage of Parliament, the debating chamber itself. Some members emerged with their reputations enhanced by the power of their oratory, commanding attention and the presence of the House. Others, however, singularly failed and were booed off the stage. They failed through rambling speech, poor diction, and argument, but also because of politics. Presenting the government's position on unpopular topics (subsidies, monopolies, the Petition of Right, for example) required a mastery of rhetoric and the institutional awareness to read the mood of the Houses.

Reading, or at least counting, these parliamentary speeches has a long established historiographical tradition. From the Namierite biographies of the *History of Parliament* volumes, to the tabulations of 'opposition' speeches counted by D. H. Willson and Williams M. Mitchell, MPs, in particular, have been ranked by the number of their verbal contributions.[12] Gradually but steadily, government speakers gave way to those who critiqued government policy in the 1620s, and by the end of the decade the official and semiofficial spokesmen for royal programs were battered down into silence or floundering rhetoric by the newly emergent 'opposition party.' More recently, Peter Mack has argued that in the Commons, traditional humanist training in rhetoric found its fullest expression sitting alongside the 'dialectic and resemble interventions in university disputations.'[13] Both approaches, however, suggest a one-way discourse, and neither method fully captures how members who commented upon speeches in the chambers, and noted down their reflections in diaries and journals, actually received them. My study argues, on the contrary, that it was all about audience. Thus, this chapter examines the ways those present in the chambers commented upon the effectiveness of individual speeches (and speakers) and what constituted 'fittest speech.' Furthermore, I situate speech in the reality of a chamber in the Commons dominated not so much by the controlled conditions of rhetoric or formal debate, but located in an often unruly and intimidating atmosphere of extemporaneous interjection and response. The chapter also demonstrates how parliamentary speech changed from Elizabethan Parliaments, dominated in large part by rhetoric and eloquent orality, to the short and sharp-witted speeches of the 'vipers' that Charles I complained about in his closing address to the 1628–29 Parliament.[14] Long-winded and often tedious orations were on the wane, replaced by frequent interventions in debate and by speeches characterized by their brevity. In part too, an institutional change had come over the Commons. As debate and more adversarial rhetoric increased, the rules of House that prohibited members from speaking more than once a day on a particular topic no longer adequately served the needs of the Commons. Growing out of this institutional need, matters of contention were pushed out of the daily business presided over by the government-appointed Speaker and into the free-flowing arena of committees, particularly the Committee of the Whole House.[15]

Unfettered from the shackles of formal debate, the oral delivery of members frequently shifted from set piece speeches (although this residual mode was perhaps predictably still valued at Joint Conferences with the Lords) to short and frequent interventions. This carried over from the Committee to the House in formal session, shifting the paradigm somewhat away from classical humanist training in rhetoric. Parliamentary practices became less and less like the university found by Mack and more a distinct rhetorical practice that began to part company in important and decisive ways with those institutions that had hitherto shaped its rhetorical paradigms. Adversarial rhetoric dominated the chamber as the residual right of performance and reaction gave way to the implicit right of response and critique. The by-product of this was an increasingly unruly and noisy Commons as MPs struggled to make themselves heard (and listened to) amid the frequent interruptions—be they vocal or otherwise. It is this soundscape of Parliament that the next chapter addresses. In the Commons in particular, noise was an ever-present element, often deliberately utilized to make a political point or to drown out those who engaged in long and tedious speech. Sound was a weapon ready to be deployed at any given moment.

Away from the general disturbance of the parliamentary soundscape caused by the to-ing and fro-ing of members and the general hum of whispered conversation, noise was one of the main avenues of social control. The House, as a collective, engaged in noisy and disruptive practices designed to force speakers to sit down and end their speeches, including heckling, coordinated humming, loud hawking, and stomping of feet. Although speakers frequently complained about the interruptions, the collective will could be curtailed neither by the orator nor even by the intervention of the Speaker of the House. Inside St. Stephen's Chapel, an often hostile and intimidating atmosphere awaited the unwary representative, and it is little wonder that the vast majority of MPs are not recorded as having made a speech at all. From a few glimpses of MPs' behavior, it is also possible to tie noise more specifically to the physical space of St. Stephen's Chapel. The Speaker at one end, aided by the Privy Council surrounding him, kept decorum and business flowing as much as possible; at the other end of the chamber, where the doors provided access to the House and a mezzanine level overflow space, less decorous behavior prevailed. At times, noise levels were so extreme and the general hubbub reached such a raucous pitch in the Commons that the din inhibited the communicative practices of the diarists. Parliamentary scribblers found themselves powerless to pass on accurate information to their friends in country because they were simply unable to hear the speeches at all.

The soundscape of Parliament also rang loudly with laughter as the House exerted social control and utilized the noise of mirth to drown out and deride speakers. Following Keith Thomas's and Quentin Skinner's analyses of early modern laughter as a form of shaming, the chapter examines how it was used in the chamber and the impact of laughter upon individual MPs.[16] From those whose wit captivated the House, to MPs forced to shout to make themselves heard above the guffaws and snorts of their fellow members, to others cowed into silence by scorn, laughter could define the reputation of speakers and thus the weight given to their pronouncements.

The communicative and political impact of sound was not always verbal. Like laughter, silence worked as a political weapon—an expression of the collective will in which the Commons expressed their dissatisfaction with government policies by refusing to speak and remaining silent.[17] Away from high politics, silence was utilized to express shock at the actions of individuals—a House stunned by the actions of one of its members. Noise (or the lack thereof) played an important part in the way in which Parliament as a body represented its views to the government and to those within the chambers, a noise that became increasingly deafening as the 1620s progressed.

In the second part of the book, I outline the material culture of Parliament both within the chambers and in the dissemination of parliamentary news through the countryside. Chapter Three concentrates on the way in which MPs and peers recorded the words spoken in the chambers. For despite the extensive historiographical tradition that situates the writings of members in the social and political world of early modern Parliament, insufficient attention has been paid to what diarists chose to record, how they selected their material, and why diaries multiplied in the early Stuart period.

Parliament had long functioned as a court in its own right with an official written record—the Parliament Roll. During the sixteenth and early seventeenth century the journals kept by its clerks (clerk of the Parliament in the Lords, and underclerk in the Commons) became more formalized and part of the official record of the house. This was also reflected in the contiguous relationship between these officers of the house and those interested in the proceedings or procedures of Parliament. MPs copied speeches from the Commons Journal while the clerks occasionally relied on diarists and those who had spoken to fill in what they had missed. MPs took notes for a variety of reasons—some to provide their patrons in the Lords with information on the proceedings of the 'other house'; some no doubt for circulation among family members and friends at home; and many for their own benefit—sometimes simply as a record of proceedings or for future reference. MPs listened carefully and copied down the arguments of their fellow members' speeches along with whatever classical and biblical references they could catch. But parliamentary diaries as a form of writing were no different from any other type of diary. Some, such as those of John Pym in the 1620s,[18] were neatly drawn into legible, seamless books, while others were the hasty hurried notes of a member busy trying to scrawl down every word. These were often riddled with gaps where the author planned to fill in the names and speeches later but never did so. Some MPs started with full annotations and then tailed away as the length of the session and physical requirements wore down the writer. Members (John Hawarde in 1624 is the obvious example) employed devices such as Law French and types of shorthand or abbreviations of common words to ease their task.[19] Hasty scrawlings over the page, barely legible writing, and shorthand leave the modern-day reader with the difficult task of reading the diaries as well as the impression of a court—the theater of state—in action.

This can further be illustrated by the amount of extant material. For the 1621 Parliament more than three thousand pages have been printed of diaries alone.[20] Even leaving aside other forms of material relating to Parliament (newsletters, separates, drafts of legislation, petitions), some of which were written and copied for sale, the surviving number of diaries gives rise to a view of the Commons awash in a sea of papers and scribbling MPs. The way in which the diarists took notes varied from those who jotted comments on parliamentary documents such as breviates of acts, petitions, or separates to those who diligently attempted to record every word. Some annotations were made in pencil, including more than the odd doodle or caricature during tedious speeches, while others used pen and ink. The latter form of writing must have been a very public and possibly cumbersome activity. Even the small writing cases of the seventeenth century needed to hold the usual implements—pen, ink, knives for sharpening quills, and sand for erasing or blotting. The clerks of the Parliament had their own tables to write upon, but MPs would have been balancing their writing material on their knees while sitting on cramped benches. The task was made more difficult as this was a theater in which the MPs were participants/actors as well as the audience. They came and went from the chamber, interrupted speeches, talked to each other, and occasionally stood up to yell and hawk at other speakers. Throughout the 1620s to this noise and confusion was added the sound of more than a dozen pens scratching on paper as the clerks and members took notes. The effect of this noise, scribbling, and motion adds a dimension to the chamber that is far removed from static representations that have come down to us today through woodcuts and other images of 'Parliament at Work.'

What went on in the parliamentary chambers definitely did not stay there. Of course, the members who scrawled, as Wallace Notestein, Fritz Levy, and Richard Cust have effectively demonstrated, did not keep their notes to themselves, but circulated them widely throughout the land.[21] However, what is missing from this story and what this book addresses is the staggering amount of information circulated and available. Parliamentary material flew out of the chambers at a hitherto unknown rate giving lie to the maxim that the debates in Parliament were *arcana imperii*—secrets of state. Through newsletters, copies of proceedings taken in the House, and separates, it was possible by the end of the 1620s to obtain the relevant information on every day's parliamentary activity. While it had not reached the formalization we find in the early 1640s with *Daily Occurrences* or *The Perfect Diurnall,* and nor was most of it printed, in many ways these scribal and sometimes printed copies provided the same news of daily proceedings.[22]

The final section of this book outlines the way in which the public interacted with Parliament, whether through physical attendance at Westminster, petitions and lobbying, or print culture. Part Three thus examines the connectedness of parliamentary activity with the physical surrounds in which the institution met. Crucial in this regard is the way in which members of Parliament interacted with the wider public and the daily activities of Westminster Palace—the bustling law courts, petitioners, sightseers, and the city itself. The beginning of this section examines the intrinsically public and theatrical nature of Parliament, from its formal public displays of ritual designed to reinforce its status as the supreme political institution, to the more casual interactions with its audience by way of the intersection of the political representatives with the denizens of London and Westminster. From this perspective, Parliament becomes less isolated and more integrated with the economy of London and Westminster, its place reinforced as one of the three main engines of the Westminster economy.[23] The orchestrated, status-driven nature of the opening and closing ceremonies as members and peers processed to and from Westminster offers a tantalizing glimpse into the political culture of display and its attendant power relations. It served both to make people part of the political process at the same time as it kept them at arm's length behind the specially constructed buntings or peering from windows on the processional route. At least that was true in theory. In practice those not specifically invited to the ceremonies often made themselves a part of them despite their official exclusion. From 'invading' the House of Lords to listening outside the doors of the Commons, Parliament was in many ways an open house. Although it has been consistently studied as a hermetically sealed enclosure, Parliament and its processes was itself in fact a permeable membrane, allowing both observation and involvement in the politics of state. Through this concentration on the space of parliamentary assembly, and the ways in which members interacted with the general populace around Parliament, we can see the development of an 'audience' watching, scrutinizing, and reporting the politics of state.

The communicative practice of Parliament changed in the 1620s, at once embracing a new-found closer engagement with those members of the public interacting with it and at the same time wary of change. Lobbying had long been an established feature of parliamentary activity.[24] But increasingly throughout the Tudor and early Stuart period, the parliamentary agenda became more packed with legislative business and matters of high politics. It became more and more difficult for individuals and pressure groups to find their way onto the docket. Adapting to this new world, lobbyists became more sophisticated, stepping up their gifts to parliamentary officials, wining and dining their representatives, and pushing their business through personal pressure in and around the chambers. But that was not sufficient—traditional practices of introducing legislation and persuading a few friends and allies in Parliament to forward their business no longer worked. And so increasingly those lobbying turned to print.

As both the recipient and disseminator of political information, Parliament shifted from a largely manuscript culture to one that embraced print. Printed petitions crept into Parliament in the late Elizabethan era but exploded in the 1620s, creating a new public sphere based around a printed culture in Parliament.[25] Petitions, lists of MPs and peers (in multiple editions), pamphlets addressed to Parliament, and, on occasion, speeches flowed off the printing presses into the chambers and through the doors of bookshops as the nation learned of parliamentary activities through print. When Charles I dissolved Parliament in 1629, in accordance with tradition, it was formally announced via a printed proclamation.[26] But by then the proclamation was competing for the discretionary shilling with dozens of scribal separates, printed speeches from John Glanville, Henry Marten and Benjamin Rudyerd, Thomas Walkley's catalogue of MPs and peers, religious and economic appeals to Parliament, and a multitude of sermons preached before Parliament.

The 1620s began with Parliament as a predominantly Elizabethan institution, one that William Cecil, Lord Burghley, would have felt familiar with, but it emerged from the decade as a more publicly aware body, deeply embedded in print culture and vigorous disputation. The 'institutional event' that Charles dissolved in 1629 was not the same one inherited by James in 1603. And while the personal rule may have put a stop to Parliament's engagement with the country (the ebbing of the post-Reformation public sphere), it did not take long in 1640 for the institutional memory to reveal itself.

PART ONE

Inside the Chambers

CHAPTER ONE

'Fittest Speech': Rhetoric and Debate

As Thomas Wentworth was concluding his oration on office-holding to the Commons on 17 March 1626, Sir Simon Weston rose to his feet and launched a virulent attack. His concern was not the substance of Wentworth's remarks or even their tone, but the manner of delivery: '[R]hetorical speeches here and amplifications take up time and are of no purpose.'[1] The House of Commons, in the midst of a fraught parliamentary session, following on from the failure and dissolution of the first Caroline Parliament the year before, did not have time for long-winded, flowery speeches. The clear implication was that Parliament was a place of business and that required debate not oratory. Two years later William Hakewill noted, '[We] should be rather logicians than rhetoricians.'[2] But it was Hakewill who also wrote that the ethos of the chamber was that 'such as speak are not stinted to any time for the length of their speech.'[3] Reconciling these two seemingly contradictory statements, to avoid excessive rhetorical flourishes but not be constrained by time, was the challenge faced by every member who spoke in the early modern House of Commons: most failed.[4]

As befitted the most prominent aspect of the parliamentary soundscape, speaking was governed by a series of rules. Sir Thomas Smith in his *De Republica Anglorum* (1583) provided an exposition on the conduct of those who wished to speak in the Commons:

> In the disputing is a mervelous good order used in the lower house. He that standeth uppe bareheaded is understood that he will speake to the bill. If moe stande uppe, who that first is judged to arise, is first harde, though the one doe prayse the law, the other diswade it, yet there is no altercation. For everie

man speaketh as to the speaker, not as one to an other, for that is against the order of the house. It is also taken against the order, to name him who ye doe confute, but by circumlocution, as he that speaketh with the bill, or he that spake against the bill, and gave this and this reason, dothe not satisfie but I am of the contrary opinion for this and this reason. And so with perpetuall Oration not with altercation, he goeth through till he do make an end.[5]

No one was allowed to speak twice to a bill on the same day, and usually debate on the bill did not take place until the second reading. However, when the House sat in committee or bills were assigned to individual committees, then members were free to speak as often as they liked (or the committee would allow). William Hakewill, in his tract on speaking in the Commons, suggested that speakers read their audience: '[He] that speaketh if he be observant shall easily perceive (even while he is speaking) how far he may presume upon the patience of the House in that regard.'[6] Sir Thomas Smith advised that

no reviling or nipping wordes must be used. For then all the House will crie, it is against the order. So that in such a multitude, and in such diversitie of mindes, and opinions, there is the greatest modestie and temperance of speech that can be used. Nevethelesse with moste doulce and gentle termes, they make their reasons as violent and as vehement the one against the other as they may.[7]

The well-nigh impossible degree of rhetorical poise demanded by this discerning, not to say hypersensitive, audience required walking the tightrope between forceful argument ('violent and as vehement') and the gentle arts of persuasion free from 'reviling' and 'nipping.' A similar code of conduct existed in the Lords, where members were not to speak in a 'personall, sharpe or taxing' manner. They too were restricted in naming other members and speaking only once to a bill on the floor of the House.[8] Members of both Houses were also expected to speak according to their conscience. The Parliament-man, John Hooker, considered that a member needed to be of 'such audacity as both can and will boldly utter and speak his mind according to his duty, and as occasion shall serve, for no man ought to be silent or dumb in that House, but according to his talent he must and ought to speak in the furtherance of the King and Commonwealth.'[9]

In order for members to be able to speak their conscience they required freedom of speech.[10] This was one of the four 'ancient privileges and liberties' that the Speaker of the Commons sued the monarch for at the opening of Parliament: '[T]hen that every one of ye house may have libertie of speech, and freely to utter, speake and declare his minde and oppinion to any Bil or question to be proponed,' in the words of John Hooker.[11] This did not mean, of course, either that members would be spared the 'crie' of 'the multitude of diverse minds' or that they were free to debate whatever subject they liked. Speeches touching on matters of the royal prerogative, especially foreign policy, were regularly admonished by the monarch and often expressly forbidden in the monarch's opening speech to the Parliament. Elizabeth bristled at the Commons meddling in the succession and her marital status; James dissolved the 1621 Parliament for criticizing his policy of a Spanish match for Prince Charles; and Charles more than once angrily rebuked the Commons for attacking his policies and his chief minister, George Villiers, Duke of Buckingham. Freedom of speech was a strictly limited notion and one, as we shall see, that increasingly became a point of conflict between the Crown and Parliament.

ORATORY

> Persuasion, explanation and argument are the province of rhetoric, the main component of Tudor grammar school education. Parliamentary oratory thus enables us to examine the impact of humanist rhetorical training in practice. At the same time, rhetorical theory can help us understand the effect of individual speeches as well as the broader implications of parliamentary discourse. (Peter Mack)[12]

Demosthenes's speeches, along with Cicero, Aristotle, and Quintilian, formed part of the early modern grammar school syllabus.[13] Pupils were taught to think of their speech in terms of persuasion and argument. 'Oratory represents, in its purest form, the proposition that *all* human speech is a form of persuasion.'[14] However, in a chamber composed of nearly five hundred people representing not only the Commonwealth as a whole but also conflicting local interests,[15] argument and persuasion could indeed change minds but not always in the way in which the speaker intended. For example, during the debate on a bill that concerned the Earl of Devonshire, Edward Bysshe claimed to have been 'unconstant and unresolved in opinion which way to give my opinion before [Christopher Sherland] spoke, and now I am against it.'[16] Similarly, Sir Robert Wingfield cited a speech by Dudley Carleton as a reason for altering his position on the union with Scotland.[17]

Mack's definition of three types of parliamentary speech—classical rhetoric (usually ornate and long), the university training of disputation (shorter argumentative orations), and formal replies, a hybrid of both—neatly captures most ideal types of verbal behavior in Elizabethan parliaments.[18] Questions about practice on the ground remain, however: did the nature of parliamentary debate and discourse alter during the period? Would William Cecil carefully listening to the debate on the Elizabethan religious settlement in 1559 have recognized the tone and nature of debate in 1628? And, to what extent was grammar school training a useful tool in the daily life of members of Parliament?

Sir Edward Coke, displaying his own grammar school training in rhetoric to the House of Commons in 1624, implied that in this regard his education was not very useful at all. He critiqued classical training and articulated a sharp distinction between classical rhetorical theory and useful discursive practice. He pronounced that 'Demosthenes orations best when longest; but not so with his speeches.'[19] For Coke, at least at this moment, 'speeches' were the pragmatic Anglo-Saxon mode of communication in the legislature, as opposed to Latinate 'oratory.' Coke's intervention, as with the many others who claimed to eschew rhetoric, was somewhat disingenuous, and he was more than capable of lengthy orations if the occasion demanded it.[20]

THE SPEAKER, RHETORIC, AND THE OPENING OF PARLIAMENT

The breakdown of both rhetorical and political ideals is vividly apparent in the troubled history of the Speaker throughout the early Stuart period. Theoretically, the Speaker was chosen by the House from among its members. However, the choice was well known before the actual day, and in practice the Speaker was a Crown appointee.[21] As Sir Edward Coke noted in his Fourth Institute, '[T]he use is that the King doth name a discreet and learned man whom the Commons elect.'[22] Coke should have known since he had served as Speaker in 1593 and was so informed by the Queen at Hampton Court some three weeks before his election by acclamation in the Commons.[23] In 1626 the designated candidate, Heneage Finch, was even asked to draft his speech and submit it to the government well before the Parliament opened.[24] John Hooker explained the task of the Speaker in the House: '[H]is Office is to direct and guide the house in good order, and to see the ordinances, usages and customs of the same to be firmly kept and obeyed.'[25] This role required parliamentary experience, tact, and an ability to tread a fine rhetorical line, acting as the conduit between the Crown and the Commons, an increasingly difficult task in the early seventeenth century. Members in the midst of heated debate found the Speaker an easy target on which to vent their frustration at royal policies. Sir Edward Phelips, the Speaker in the first Jacobean Parliament, 1604–10, had lost so much respect in the House by the end of the Parliament that one member 'challenged him on the stairs' and, in a gesture singularly absent from the precepts of Ciceronian oratory, 'popped his Mouth with his finger in scorn: Did again this morning do it in the Street on Horseback.'[26] The 'duel' between the House and the loyalty of its Speaker reached a climax in 1629 when Speaker Sir John Finch, attempting to adjourn the House by leaving the chamber, was dragged back to his chair and forcibly held down.[27] The 'dual' role of serving both the King and Commons often became a matter of choosing sides, and when the Speaker erred in favor of the monarch, his authority in the Commons waned.

Whatever the limitations of classical/humanist rhetoric, every utterance within St. Stephen's chapel was institutionally framed and inaugurated by the ritual orations that attended the opening procedures of Parliament to which the Speaker was key. Members of both houses fell to debate only after these formal declamations. The most conspicuous aspect of these proceedings was the opening oration by the newly appointed Commons' Speaker, or what was customarily called the 'disabling speech.'[28] The election of the Speaker occurred on the first day of Parliament after the Commons had listened to the Lord Chancellor's opening speech given on the monarch's behalf. After which the Commons were willed to return to St. Stephen's Chapel and choose a Speaker. Contemporary parliamentary commentators suggest that it was the foremost privy councillor who should commend one man to the House. If none other was named (and generally they were not),[29] then the member should rise and humbly stress 'his defectes both of nature and arte are such as he is altogeather unable, and therefore praieth them to chuse another more fitt; which peticion is comonly answered with a full concent of voyces upon his name.'[30]

The disabling speech followed the rhetorical formula of the Introduction and Division (Exordium); Three points (Narration); Why there was a need for change (Proof and Refutation); Conclusion and apology for length of speech.[31] The rhetorical strategy of 'disabling' occurred in the opening remarks, in a declaration of unworthiness for the task at hand, whether as a learned man, an orator, or simply for the assigned duty. This now culturally remote but carefully coded gesture of obeisance before Crown and Parliament betrays the shifting rhetorical terrain between Henrican and Elizabethan Humanism and the 1620s.

Perhaps the most vivid example of this is the speech of Sir Edward Phelips before the King and Parliament when he was appointed Speaker in 1604. After a lengthy enunciation on the divine sovereignty of the monarch, Phelips launched into his own state: he described himself as 'worthless, unworthy, defective with secret imperfections, estranged from virtue, labouring under the weight of a so heavy a burden, under which [he] already do groan, and shall both faint and fail.' The Commons, he noted, was 'misguided' in their wisdom and 'favours'; 'unwarranted' in nomination; and 'misled' in its opinions. Unsatisfied with these pejoratives, he went on metaphorically to throw himself at the feet of the King, claiming how he would want to be 'cooled by death' rather than neglect James's service, and not only that, but his body suffered 'through frost-bitten Defects of [his] own Imperfections.' Fortunately, Phelips had recovered from frostbite by the next paragraph, to be warmed by his zeal, which 'resembled fire, hot yet trembling: hot in my Desire to discharge the full Measure of my Duty; but, Pisander[32] like, trembling, in my fear, lest, through my Imperfections, I fail in that, which I should perform.'[33] Clearly, Phelips was suitable for the task at hand and was duly appointed. His oration was described by Sir Edward Mountagu as 'an eloquent speach in disabling himselfe,'[34] in which in the exordium Phelips had established his ethos as the appropriate and skilled candidate by disparaging his own rhetorical skills. In contrast, Speaker Sir Robert Bell in 1572 had failed to tread the fine rhetorical line. It seems that it was possible to 'disable' oneself mightily, and yet avoid being seen as too obsequious toward the monarch or as diverging too far from the customary trope. Bell, named as 'the orator' in the parliamentary satire *Lewd pasquil*, was criticized for being 'too full of flattery, too curious and tedious.'[35]

Even in the more fraught circumstances of the early Caroline Parliaments, the disabling strategy on the theme of unworthiness did not lose its essence. Perhaps it lost some of its rhetorical flourish and amplification, although this may be dependent, as we have seen, on the individual Speaker rather than political circumstance. Sir Heneage Finch, chosen Speaker in 1626, noted his 'unworthiness' as well. He, too, spoke of weight and burden, weakness and inability, and casting himself at the foot of the royal throne, but certainly with less recorded enthusiasm than Phelips in 1604.[36] By November 1640, the opening of the Long Parliament, the strategy of disabling, while still utilized, was greatly diminished. In a speech that was immediately printed, Speaker Lenthall threw the entire House at the King's feet in a noticeably less obsequious fashion than his predecessors. He even went so far as to 'lament to thinke how great a mist may overcast the hopes of this Session.'[37] The tenor of the 'disabling speech' had changed when Lenthall could speak of the Commons 'endeavour[ing] a sweet violence which may compell your Majestie to the love of Parliaments.'[38] Although violence here should be taken to mean 'intensity' rather than 'physical force,' the rhetorical barb barely concealed in the double meaning of 'violence' was probably not lost on anyone present.

This notion of the disabling speech extends beyond the ceremonial and into the debating chamber itself. One of the major characteristics of speech in Elizabethan Parliaments was that of apology and unworthiness to address the subject. Henry Jackman's 1589 speech on the subsidy started with a long apology in which he hoped the House would show 'consideracion of my manifold defectes, I maye iustlye feare once to open my mouth in this honorable and grave assembly.' Later he continued, 'hopinge that if any thinge have escaped me worthye reprehension throughe ignorance, it shalbe excused by reason of myne infancy in this practise of speakinge.'[39] As Markku Peltonen has noted, Jackman's speech was a model of oratory. In the exordium he utilized *insinuatio* to deflect from his controversial point of opposing the subsidies and distinguished between hypothesis and thesis. Throughout Jackman presented his argument just as the classic rhetoric manuals suggested, with a deliberative style of necessity and utility argued through commonplaces to build an emotional and persuasive effect.[40] Soon after, in another speech in 1589, Jackman continued his theme, 'in regard whereof, together with the consideration of my manifold defectes and disabilityes both in nature, arte and exercise of speaking itt might better beseeme me to lende myne eares to receave instruction, then to bende my tongue to geve information.'[41] Jackman continually followed this method; speaking on the Tillage Bill in 1598, he opined that 'I am not ignoraunt howe difficult, and how dangeros, a thinge itt is for any one man in so deepe a dumnes of so greate and so grave a counsell to undertake and, as itt were, to professe that he onely is to be hearde. The conceypt wherof together with the conscience of my manifold defectes and debilities had *almost* indicted unto me a perpetuall silence in this place.'[42]

Jackman was certainly not alone. Sir Robert Cecil on the London retailers' bill of 1593 noted that 'he had promised himself silence, for it spake of trades wherein he had no skill. But . . .'[43] In 1601 Cecil proclaimed, 'I am sorrye and very loath to breake a resolution which I had taken, that is ffor some respectes to have byne silent or verye spareinge of speeches all this parleamente: but . . .'[44] Doctor Bennett the same year addressed the chair: 'Mr Speaker, although I had noe meaninge to speake, yet I will nowe speake to the obiection that was last made.'[45]

Disabling speech was indeed a formal rhetorical strategy—but, as we have seen from the above examples of the Speaker's disabling oratory—such strategies could and did go awry, or at least have unintended consequences. Only on certain occasions did Parliament function according to the textbook example of debate, persuasion, and rhetoric. In 1533 Henry VIII invited the Papal Nuncio to attend a day in the Commons to witness the debates there. The day was stage-managed to avoid any hint of religious controversy, and the nuncio was treated to a debate on a bill against thieves.[46] Yet only one year later, Henry pronounced to the imperial ambassador, Eustace Chapuys, that it was against the English custom for foreigners to hear the debates of Parliament. That the bill under discussion was to strip Catherine of Aragon of the title of Queen may have played a part in this decision.[47] A set piece debate was staged for Francis de Montmorency and his delegation in 1572, and Montmorency was actually permitted to go beyond the bar and sit by the privy councillors while two of the house's greatest debaters, Henry Yelverton and William Fleetwood, argued *pro et contra* on a bill.[48] These instances were not only unusual events; they were also actively staged-managed ones, and as such were far closer to the ideal paradigms of rhetoric learned in the grammar school and far removed from the normal cut and thrust of daily debate.

The residue of classical oratory, then, continued to resonate not only in speeches on ritual occasions but also in the wider chamber of debate. For all that, there were shifts in patterns of speech that are identifiable over the period. Most recorded parliamentary speech is a long way from fully fledged classical oration. The practice of disabling, as we have seen, carried over into the early Stuart Parliaments, and certainly there were still many instances of it; even John Pym in 1621 noted how 'it hath always been a burthen to me to speak in this House.'[49] Similarly, Sir James Perrot desired 'not to hear myself speak,' and Sir Edward Giles was moved to his feet by 'that which I heard publically delivered.'[50] But these speeches are certainly less frequent than they were in Elizabethan Parliaments as rhetoric took on a more adversarial tone and diarists in the chamber recording the words of MPs concentrated more on the substance of speeches rather than rhetorical flourishes.[51]

THE ETHOS OF THE CHAMBERS

Lofty ideals of free and bold speech, what the Parliament-man John Hooker had called the right of a member 'freely to utter, speake and declare his minde,' gave way to the practical realities of speaking in a small chamber packed with eminent lawyers, experienced Parliament-men, royal courtiers, and privy councillors. It did indeed require boldness for a newly elected burgess from far away from London to feel confident enough to stand up and speak to a House that answered poor speech by humming, hawking (spitting and noisily clearing the throat), and heckling. The House quite simply evinced an intimidatory ethos. On 3 December 1601 Zacharias Locke almost delivered his second speech as an MP, but 'whoe for verye ffeare shooke, that he could not proceed, but stood still a while and at length sat downe.'[52] Locke did not stand for election again. Two weeks later, during a debate on whether a malefactor should be cleared of offending the House, 'all cryed "I, I, I," but onlye younge Mr Francis Grantham, whoe gave a great "Noe," at whome the Howse lawghed, and he blushed.'[53] This was Grantham's first and last word as an MP. Because of the nature of the surviving evidence, it is impossible to know exactly how many members refrained from speech during any Parliament—the figures that we have must be viewed as highly unreliable and on the conservative side. However, it is worthwhile noting that the highest recorded percentage of speakers in an Elizabethan Parliament was 20 percent, in 1601.[54] In other words, in a chamber of 462 MPs, there were 370 who made no recorded intervention; a substantial portion of those, we must conclude, never spoke at all.

Elizabeth, though, strived to keep her parliamentary sessions short and nongovernment business to a minimum. By contrast, the Jacobean sessions were considerably longer and commensurably more people spoke. Furthermore, the survival of a greater number of parliamentary diaries also allows us to add to the statistics. Williams Mitchell calculated that 259 members spoke during the long 1621 Parliament (approximately 54 percent). But of the 3,349 speeches, twenty-one men delivered 1,741 of them (52 percent).

The following Parliament, in 1624, saw only 137 speakers recorded in the *Commons Journal*, despite its three and a half months in session. And even in 1628, the most volatile Parliament before 1640 and one that remained sitting for over three months, only 32 percent of members are recorded as speaking.[55] The vagaries of the evidence on speaking, especially through patchy recordkeeping by the clerks and the House's clampdown on committing speeches to the *Journal* in the late 1620s, make all these figures at best tentative. Nevertheless the record reveals that the vast majority of speeches were given by a few members and that for most in the House, it was a place of performance by a small proportion of the House or, at least for the occasional intervention rather than speech-giving. The majority of the members formed part of a noisy audience who hummed, murmured, and shuffled their feet, but they rarely stood to speak on the stage.

'FITTEST SPEECH'

Being 'gracious with the House,' as one contemporary put it, was a necessity.[56] Speaking seasonably and capturing the mood of the House were other important aspects of parliamentary speech. These political necessities of speech were also stressed in the formal rhetorical training of grammar school education, which included learning the forms, structuring arguments, and relying upon reasoned persuasion. Those who could hold the attention of the Commons through eloquence and learnedness received its plaudits. Both diarists and the Common's clerk repeatedly praised both these qualities in Sir Francis Bacon. On 26 March 1604 Sir Edward Mountagu noted in his diary how Bacon 'in a very good speech delivered unto [the Lords] the manner of how proceeding,'[57] and in 1614 the clerk described him as 'the heir apparent of eloquence.'[58] Mountagu also considered Sir Oliver St. John to have made 'an excellent speech' on the poverty of former military officers. Even greater praise was lavished upon Sir Thomas Wentworth by Sir John Eliot in 1625:

> There was in that gentleman a good choice of parts, natural and acquisite, and no less opinion of them. A strong eloquence he had and a comprehension of much reason. His arguments were weighty and acute, and his descriptions exquisite. When he would move his hearers with the apprehension of his sense, he had both *acumina dictorum* and *ictus senteniarum* to affect them. His abilities were both great in and persuasion, and as great a reputation did attend them.

Wentworth, it seems, while able to deliver a speech worthy of university oration, was unable to maintain his rhetorical composure when faced with disagreement and opposition. His enraged responses had the effect of undoing his eloquence. Eliot goes on to deliver the sting in the tail of his praise for Sir Thomas:

> But those many and great virtues, as Livy says of Hannibal, as great vices paralleled, or rather they were in him as Cicero notes in *Catiline, signa virtutum*, forms of virtue only, not the matter; for they seldom were directed to good ends, and when they had that color some other secret moved them. His covetousness and ambition were both violent, as were his ways to serve them. And those affections raised him to so much pride and choler, as any opposition did transport him, which rendered him less powerful to his adversaries, where the advantage was followed and perceived.[59]

Rhetoric here is regarded with some skepticism, as nothing other than flannel and spin. Perhaps because of the greater constitutional issues in the 1620s, overly stylized forms of rhetoric were now marked as the likely tactics of the parliamentary machiavel whose use of rhetorical ornament and flourish is not only distinct from the substance of his speech but also a cunning distraction from it. But not even eloquence could persuade the House when the mood of the Commons was contrary to the locutor's thoughts. As Sir John Eliot wrote of his fellow member in 1625, Sir Humphrey May, '[He] concluded with an apothegm (whereof he was never without store): The wit of this gentleman always drew the attention of the House, though his motions seldom relished it.'[60] Even that most eloquent of speakers, Sir Francis Bacon, could not dissuade the Commons from following its determined course of action: '[T]hese reasons and persuasion (though delivered by an excellent speaker and with all advantage that wit, words or eloquence could add to them) moved the House no wit.'[61]

If the house ostensibly valued plain speaking, it was also the case that intemperate speech could lead not only to censure but also expulsion. A ruling in the Commons in 1604 spelled out the protocol: '[If] any man speak impertinently it stands with the orders of the House for Mr Speaker to interrupt him.'[62] In practice, a member could get away with more if he captured the mood. Certainly Christopher Sherland's attack on John Baber in 1628 warranted the House's censure—he called him a 'coward' and a 'knave' and told the Commons 'that any such whitelivered creature should [not] sit in that Council.'[63] However, Baber had been responsible for the forced billeting of soldiers in Sherland's hometown, Wells, an issue that the Commons viewed as illegal, and so no action was taken against him.

Flattery of the House could also save a member from expulsion or censure. According to the rules of the Commons, a sitting mayor as the return-
ing officer was not entitled to stand for election.[64] This rule, honored more
in the breach than observance, was brought to the Commons' attention in
1614 when a Mr. Byng questioned the right of the mayor of King's Lynn,
Matthew Clarck, to sit in the Commons. Clarck rose to his feet and defended himself. He 'submitted himself to the pleasure of the House and declared that forasmuch as he had considerable business committed unto him
that much concerned the town's good, his fellow burgess not yet come up,
he might be continued in the House till the next session of Parliament to
make his affairs known to the House, notwithstanding.' Clarck 'protested
he had rather continue to be a scholar in this school of wisdom than governor of the best town in the realm.'[65] The case was referred to a committee.
Possibly impressed by his flattering references to the Lower House, the
committee took no action against Clarck and he remained an MP throughout the Parliament. Despite a clear breach of the electoral rules, Clarck had
ingratiated himself with the House. Clarck's case can be neatly contrasted
with that of Griffin Payne. Payne's position in the House was questioned
after he made a 'bitter invective' about the purveyance bill in 1604.[66] A purveyor himself, as well as a new Parliament-man, Payne attacked the Commons' right to discuss the subject. Upon examination by the House, he was
found to be the mayor of Wallingford, Berkshire. This excuse was used to
sequester Payne from the House until the committee of privileges reported
on the matter. The session ended without any report, as did the following
two parliamentary sessions, and it was not until March 1610 that Payne
was allowed back into the House upon his petition.[67] Payne, in contrast to
Clarck, had neither captured the mood of the House nor praised its worth
and so suffered the consequences.

John Pym was quite candid in his attitude toward those who spoke in the
House. When in 1624 Sir George Chaworth fervently upheld James's policy
on war with Spain but criticized the Duke of Buckingham, Pym noted in
his diary that 'if there had been bad humours enough in the House, [his
speech] might have done some hurt.' Although it passed without comment
at the time, Chaworth considered his speech to have given the Commons
the excuse to investigate irregularities in his election for which he was later
excluded from the House. As he noted, '[T]hey were glad to be shut of me,
giving me the title of a Royalist.'[68] Speaking in favor of unpopular govern-

ment ministers or royal policies, as Chaworth found out to his cost, was a dangerous pastime in a House with contrary opinions. Edward Clarke suffered a similar fate in his maiden (and final) parliamentary speech. On 6 August 1625 he complained 'that some of this House did use particularities with bitter invectives and unseasonable not fit for this time, and that against the officers of state in this kingdom, which he, for his part, as being advanced by him, was bound to oppose.'[69] Despite being interrupted throughout his speech and asked to control himself, Clarke continued in the same vein until he was ordered to withdraw from the chamber and committed to the custody of the sergeant at arms. Clarke was permitted back into the House the following day but only after he had apologized for his speech.[70]

Members were quick to react to offense if they chose to do so. The young firebrand lawyer Thomas Sheppard wasted no time after election to his first Parliament (1621) attacking his Dorsetshire nemesis, Sir Walter Earle. Earle had introduced a bill for the keeping of the Sabbath (Sunday). Sheppard immediately attacked it:

> This bill was idle and indiscreet, first, for the title of it. Every one knoweth that *dies Sabbati* is Latin for the Sabbath day, and *dies Sabbati* is Saturday, as it is taken in all writs, returns and amongst lawyers. So as it is no otherwise than if it should be titled An Act for the Observing of Saturday, otherwise called Sunday. So much for the title. The body is no better than the head. This is first an Act made in the spite of the face and teeth of the King's Book, which allows of dancing on the Sundays; and King David says let us praise God in a dance.[71]

According to the notes taken by Pym in the chamber, Sheppard's attack quickly became even more vitriolic:

> The occasion of the bill growes from a kind of cattle that will not submitt themselves to the ceremonyes of the Church. It savours of the spiritt of a Puritan. I call not those Puritans that speake against druckennes, those that terme them Puritans are themselves Atheists, but such as are refractory to good order. Foxes tyed by the tayles while their heades are devided with factions, their tayles are ioyned with fyer brands to set fire on the good corne. Shall we make all these engines and Barracado's against Papists and not a Mouse-trappe to catch a Puritan. The griefes and cries of the people is greate. Now sooner is any Complaynt made against this kind of people but some Justice of Peace or other is redy to protect them. This was the humor that gave occasion to the Bill and he that preferr'd it is a perturbator of the Peace.[72]

This was enough to enrage the House, especially as Pym noted, this was spoken 'with a greate deale of scorne and Malepeirt gesture; and thowgh

the mislike and mutteringe of the Howse troubled him often, yet he protested he would speake and if he did offend, his bodye and his Fortune
should answere it.'[73] Sheppard's suggestion was indeed taken up, and he
was commanded to leave the chamber.

Parliamentary speeches certainly could be dangerous. At least according
to the report of Sir John Evelyn, during an apoplectic maiden speech in the
House on 11 May 1604, Sir Richard Browne ruptured a vein and died two
days later.[74] Similarly famous, though in this case only for the vehemence
of his public speeches rather than the untimeliness of his death, Sir Richard Bulkeley was described in the satirical verse known as the 'Parliament
Fart,'[75] as 'an Anglesey lad, Rose up in a fury and rose up half mad.'[76] Others did themselves no favors by speaking in the House. Sir William Cornwallis's maiden speech in 1604 was a defense of the Anglo-Scottish Union
proposal, a subject upon which he had published a book, *The Miraculous
and Happie Union of England and Scotland*. The report of his speech was
unflattering: he 'hath taken upon him to answer the objections against the
Union, but they are done so lamely, and, although it seem scarce possible,
so much worse than his book .... It is incredible to think, if it were not true,
that such simplicity of conceit could not be joined in him with so impudent
utterance.'[77]

Parliamentarians frequently complained about long, boring speeches.
When the monarch trespassed on the time and patience of the House, such
as Henry VIII in 1531, who spent an hour and a half regaling the Lords
about the poisoning of Bishop Fisher,[78] there was nothing to be done but
sit in silent submission. Not so with fellow members of the House. The
author of an anonymous Elizabethan parliamentary diary considered Sir
Francis Knollys's subsidy speech of 1571 'a longe, needeles discourse,'[79] and
in the same year the Lord Keeper, Nicholas Bacon complained:

> And therewith that you will also in this your assemblye and conference clearely
> forbeare and, as a greate enemye to good councell, flee from all manner of
> contentious reasoninges and disputacions and all sophisticall, captious and
> frivolous argumentes and quiddities, meeter for ostentation of witt then
> consultacion in weightie matters, comelyer for schollers then for counsellors,
> more beseeminge for schooles then for parliament howses; besides that
> commonly they be great cause of much expence of tyme and breed few good
> resolucions.

What Bacon insists on is, again, the distinction between the idealized forms
of classical rhetoric and the speech fit for specific purposes of the House,

a chamber that was developing its own distinct forms of speech and discursive style, albeit influenced by the rhetorical training found in grammar schools.

There were signs throughout the period of mounting impatience with tedious and long-winded members. Diarists, and even the official clerk of the House, did not shy away from recording the flaws, real or perceived, in the speaking abilities of their colleagues. William Morrice, descriptively or perhaps derogatorily, described as a 'Welshman,' gave 'a longe unnecessarie weake speache' on the Union debates in 1606, noted Robert Bowyer.[80] The clerk agreed and described it as 'a long speech to little purpose a repeticon sermon.'[81] Sir Henry Poole came off no better in Bowyer's opinion, giving 'a labored speech, and preamble somewhat farre fetched and premeditated.'[82] Sir Robert Hitcham too tried Bowyer's patience during debate in 1606, 'a long, senseless declaration,' he wrote in his diary.[83]

In the foreign policy debate of 1621 the temper of the House was missed by Sir George Hastings, of whom John Pym noted in his dairy, '[H]ere were interspersed some unseasonable motions.'[84] Dudley Carleton commented in 1607 that 'here be some gentlemen are enemies to long speeches, if they concur not with their own sense.'[85] Attitudes toward the length of speeches varied and depended heavily on the skills of the orator. London's Recorder, William Fleetwood, much given to lengthy orations, clearly entertained the chamber and for the most part did not fall afoul of the House.[86] Occasionally speeches were described as a 'long and learned discourse'[87] or 'long and good.'[88] Overall, the mood of the House determined whether verbose speeches were tolerated. In the midst of attacks in 1621 on the notorious monopolist Sir Giles Mompesson, Christopher Brooke showed concern that 'long speeches prevent our endeavours to get Sir Giles Mompesson again.'[89] He was eager to avoid flowery rhetoric and to replace it with action and debate.

Formal rhetoric was often used to bide or waste time and to filibuster. The theme of 'much eloquence upon little matter' had been employed by Bacon in 1571,[90] and the policy, repeated again a decade later when members were reminded to 'use reverent and discreet speeches, to leave curiosities of form, and not to spend too much time in unnecessary motions or superfluous arguments,'[91] clearly suited the government agenda of pushing through legislation and supply without distraction. In many Elizabethan Parliaments, it also played into the hands of the government, which could count on many of the most eloquent speakers, such as Bacon, Sir Walter

Mildmay, and Thomas Norton. Elizabeth herself also lectured the House on wasting time through rhetoric: '[H]er highnes thinketh that they sholde leave to talk *rhetorice* and speke *logice* to leave longe tales w[hic]h is rather an ostentacon of wytt then to any effecte.'[92] Even James I, impatient at the long debates over the Union proposal, weighed in on speaking practices:

> Studied Orations, and much Eloquence upon little Matter, is fit for the Universities; where not the Subject that is spoken of, but the Trial of his Wit that speaketh, is most commendable: But, on the contrary, in all great Councils of Parliaments, fewest Words, with most Matter, doth become best; where the Dispatch of the great Errands in hand, and not the Pray of the Person, is most to be looked unto; like the Garment of a chaste Woman, who is only set forth by her natural Beauty, which is properly her own; other Deckings are but ensigns of a Harlot, that flies with borrowed Feathers.[93]

In a long and angry speech in which he contrasted the length of English Parliaments unfavorably with the brevity of their Scottish counterparts, James admonished the Commons to find a middle way in speaking between 'foolish rashness, and extreme Length.'[94] Ironically, in urging brevity, James failed to follow his own advice and tried the patience of the assembled listeners with a long oration.

Increasingly, the audience of Parliament required spontaneity and vigor of address (rather than the disquisition and recitation) within the bounds of the House's (un)written rules of rhetorical decorum. On 23 May 1614, William Cavendish was admonished by Sir John Savile for reading aloud [to the House] from his table book.[95] The anonymous author of 'A true presentation of forepast parliaments' similarly chastised those who 'shall come with long, premeditated, set, penned orations,'[96] and Richard Grosvenor delivered 'a large lecture' 'out of his papers' in 1621.[97] It has also been suggested that many of the legally complex speeches given on the Great Contract in 1610 and the Petition of Right in 1628 were not only prepared in advance but also read verbatim in the House.[98] Custom and practice dictated that speeches were not to be read, but it was acceptable (and probably commonplace) for notes to be used.[99] The occasional apology for doing so should not blind us to the myriad contemporary examples. Thomas Wilbraham in 1572 begged the pardon of his fellow members for not providing a full relation of the proceedings against Mary Queen of Scots, as he had not taken notes in writing and expected not to be able to report fully.[100] Hakewill's experience of Parliament as he set down in his treatise on speaking allowed that 'any man may in speaking help his memory with notes,' and Nicholas Fuller used notes when speaking to the High Commission bill in 1607.[101] Although notes aided the memory, speakers needed the ability to adapt to the fast-paced nature of debate. Sir Benjamin Rudyerd came in for particularly harsh criticism in the 1625 Parliament. Rudyerd, Sir John Eliot commented, 'did speak never but premeditated, which had made more show of memory than affection and made his words less powerful than observed.'[102] It was clearly not sufficient just to be eloquent and well prepared.

Classic humanist eloquence could be understood in itself as a form of tedium. One example of this, London's Recorder, William Fleetwood, a man often remarked upon to 'speak learnedly and withall pleasantly,'[103] was also notorious for giving 'a longe tedious talke nothing towching the matter.'[104] Fleetwood, who has been aptly described as an 'incorrigible raconteur' and an eloquent speaker, must have tried the patience of the House during his frequent two-hour discourses—even he admitted, '[B]ut now you will say, I am out of the matter; yet the best is, I will come in again.'[105] The Recorder was wont to pursue his diversions. When opining on how lengthy bills were, he started discussing an old Parliament-man, Mr. Temple, who thought the same way; as Fleetwood noted, 'I remember him: he was a very honest gent and he was buried in the churchyard very honorably.'[106] Fleetwood again in 1585:

> You would think I had studied this year I am so ready and perfect in it, but I promise you I never heard this bill before, but I could keep you here till two o'clock with like cases, for I had a collection of them till my book was picked from me.

He then opined at length on

> the bishop of Winchester's cook [who] had spurge comfits given him. Do you laugh at it? I tell you it is no laughing matter when you hear the end. He in revenge hereof made certain porridge which an old woman died after she had eaten of them and so I think she would [have died anyway] though she had not eaten of them, for she was very old. But then [there] was a statute for poisoners that they should be boiled to death in hot lead, let down by little and little. I remember I saw one once when I was a little boy sitting behind [my] grandfather upon a horse, and was taken away when I cried for fear, for I tell you it was a terrible matter to behold. . . . I think you would be content to hear me these two hours.[107]

Fleetwood's speech amply illustrates that long speeches, digressions, and rhetorical persuasions were the norm in most Elizabethan Parliaments. But even then, Jacobean style came into play, and practices in the chamber did not fit any neat schematic. The House moved at its own pace and according to its own whim, and on most days digression and intervention on another topic was just as common as point by point debate of a single issue.

There is a tonal, even auditory, difference in speech between Elizabethan and Jacobean Parliaments. Short, sharp debate and adversarial rhetoric sit alongside more conventional rhetorical formulae. This is not necessarily an exact quantifiable science, a case of statistics, nor because of the difference in surviving records and among those who recorded debate is it possible to identify a particular moment of change. It may also be true that these rhetorical flourishes ceased to be recorded even by diarists who attempted to write verbatim and to record only the substance rather than the rhetorical ornament—this itself is a telling factor as to the new importance of direct, substantive speech.[108]

THE COMMITTEE OF THE WHOLE HOUSE AND PARLIAMENTARY MANAGEMENT

This is not to say that either long speeches or rhetoric disappeared from the chamber, as many of the above examples demonstrate, but parliamentary discourse had shifted from the early Elizabethan to the Caroline Parliaments. One of the main factors in this change was the development of the Committee of the Whole House. As its name implies, this committee consisted of all members of the House. It differed from the regular procedure of sitting in that the Speaker left his seat and was replaced by a chairman named by the House. This procedural device used to discuss a particular matter had the advantage of freeing the House from its own etiquette on speaking. In a committee, members could speak as freely and often as they liked. The formality of the House's structure was removed, as was the authority of the 'official' Speaker to control the agenda. This substantially changed the nature of proceedings from a place in which members gave set-piece speeches to one in which, more often than not, they reacted to previous locutors, referred to them by name (this was forbidden in the House), and spoke more than once. It also increased the dominance of a select few who held the respect of the House, making their interventions more significant and domineering. As the Parliament-man Sir Herbert Croft commented, '[In] Committees where every man may reply, some speciall Persons of

Place by speaking often and countenance doe prevaile more than by their reasons.'[109]

Wallace Notestein, in particular, saw this new procedure of the Committee of the Whole House as an integral part of the Commons' 'Winning of the Initiative' in the early Stuart period. He viewed its development in the light of battles between the Crown and Commons for control of the parliamentary agenda.[110] More recently, this view has been challenged by Sheila Lambert, who found its origins in the large committees appointed in the later Elizabethan Parliaments. For Lambert, the Committee was an efficient procedural tool, not a stick to beat the government with.[111] This attention to the genesis of the committee, however, has overshadowed the crucial and historic ways in which it changed forever the nature of debate, and in doing so how it played into the hands of those who could sway the House through powerful speech and force of argument.

For example, on 8 November 1610 the Speaker, Sir Edward Phelips, suggested to the House that a committee should be formed to send an answer to the King on his demand for a subsidy of around £500,000. Sir Edwin Sandys immediately leaped to his feet; '[It] was matter of too great weight for a few to take upon them at the first without the direction of the House.'[112] He proposed a Committee of the Whole House followed by a subcommittee to draft the answer. This motion was approved, and the desire of Phelips, and no doubt the government spokesmen in the Commons, to control debate in a small committee was quashed. By 1628 the House was utilizing the device more and more to the extent that the majority of the debates were carried out in the Committee and on most days, the Commons broke into committee at some point.[113]

The effectiveness of the procedure is clear. For example, on 6 May 1628, at the height of political tension over the King's answer to the Commons questioning their liberties of speech, the House brusquely discarded the opinion of the Secretary of State and former university orator Sir John Coke that their reply should be debated in the House, and ordered itself into committee with the doors locked. Despite a valiant attempt by Coke in the subsequent proceedings to put the government's side, he was totally eclipsed by the dominant leadership of the Commons: Sir Nathaniel Rich spoke four times; John Pym also spoke in favor of a Petition of Right on four occasions; Sir John Eliot intervened three times, as did Sir Edward Coke, while Edward Littleton and Edward Alford spoke twice.[114] The tone of the debate was also significant. This type of committee, usually not planned in advance, was not the place for formal set-piece debate or a pre-pared speech introducing a piece of legislation. The recorded speeches are usually brief, and a comparison of the speeches between the diarists who were taking notes while sitting in the Commons illustrates that it was not the vagaries of recording that made them so.

Furthermore, the Committee of the Whole House made government management of the Parliament much more difficult. Short, sharp inter-ventions and extemporaneous debate were much harder to control than a chamber in which individuals could speak only once and were governed by the authority of the Speaker. But procedural change would account for little if members had nothing of political significance to debate. Some of the changes between oratory in Elizabethan and early Stuart Parliaments might be ascribed to the contested nature of the subjects under discussion, rather than to the more nebulous process of parliamentary procedure and change I have been describing. Certainly through abbreviated sessions and effective Privy Council control, Elizabeth kept a tight rein on Parliament. She too had the advantage of focusing the attention of the Commons on the need for supply to fight the lengthy war with Spain. Her personal management skills were also sufficient to temper any trouble that arose, for example in the 1601 Golden Speech, in which she deflected the ire of the Commons on the royal grants of monopoly patents.[115] In contrast, James I, eager to make a mark on his new kingdom and push through a policy of Union with Scot-land, immediately found himself embroiled in controversy. Nor was the Union the only cause of parliamentary strife. Wardship, free trade, purvey-ance,[116] and impositions were all troublesome points of friction between the Crown and Parliament.[117] After peace was signed with Spain in 1604, the fiscal arguments for supply were harder to make, despite a huge debt left by Elizabeth. Radical attempts to permanently change royal finances and the taxation system through the Great Contract foundered partly on mistrust between James and the Commons, while allegations of electoral interference by the government helped ruin the 1614 Parliament.[118] These were issues far more substantial than those found in the last decade of Eliza-beth, and the debate was, as Notestein put it, 'more pungent.'[119]

Hotly contested political speech became even more of a factor during the 1620s. Issues of foreign policy, the religious policies of James and Charles, mismanaged wars, the influence of favorites, and illegal taxation all pro-vided flashpoints between the Crown and Parliament culminating in the Petition of Right in 1628.[120] But Elizabethan Parliaments had shown that unpopular views expressed in the Commons, and ones that criticized royal policies, did not have to lead to the dissolution of Parliament. However, orderly debate required parliamentary experience and good management. Through the Privy Council, and especially the efforts of William Cecil, Lord Burghley, the mid-Elizabethan era was blessed with these qualities. Michael Graves has termed the cohort of effective Commons speakers who helped manage business in the House and kept the government agenda on track 'men of business.'[121] Led by Thomas Norton, William Fleetwood, and Robert Beale, this group drafted legislation, spoke on government issues in the Commons, and generally guided the proceedings. They were able to act on the government's behalf without holding an official position, such as being a privy councillor. This gave them a greater air of authority in the House and the ability to speak without being too closely identified with the government. But the influence of the men of business on the House and the generally sound top-down management was an all too brief period in the history of the early modern Commons. The last two Parliaments of Elizabeth's reign were disorderly and poorly managed.[122] The Parliaments did not lack great orators, Sir Walter Raleigh and Sir Francis Bacon among them, but without a firm guiding hand the debates grew disorderly.

The lack of effective management from the government was a problem in the Jacobean and early Caroline Parliaments. and no doubt some of the change in the nature of the debate and the move toward more adversarial rhetoric and away from classical oratory may in part stem from a lack of direction. Some of the fault for this must lie with the government for failing to provide an agenda that addressed general grievances in the Commonweal at the same time as pushing the government needs of fiscal supply. Perhaps, too, it can be said that the number and quality of privy councillors in the Lower House was insufficient to manage the Commons effectively. Although the lack of privy councillors should not be labored too greatly, it is accurate to say that in general the quality of speaking with eloquence and persuasion belonged more to those who came to oppose government policy than it did to those who were responsible for defending it. Sir John Coke, although a skilled orator, represented increasingly unpopular government policies, and this hindered his ability to utilize his formidable eloquence in defense of those policies. In the House, no other great, eloquent, or effective speakers could be said to come from the privy councillors in the 1620s.[123] In contrast, many of those who critiqued government policies and were involved in the major constitutional debates of the late 1620s were some of the House's most persuasive orators, including Sir Edward Coke, Sir John Eliot, Sir Robert Phelips, and Sir Dudley Digges.

Certainly, those opposed to the increasing criticism of royal and government policies considered that the House was dominated by a few popular or fiery spirits. As the memorandum 'To his sacred Majesty, Ab Ignoto' stated, '[No] honest patriot dare oppose them, lest he incur the reputation of a fool or a coward in his countrie's cause.'[124] Charles I warned the 1626 Parliament that the cause of trouble between the monarchy and the Commons was a small number of disaffected spirits, blaming specifically the few rather than the many, whom he praised as 'wise and well tempered.'[125] Some sixteen years earlier, Lord Chancellor Ellesmere had also ascribed the failure of royal policies in the Commons in this way: '[S]ome particular persons (desirous to be remarkable and valued and esteemed above others for their zeal, wisdom, learning, judgment and experience) have presumed to use in the lower house publically very audacious and contemptuous speeches against the King's regal prerogative and power.'[126] Ellesmere even considered that a plot to refuse to grant the King any money was hatched in secret by 'six of them who had great countenance and did bear great sway in the House.'[127] From the standpoint of the government and monarchy, the House could be, and often was, controlled by a few members who commanded attention. And it was upon these few that the royal ire was directed when Parliament was dissolved. In 1621, after an angry King James closed the Parliament, he ordered the imprisonment of those whom he thought had spoken against him. MPs Sir Edward Coke, Sir Robert Phelips, John Pym, William Hakewill, and William Mallory all spent brief periods incarcerated.[128] Similarly, in 1629 the wrath of Charles fell upon nine members of the Commons, who were imprisoned after the Parliament ended. In his closing address he informed Parliament that 'some few vipers amongst them did cast this mist of undutifulness over most of their eyes.'[129]

∽

Ideals of parliamentary speech, whether they be of rhetoric or disputation, were paradigms that could break down in the chamber. The day to day business of Parliament required a combination of persuasive rhetoric, but also to 'speak shortly as is fittest in Parliament.'[130] Increasingly, this came to mean not only speaking concisely but also speaking often and even with frequency in the same debate. Even Peter Mack, after a thorough analysis of rhetorical practices in Elizabethan Parliaments, is forced to conclude that in

'Elizabethan parliamentary oratory the distinction between display and persuasion is very fuzzy.'[131] Political argument does not fit into neat categories. Hence the limitation of a schematic approach like Mack's. Further, in terms of parliamentary speeches we cannot examine the behavior of the body as if it were a unified whole. This is to take the institution's propaganda about itself at face value, to mistake an ideal of parliamentary government for the reality of political process. The body was not a representative of the nation but rather the milling throng of representatives of the nation. Members engaged in all forms of verbal and physical communication: rhetorical speech on occasion; debate; interjections; interventions; long-winded speeches full of classical and biblical allusion; silence as protest; absence as protest; hemming, hewing, and hawking (spitting). Parliament, as a brief glance at any day's records will show, seldom followed logical patterns of subject nor often of discourse. Thus the main intervention by most MPs in the chamber is in the interruption of speech by others through coughing, talking, or spitting—through noise rather than speech, the subject of the next chapter.

CHAPTER TWO

Audience Reactions: The Noise of Politics

'Tis worse than the noise of a saw.'[1] Although Ben Jonson's character, Morose, in *Epicoene* (1609) is talking about the raucous sounds emanating from musicians, his complaint could be equally applied to the chambers of Parliament. Indeed, Jonson frequently wrote about the ubiquitous background noise that permeated the environs of Westminster. This cacophony in the streets carried over into the chambers of Parliament. The soundscape of Parliament was constituted by far more than frequent voluble speech, rhetoric, and debate. Noise was not just a characteristic of the scene but also, at times, an instrument that could be used to pointed and deliberate political effect. Noise might be marshaled to drown out an unpopular speaker, to register support for a cause, or to force the House down a particular avenue. The impact of noise also had practical consequences that led to confusion through misheard speech and difficulties for diarists who attempted to record the debates as the general hubbub of Parliament inhibited auditory cognizance. The communicative practices of its members were hindered by their inability to copy down the words of speakers and convey vital information to a wider audience of friends, relatives, and patrons. Nor were the clerks of the Commons immune to the din as they endeavored to provide an accurate and official record of proceedings. While decorum in the House of Commons was an ideal spoken about in the manuals of parliamentary commentators, it was rarely found in the noisy day-to-day life of Parliament. The sheer numbers elected to the House of Commons led to a chaotic racket. The Spanish ambassador remarked that James himself complained about the chaos in the Commons:

King [James I] at once began to say to him [Sarmiento] that although your Majesty [Philip III] had many kingdoms, and more subjects beyond comparison than he had, yet he had one thing greater than your Majesty, and that was a greater Parliament, for the Cortes of Castile were composed of little more than thirty persons, whilst the Parliament was made up of little less that five hundred. Of these men there was no head, and they voted without order, nothing being heard but cries, shouts, and confusion. He was astonished that the kings his predecessors had consented to such a thing.[2]

Of course, if the Spanish ambassador is to be trusted, then James was obliquely critiquing his own government and the lack of leadership from privy councillors and royal officials in the Commons.[3]

Spaces that we would now regard as 'sacred,' or refuges from noise—the communal gatherings in church services, the theater—public preaching, and politics were not immune from disturbance. Indeed, in many ways it defined them. This is especially true of Parliament, where noise and commotion increasingly became a signifier of parliamentary protest and opposition. Understanding the dynamic of difficult auditory conditions in which MPs conducted the business of the nation reveals not simply the ubiquity of noise, but the politics of opposition.

THE SPACES OF NOISE

Parliament, with it assemblage of more than 500 often raucous members and continual hubbub, was not a unique environment. Sir Robert Cecil described the behavior of MPs in 1601 as 'more fit for a Grammar-School than a Court of Parliament,' and as Keith Thomas commented about the church, '[T]he tone of many Elizabethan congregations seems to have been that of a tiresome class of schoolboys.'[4] John Donne was particularly scathing: '[A]ll that had formerly been used in Theaters, *Acclamations* and *Plaudites*, was brought into the *Church*, and not onely the vulgar people, but learned hearers were as loud, and as profuse in those declarations, those vocall acclamations, and those plaudits in the passages, and transitions, in Sermons, as ever they had been at the Stage, or other recitations *of their Poets or Orators*.'[5] Of course some churches, St. Paul's Cathedral for example, fulfilled a wider role in the community than just a religious one. St. Paul's was the commercial center of the London book trade and the home of news and gossip. Hence, John Earle's description: it contained a 'strange humming or buzze-mixt of walking, tongues and feet: It is a kind of still roare or loud whisper.'[6]

In the public space of the theater, where people went both to see and *hear,* the playhouse was a convivial, noisy, and social arena. Hawkers sold food and drink, moving freely among the crowds while audiences thought nothing of making their opinions heard by the actors, even on occasion barraging them with pippins. Aware of the noisy soundscape, playwrights often inserted into their prologues appeals for the audience to refrain from excessive and noisy behavior during the performance. William Fennor roundly condemned the excessive disturbance at amphitheaters:

> Clapping and hissing, is the only meane
> That tries and searches out a well writ Sceane,
> So it is thought by *Ignoramus* crew,
> But that good wits acknowledge's untrue;
> The stinkards oft will hisse without a cause,
> And for a baudy jeast will give applause.
> Let one but aske the reason why they roare
> They'll answere, cause the rest did so before.[7]

Even in the more genteel surroundings of the indoor playhouses in which the social status of the audience was higher, there were problems resulting from loud applause and hissing.[8] Such disruption was not deterred even by the endeavors of playwrights to control crowd behavior with demeaning references to the noise of the more down-market amphitheaters in works written for performance in such privileged indoor venues as Blackfriars.[9]

Theaters and sites of preaching were enclosed communal spaces with a deliberate and captive audience. But the noise did not relent in the more fluid spaces, such as Westminster Hall, which adjoined the chambers of Parliament. Westminster Hall housed the major law courts, King's Bench, Chancery, and Common Pleas all in open structures from which the words of judges, plaintiffs, defendants, and lawyers echoed around the Hall. Laughter, applause, and shouts from the courts mingled with the commercial transactions of stallholders, the conversation of sightseers, and the scribbling audience of lawyers-in-training making notes on cases. In Thomas Dekker's dialogue between the cities of Westminster and London we get an indication of just how noisy the Hall must have been: 'If the sounde of lawyers tongues were but one whole twelve month in thine eare, though thy selfe wouldst even loath it, tho it were unto thee never so delicate Musicke.'[10] Pickpockets roamed the area, and the likes of Samuel Pepys found it a good place to womanize. The customary legal and commercial affairs of the nation were carried out while Parliament was in session, a noisy and scant sixty feet from the Commons' chamber.[11]

Outside the doors of the Commons, the activities in the lobby contributed to the soundscape. The lobby of both the Lords and the Commons was open to the general public and frequented by curious onlookers as well as officials of Parliament, and those having business with the Houses. Petitioners, suitors, and servants crowded the lobby often in large numbers, causing congestion and undoubtedly noise. In addition it served as a place where interested parties as well as MPs and court officials could obtain copies of committee reports, proceedings, and notable speeches—all for a fee. Off the lobby MPs came out of the House to use the smoking room and 'bog,' or receive messages. After MPs and peers had traversed Westminster Hall and the lobbies and entered their chambers, MPs probably found little respite from the noise.[12] For the Lords, however, greater auditory sanctuary was to be found.

DECORUM IN THE HOUSE OF LORDS

In the Lords, a much more intimate and status conscious gathering than the Commons, noise and disturbance were not significant factors. Although the paucity of diaries detailing the daily workings of the House inhibits our ability to sense the overall demeanor of the chamber, instances of unruly speech and behavior were recorded. These, though, are very rare. The Lords was a more formal chamber in which strict rules governed behavior. The House even went so far as to institute mandatory reporting of any dispute between its members that took place in the environs of Parliament.[13] Nevertheless quarrels did break out. In 1621 the Earl of Berkshire, seeing his path blocked into the House by Lord Scrope, forcibly shoved him aside. The Lords took grave offense at this violence and committed Berkshire to the Fleet. In the eyes of the Lords, the affray was made even more heinous because it took place while Prince Charles was sitting in the Lords. Upon his release, Berkshire was ordered to apologize both to the House and to Prince Charles. The public apology was followed by a personal, although inaudible, submission to Charles: he 'went up to the Prince, in the upper end of the House, and on his knee, used private speech unto his highness, with a low voice not to be heard . . . which seemed to be an acknowledgement and submission.'[14] Berkshire and Scrope were then reconciled in front of the Prince.

While the Berkshire and Scrope incident was an atypical case of disturbance, noise could also fill the chamber at moments of high political tension. The Earl of Arundel's imprisonment in 1626, for his son's unauthorized marriage to a member of the royal family, caused tumult in the House, as many peers considered the true cause of Arundel's imprisonment was his opposition to the Duke of Buckingham: 'My lord Duke, my Lord of Dorset, my Lord of Carlisle, my Lord of Holland, stood all up, one after another to have spoken, but could not be heard.' These rare instances of a lack of decorum in the Lords stand in stark contrast to the continual hubbub that permeated the Commons.

AUDITORY CONDITIONS IN THE HOUSE OF COMMONS

In 1576 Thomas Cromwell, the parliamentary diarist, was dismayed to miss the Queen's closing speech when the 'greatest company went forth, and after her Majestie made an oration, but I could not here the same, scant one word in xx[ty], no one perfect sentence.'[15] Cromwell was not alone in his failure to record the Queen's speech or to catch the words of other speakers. It is through the pens of these diarists that the general hubbub of daily activity becomes clear. Of course, the unknown hearing problems of individual diarists as well as the scratching of quills, the sharpening of pens, and rustling of sheets of paper also contributed to the soundscape and affected the hearing of parliamentary writers. When we add to this the continual to-ing and fro-ing of members, the jangling of spurs, clanking of rapiers, stomping of boots,[16] and 'private murmurings,' it becomes clear that close attention and excellent training must have been required to record anything at all. It was possible for members of the public standing outside the doors of Parliament to hear what was said in the chamber, even at times with the doors closed.[17] But the occasions on which the clarity of sound in the lobby cut through the Commons 'cacophony' to the extent that it was possible to understand more than brief snatches of debate were probably limited.

The Commons' soundscape was often confused during formal speeches where the press of numbers inhibited aural cognizance. Cromwell again missed out in 1585 when of the Queen's speech 'I colde not well heare the contentes therof.'[18] An anonymous diarist fared no better in 1593, when with 'ill-fortune was I stood so as I could not heare but litle of it.'[19] These ceremonial occasions were marked by the presence of the monarch and the court, interested crowds of onlookers, and a high attendance among MPs and peers. Thus overcrowding was the result, and the proceedings were inaudible. The Lords chamber in which the opening oration took place was simply not large enough to accommodate the press of members, let alone the strangers who occasionally and illegally pushed their way in. The opening speeches offered no better auditory conditions, although experienced Parliament-men often left the Commons early to get a good position to hear the speech.[20] In 1593 the door to the Lords chamber was closed before many of the members had arrived, and the excluded throng gathered outside 'murmured so loude that the noise came to her Majestie's hearing, who presentlie commaunded the dore to be lett open.'[21] Those in the Commons hoping to take notes on the opening speech in 1601 fared no better, as the door was barred with many still outside and 'theruppon every man went out discontented.'[22] This problem reoccurred in 1604, when the door was closed on MPs attempting to hear James's speech.[23] Similar auditory problems were also apparent among those who sought to copy notes from sermons. Robert Saxby, an avid sermon note-taker, was hindered at St. Bartholomew's Church in London by not sitting near enough to the preacher and on another occasion by the low voice of the minister.[24]

Hearing formal speeches in Parliament was clearly problematic because of the number of people, 'confusedly,' as one diarist described it, trying to witness the monarch's oration. But sensory capacities might be also inhibited during debate in the Houses. A surviving fragment from a speech in 1585 sums up the auditory conditions MPs encountered:

> I am bold to move yow for my self and those that sitt about me in the lower part of the House that it would please yow to move such as mean to speak to any bill that they would speak as loud as reasonably they can and for so short tyme rather take some paynes and not respect ther owne ease and as it were to enforce them and strech their voyces, though it [be] to their payne, rather then that we should lose the profitt of their speech. I doubt not but they that speak to any bill their meaning is to draw the hole Howse to their mynde, which they can hardly bring to passe except we heare them, for without hearing we can not understand them, nor without understanding can not give our consentes, but shalbe like those that hear service in a strange tonge, and say Amen to that they understand not, when they think they pray to our Lord they shall saye Amen to a prayer made to our Lady. . . . We se by experience that we are dryven many

tymes to rise both to our disease and disturbance of those that sitt beneth us.
We see also we ar constrayned many tymes, as seems against good manner and
not without parent offenc, to crye 'Speak out, speak out,' wherunto as it hath
bene sayd that we must bring our eares with us, so [they] may better bring ther
tonges with them.

It was moved that to know how farr men might tell the secrettes of the
Howse: it is nedlesse to us for we can tell none for we hear none.[25]

This debate on 8 February 1585 on fraudulent conveyances, and ironically
coming shortly after the reading of a bill on hue and cry, illustrates the
cacophony in the House when contentious matters arose. The conveyances
measure was 'greatly impugned' and failed narrowly upon division, after
much contentious debate.[26] A similar occurrence in 1607 after the commitment of the bill for the repeal of Hostile Laws, meant that John Hare could
not be heard over the noise in the House.[27] Hare was not alone, although
the reasons for the auditory problems were many. Fleetwood accused one
person who cried out that he could not hear, of being distracted by reading
a book.[28] Sir Henry Unton was accused of speaking in a low voice,[29] while
the general shuffling and noise of the Commons as MPs came and went and
talked among themselves led to difficult conditions for hearing. The House
was certainly no respecter of age; in 1601 'an ould doctor of the civill lawe
spake, but because he was to longe and spake to lowe, the Howse hawked
and spitte, and kepte a great coyle[30] to make him end.'[31] This then was the
general hubbub of debate that frequently inserted itself into parliamentary
proceedings. Mostly it occurred in circumstances when the House found it
self divided over a particular issue and both sides sought the advantage of
shouting the other down.

LAUGHTER

Amid the speech and politics in the parliamentary chambers came moments of laughter, occasionally humorous but more often designed to
shame. One of the methods of social control in early modern England was
laughter—the sound of mocking, scorn, and derision. In his 1976 Neale
Memorial lecture, Keith Thomas examined this point in relation to English
society. He noted that it 'did not only reflect contemporary anxieties. It
also played a more positive role as a crucial part of the social process. Very
often that role was a conservative one, for in its affirmation of shared values

laughter could be a powerful force for social cohesion.'[32] Thomas Wilson's *Arte of Rhetorique* (1554) included a passage on 'delityng the hearers, and stirryng them to laughter,' in which he maintains that we experience feelings of contempt whenever we perceive 'the fondnes, the filthines, the deformitiee' of someone else's behavior, with the result that we are prompted to 'laugh him to skorne out right.'[33] As Quentin Skinner notes, quoting Hobbes, '[T]he passion of Laughter is nothyng else but a suddaine Glory arising from suddaine Conception of some Eminency in our selves, by Comparison with the Infirmityes of others.' Skinner sums up Hobbesian laughter by seeing that 'these feelings of glory are always scornful and patronising, always a matter of glorying over others,' so that 'to be laughed at' is to be 'derided, that is tryumphed over.'[34]

We have seen in Chapter One the problems faced by young Mr. Grantham and Zachiarias Locke, but others too were cowed by the derisive laughter of the House. Sir Richard Knightley also endured the mocking laughter of the Commons when he became confused and shouted 'noe' instead of 'aye' during a debate.[35] Ignatius Jordan, a severe puritan, introduced a bill in 1628 to make adultery punishable by whipping and a fine. John Pym, commenting on the bill, 'said that he did not like the frame of the bill, but since the sin required the judgement of God on this land, they should commit it.' The House burst out laughing and cried, '[C]ommit it, commit it.' An infuriated Jordan was left complaining to the House that this was 'no laughing matter,'[36] while an embarrassed Pym rather pedantically explained that he wished to see the bill committed, not the offense. William Fleetwood too felt the scorn of the Commons, complaining, 'Do yow laughte? Laught not at me no more then I do at yow. Yow dele uncivilly with me, it is yow allwayes ther in that corner of the Howse. If it do not fall out so, hang me up at the parlyment dore.'[37] But the instance of derision is best seen in Henry Doyley's earnest attempt to inform MPs that a scandalous libel had been printed about the House entitled 'The Assemblye of Fooles.' This caused a great stir and murmuring in the House. An investigation was launched. After the offending book was found and examined by the privy councillors, 'it was ffound to be a meere toye and an ould booke entiteled, 'The Second Parte of Jack of Dover,' a thinge both stale and ffoolishe, ffor which the said My Doyley was well lawghed at, and therby his creditt muche ympeached in the oppinyon of the Howse.'[38] In these instances of laughter, we can see not only the exercise of shaming and social control but also the politically weightier consequences of 'impeaching credit.'

The Commons too suggested derision as a punishment, if the fault were found to be heinous. In 1621 while in the Fleet prison, Edward Floyd insulted the Queen of Bohemia, laughing as he remarked that 'he heard that Prague was taken, and that goodwife Palsgrave (Princess Elizabeth) and goodman Palsgrave (Prince Frederick) have taken their heels and were run away . . . . What would now become of the lad, Bess must come again to her father.'[39] When Floyd's words came to the attention of the Commons, members fell over each other in an attempt to inflict unique forms of punishment. Sir George Goring proposed that Floyd should be hung with an ass's tail, while, creatively, John Whitson proposed dropping hot bacon on him while he was being lashed.[40] Floyd was eventually punished by the Lords and forced to ride through London backward on a horse with the tail in his hand.[41] But the Commons could be mindful of gravitas. After a page had threatened to throw Sir Francis Hastings down the stairs outside Parliament, the House debated how to punish the page: 'It was moved, because his hayer was extraordinarye longe, he might be carryed to a barber, and close cutt before his dischardge, but that was thought to be very unfitt ffor the gravitye of the Howse to take notyce of soe slighte a ffaulte.'[42]

Derision was not the only form of laughter in the Commons. But because of the preeminence of laughter as social scorn, diarists were often quick to note mirth and distinguish it from mocking, although one commentator thought that laughter 'was a thing very ill beseeming the serious gravity of so great an assembly.'[43] Townshend in 1601 noted pointedly in his diary that when the House laughed 'hartelye' at his speech, it was 'done for mirthe.'[44] Similarly, it was commented that 'generall laughing' followed Mr. Stevenson, who protested, 'I no more meant to speak in this matter then I did to bidd yow all to breakfast.'[45] As with the dry humor of Sir Robert Wroth who under question of one of his servants claiming parliamentary privilege noted that 'he is one of the most necessariest servantes, ffor in truthe . . . he is my taylor.'[46]

VERSIFYING NOISE

Keith Thomas also identified crudeness as one of the main elements of laughter as mirth. In parliamentary terms, the soundscape of laughter, background noise, and speech coincided with the most famous pre–civil war parliamentary satire, 'the fart censured in the parliament house.' As one nineteenth-century editor commented, '[T]his escape' led to 'forty stanzas of the most wretched doggrel.'[47] Its interest lies in not only affirming crudeness as a matter for laughter, and that noise in the House was commented upon (although these in themselves are important), but how it identifies MPs with both their modes of speech and their interests. The latter is significant, as it attests to what individuals often spoke about. Hence the Corporation of London Recorder is noted as speaking for the city; the lawyer William Noy on entails; and the privy councillor Sir Thomas Lake on the Council. But it also mentions how some MPs, Nicholas Fuller for one, spoke with eloquence; that Sir Robert Cotton favored quoting from records; George More was known for calling the House to order; Thomas Mounson and Bennett for their sageness, and so on. The poem, which contains so much detailed information on the members that it was obviously penned by individuals intimately familiar with the chamber, illuminates a House in which the soundscape was noisy and the MPs were 'wind-bags.'

The verse was occasioned by Henry Ludlow's loudly breaking wind on 4 March 1607, just as the messengers from the Lords arrived with a communication on the Union with Scotland and naturalization.[48]

> Never was bestowed such art
> Upon the tuning of a Fart
> Downe came gave auncient Sir John Crooke[49]
> And redd his message in his booke.
> Fearie well, Quoth Sir William Morris, Soe:
> But Henry Ludlowes Tayle cry'd Noe . . .

The parliamentary diarist, Robert Bowyer, noted in his journal the following:

> As the messenger had spoken the Words (their Lordships) one at the nether end of the House *sonitum ventre emisit*; whereat the Company laughing the Messenger was almost out of Countenance. It is said to have been young Ludloe; not that this seemeth done in disgrace, for his Father Sir Edward Ludloe before at a Committee fell on sleepe and *sonitum ventre emisit*: So this seemeth Infirmity Naturall, not Malice.[50]

The initial verses were penned by a coterie of wits, including Christopher Brooke, John Hoskins, Edward Jones, Richard Martin, and possibly John Donne.[51] Brooke, Hoskins, and Martin were MPs in 1607, while both Jones and Donne had previously sat in the Commons and thus were no doubt familiar with the various members referred to in the poem and the

nuances of parliamentary procedure evident in the stanzas. It is likely that
the poem started as a coterie game by members of the dining group that
met at the Mitre and Mermaid taverns in the early seventeenth century.[52]
Twenty-seven copies are extant, and it was printed as part of miscellany collections in 1655, 1660, and 1699.[53]

Michelle O'Callaghan has stressed that much of the verse shows how
the disturbance in the House was treated in a 'decorous and orderly' manner,[54] and Ralph Starkey's headnote in his own copy reads 'A Censure of a
Fart (that was lett in the Parleament howse by mr Henry Ludlowe) by a
worshipfull Iurie each speaking in theire order as foloweth.'[55] However, this
clever juxtaposition of the theory of parliamentary practice (order, civility,
decorum in speech) with structured metrical rhyme, owes more to the medium of versifying and rhymed couplets than to the content of the stanzas.
The poem actually stresses the noise of the chamber. The most obvious
reference is through the opening 'explosion' of Ludlow, which gave rise to
the wits penning the verse. But also in the references to his father's similar
behavior and the incident in which Edward de Vere, Earl of Oxford, far-
ted in front of Queen Elizabeth.[56] Sir William Lower's couplet ends 'with
a loud shout,' while Sir John Hollis 'said, on his word, It was but a Shoo
that creak'd on a board.'[57] We also see the obverse of noise, silence, in the
couplets attributed to John Bond and Sir Thomas Mounson:

> Sylence quth Bond thoug words be but wynde
> Yet I much mislike of this motion behynd
> For quoth hee it stincks the more you stirr it
> Naturam Expellas surca licet usque recurrit
> Then gan sage Mounson silence to breake
> And said this fart would make as Image speake[58]

Continual references as well to rising and being seated all add to the sense of
clamor in the poem. Noise in the chamber is used to define the body politic. The verse describes the obverse of dignified rhetorical oratory from an
august organ of state; indeed it was penned as a parody of dignified oration
in which the fart stood for disorderly speech (its logical inversion) and as a
metaphor for much of the cacophony in the House. That the fart represented speech, and disorderly speech at that, can be seen from the final stanzas in
one version when the fart as a traitor was committed to the Tower:[59]

> But all at last said, it was most fit,
> The Fart as a Traitor, to the Tower to commit:

Where as they say, it remaines to this houre,
Yet not close prisoner, but at large in the Tower.

The poem also warns against too rambunctious speech in the House, as in the instance of Christopher Pigott, who was committed (like the fart) to the Tower for outspoken speech:

Then Sir Edward Hoby alleag'd with the spigot;
If you fart at the Union, remember Kit Pigot.[60]

SILENCE

Ludlow's fart punctuated the chamber with noise. In the Commons, silence, the obverse of noise, was a deliberate signifier of shock and protest. It was used to register displeasure with a speech; amazement at the audacity of the orator who had stepped outside the bounds of accepted rhetorical behavior; and protest—usually as an implicit criticism of government or Crown policies. The criticism may have been *unspoken*, but it can not have been *unheard*. As Christina Luckyj notes, '[S]ilence in early modern England was an unstable and highly contested site. . . . Silence [could be] an antirhetorical space of resistance, inscrutable, unreadable and potentially unruly and chaotic.'[61] This then is the dominant type of silence found in the Commons.

In 1523 in response to the King's demand for a huge subsidy, conveyed in person to them by Cardinal Wolsey, it was answered with 'a mervailous, obstinate silens.' The Speaker, Thomas More, was forced to apologize to Wolsey, proclaiming that it was contrary to their dictum of free speech to debate in front of others: 'They could not answer for it would have been inexpedient and he could not answer as they had not commanded him to.'[62] Wolsey went so far as to pick out a member of the royal household whom he knew personally, 'How say you, Mr Marney?' Wolsey asked but still received no reply.[63] In 1566, the House showed its displeasure with Elizabeth's refusal to discuss her marital status by hearing William Cecil's message from the Queen in complete silence. Two days later on Saturday, after the Queen had curtly commanded the Commons to desist, the House again descended into silence. The following Monday witnessed Paul Wentworth's strident defense of the liberties of the House.[64] In 1606 after the delivery of a message from the Lords on the unpopular proposal for Union between England and Scotland, the Speaker was forced to rise and request the pleasure of the House be known after a 'great silence.'[65] Similar outbreaks of political silence can be found in 1621 and 1626, when both Houses refused to transact any business after Charles had arrested MPs and peers. On 3 June 1628 the House registered protest at the King's answer to the petition of right by sitting in silence until Sir John Eliot broke the quiet of the chamber, '*Curae leves loquuntur, ingentes stupent.* At this time I must confess I know not how to deliver my opinion; but some must break the ice and, in this great silence, I first attempt it.'[66] A clear way of how to proceed through the minefield that was the King's unsatisfactory answer to the petition had still not emerged two days later. On an extraordinary day in which Sir Robert Phelips wept fearing that it would be the last time he ever spoke in the Commons, and Digges claimed he was sorry to have ever sat in Parliament. Digges also proposed that the House should sit in silence—'we are all so miserable, we know not what to do.'[67] After the House 'sat in sad silence for a while,' and various MPs had called out for this to be made an order, business resumed as Sir Nathaniel Rich, a confirmed bachelor, nonetheless remembered the words from the marriage ceremony in the Book of Common Prayer and swayed the Commons toward action: '[E]ither we must speak now, or forever hold our peace.'[68]

Political shunning of the monarch or the other House was only one cause of silence in the Commons. On occasion, the House was unwilling to proceed without direction or knowing the mind of the privy councillors. During the debate on the subsidy in 1601, the House 'sate silent a good while' waiting for the councillors to speak; one councillor awaiting the House whispered, '[H]ave they not tongues as well as eares.'[69] This lack of direction in a poorly managed Parliament exemplifies the Commons' soundscape, for rapidly silence became tumult. The absence of formal speech gave way to private entreaties when Sir Walter Raleigh beckoned Sir Edward Hoby to come and sit by him at the top end of the House. Unfortunately, Hoby's elevation to a better position was foiled by the lack of a seat, and he returned sulking to the lower end where he cried out after Raleigh had spoken, '[We] cannotte heare yow, speake out.' An affronted Sir Robert Cecil declared that if Hoby wished to sit near the front, he should also have the duty that went along with it, while Raleigh, who seems to have instigated the confrontation, 'with a countenance full of disdayn,' implied that Hoby might have been better behaved had he consumed less drink at lunchtime.[70]

The afternoon proceeded noisily before a 'confused' House rose after dark and 'would sitt noe longer.'[71]

Silence was often the consequence of failure of parliamentary management. If the opening day of Parliament often typified the crowded, noisy environment in which MPs found themselves, so too silence was a predominant feature that surrounded the choice of the Speaker of the Commons. Traditionally the Speaker was known well in advance, chosen by the monarch and the 'election' on the opening day a mere formality.[72] It was also customary for the nomination to be made by the senior privy councillor in the Commons. However, this procedure was often surprisingly poorly managed, which led to periods of silence. For all the ritual ceremony of the first day, well-known and mapped out in advance, on this day the soundscape of the Commons was generally confused, as we have seen from the difficulties of hearing and gaining access to the monarch's speech. The exemplar of poor management occurred in 1601, when the Commons returned to their House and far from leadership, the Privy Council whispered among themselves until finally the Comptroller of the Household, Sir William Knollys, rose to nominate the Recorder of London, John Croke. Confusion continued after Knollys's speech, when the chamber again sat silent as the councillors whispered to each other. After a while Knollys was forced to rise again and ask whether the House would accept Croke, to which 'everye man cryed I, I, I.'[73] Further silence followed Croke's disabling speech, and again the councillors conferred among themselves before Knollys again asked the House to approve Croke. Poor management in a house of novice Parliament-men led to mute members and confused procedure on the opening day. Little had changed by the start of the next Parliament in 1604. Despite Secretary Herbert informing the House that the King preferred Sir Edward Phelips to be the Speaker, MPs again sat in silence before a host of other names were called out, although Phelips was eventually elected.[74]

Silence also helped to protect the Commons' secrecy in debate. When the counsel of the Virginia Company, Mr. Martin, presented the Company's business before the House in 1614, he was accompanied by three members of the Lords who were also on the Virginia Company Council. The Commons treated their lordships with great respect, allowing the Lords to sit and be covered. But the House also ordered that Martin be heard in silence, as members of the Lords were in St. Stephen's. Remarkably, the

House maintained this silence even though Martin digressed from Company business and launched an ill-advised attack on the Commons. Stoically sitting through Martin's tirade, the House maintained an unusual degree of composure, and he was 'not interrupted because it was agreed by the House before he came in to hear him with silence.'[75] Nevertheless, a speech with Chamberlain described as 'taxing them for theyre slow proceding, for theyre disorderly cariage, and schooling them what they shold do, with divers odde glaunces' was not going to go unpunished. Martin was called before the Commons and forced to make an apology. He found the Commons a daunting body before which to present his argument, and, nervous at his appearance there, he had consumed a quantity of wine. As Sir Robert Hitcham commented, '[In] this perplexity he might be carried to say he knew not what.'[76]

Speeches at which the House took offense provoked one of two responses, the humming, hawking, and hemming we discussed above, or silence. Raleigh's 'sharpe speeche' on monopolies in 1601 elicited a 'greate silence.'[77] Raleigh again managed to shock the House into silence when he announced that he had often forcibly prevented MPs from voting by physically holding them back. This caused both 'lowde speech and stirre' and an ensuing silence.[78] In the Commons the silence of the whole House signified both protest and astonishment. During the debates on the Union with Scotland in 1606–7, Sir Christopher Pigott offended the House by noisily interrupting the proceedings. That he made his interjection while seated was a clear contravention of the manner of addressing the House, where MPs stood to be acknowledged by the Speaker before they spoke. After rising to continue his comments, he violently attacked the Scots, 'much to the dislike and greefe of the whole house.' His speech was so offensive that a shocked House became mute.[79] When the King complained that Pigott had been allowed to proceed with his diatribe, the Commons protested 'that the dislike appeared sufficiently by that *maestum silentium*.'[80] Quoting Seneca, *Curae leves loquuntur, ingentes stupent,* the Commons answered the charge by this no doubt familiar concept, that 'light griefs are communicative, great ones stupefy.'[81] The House then sent Pigott to the Tower for his impertinent speech. Silence thus punctuated and framed political opposition and debate. But so too could the collective will of the House be expressed through disturbance.

POLITICAL NOISE

Noise was a tool utilized to express the opinion of the House on the actions of an individual member. In 1628 the speakers at a joint conference with the Lords on the Petition of Right received the applause of the entire House 'with acclamation and putting off of hats.'[82] Such instances of unanimous approbation were rare. In most instances the general body of the Commons was united in opposition and employed both rhetoric and disturbance to show disapproval and force an end to speeches.

Perhaps the most famous instance of this is Arthur Hall's speech in 1572. Hall aptly described himself as 'overweenyng of himself . . . furious when he is contraried, without patience to take tyme to judge or doubte the daunger of the sequele . . . [and] so implacable if he conceyve an injurie.'[83] These traits he carried over into his parliamentary career. In 1572 the overwhelming majority of the Commons clamored for the Duke of Norfolk's execution to be carried out and for Elizabeth to take action against Mary Queen of Scots. Hall, though, defended both vigorously and was subjected to the displeasure of the House, which attempted to drown him out—'the House misliked so mutch of his talke that with soflinge of feet and ha[w]kinge thei had wellny barred him to be hard.'[84] Another diarist remembered it as 'a greate murmur, spitting and coughing.'[85] Charged with 'lewd speeches,' Hall claimed that he had forgotten himself, as so much noise greeted his oratory that 'he spake he knew not what.' Later in his career and again drawing the ire of the House, he printed a series of advices to the House that accused MPs of rowdy behavior through drunkenness and too much tobacco.

Hall had riled the House by speaking against its will on controversial issues. But boredom and long oratory could also move the Commons to disturbance. London's Recorder, William Fleetwood, whose frequent speeches often lasted hours and wandered off the topic at hand, was a particular target.[86] He exploded at the 'hacking and hewing' in the House 'by the faith yow shall all lye by the heles before I will speak for any of yow.'[87] In 1593 James Dalton complained about the House's behavior during Sir James Morice's speech: '[It] was straunge and shamefull to see howe a number of the House without all modestie or discretion coughed and hauked, of purpose to putt him out.'[88] Sir Robert Cecil then complained about the noise made during Dalton's speech. The problem might have been, as Townshend recorded in 1598, 'the rebellious corner in the right hand of the Howse.'[89]

Perhaps unsurprisingly, the area closest to the door and farthest away from the Speaker and the privy councillors at the other end of the chamber seems to have been a specific site of disturbance, although this may have shifted to the gallery after it was built in 1621. Bulstrode Whitelocke termed it 'the resort of mutineers' and noted his dislike of sitting there.[90]

Hissing seems to have been one of the most effective and oft utilized disruptive techniques. In 1606 Mr. Hext complained of the House 'hissing' at him when he spoke.[91] Mr. Bond also complained in 1610 that a speech had been met with 'much hissing and spitting' and called for the Speaker to stop 'impertinent speeches.'[92] Leonard Bawtrey in 1614 suffered the same fate for telling the Commons it could debate only matters the King had approved.[93] The use of noise in the Chamber to end the long-winded or boring speech of an MP was recognized as a facet of debate by contemporary commentators such as William Hakewill:

> Such as speak are not stinted to any time for the length of their speech: but he that speaketh if he be observant shall easily perceive (even while he is speaking) how far he may presume upon the patience of the House in that regard, for if they be well pleased with the speech there will be great silence and attention; if otherwise, they will talk one with the other, which will cause a murmuring noise and sometime they will hawk and hem or make some noise by scarping with their feet, that he which speaketh shall hardly be heard but by those that are near him, against which misdemeanour there have been divers orders made.[94]

The Commons also used shouting and interruptions in order to enforce the rules of the House. It was generally recognized that MPs should speak only once in a debate unless the House was in committee, where it was permissible for members to speak more frequently. Those who attempted to speak again during ordinary debates in the House were usually shouted down and interrupted, a fate suffered even by such an experienced Parliament-man as Sir Francis Bacon in 1604.[95] Sir Edward Coke's son, Clement,[96] and John Bankes in 1626 also fell afoul of the House for this reason.[97]

On occasions of high political drama the usual commotion, bustle, and auditory difficulties of the Commons were also punctuated by wailing and weeping. The King's message to the Commons on 5 June 1628 that he intended to keep to the fixed date to end the session, 'that black and doleful Tuesday,' as Joseph Mead called it,[98] caused an uproar in the House. Not only was the soundscape confused as many cried out but Sir Robert Phelips had difficulty marshaling his speech through his tears and Sir Edward Coke 'was forced to sit down when he began to speak, through the abundance of tears; yea the Speaker in his speech could not refrain from weeping.'[99] The passions were so great, according to Mead, that silence befell the chamber.[100]

The furor in the Commons surrounding monopolies in 1601 caused the house at times, as Sir Robert Cecil complained, to act 'more like a grammar school than a Court of Parliament.' In addition to the controversy over monopolies, the House was not well served by its choice of Sir John Croke as the Speaker. Croke, though grave and learned, does not seem to have had the authority or personality to stamp his mark on grammar school behavior. After fumbling his way through the opening day and a messy election dispute, Croke failed to read the mood of the House on 20 November and was overwhelmed by the noise in the Commons.

> The Speaker gave the Clarke a bill to reade and the Howse called for the Chequer bill; some said Yea, some said Noe, and a greate noyse ther was. At laste Mr. Lawrence Hide said, 'Mr. Speaker, to end this controversie because the tyme is verye shorte, I would move the Howse to have a verye shorte bill read entitled "An acte for the explanacion of the common lawe in certayne cases of lettres patents."' All the Howse cried I, I, I.[101]

The chamber and the business of Parliament must have been a daunting space, especially for a new MP unfamiliar with its habits and procedures. There were no orientation tours or manuals specific to parliamentary conduct. In 1584 it was claimed that the opening ceremonies were disorderly, with MPs milling about in 'troops,' as no one knew what to do, 'there being not past vij or viij of the old parliamentes.'[102] Negotiating the Commons' soundscape was a learned experience that required skills of oratory and of experience and a general consensus of speaking with the voice of the House.

The early Stuart Parliaments began with noise and disturbance (epitomized in the chaotic opening ceremony),[103] and they ended in 1629 in loud clamor, tumult, and violence. The first Parliament of James was marked by confusion, mismanagement, and misunderstanding. The final day of activity before the Personal Rule brought a halt to Parliaments for eleven years occurred amid uproar and orchestrated political noise on 2 March 1629 over what was, in the minds of many MPs, a premature end to the Parliament.

Immediately after prayers the Speaker, Sir John Finch, attempted to follow the King's orders and adjourn the Parliament. This precipitated a noisy confrontation between the majority of the House, who voiced their disapproval by shouting down the Speaker and further calling with a 'loud crye' for Sir John Eliot to speak. Finch's refusal to hear Eliot and his sudden departure from the chair prompted Holles and Valentine to seize him by the arms and force him to stay seated. This level of violence and disturbance continued in the House as not only Hollis and Valentine leaped toward the Speaker but many in the House shot out of their seats and flocked toward the chair. Urged on by the cries of the House, in a tub-thumping performance, Eliot threw a paper he had intended to read into the center of the chamber from his seat high up in the House. Again the House erupted urging Eliot to speak—as one source has it, the Speaker was 'violently called upon by many to have the paper read.'[104] At some point in the proceedings William Coryton scuffled with Francis Winterton, who attempted to assist the Speaker.[105] Further noise and confusion ensued when calls were made for the door of the House to be locked, and a cry of 'All, all' urged Eliot to continue his speech. The mood of the House did not improve when Sir Dudley Digges, in an attempt to provide a modicum of reason to the day's proceedings, was hissed at for suggesting that the Lord Treasurer Sir Richard Weston was innocent of the charges laid against him unless they were proven. By this point Eliot had somehow burned his paper (perhaps in the Commons fireplace) while the Speaker maintained his political silence and refused to read Eliot's charges, or to engage in the debate. The day ended with the House yelling approval to Holles's summation of the points of Eliot's paper, the Speaker in tears, and 'confused noyse and stirre' before the adjournment and subsequent imprisonment of the overly vocal leaders of the Commons.

Despite the ramifications of 2 March, Eliot had utilized a proven tactic to coordinate the natural clamor and shouting of the House to achieve his goals. Eliot and his friends won the day, for noise was a legitimate and accepted part of political life in the Commons. Shouting, hissing, and creating a disturbance were employed both for purposes of 'oppositional' politics and also as an effective way in which the collective political nation enforced its will against its own members. Ironically, Eliot, Holles, and Valentine ultimately relied upon silence to defend themselves from the King. Refusing to plead to charges of sedition in King's Bench, as they did not recognize the authority of the court over the affairs of Parliament, they were condemned by their silence; the judge took their muteness as a signifier of guilt.[106]

~

In 1614 Sir Herbert Croft compared the noise in the House of Commons to a cockpit.[107] Although roundly condemned, MPs certainly shared some traits with audiences at theatrical and sporting performances.[108] In these venues too, noise dominated the soundscape. Perhaps the resemblance was inevitable in a political body of nearly five hundred members surrounded by parliamentary officials, petitioners, hundreds of servants, and interested onlookers. But more important, noise (and silence) were political tools used by the House to control its members, and to register disapproval at the policies of the Crown.

Freedom of speech might be curtailed but noise could not be silenced, and a mute House could not be compelled to speak. As we have seen, the vast majority of members did not speak in the House but through acclamation, hawking, murmuring, or sitting silent, they did, nonetheless, participate in the political business of the nation. Their 'voices' were heard and registered through their actions rather than in speaking in the intimidating environment of the Commons. Moreover, even the 'trivial' noises of Parliament turn out to be political when they operate in concert, and when they are orchestrated to operate as an instrument of the body politic—as an expression of its collective will. Even dissent 'in the corner or lower end' of the House emanates not so much from individual members but as an identity expressed by the vocal powers of a smaller group within the collective of the Commons. Noise did not replace speech as the dominant trope of opposition, but it increasingly joined with it as a tactic to thwart individual speakers, or the policies of the Crown, and as a way in which the House as a single body reacted to unfavorable news. What defined gatherings, be they political, religious, or cultural, was participation. As we saw in the last chapter, for the vast majority of MPs their verbal participation was limited to sounds other than speech.

PART TWO

Writing Parliament

CHAPTER THREE

Swift Pens: Recording Parliament

Sir Bulstrode Whitelocke's diary of the 1626 Parliament was intended as a reference work for his son and as a permanent record of the session. The diary being written in three cheap paper books that he later copied into his Annals, Whitelocke clearly felt part of an important enterprise—namely, that of parliamentary recording and reporting. He labored over his account: 'I have been the longer in relating passages of it because I was an actor and a constant attender in it and can leave it to you for an example that in all debates I was neither by court flattery nor popular vanity, but only by that reason and conscience which God hath given me.'[1] Whitelocke was keen to emphasize that his diary was intended not only as an educational tool for his son but also as a record of his work and participation. In the context of the 1620s, when the 'Parliament-man' became a scribbler and the Commons resonated with the sound of quills scratching on paper, neither Whitelocke's recording of parliamentary debates nor the value he placed on their posterity were unusual events.

Before the 1620s, private parliamentary diaries were largely just that, personal records kept by members with antiquarian leanings interested in procedure, bill readings, and the minutiae of the House's work. Few in number and largely uncontroversial jottings of legislative or procedural manners, the diaries resembled and closely followed the official Commons Journal. From 1621, this limited method of engagement with activity in the chamber no longer reflected the interests of MPs nor the importance of events discussed in Parliament. A news-hungry gentry demanded more information, and MPs saw themselves as more central to the political process, as witnesses and actors in history. This is reflected in the changing nature of diaries throughout the 1620s. In the increasingly contested political atmosphere of that decade they proliferated and became records of speeches made on the floor on the chambers, rather than legislative business and procedural minutiae.

$\sim$

The proceedings of Parliament were *arcana imperii* (secrets of state), a statement in jarring contradiction to the more than 120 extant copies of detailed notes and diaries people took in the House between 1571 and 1629. 'Every person of the Parliament ought to keep secret and not disclose the secrets and things spoken and done in the Parliament House, to any manner of person unless he be one of the same House.'[2] This edict, however, was honored more in the breach than in the observance[3]—from George Strode in 1593 who copied 'certaine briefe things w[hi]ch I observed at the parlam[en]t,'[4] to Edward Nicholas, Secretary of State, who in the 1620s ensured that his notes made their diurnal way into the hands of the King, personal and state papers are awash with the proceedings of Parliament.[5] Similarly, Edward Alford scribbled notes, comments, and doodles on the backs of committee lists and bill breviates, and Sir Richard Grosvenor, who in 1628 laboriously attempted to capture speeches verbatim, scrawled furiously in his diaries. The chambers of Parliament played host to a myriad of MPs and peers who wrote as 'journalists,' recorders, and compilers of potentially dangerous political information.[6] Amid these scribblers were the serial diarists, the proceduralists, high politicos, gentry, or family 'informers,' and those whose antiquarian interests led to the minutiae of rule recording. Diarists' methods of recording information were as individual as they were.

Parliament was built on a foundation of paper and staffed by professional scribblers. Parliamentary clerks in the Lords and Commons recorded the official proceedings. A deputy clerk sat in the Commons' lobby transcribing the Journal and offering copies, for a price, to those who required committee lists, copies of speeches, and official memoranda. For the clerks, their primary role was to keep the official journals of proceedings in the chambers. These started life as rough sets of notes with the clerks recording a mixture of speeches, procedure, the business of bill readings, and committee reports, as well as the onerous and difficult task of writing down the names of committee members as they were shouted out by MPs. As William Hakewill commented, the clerk recorded the 'names (in that confusion) he can distinctly heare.'[7] The clerks then drafted their notes into fair copies of the Journal, usually eliminating much of debate, and theoretically anyway, the names of members.[8]

Parliament was not a cheap institution. Between 1640 and 1642 paper, when the accounts are most detailed, consumption of books and other supplies came to a staggering £763 15s 2d.[9] The parliamentary need for paper, printing, and stationery supplies was so high that the King's printer moved to Westminster during parliamentary sessions and set up a press in Westminster Palace.[10] Paper was delivered on a weekly basis, more often if required, and other parliamentary supplies included pens, pen knives, cedar pencils, ink, standishes, ink horns, and sand (black and white). Acts of Parliament, orders of the House, votes, committee lists, and reports piled up on the clerk's desk necessitating bags and trunks to store such quantities, and, of course, a key to lock the chamber at the end of the day to prevent pilfering. These were usually of the highest quality: a 'turkey' (goat) skin bag with silk strings to hold bills, two boxes covered with leather with locks also for bills, 'fine' paper, and 'best' or 'fine' parchment were all at the disposal of the clerks.[11] Essential to the smooth running of business, the clerks of the Lords and Commons obtained bibles, books of common prayer,[12] almanacs, and copies of statutes. In a similar fashion, the Speaker was provisioned with books relevant to his position. William Lenthall, the Speaker in the Long Parliament, also obtained bibles, books of common prayer, legal treatises, and copies of statutes. However, other book purchases seem to have little relevance to the immediate work of Parliament. In 1614 the Clerk of the Commons also had at his disposal copies of John Speed's new work, *History of Great Britain*, Raphael Holinshed's *Chronicles of England, Scotland and Ireland*, and John Foxe's *Acts and Monuments*.[13] Speaker Lenthall's extraneous purchases at the Crown's expense were, as Elizabeth Read Foster has noted, very extensive.

> [Lenthall] began to buy a library at the expense of the Crown: three almanacs, statutes, abridgements, several bibles, a service book, registers of writs, Fulbecke's *Law*, Coke on Littleton, Pliny's *History*, Plutarch's *Lives*, the works of Seneca, an English translation of Tacitus, a *French Academy*, *Flores Doctorum*, *Office of Executors*, Kitchen's *Court Leets*, Matthew Paris, the *Adages* of Erasmus, Du Bartas, *The Souls Solace*, and Gerard's *Herbal*.[14]

In all, Lenthall added more than sixty works to his collection, including another copy of Du Bartas.[15]

OFFICIAL JOURNALS

Both the Commons and the Lords Journals pose substantial problems of evaluation. As the focal point of the medieval Parliament, the Lords was quicker to develop its own official journal, and a more or less continual record exists from 1510.[16] However, the Lords Journal was simply a record of official business, and its content is little more than a register of daily attendance registers begun in 1515, as well as proxies, legislative proceedings, and the occasional record of rules and orders of the House. The clerk did not note speeches or debate, because it did not help him fulfill his responsibilities to track the process of legislation through the chamber. The paucity of the Tudor Lords Journal improves only marginally under their early Stuart successors. However, the antiquarian interests of two clerks of the Parliament, Robert Bowyer and Henry Elsynge, offers a much greater insight into the debates in the Lords. Both clerks appear to have kept much fuller notes than their predecessors, and their moves toward professionalized record-keeping ensures that we have available some of the actual debates in the journals. Furthermore, their notes from debates and speeches in committee survive in many fragments in the Main Papers. Two factors are at work here. First, as Parliament became more and more part of the political nation and took upon itself greater responsibilities (revival of impeachment; standing committees in the Commons and Lords), so the paperwork multiplied. The records generated in the House of Lords, and now extant in the Main Papers, grew exponentially in the 1620s as the Upper House investigated a host of new complaints. The clerk was now responsible for keeping extensive files on the impeachment process, petitions submitted to the Lords Standing Committee on Petitions, and grievances presented to the Houses.[17] Increasingly too, legislation was promoted (and opposed) by interest groups via supporting documentation, both scribal and printed.[18]

The clerks and the institution itself became more professional and more adept at dealing with the ever more contentious business in the House. Part of this process came through the individual efforts of Bowyer and Elsynge. In 1604, they were appointed as Joint Keepers of the Records in the Tower.[19] Bowyer was elected an MP in 1605 and became a keen observer of parliamentary behavior, keeping a journal of the proceedings of the Commons.[20] He had held the reversion to the office of Clerk of the Parliaments since 1597, and he succeeded to it in 1610. It is difficult to overstate either the professionalism, experience, or interest that Bowyer brought to the office, or his importance in starting a system of full and accurate record-keeping that he bequeathed to his successors and that today stands as testimony to his work. Bowyer was undoubtedly helped by his experience as an MP and as the Keeper of Records in the Tower. While a member of the Lower House, Bowyer had assisted the underclerk in completing the final version of the Commons Journal. Bowyer made notes in the margins of the draft journals, correcting errors and adding his own recollections so that the final copy was vastly improved. He brought a similar professionalism to the Lords Journal. Bowyer worked furiously to record verbatim the words spoken in the Upper House, and later reviewed his 'scribbled books,' noting in the margins the material that should be included in the fair copy. Often critical of his predecessors' laxity, Bowyer examined his notes for accuracy, and his text is grounded thoroughly in procedure and precedent. 'Although only one of the scribbled books has survived for the 1610 session, it provides a vivid illustration of events, speeches and happenings in the Upper House. It also shows the course of events (often different from the final Journal), the order in which Lords were named to committees and his impressions of important speeches.'[21] But as Bowyer commented, '[I]nto the Journal book which is the record, he [the clerk] doth in discretion forbear to enter many things spoken, though memorable, yet not necessary nor fit to be registered and left to posterity to record.'[22] In the scribbled books, '[T]he House of Lords comes alive through the diligence of its clerk.'[23]

As both Clerk of the Parliaments and Keeper of the Tower Records, Bowyer received many letters asking for favors or assistance. During the 1610 session of Parliament, Lord Lisle asked him to write to the London sheriffs about a matter of privilege for one of his servants, while Lord Saye and Sele requested copies of the bills against pluralities and that for disuniting the parsonages of Dean and Ashe. For the latter, Bowyer received not only his fees but also a piece of venison as a gift.[24] On 5 March, a servant of the attorney general, Sir Henry Hobart, wrote to Bowyer asking him to discuss the bill for restoring in blood the children of George Brooke, which Hobart had penned but that was incorrectly titled. Later in the session, Hobart again contacted Bowyer, this time on a private matter, stating that he had sufficient fees to pay Bowyer to proceed with haste on Hobart's own bill for draining marshland in Norfolk.[25] Lord Eure was interested in a copy of the bill for JPs quieting of possessions, and Justice Walmesley asked Bowyer to do what he could to further the bill against 'Barwicke,' for which he would be 'paid what I said if the bill is enacted.'[26] Sir George Rennell received a copy of the Thetford School bill, and the King requested Bowyer to inform him how the bill for naturalizing Margaret Clark was proceeding. William Noy asked Bowyer to provide certain records to assist the procedure of Lord Abergavenny's bill, and the Earl of Bath requested a copy of the River Tow measure.[27] Bowyer was also busy assisting the Lords, who ordered him to search for precedents for punishing Dr. Cowell (5 March) and to copy Commons documents on tenures and wardships (31 March).[28] In the fifth session of the 1604 Parliament, Bowyer was in receipt of a letter from the underclerk in which the Commons ordered Bowyer to copy and endorse the answers of the King to the grievances petition of 1610. The Lords, justifiably upset at the effrontery of the Lower House in issuing sending orders to its clerk, allowed Bowyer to pen a draft but in no uncertain terms informed the Commons that it had no jurisdiction over officers in the Lords.[29]

With Bowyer's death in 1621, Elsynge succeeded to the office, taking for the first time a recently devised oath of office.[30] Although much of the clerk's preparation for the 1621 Parliament had been undertaken by Bowyer, Elsynge was left to cope with a much greater workload as the House instituted standing orders, dealt with the revival of the impeachment process, and accepted its role as a court, allowing petitions from those who considered themselves harmed by the legal system. These new categories of business meant that the House both generated and received many more documents than it had before. Elsynge's training as a clerk under Bowyer stood him in good stead, as he kept meticulous proceedings on bills, a daily agenda, committee books, orders of the House, legal proceedings, and grievances. Elsynge also authored a tract on parliamentary procedure, *The Manner of Holding Parliaments in England*, and other parliamentary commentaries in a similar vein.[31] The sheer volume of material in the 1620s dramatically increased the clerk's workload and the amount that peers needed to read and debate. With the revival of the House of Lords as a judicial body in the 1620s, 207 legal cases were heard. All these involved the receipt of the original petitions and multiple supporting documents, including the often lengthy 'articles of grievance,' testimonies of witnesses, and records from earlier court decisions.[32] In addition to the forty-seven legal cases reviewed in 1628–29, the House also obtained copious records on the Commons' claims on the liberties of the subject. On 9 April 1628, for example, from the Tower the Lords ordered brought to Westminster copies of Rolls from fourteen different Parliaments ranging from 1 Edward I to 42 Edward III, Treasury records from the reigns of Edward I and Edward III, eleven sheets of precedents out of King's Bench, the report of Sir Dudley's Digges speech at the 7 April Joint Conference, twelve sheets of Edward Littleton's report, and nine sheets of Sir Edward Coke's the same day. In addition, William Cavendish, the Earl of Devonshire, furnished '60 sides close written' of John Selden's speech on 7 April.[33]

The Commons was not as meticulous or experienced as the Upper House in record-keeping. The Underclerk of the Parliaments and his assistant, who also sat in the chamber, kept records of proceedings and debate, as well as a book of orders, and from 1621, a separate record of debates in the committee of the whole House. But the Journal itself did not reach a settled format until the Restoration, and much depended on the vagaries of the clerks. It is also more difficult to trace the development of the Commons' records than that of the Lords because fire consumed the old Westminster Palace in 1834 and destroyed much of the Commons' material. Furthermore, many of the Commons Journals are missing for other reasons. The antiquarian and parliamentary diarist Sir Simonds D'Ewes purloined the late Elizabethan journals to write up his own journals during the 1620s, and it is also possible that in the 1620s, when generally only rough drafts of journals are extant, D'Ewes too 'borrowed' the fair copies.[34] The first Commons Journal is extant from 1547, in contrast to 1510 in the Lords. The early journals are little more than procedural lists, and although they become somewhat fuller in the Elizabethan period, very little debate is captured, let alone the tone and atmosphere of the House. Thanks to the interference of D'Ewes, no Commons Journal is extant between 1584 and 1601. Although very few of the finished fair copies are extant, we are more fortunate during the early seventeenth century with the survival of numerous draft journals.

Both houses kept a wary eye on what their respective clerks were recording. It was during the first Jacobean Parliament (1604–10) that the Commons started to take cognizance of its own written record. This may well have been in response to concerns that the then clerk, Ralph Ewens, served the King rather than the Commons.[35] The position, however, was not in the control of the Commons but was a royal gift. Concern first arose in 1607 after the Commons refused to enter into its Journal the King's letter ordering a stop to proceedings on the part of the Hostile Laws bill, which concerned offenders fleeing from England into Scotland or vice versa. This, along with a similar royal commandment against the Commons petition on

Jesuits, prompted the House to establish a committee to review the clerk's work. The subcommittee reported on 3 July:

> Sir Edwyn Sandys maketh Report of the Travel [*sic*: travail] of the Committee appointed to peruse and consider of such Entries as are made by the Clerk in his Journal Book, &c. e said, they considered of Matter of Privilege, Matter of Order, and Matter of Message; and conceived, that, as in this Parliament there had as many and as weighty Matters come in Question, as ever in any former Parliament; so it were fit, some extraordinary Care and Regard were had in keeping a Memorial of them. For the present, they had set down in Writing, what Course they thought meet to be held, with a Desire that it might be read, and entered, if the House did approve it: And so delivered from the Committee, a Paper; which was presently read; and, upon Question, resolved to be entered, in these Words: THOUGHT fit and convenient, by the Committees, that this Order should be entered; viz.
>
> That, between this and the next Session of Parliament the Clerk shall perfect his Journal for these Three first Sessions; and that no Matter, concerning Privilege, Order, or Matter of Message, or Conference, or Resolution of the House, proceeding thereupon, shall be of Record, or in Force, till such Time as the same be perused, and perfected, by a Committee to be chosen the next Session of Parliament, and approved by the House ; and that from henceforth the Committee for Privileges do, every Saturday in the Afternoon, peruse and perfect the Book of Entries in all such Matters as aforesaid; and that, in regard to the great Pains, which the Clerk is to take in perfecting the said Journals, some Course be taken, the next Session, for his better Encouragement.[36]

Despite the potential (and later realized) danger to speakers in the Commons who criticized government policies and the appointment of a committee to peruse the clerk's book on the opening day of the 1610 session,[37] the clerks continued to record debate and to name speakers. Thus the clerk's record provided a valuable source of information for the King. Most dramatically, on 30 December 1621, the clerk, John Wright, was summoned to Whitehall and ordered to bring along his Journal. There, after a lengthy diatribe against the Commons entering its protestation about the privileges of the House in the Journal, James seized the offending book and tore the pages out.[38] Wright later found himself imprisoned along with those regarded as troublemakers in the Commons, Sir Edward Coke and Sir Edwin Sandys.[39] In 1628, during the debates on the Petition of Right, Sir Edward Coke moved that according to previous orders, the clerk was not to take down the speeches of members, only the orders of the House.[40] Elizabeth Read Foster has noted that 'the Journal is a record of the Commons ways of doing business, of the privileges of the House, but not a record of its members.[41] This may have been the official line, but in practice it was not the case; MPs turned to the clerk for copies of the Journal to fill in gaps in their own diaries, and until the tense political climax of 1628–29, the Journal served both as a record of procedure and a readily available record of speeches.

It is also possible that 1621 marked a watershed in another way. Although it is likely that the parliamentary records had been kept in the Jewel Tower at Westminster since the late Elizabethan period, in 1621 the repository was expanded and fireproofed. As Andrew Thrush has surmised, this action was no doubt spurred by the disastrous 1619 fire in Whitehall that destroyed innumerable government records.[42] But it also bespeaks a growing concern that the records of Parliament needed safekeeping and most likely a larger, more organized space to cope with the increasing number of documents before the Parliament. It was also in 1621 that the Lords established a subcommittee of Privileges to examine the clerk's Journal every week.[43] Notes such as those on the bitter words between Lords Arundel and Spencer in May 1621 were expunged from the record by the subcommittee.[44] The permanence of the record and its safekeeping is further apparent in that from 1621 the clerk's fair-written Journal, perused and corrected by the subcommittee, was enrolled onto parchment.[45]

DIARISTS

While the clerks in both Houses had the advantage of tables to write on and store their equipment, MPs and peers in the chambers arrived each day laden down with writing implements. Most writers in the House seem to have used pen and ink, necessitating paper, quill, ink, sand, and a knife. This was a somewhat cumbersome process, especially on occasions when the House was packed and space for writing was at a premium. Most MPs probably balanced their notebooks and materials on their knees—something that would account for the appalling script—but others may have availed themselves of writing boxes. Some of these little table desks (as they are known) can be found at the Victoria and Albert Museum.[46] While the standard usage has been held that these were placed on tables, they would have been quite as effective as a portable writing surface.[47] Physically, as might be expected, most diaries that we can ascertain were written in the

House were quite small—the most common size seems to be 5½ x 3½ inches. Occasionally the more effusive purchased books that were 7½ x 5½ or even larger, but in the cramped conditions of Parliament, bulk was to be avoided.

Of course, diarists and clerks struggled to record those who spoke softly, quickly, or whom they considered inarticulate.[48] Robert Bowyer managed only broken notes when Sir Edward Coke was delving into a very elaborate argument about the legality of impositions, and he had to ask the Earl of Arundel for a copy of his speech in 1621, as 'I did not well hear nor understand my Lord.'[49] Sir Francis Bacon 'professeth to omit some answers by reason that his tables failed him,'[50] and even James I slowed his speech to Parliament, 'because I see many writing and noting I will hold you a little longer by speaking the more distinctly for fear of mistaking.'[51] One member reporting news commented, 'I did diligently employ my tables, and made use of the like collection of two gentlemen of the lower house who had better brains and swifter pens than I.'[52] Richard Martin used a table book,[53] as did William Holt, who on 13 March 1607 attempted to excuse himself from reporting a conference; but as he had been seen with 'tables in his hand, and was seen to write diligently,' his excuse was not allowed.[54]

The references here to table books may refer to the use of erasable tablets to take notes in the House. Although because of their very nature as erasable, no direct evidence survives that MPs utilized this technology, the cumbersome nature of writing with pen and paper in cramped conditions certainly makes it likely that some MPs adopted this technique. These tablets were widely available, portable, and ideal for writing in the House, provided of course, that the diarists were sufficiently organized to copy their notes into a more permanent format every evening. Whether they were actually used will remain a matter of speculation, but Peter Stallybrass has argued that 'tables' and 'table-books' were synonymous in the early modern England lexicon with erasable writing surfaces.[55]

The graphite pencil was one new technology adopted by some MPs. Certainly a number of members used pencil in the House. Edward Alford took most of his notes in the margins and on the dorso of parliamentary papers using a pencil,[56] and Sir Nathaniel Rich's 1614 diary is written completely in pencil.[57] Obviously this was a far easier method of note-taking than the messy, bulky use of quill and ink. For Alford pencil was simply a convenient method; perhaps for others like Rich, it portended the later copying of notes into a more formal and permanent record. Certainly by the mid-1640s, the Clerks of Parliament found pencils extremely useful. John Browne, the Lords clerk, took delivery of twelve 'cedar pensills' in 1646; pencils formed part of the stationery of the Commons clerk in 1640.[58]

One recent technology that diarists did not readily adopt was the use of shorthand. No doubt as Michael Mendle has demonstrated, this related to the enormous difficulties of learning the complex early systems, such as John Willis's *Art of Stenographie* (1602), and the fact that for all but the extremely skilled practitioner, shorthand slowed writing down.[59] Also mitigating against its use may well have been that even those who were adept struggled to cope with verbatim speech. And while the shorthand systems of the day advertised their ability to copy down speeches, they also warned that the speaker must speak 'treatably.'[60] Given the continual clamor, interjections, and auditory difficulties of the Commons, shorthand was not an effective option. However, our knowledge of this is limited in that many of the diaries are fair copies written up later from notes. Nevertheless, of the forty or so we can determine to have been written in the House, only a very few—for example, those of John Hawarde and Sir Edward Nicholas—delved into a standardized system of abbreviations.[61] Hawarde was an unusual diarist in that he wrote in a combination of Law French and English with the occasional Latin phrase thrown in to confuse those attempting to decipher his appalling handwriting. Edward Whitby too in 1626 drafted his notes as chair of the grievances' committee in Law French, as did Henry Sherfield's part ink/part pencil diary of 1628.[62]

Some MPs had their own convoluted method of recording information. Bulstrode Whitelocke's 1626 diaries provide a good example. Whitelocke started his small 5½ x 3½ paper diary with the proceedings of the Commons, writing only on the recto side. Turned upside down, and starting at the other end of the book, again only on the recto, were notes on afternoon committee meetings. When the two met, he turned the book over and reversed direction. When he ran out of space for the daily proceedings he moved to the next available space in the afternoon committee meeting pages—interspersed are a variety of separates and keynotes speeches copied in by him from other sources. This not only confuses the historian but it clearly caused Whitelocke a few problems as well. When he started a second book he worked in chronological order, writing on both sides of the page, and placed committee reports within his daily proceedings. This system Whitelocke found more amenable and continued on with it through Book Three. As he told his son, '[T]his was your father's beginning in public action and thus early was he entered in the best school in Christendom, which he constantly attended and took notes of all that passed. But they being imperfect though laborious, and the matters being here set down in the generality of them, the labor of those notes is not inserted.'[63] Sir Simonds D'Ewes, one of the keener observers of parliamentary behavior, and famed for his important diary of the Long Parliament, actually went so far as to compile his own diaries even when he was not an MP.[64] Significantly, these are not just the rather formal copies of the Commons and Lords Journal which D'Ewes compiled for the Elizabethan Parliaments, but much more elaborate diaries with speeches, debates, and summaries. Not satisfied with his own work he even offered advice on the genre: 'The greatest part of October [1625] was spent visiting and discoursing, although whilst I was with Sir Nathaniel Barnardiston, at Kediton, the first week of the month in part, and the whole eighth and ninth days of it being Saturday and Sunday, I laboured on the week days to direct him how to frame a journal of the last unfortunate and successless Parliament, in which he had been a burgess.'[65] Diarists too gained more knowledge and experience as the Parliament progressed: Sir John Newdegate's diary in 1628 improves noticeably as the Parliament goes along; his notes and summations become clearer, and more and more MPs are identified as he gains familiarity with his fellow members.[66]

One of the major differences between those accounts taken in the House and those 'written fair' later is the degree to which debates are altered and summarized. Occasionally with rough notes we find diarists such as Sir Thomas Wentworth in 1621 not so much recording speech but merely paraphrasing a whole debate into a conclusory paragraph,[67] but mainly they attempt to record speech verbatim or snatch at phrases and key points in a way that often makes the debate difficult to follow. But those who took due diligence to write their notes into more formal prose either every evening—such as Sir Walter Yonge in 1629—or draft them into a coherent whole at the end of Parliament were concerned with how and what the House decided. The best example of this is John Pym. As the editors of *Commons Debates 1621* noted, '[H]is method is a combination of analysis and of speeches analyzed.'[68] His dairies go far beyond the works of others to lay out debate, providing both sides of the argument, and then noting why the Commons reacted the way it did. Left out is anything that does not advance the argument. Pym, as we know from his own admission, wrote from the benefit of hindsight, possibly some years after the events. Despite this, and his clear sympathies with those who sought to preserve what they regarded as the ancient liberties of Parliament against the encroachment of the monarchy, his diaries are not the work of a partisan hack but a clear and logical rendering of proceedings.

Why then were there so many diaries drafted? One of the widely acknowledged reasons that people were elected to Parliament was to represent the interests of the town or corporation they served. Corporation and personal archives record the details of town business in Parliament as well as wider national concerns.[69] With Parliament increasingly moving toward center-stage, the desire for news in the provinces impacted Westminster. In tandem with the rise of the coranto and the professional news-letter writer we can trace the development of parliamentary diaries.

The contrast between the extant parliamentary diaries of the 1620s and previous parliaments is stark. If we compare the second Jacobean Parliament of 1614 with the third (1621), there are immediate and significant differences that reflect the increasingly important role of Parliament as the central location, the 'point of contact' between the government and the governing class. Numerically, the five diaries of 1614 are dwarfed by the thirteen that survive for 1621. But much more important is the nature of the record. In 1614 only one of the diaries can be said to be a substantial account of the parliamentary proceedings. The anonymous diarist of MS E237, at the Kenneth Spencer Research Library (University of Kansas), covers all but the first two weeks of the Parliament—as the diarist notes, he arrived only on 18 April, when Parliament had opened on 5 April. Significantly, like many of its 1620s counterparts,[70] the fair-written diary was copied in such a way as to leave a margin for annotating the record, primarily in this case to provide titles of subjects for ease of reference. The marginal indexing of the diary in such a fashion suggests that it was intended as a reference work to be referred to again and again as required. The diary gives good accounts of speeches and debate. Thus in style and content it is more in keeping with the diaries of the 1620s than those that preceded it. Of the other accounts, none can be said to be a full record of proceedings. Additional manuscript 48101 is a fair copy that covers only 13–16 April and then 3 May 1614 until the close, just over a month later. Another fair copy account records only twelve days' activity, while Sir Nathaniel Rich's notes last for a paltry three days and Sir John Holles's account for a week.[71]

In stark contrast, thirteen accounts of 1621 are extant of which eleven contain lengthy, detailed proceedings. For the development of diaries in the

1620s, culminating in the *True Relation*, the most significant work is the 'X' diary. This, like its more famous 1629 relative, is a compilation drawn from at least two diaries taken in the House (and no longer extant) to which the 'author' has added copies of speeches, separates, committee records, petitions, and miscellaneous other material. The record is the fullest account to that date both in detail of proceedings and the new skill of weaving separates and set-piece speeches into a parliamentary record. Significantly as well, five different copies of the dairy exist. Some contain only fragments, but it certainly appears that the original was in widespread circulation, emphasizing the eagerness for parliamentary news and the desire to own a copy of the proceedings. Five copies also survive of John Pym's diary. Pym wrote his diary sometime after the Parliament, most likely from notes that he took in the House and at committee.

The contrast between the 1621 diaries and those for previous Parliaments is too great for it to be simply a matter of surviving documentation. The pattern of 1621 is repeated throughout the 1620s. It shows an increasing desire on behalf of the political nation to record parliamentary proceedings, to disseminate them, and to preserve them for posterity. What it illustrates is the degree to which diarists saw themselves as important actors playing a role in an increasingly vital political forum. Two further points bear this out. First, the status of most of the diarists. Figures such as Sir Nathaniel Rich, Sir Thomas Barrington, John Pym, Sir Thomas Holland, Sir John Lowther, Sir Edward Nicholas, Sir John Holles, Sir William Spring, and Sir Richard Grosvenor were not minor gentry figures but of considerable standing in their regions and in some cases on a national scale. In many cases, too, they were long-serving, senior, and vocal MPs; very few of the 1620s diaries were written by those without substantial influence or status. Second, most diarists who composed notes were not motivated by an isolated interest in one particular session or issue. Lowther, Holland, Rich, Pym, Sir Richard Dyott, and Grosvenor were serial diarists.[72] Returned frequently to Parliament, they arrived armed with pen and paper to record the proceedings.

Looking at the 1624 records illustrates the particular interests of diarists and the ways in which their focus varied considerably. The Commons Journals are particularly full accounts, largely because the fair (and thus sanitized) copies have not survived, and the fuller rough notes taken in the House are available. John Wright, the clerk, was not the most efficient or effective note-taker, but he did manage to capture many of the speakers in each debate.[73] Furthermore, his notes can be supplemented by those of his eponymous son, the deputy clerk, who more often than not achieved a higher degree of accuracy in recording the proceedings than his father.[74] As was customary with the official records of the Commons, the journals are a mixture of debate and procedural matters with the emphasis on the latter. While they do not reach the depth in reporting speeches that many of the diaries achieved, they often record many more speakers per debate than any other source.

The major diary accounts of 1624 vary considerably in their ambition, content, and compilation, providing a microcosm of how and why diaries were constructed in the 1620s. Sir Edward Nicholas continued to record diligently the proceedings in order to provide the King and most likely his patron, the Duke of Buckingham, with information from the Lower House. Present on seventy-four of the seventy-nine days of the Parliament, he took copious notes in the House, using a mixture of shorthand symbols and longhand, on everything from constitutional issues to bill readings.[75] In doing so, his diary is in many ways a fuller account of the proceedings than the Commons Journal. John Pym, picking up where he left off from 1621, continued his policy of taking notes in the House and then drafting them into a synopsis. The three Pym accounts from 1624 illustrate his methodology. His rough notes taken in the House constitute the diary fragment from late February.[76] A second more polished but still unfinished diary exists for 13 April to 10 May,[77] while his final record starts on 19 February and runs through 7 May.[78] In compiling the diary, Pym shifted from identifying speakers and as much of the content of the debate as he could record, to his standard refinement to synoptic paragraphs, largely devoid of the identities of individuals or the length of the debate. Pym's diary was a comprehensive account of the session, arguments raised, and decisions made, rather than a verbatim record.

More effusive was the antiquarian Sir Simonds D'Ewes. His diary was partly copied from the Commons Journal and from another account (or accounts) no longer extant.[79] D'Ewes sought to record all the proceedings from speeches on matters of state to details of orders made in the House and the passage of legislation to provide a comprehensive account.[80] However, he did not sit in the Commons in 1624 and crafted his diary at a later date. The diary reflects D'Ewes's intense interest in early modern Parliaments but is a significantly different record than his Elizabethan accounts. The latter reflect the limited information available to D'Ewes—bare-bones accounts of procedural issues, only rarely interspersed with debate and largely lacking in the exact words of members. In contrast, the number of diaries available in the 1620s and the vast amount of information recorded allowed D'Ewes to expand his parliamentary accounts. Another who followed the principle of full note-taking of all events was Nicholas Ferrar. Even though the surviving portion of the diary lasts a little under a month, it provides a concise and accurate account of all the daily business in the House from legislation to foreign policy. Ferrar's own interests as a council member of the Virginia Company, are evident in the remainder of his parliamentary papers from 1624 as he sought to advance and protect the interests of the company.[81]

Nicholas, Pym, Ferrar, and D'Ewes provide the all-encompassing record, but others focused on their own interests. Sir Walter Earle, whose diary is a later fair-written account, concentrated on high political events, such as impeachment proceedings and foreign policy.[82] Largely silent on legislation, except to note bill readings, Earle however did enter into his diary whenever the House determined precedents, and his interest also stretched to encompass reports from joint conferences with the Lords and the debate in grand committees. John Holles followed a similar pattern on the 'great affairs' of Parliament, although on the occasions that he noted legislative activity, the account provides an invaluable record of the speeches of MPs.[83] This form of high political diary was also adopted by Sir Thomas Jervoise and Sir Richard Dyott.[84]

Away from those who concentrated on politics were MPs who closely followed the procedural business of the House. Sir Thomas Holland originally started his diary as a full record but clearly had significant problems keeping up with the speed of proceedings in the chamber. His pen was unable to keep pace with the member who was speaking, and the pages are littered with blank spaces where he moved onto the next orator. Presumably he intended to fill in the speeches later but never achieved his aim. Holland shortly afterward abandoned his attempt at verbatim recording, and the lengthy passages of incomplete notes were replaced by brief annotations of bill readings and committee reports.[85] In contrast, Sir William Spring never attempted to record more than brief summations of debate and the procedure of the House. He kept notes throughout the Parliament although two of his books 'hastely taken in the house' are now missing.[86]

John Hawarde's diary reflects his career as a lawyer in Star Chamber and his experience in taking notes in the courtroom.[87] The diary, primarily in the Law French that Hawarde also used in Star Chamber, provides pithy, accurate synopses of speeches and legislation scribbled as he sat in the chamber.[88] Hawarde by no means recorded all the proceedings but focused on his interest on the law. Sir Nathaniel Rich continued his tradition of noting the proceedings of the House, focusing, as with all his diaries, on religious matters.[89] However, the diary covers only 23 February to 6 March, and he may have given up or the remainder may be lost.

There are also two anonymous diaries for the Parliament. MS E 237 at the Kenneth Spencer Research Library is a collection of diary entries covering the first month of Parliament, with a number of speeches by the King, Prince Charles, and the Archbishop of Canterbury copied in.[90] The Rawlinson diary, D723, is even shorter, recording proceedings only between 19 and 24 February and is most likely a surviving fragment copied from a much fuller version.[91] A summation of the major political events of the Parliament can also be found in the Rawlinson Manuscripts. B151 was transcribed from an unknown source by the Shropshire clergyman Richard Horne.[92]

There was also a shift away from recording procedure and bill readings toward debate and attempts at verbatim speech recording. It is possible to trace both interest and motivation in some of the diarists—a good example is Sir Thomas Belasyse, MP for Thirsk in 1621. When Belasyse arrived in Parliament for the first time he started recording notes on loose sheets of paper—a somewhat haphazard method that he abandoned after the Easter recess in favor of systematic recording in a diary. His was the fairly standard procedural diary—records of bills, precedents noted for his own use, a veritable fount of knowledge useful to any county magistrate. But when the Parliament recommenced in November and became embroiled not in bill readings but constitutional issues, Belasyse's diary changes. Bills fall by the wayside as speeches and debates start to dominate his penmanship. We also find him purchasing copies of major speeches given at this time and engaging in partisan coverage of the debates; some days he can be seen as swaying toward the King's supporters and other days his diary is heavily weighted in favor of those challenging James.

One clear example of how the diarists differed in their recording practices is the second reading of the transportation of wool bill on 30 April 1621. The Commons Journal, of which we have the rough notes taken in the House by the clerk, John Wright, unsurprisingly lists a far greater number of speeches than any other source, eleven speakers in total.[93] However, in the hectic pace of the debate of many speakers, Wright managed to scribble down only a few terse points by each. More detail of the arguments was captured by Sir Edward Nicholas, but he recorded only what he considered the key speeches: Nyell, who suggested adding to the bill a clause about transporting sheep not just wool, and the debate between Sandys and Coke as to whether the crime should be felonious.[94] Sir Thomas Belasyse too gravitated toward the crucial interventions of Sandys and Coke, although that is unsurprising given his propensity to record their speeches throughout the Parliament.[95] Belasyse also included a part of Giles's speech but without attribution, and he clearly did not recognize the Bristol MP, John Whitson, who Belasyse referenced anonymously as 'moved by one.'[96] John Smyth's diary contains nothing but a key sentence from Coke's oration, and neither is the bill mentioned or Coke referred to by name. Thus without cross-referencing other sources, the context is only apparent to Smyth.[97] The compiler of the 'X' diary failed to improve on this, confusing Coke's speech on wool with the following debate on ordnance.[98] The other diarist who covered the debate was Pym. Characteristically, his diary is a model of summation. No speakers are named, but all the relevant issues are incorporated into the proceedings. Pym noted that three 'things were desired to be added.' His second section neatly characterizes the objections to making the law a felony and the final part of the outcome of the debates on the felony argument before he records the bill's committal.[99]

On 4 April 1628, the main business of the House was the second reading on the subsidy bill. The matter of taxation was sure to draw a crowded house of speakers and to ensure that the diarists were busily at work capturing the mood of the Commons. The contrast between what they recorded also epitomizes their varied interests as well as the fundamental difference between the diarists and the clerk's journal. The morning opened with a procedural matter, two election disputes (York and Droitwich) both of which the clerk gave a substantial account of in his journal. But the diarists largely ignored the issue; only Stowe MS 366 (probably the diary of Sir William Borlase) mentions the elections and then only one sentence on the York dispute. The House then turned to the fast preparation for the following day, again a matter of procedure, and passed over in all accounts but the Commons Journal. Sir Edward Coke's report on how to approach the Lords to discuss the matter of the liberties of subjects received a little more attention, appearing in summary form in the Journal, Stowe 366, and Harleian 2313. The Secretary of State, Sir John Coke, then rose to deliver a message from the King urging the Commons to proceed with the subsidy bill, as he noted that 'we are now preparing for the great business, and I hope that none here sits unprepared.'[100] Certainly the diarists were prepared, and the emphasis switches from the journal to the pens of MPs. In the journal, Coke's message is relegated to a terse sentence with an order for Coke to deliver the message in writing so the clerk could enter it in the official record. The subsidy itself is recorded as having a second reading and being committed before the House adjourned for the day. However, as the diarists reveal, the Commons entered into a lengthy debate. *Proceedings and Debates* gives substantial accounts of twenty-five speeches, and sixty-one interventions are captured in Stowe 366, although many of these are abbreviated as the debate wore on and pens failed to keep pace with the spoken words.[101] Newdegate recorded forty-four speeches, Harleian 2313 twenty-eight, and Sir Edward Nicholas thirty-three. Comparing the diaries, a remarkably high number of sixty different members intervened in the debate. Given the detailed notes recorded by all the diarists, it seems likely that all the speakers in the debate were represented through the written word. Of course, the subsidy debate was one of the issues of which MPs took particular note and thus could be expected to have attracted significant attention.

The various accounts also showed a degree of heightened sophistication in summing up the main content of speeches. Those who contributed little to the debate, such as Sir Thomas Hoby's brief intervention on the amount of the subsidies, received no more than a passing mention. But despite adding little to the debate other than Hoby's opinion, it was recorded in four of the five accounts. More significant or novel arguments, such as Sir Edward Coke's reference to Wat Tyler's rebellion in 1381 over subsidy grants and the slaying of a subsidy commissioner in 1489, received more space in the diaries. Similarly, experienced Parliament-men who spoke frequently—Sir Henry Mildmay, Sir James Perrott, and Sir Robert Phelips, for example—appear at length in most accounts. Thus the diarists noted in detail Mildmay's proposal to support the King through subsidies but regulate his finances, because he was the Master of the Jewel House and someone with intimate court connections. Similarly, Phelips's suggestion to impose conditions of use on the subsidies found its way into all the accounts—'supply and liberty' are twins, the Stowe 366 diarist noted.[102] Perrott too captured the diarists' attention with his speech, which queried whether supply should be given without limitation, something Charles I's message had specifically requested. No doubt the debate was well recorded because it concerned the important issue of taxation; as it was linked to the liberties of the subject, it moved beyond a discussion of finances and into the relationship between Parliament and the Crown. It is also evident that the most vocal MPs were, in Sir John Coke's words, 'prepared' and ready to speak. Sir Edward Coke, Sir John Eliot, Sir Dudley Digges, John Selden, Sir Francis Seymour, Sir Benjamin Rudyerd, and Sir Henry Marten (among many other frequent speakers) all offered their viewpoints.

The degree to which the diarists captured the main ideas in the speeches, and in some cases their actual words, is remarkably consistent in comparing the accounts. The styles vary considerably, from the neat prose of the compilation *Proceedings and Debates* to the staccato notes of Harleian 2313 and the careful summations of Newdegate—a feat more impressive as the diary shows evidence of having been written in the House as the members spoke. For example, Christopher Clitherow's reminder that Baltic trade needed to be protected, and his introduction of a paper to that effect, received a full report covering the Baltic, Zeeland, the Low Countries, and Austria's designs on the region in *Proceedings and Debates*, an analysis of the importance of the Baltic to England in Stowe, and short terse summations—'that the supplying and aiding the King of Denmark as necessary as any'—in the other accounts.[103] Significantly, though, apart from Nicholas, who ignored Clitherow, all captured the clear intent of his intervention.

The subsidy bill not only raised questions about matters of state; MPs also sought to protect their parochial interests. On 31 May when the House again looked at supply, the diarists and Stowe in particular were captivated by whether Cambridge should proceed Oxford in the bill or vice versa—a debate that dragged on well into the afternoon. Stowe recorded forty-nine speeches of increasing partisanship until Sir Nathaniel Rich 'resolved' the issue by staging a walkout of Cambridge men.[104] But while most of the Cambridge contingent left the House, 'hot words' continued until the committee was adjourned.[105]

Of course it is not always, or indeed often, possible to recover why some diarists penned their compilations. Sir Nathaniel Rich remains one of the most enigmatic and elusive. Five times in the early Stuart period he seems to have entered the House filled with enthusiasm to record matters of interest. In Rich's case, a man of strong Puritan beliefs and a fervent supporter of godly reform, his notebooks detail (in a hastily scribbled fashion) debates on religion. But five times his early enthusiasm waned, leaving us with little beyond a few weeks of his musings. That Rich was an astute observer and detailed recorder is clear—his diaries reveal committee of religion discussions unrecorded elsewhere and nuanced captures of speeches. But in every session his pages peter out, the blank spaces grow longer, and finally Rich's voice appears only in the words of other diarists.

THE HOUSE OF LORDS

In stark contrast to the Commons, very few diaries survive for the House of Lords. The most prolific of the diarists was Sir Edward Montagu, the Northamptonshire magnate who had been raised to the peerage as Lord Montagu of Boughton in June 1621. Montagu, the dominant figure in eastern Northamptonshire, was an experienced Parliament man. He was elected as an MP on six occasions and served as a Knight of the Shire for his home county in the first three Jacobean Parliaments.[106] Furthermore, he was already an established parliamentary diarist, having compiled a journal of the first Jacobean Parliament.[107] Montagu's Commons diaries reveal a preoccupation with the business of a county magistrate. He faithfully recorded bill readings and offered only brief summations of speeches. Montagu was not much more forthcoming after his elevation to the Upper House. In part this may be because he collected separates of speeches he deemed significant rather than attempt to transcribe them in the House. It may also be that Montagu wrote his notes after the day's proceedings had ended, as some of his diary entries for 1626 suggest; thus he could only remember a brief summary of debates.

When Montagu entered the Lords in November 1621, he found another parliamentary diarist hard at work. The parliamentary journals of Henry Hastings, 5th Earl of Huntington, survive from 1610, 1614, and 1621. Huntington, who had the benefit of an impeccable classical education, took a series of notes while he was in the House, later writing these into a fuller account with the help of his secretary, who obtained separates and adding material he had missed from the Lords Journal. Huntington noted bill readings but paid closer attention to speeches, particularly those that engendered controversy. In 1610, he provides the fullest account of the joint conferences on the Great Contract and often very detailed notes on speeches in the House. The pattern was repeated in 1614, although the diary started off more as a record of business and only engaged in the lengthy reporting of speeches once the Lords was embroiled in the debate over the contentious matter of impositions. In 1621, Huntington concentrated on the privileges of the House of Lords and the debates, including the King's speeches to the House on the controversial issue of monopolies. Although he occasionally dips into bill proceedings, this was not his main focus. The pattern of Hastings's diaries reinforces the changing nature of 'personal' parliamentary accounts during the period from records of business to debates over constitutional issues.

The Earl of Bridgewater's notes for 1628 are fragmentary, covering only twenty-three days of the session. Nevertheless, his interests in what he saw as the major issues of the Parliament are clear. Bridgewater's diary reflects the dominant concern of the Parliament—the Commons fight for their 'liberties' and the debates over the Petition of Right. He took extensive notes at the Joint Conference on 7 April from the presentations of Sir Dudley Digges, Edward Littleton, Sir Edward Coke, and John Selden, detailing especially the legal precedents they cited.[108] Five days later he again made careful notes on the answer to the Commons' arguments on the liberties of subjects given by Sir Robert Heath, the attorney general.[109] This pattern of concentrating on the large constitutional issues that engulfed the 1628 Parliament is repeated throughout the diary—the 'minutiae' of general legislative procedure did not occupy his pen in the chamber.

SEPARATES AND THE *TRUE RELATION*

The multiplication of diaries was not the only significant development of parliamentary manuscript culture in the 1620s. Separates of speeches, debates, and proceedings grew exponentially from their few forebears. In the Elizabethan and early Jacobean periods, the most common form of parliamentary writing was the oft-copied opening and closing speeches made by the monarch or Lord Keeper. But as with diaries, the tone shifted from an emphasis on the final outcome of issues to an interest in the decision-making process itself. By the time of the constitutional debates of 1628, interests in separates had developed to such an extent that Sir Richard Browne was able to collect thirty-one pieces.[110] A student at Gray's Inn in 1628, Browne assiduously collected separates from the Parliament. Browne obtained thirty-one different pieces from the opening speech of the Lord Keeper to the King's closing address in June 1628, including Commons' petitions to the King along with his answers, Roger Mainwaring's submission to the Commons and reports of Joint Conferences between the Houses. Browne's papers also include the speeches of many of the Commons luminaries: Sir Francis Soames, Sir Robert Phelips, Sir Edward Coke, Sir Dudley Digges, Sir Benjamin Rudyerd, and Sir Henry Marten on the petition of right, 'without alteration.' It also seems to have been possible to order a day's worth of speeches on a particular topic, Browne making sure he had all the speeches on supply for 2 April 1628. Included among his papers was a string-bound copy of the Commons' Remonstrance as well.

By 1629 the copying and compilation of parliamentary procedure had reached another pinnacle. Spurred on no doubt by the clashes between the Commons and the Crown in 1628 and the printing of the Petition of Right, the country was eager for news of Parliament. The *True Relation*, which was printed in 1641 and again in 1654, was a compilation of parliamentary proceedings taken from two different sets of serial (possibly daily) newsletters and separates. Of the *True Relation*, forty-eight copies survive in four different groups, indicating multiple copyists. This is the first parliamentary session for which we have evidence of a daily newsletter intended for copying and circulation. Although the content of the *True Relation* varies across the copies, all are characterized by including reports from the newsletters and the increasingly common practice of supplementing daily proceedings with separates of speeches. Although parliamentary newsletters became increasingly common in the 1620s, daily news reports are a particular feature of the 1629 Parliament and serve as the precursor for *Diurnall Occurrences* in the 1640s.

The *True Relation* may be the pinnacle of multiple copies from a single source (or at least closely related sources), but copies of individual diaries were in circulation much earlier. In the mid to late 1620s, as Parliament became increasingly a focal point of political debate and a topic of news, more and more people sought out diaries and separates for their collections, both topically of the Parliament at hand and with a certain antiquarian fascination with past news. D'Ewes was not the only one to obtain and copy the journals and diaries of earlier Parliaments. Pym's close friend, Francis Russell, later 4th Earl of Bedford, obtained one copy of John Pym's 1621 diary, of which five distinct issues survive. Russell copied the diary in his own hand making numerous marginal annotations.[111] Internally, references to the Petition of Right suggest that he copied this after 1628.[112]

~

There seems little doubt that as Parliament became a more self-aware body in the early seventeenth century diaries and diarists multiplied in number. Even monarchs seemed conscious of the propensity for note-taking, from James, of course, slowing his speech for the benefit of parliamentary scribblers, to Charles in 1626 sending for 'four, five, six notebooks, and therein found those words, or such in effect.'[113] The words of members, the cut and thrust of debate, and the report of who said what to whom increasingly came to be copied and circulated. Those wishing to read, understand, and discuss Parliament no longer relied on copies of the Commons Journal, although these were still prominent, but for news-hungry gentry the sterility of the official journal was no longer sufficient.

Of course, there is a close connection between copied diaries full of speeches, highlighting those of Coke, Phelips, Eliot, and Rudyerd and the well-documented rise of the parliamentary separate whether in print or manuscript. Parliamentary news ceased to be the traditional concern of county magistrates, eager to learn of new statutes affecting their work as justices of the peace, and became instead part of a national debate on monopolies, taxation, billeting, and the privileges of Parliament. This exploration of the early Stuart diarists leads to a number of important conclusions. Diaries changed in the period—their sophistication increased as Parliaments were held more frequently in the 1620s. The interests of those involved in the scribal culture of Parliament altered as constitutional and political issues occupied space previously 'rented' by local concerns and private legislation. Living in dangerous times of early Caroline England placed more of an emphasis on being a witness to history and recording that history: a history that was increasingly disseminated to an interested outside world. Supply and demand were closely intertwined in the world of parliamentary news.

What is clear in the 1620s is a shift from the concept of private diary, written for the benefit of the author and perhaps his close acquaintances, toward proceedings meant to be disseminated more widely and made public. This change can also be seen in the shift from diaries recording the outcome of debates on issues to the insertion of speeches and interventions involved in the decision-making process. The words of MPs became just as important as the record of the final decision—if not more so. In conjunction with this is the rise of the number of separates of speeches collected by

MPs and in many cases copied or inserted whole into their private diaries. The culmination of this was the shift to the medium of print. What the changing nature of diaries and the journals portend is a change in the nature of political communication. A shift from a generally private or intimate discourse to a public one.

CHAPTER FOUR

Procreative Pens:
Disseminating News from Parliament

'From the Parlyment I knowe you expect lyttle from me for you know I am not Parlyment man.' Samuel Albyn's modesty was either rhetorical or misplaced—three pages of detailed notes of parliamentary business follow in his letter to John Rawson in March 1621. 'I could wright you a great deale more,' he continued and then named his well-placed sources, Sir Thomas Richardson, Speaker of the House of Commons, and Sir James Ley, the Chief Justice of the King's Bench and legal assistant in the Lords, both of whom passed him parliamentary news.[1]

By the early 1620s, news was all the rage as the printed coranto kept the gentry informed of events abroad, and professional newsletter writers like Sir John Pory plied their trade.[2] The news revolution of the 1620s encompassed more than just the rise of the coranto and the widespread accounts of foreign events. As Parliament moved more and more toward the center stage of domestic policies, and disputes between the governing class and the Crown dominated the parliamentary agenda, so news spread more widely and rapidly than it had before. This is reflected not only in the rise of parliamentary diaries but also in the availability of separates relating to Parliament and the concentration, scope, and frequency of newsletters and information concerning activities in Westminster Palace. In the same way that the Thirty Years' War drove the embryonic newspaper industry, so Parliament provided the raw material of the manuscript political letter. As Thomas Fuller noted in his collection of more than two hundred speeches and documents from the 1628–29 Parliament, 'Some gentlemen Speakers in the Parliament, imparted their speeches to their intimate friends; the transcripts thereof were multiplied amongst others (the penne being very procreative of issue of this nature.)'[3]

~

The 1620s were all about news. The first printed coranto of foreign news arrived in England in early December 1620 from an Amsterdam publisher, Pieter van den Keere.[4] Printed in Amsterdam, the first corantos were single sheets that concentrated on news from the battlefields and royal courts around Europe. Their success in England was immediate, and news quickly became an established industry. In 1621 Nathaniel Butter and Nicholas Bourne emerged as the leading publishers of corantos, employing Thomas Gainsford to translate and edit the Dutch news sheets. Despite obtaining a license to print corantos in September 1621, the government was wary over the publication of news. One of the first involved in the trade, Thomas Archer, had been imprisoned in summer 1621, and Butter and Bourne frequently ran afoul of the authorities. James I, worried that the impact of news about the war on the Continent might inflame public opinion toward a more interventionist stance, asked the Dutch government to ban the export of corantos.[5]

The government's pro-Spanish foreign policy had already drawn widespread criticism, and the publication of Thomas Scott's controversial and popular anti-Spanish treatise, *Vox Populi*, had further heightened tensions.[6] With news of the Thirty Years' War, debates on English foreign policy and the buzz surrounding the forthcoming Parliament, news was very much to the forefront, and the government reacted quickly. A proclamation was issued on 24 December 'against excess of lavish and licentious speech of matters of state.'[7] The proclamation had been recommended and then drafted by Sir Francis Bacon, who was concerned that the forthcoming Parliament would pick up on the general hubbub about matters of state.[8] Initially at least, the proclamation did have some effect on the availability of parliamentary information. Certainly, the Venetian ambassador, Girolamo Lando, was surprised at the difficulties he had in procuring a copy of the King's opening speech: 'I enclose a copy of the substance of the king's speech to this parliament, which I have translated. I had great trouble in getting it owing to the efforts to prevent its circulation, contrary to the general custom, for such things are usually printed.'[9] The inveterate letter-writer John Chamberlain encountered the same problem: '[We] expect it in print, though (by that I have heard) there are divers passages in it that perswade the contrarie, or at least are likely to be omitted.'[10] In contrast to most royal orations at the opening of Parliament, which simply stated why they had been called, James had seen fit to lecture the Commons on the nature of a Parliament, and it was most likely this material that caused a delay in printing.

Given the extraordinary lengths that the government had gone to in order to manage the Parliament and ensure its tractability, it is unsurprising that information was slow in forthcoming, at least initially. With Bacon acting as the chief parliamentary manager, not only had the 'lavish and licentious speech' proclamation gone forth, but another was issued to regulate the elections.[11] Chamberlain referred to it as one of the 'gentlemen ushers' that went before the Parliament, and if Bacon's licentious speech proclamation that limited discussion of matters of state met with royal approval, then his attempt to bring electors and Parliament into the debate on foreign policy certainly did not. What Bacon proposed, drafted, and submitted to the King was a detailed explanation of royal policy toward the Palatinate in order to enlist the assistance of Parliament in regaining Bohemia for Frederick and Elizabeth. Bacon of course acknowledged the King's power: '[F]or although the making of war and peace be a secret of empire, and a thing properly belonging to our high prerogative, royal and imperiall power: yet nevertheless, in causes of that nature which we think fit not to reserve but to communicate, we shall ever think ourselves much assisted and strengthened by the faithful advice and general assent of our loving subjects.'[12] Communication with his subjects in such a clear form, was not, however, how James felt a King ought to rule. Bacon received the King's response in a letter from Buckingham: 'I have shewed your letter & the Proclamation to his Majestie, who expecting only, according as to his meaning was, directions therein for the well ordering of the Elections of Burgesses, findeth a great deale more contayning matter of State & the reasons for calling the Parlement, whereof nether the people are capable, nor is it fitt for his Majestie to open now unto them . . . . His Majestie hathe therefore extracted somewhat of the latter part of the draught you have sent purposing to take a few dayes space to sett down himself what he thinketh fitt.'[13] James, having dismissed the intellectual capacity of his subjects to understand European affairs, then embarked on an extraordinary course of royal authorship and management. Thus summarily dismissed was advice of his Privy Council committee on Parliament and his senior government officer, while James bent himself to the task of writing a proclamation. Out of course went any reference to why Parliament was being called as James endeavored to control the information on matters of state. Despite this and the subsequent attempt to delay the transmission of the King's opening speech, by 10 February Joseph Mead informed his correspondent that he expected a printed copy in Cambridge, and in the meantime transmitted in his letter the principal points of the speech.[14]

Parliament contributed significantly to the news revolution of the 1620s. First, many of its MPs were avid writers, scribblers, and correspondents who also collected the material output of Parliament either through separates, diaries, or other parliamentary documents. Second, the raw material of parliamentary debates provided both professional and amateur newsletter writers with much of their domestic news while Parliament was in session. Third, and by default, as the fractious relationship between the Crown and sections of the governing class turned Parliament into a battleground of wills in a dispute conducted both verbally and via furious exchanges of documents, so the words of MPs and parliamentary papers came to be copied more and disseminated more widely.

The relationship between Parliament, the news revolution, and the social networks of communication has had a long historiographical tradition, especially for the 1620s. In 1921 Wallace Notestein and Frances Helen Relf identified the widespread survival of what they deemed separates, parliamentary documents on an individual subject. A separate, as originally defined by Notestein and Relf, was a 'parliamentary document or speech to be found in a single manuscript. It might be a declaration, a message, a set of grievances, a protestation, a legal argument, or most commonly the speech of a member.'[15] However, the majority of early separates were uncontroversial renderings of the opening and closing speeches made by the monarch or the Lord Keeper. Only occasionally do the words of members in debate appear in separates. They were viewed, as Richard Cust has noted, as an 'authoritative record' and often copied into journals or commonplace books, or kept as a collection.[16] These separates, along with manuscript news and other printed material, circulated widely among the gentry and were deliberately collected, copied, and discussed. As Fritz Levy's ground-breaking article 'How Information Spread among the Gentry' points out, the Thirty Years' War spurred on the growth of the news industry; as Parliament was involved in debates over English intervention and funding, it became one of the foci of news reporting.[17]

The ways in which the public engaged with Parliament metamorphosed during the early modern period. So too did the flow of information about and around Parliament. In a fundamental way the balance had tipped between Parliament as a recipient of information from the governing class and the repository of its concerns, to a disseminator of those concerns. For the Elizabethans, Parliament was a legislative and financial instrument. To it, MPs, corporations, and the government submitted bills and in return, received acts.[18] The paper trail was primarily legislative and official. Private diaries of parliamentary business were few and far between, and although MPs wrote to their constituencies and corporations, the output of their writing activities was minimal and focused among the practical concerns of individual and local interests.[19] This was a pattern largely maintained through the early Jacobean Parliaments of 1604–14. But 1621 witnessed a steep rise in the parliamentary consumption of paper. The initial phases of the news revolution and information gathering swept into Parliament as MPs started in earnest to collect separates, keep diaries, and obtain other parliamentary material. In combination with new techniques of lobbying for private interest groups as well as public legislation, Parliament was awash in a sea of paper and the recipient of innumerable *printed* and manuscript documents. The escalating professionalization of Parliament and its more deliberate and systematic collection of its own records as well as its revived judicial role also dramatically increased the flow of paper. Members too had easier access to material to write on as petitioners to Parliament distributed printed briefs. This seems to have had the effect that more people took notes of the proceedings on these documents. This combined with the impact of the Thirty Years' War and parliamentary discussion of foreign policy, particularly the wisdom of the prospective Spanish Match and England's involvement in the war, created an atmosphere of information gathering and frenetic note-taking.

This pattern of engagement with Parliament was repeated in 1624. Parliament was still fulfilling its 'traditional' role as a legislative arena, and thus paper flooded into the chambers. In part the 'paper wars' that ensued and the amount of material available was a response to the ever increasingly packed parliamentary agenda. Legislative interests were in competition with foreign policy debates, impeachment proceedings, and the general grievances of the political nation.[20] But the nature of parliamentary activity changed after 1625. In part the early Caroline assemblies were 'war Parliaments,' and thus legislation was the priority of neither the government nor the governing classes. This had the practical effect of limiting the degree to which lobbying took place, of which a by-product was that less and less paper came into Parliament. Conversely, as the newsletter industry changed from private communication between friends and kin to a professionalized subscription service, more and more paper left the chambers and was transmitted to the provinces. The heightened tension around parliamentary sessions created political news and increasingly the desire to read and hear about the events taking place within Westminster Palace. This was not only reflected in the transmission of news via letters and professional news-writing services, but in the dissemination of parliamentary separates.

The traditional starting point for the flow of information from Parliament to the countryside came from members of Parliament acting in their capacity as representatives of towns and boroughs. Parliament served as an important 'point of contact' between the Crown, governing class, and constituencies with either a legislative agenda or petitions and grievances to express. Furthermore, individuals advanced their own interests by way of promoting bills, lobbying against measures, and often maintaining a physical presence around the parliamentary chambers.[21] For many towns, such as Exeter, both its MPs regularly communicated news back to the corporation.[22] Traditionally, many MPs, and especially those for major corporate towns who often had a vested interest in parliamentary legislation, such as Hull, Bristol, and Norwich, kept their constituencies informed about the progress of individual pieces of legislation that affected the town, as well as the all-important matter of subsidies. Other constituencies, York for example, regularly prepared an agenda for the parliamentary session and gave their MPs specific written instructions. Increasingly, MPs also collected parliamentary documents of national interest and forwarded news of major parliamentary events. In the second sitting of 1621, Ignatius Jourdain and John Prowse reported how the Commons viewed the issue of supply, war with Spain, and other matters they considered of interest to Exeter.[23] Bridgwater in Somerset obtained a copy of the proclamation for the arrest of the notorious monopolist Sir Giles Mompesson, who had been condemned by Parliament through the efforts of its MP, Roger Warre.[24] One of the Yarmouth (Norfolk) members in 1624, Benjamin Cooper, traveled home during the Easter recess, making a full report on supply and the fishing trade as well as presenting the town corporation with copies of the King's and Prince Charles's speeches in Parliament.[25] Bristol's members in 1628 carried back to the town 'six paper books' that presented the arguments in the Commons on the liberties of the subject.[26] News also found its way out of Westminster and into the country as many corporations sent representatives to Parliament to liaise and assist their MPs. For example, in 1610, after the town of Lowestoft had introduced a fishing bill hostile to the interests of Great Yarmouth, a copy of the measure was obtained in Yarmouth and counterarguments were drafted; two aldermen were dispatched to Parliament with the written briefs to assist its MPs in thwarting Lowestoft's ambitions.[27] Hull as well, anxious to protect its important mercantile interests, regularly sent aldermen to London to assist its members.[28]

Those without access to corporation records gleaned their parliamentary information from newsletters. From the 1590s, when regular newsletter writers such as John Chamberlain and Rowland Whyte were starting to ply their trade, parliamentary news expanded. This was aided by the development of the professional and paid newsletter writer, such as John Pory, along with those for whom the correspondence of news formed a major part of their weekly activities—for example, Matthew Moreton.[29] Those most heavily involved in the newsletter trade all had some close connection to Parliament. John Pory had served as an MP for Bridgwater, Somerset, being seated after a by-election on 5 November 1605. Pory made only rare contributions in Parliament, but he did start writing about parliamentary business. During the debates on the great contract in 1610, he wrote to Sir Ralph Winwood, '[T]his day [17 July] in the success may prove either the happiest or unhappiest Parliament day since His Majesty's coming in.'[30] Like his later newsletters, this was filled with the details of the discussions in the Commons. Pory gained further experience of parliamentary assemblies in 1619, when after his posting to Virginia as the Secretary of State for that colony, he was appointed as the first Speaker of the newly constituted Virginia Assembly. Pory's role as the Speaker turned him into an active Parliament-man. He set the agenda for the session and guided the procedures that the assembly would follow. In addition, like so many of those he would later associate with in England, he kept a journal of the proceedings, compiling and sifting out what was of importance—something that no doubt kept him in good stead when he later obtained and passed on news from Parliament. Pory's correspondents throughout his life numbered many who had an active interest in Parliament: Sir Robert Cotton, Sir Dudley Carleton, Sir Edwin Sandys, Sir Thomas Edmondes, Sir Thomas Puckering, George Garrard, Sir Thomas Lucy, and John Viscount Scudamore.[31] This social network was augmented by Pory's operation from the shop of Nathaniel Butter, the printer of corantos. As Sabrina Baron has noted, as Pory received his intelligence and sent his letters from Butter's shop, no doubt it was possible for those interested to see and buy his parliamentary news there.[32]

John Chamberlain trawled for intelligence in Saint Paul's walk, near his domicile, but he too had a well-connected circle of friends who could supply him with parliamentary information. In the Lords, he could call upon the Bishop of Winchester, Lancelot Andrews, and Oliver Lord St. John of Bletso. His correspondents and intelligence sources around court included his great friend the MP Sir Dudley Carleton and other prominent Parliament-men: Samuel Backhouse, Sir William Borlase, Sir Thomas Edmondes, Sir Rowland Lytton, Sir Henry Savile, Sir Henry Wallop, and Sir Ralph Winwood.[33]

As Fritz Levy has noted, in the 1620s 'the Reverend Joseph Mead's letter to Sir Martin Stuteville show a further development in the spread of news.'[34] Mead, domiciled in Cambridge, collected whatever news he could from travelers passing through town, from printed corantos received from London and in letters from his correspondents there. These he turned into a weekly newsletter to Stuteville. From looking at the Mead letters for 1626, it is possible to analyze the amount of information in circulation. In total twenty-five letters are extant, covering the four months that Parliament was sitting. Mead usually dated his letter on every Saturday of the session, occasionally sending more than one letter a week and enclosing what he considered the most important separates. The initial letters offered the popular gossip about the date that Parliament would actually open and news of the election of Dr. Thomas Eden and Sir John Coke as the burgesses for Cambridge University.[35] On 28 January, as more election news trickled in from around the area, Mead added this and enclosed the latest coranto, but as the Parliament had yet to begin, most of his information involved foreign and court news. Parliament opened on Monday, 6 February, and Mead's next letter briefly rehashed the King's speech and that of the Lord Keeper. On 18 February, Mead passed on news about the election of Sir Heneage Finch as the Commons Speaker, bill readings, the paucity of MPs at the opening, and how Sir Edward Coke's election to Parliament was challenged as he was pricked a sheriff and thus ineligible to sit. Mead quickly latched on to the potentially hot topic of whether the Commons would attack Buckingham, passing on the news that the House had not liked the first salvo. In the following dispatch, Mead also enclosed a letter of parliamentary news from Stuteville's friend and avid Parliament-watcher, Sir Simonds D'Ewes.[36]

Coke's status again was in the news, but Mead complained that he had been unable to garner much Parliament business, although he was sufficiently informed to be able to relay the speeches from Eliot, Digges, and Rudyerd. Mead's news was certainly delayed getting to Cambridge at this time, as Eliot's intervention on the mismanagement of royal finances was given on 10 February, as was Rudyerd's desire to examine the livings of ministers.[37]

By the time that Mead next wrote to Stuteville, for the first time Parliament dominated his news. He transcribed the Lords' petition to the King on the precedence of English nobility, noting that the reasons they presented alongside the petition were 'too tedious to transcribe,' although Mead did provide a lengthy summation. As 'great matters' started to emerge in Parliament, and perhaps as his intelligence improved, so Mead slipped into daily reports: 'On Thursday . . . the next day, Friday.'[38] Mead also informed Stuteville that he still awaited the arrival of the printed catalogue of MPs and peers sitting in the Parliament but would forward it as soon as it became available.[39] By 4 March Mead was complaining about the lack of progress in Parliament creating newsworthy events, 'I never knew a Parliament so still,' he told Stuteville.[40] Mead though was disingenuous, for his letter updated Stuteville on Coke's election, the privilege case of Lord Vaux in the Upper House, details of the examination of Richard Montagu's treatise on Arminianism, and discussions in Parliament about the French stay of English shipping.[41] These issues also dominated Mead's following correspondence as high politics embroiled Parliament over the examination of the Council of War by the Commons, Montagu's actions, and the seizure of the French ship, the *St. Peter* of Le Havre. Mead was sufficiently well informed to learn that Buckingham was soon to come under severe scrutiny, 'I have heard that one of the House of Commons hath thirteen articles to put in against a very great person which will either break him or dissolve them.' His sources were not hopeful of success against the Duke, nor of the continuation of Parliament: '[S]ome are of opinion that the Parliament cannot last above a fortnight, so many things beginning to be propounded, which thwart the King's mind.'[42]

As the atmosphere in Parliament continued to heat up, news now flowed freely from Westminster and did so in great detail. Mead's newsletter of 17 March covered all the continuing news from the previous epistle as daily accounts of Parliament. Another letter followed the next day, and parliamentary business was enclosed that was compiled from three different sources: 'authentical letters,' Mead called them. Also he had personal sight of a table book that someone in the Commons had brought to Cambridge the Wednesday before (15 March), from which he copied the 'questions propounded by Dr Turner in the House of Commons.'[43] The following week brought more of the same news, concentrating on Buckingham and the King's reaction to Turner's questions.[44] By the start of April, Mead was reporting in a gloomy fashion that the Commons feared dissolution after the King had roundly condemned Parliament's willingness to allow the attacks on Buckingham and the 'mean and insufficient' amount of subsidies that the Commons had proposed.[45]

Mead felt matters had sunk even further by 8 April. A long report on the clashes between Charles and the Commons opened with this sentence: '[F]or news it ever as bad as it was.'[46] The combination of despair over the Parliament and the continual attacks of Dunkirkers led Mead into biblical woe: '[W]hat shall we say or think when the chariots and horsemen of our Israel are confounded and of the wheels at a time as this? Lord have mercy upon us and open our eyes.'[47] At this point Mead seems to have had some trouble obtaining information, and he commented that 'they have been very secret and silent, and, as it were, surcharged with the difficulties then arising in their consultations.'[48] Those issues that occupied the most parliamentary time unsurprisingly dominated the remainder of the April letters. Buckingham was of course to the forefront ('businesses against the Duke came in very fast'),[49] as were the negotiations over the subsidy and the Earl of Bristol's attack on Buckingham in the Lords. Mead took time out to pass on some legislative news that had come to him, including the passage of bills against citations issued in ecclesiastical courts, butchers, and drovers, as well as the continuing matter of Montagu's suspected Arminianism and the fitness to hold office of Lewis Bayley, the Bishop of Bangor.[50]

Early May was filled with news of Bristol and Buckingham. Mead's intelligence was sufficient enough to allow him to quote from Bristol's accusation against Buckingham in the Lords on 1 May.[51] As May progressed, Mead's letters increasingly show the Parliament turning against Buckingham, and his own notes to Stuteville convey detailed and sometimes verbatim parliamentary speeches. On 13 May he conveyed the information that Bristol had acquitted himself well in the Lords, 'but the Duke is said to jeer openly in Parliament all accusations brought against him with too much appearance of insolency.'[52] Certainly Mead reported that, during the opening preamble, Digges (whom Mead confused with Glanville) lost his patience with Buckingham, who openly 'jeered and fleered him,' causing Digges to abandon his set speech to address the Duke directly as to his behavior.[53] On the following day Mead noted 'four sharp speeches' against Buckingham in the Commons and Thursday's refusal to continue parliamentary business because Digges and Eliot had been taken away and committed to the Tower. Mead ended his weekly news on the despondent note that it was rumored that Buckingham had asked the King to dissolve Parliament, and his letter writer informed him that 'it is generally thought . . . that the last Parliament of King Charles his reign will end this week. Is it not time to pray?'[54]

The following week, Mead passed on the news that Digges had been released from the Tower, along with a rather outdated gossipy story from the House of Lords concerning Lord William Spencer's support of Buckingham in the Upper House and his son's (Richard Spencer's) involvement in the charges against Buckingham in the Commons where he sat as an MP. On 25 May the letter contained news of Bristol's answer to the Lords and the adjournment of the Commons. The brief details in this letter were fleshed out in more detail two days later, after Mead had received a letter from D'Ewes that had originally been directed to Sir William Spring. D'Ewes sent it to Mead so that he could copy it to Stuteville and then it could be recopied and further circulated. Mead had further correspondence from one of Cambridge University's MPs, Dr. Eden, which also added to his intelligence. Much of the letter of 3 June was taken up with Mead's report on how Buckingham had been elected the chancellor of Cambridge University and the pressure put on the fellows to accede to the King's demand to appoint him. However, even such momentous news in Cambridge could not halt the flow of parliamentary detail. Mead had obtained the speeches of Digges and Eliot and 'many of the like' but lamented that without a scribe he could not forward copies.[55] Some of Mead's news on 10 June came from Sir Alexander Temple, MP for Sussex, who had arrived in Cambridge. The university's role in Buckingham's appointment was still very much at the forefront, and Mead anxiously pondered further reaction from the Commons. Dr. Eden's attempt to buy time in the Commons to discover what had happened during the election had not gone down well in the House, and Mead was anxious that the university explain its position.[56]

'I shall tell you the last and the worst first.' So Mead opened his final letter relating to the Parliament. It had been dissolved on 15 June,[57] and neatly sums up the cause: 'when the Commons had made a remonstrance to his majesty, but would not grant him any supply for his necessities, unless they might have justice against the duke.'[58] News of the Parliament ended rather abruptly, but there was no need for Mead to go into elaborate detail. His letters to Stuteville had comprehensively covered the flashpoints of the session from Bristol's accusations against Buckingham, the Commons actions on the matter, debates over the subsidy, and the committal of Digges and Eliot. Stuteville was in possession of separates of the most important speeches and other documents and from his home in Dalham, Suffolk; he knew all there was to know about the second Caroline Parliament.

If the 1626 Parliament marked a watershed in being able to keep fully abreast of parliamentary proceedings, then the last Caroline Parliament of the 1620s pushed information gathering to a pinnacle. Opening after the debacle of military defeat at the Île de Rhé and in the wake of the hugely unpopular Forced Loan and subsequent Five Knights' case, news of a prospective Parliament set the nation abuzz even before it opened. As Conrad Russell pointed out, '[In] seeking the renewal of their liberties, the Commons showed a unity of purpose unknown in any other Parliament of the 1620s.'[59] Benjamin Rudyerd's prophetic statement in the Commons on 28 March 1628—'[T]his is the crisis of parliaments; by this we shall know whether parliaments will live or die'[60]—was echoed in the extent of Mead's reports to Stuteville in 1628. Information from London was transmitted to Mead's home, sometimes daily. The extent of Mead's intelligence-gathering network was such that he was able to provide a continuous flow of parliamentary news beginning with his letter of 17 May 1628 to Stuteville: 'I will begin now where I think I left you in my last.'[61] As he wrote to Stuteville on 19 April, 'Because I have seen a letter or two more besides those of last Saturday, namely one written on Monday, another on Tuesday at night last, I will out of them all contrive an orderly relation according to the days of the months journal-wise.'[62] Although Mead's writing still reads like a letter, the organization of daily news from Parliament resembles more a parliamentary diary than a weekly report in a newsletter. The news of Monday, 7 April included the speeches of Coke, Selden, Littleton, and Digges at a joint conference with the Lords. For Wednesday (two days later), Mead felt confident enough to quote Christopher Sherland's attack on the Recorder of Wells, John Baber, for his role in the forced billeting of soldiers in the town. The extent of Mead's intelligence is clear—his account to Stuteville is the longest extant record of Sherland's speech:

> Whereupon one Mr Sherland, of his own coat, stood up and said: I must fling the first stone at my brother—a coward he is, and was. Always a knave, and knowing the law and not having the heart to do according to it, it is

worthy double punishment. Nor was it fitting, said he, that any such white-livered creature should sit in that council, but only such durst speak what they thought, and according to their conscience. Therefore his opinion was he should be expelled the House.[63]

Of course, as John Morrill has pointed out, we should be wary of attributing the exact words recorded by parliamentary scribblers to members themselves—the process of listening and writing led to many variations in the accounts even when they seem to be their actual words.[64] However, the writer of Stowe MS 366, possibly Sir William Borlase (MP for Chipping Wycombe, Buckinghamshire), did record similar words:

> I would not have flung a stone at him, but that he is one of my own coat. He hath had a finger where he had nothing to do. That which aggravates me is his extenuation for pursuivanting. I hold no man incorrigible but a coward, and a coward because there is no hope of him. I am with those that stand for his severest censure.[65]

Other diarists, such as John Newdegate and Edward Nicholas, also picked up on Sherland's reference to Baber as a coward.[66] Whether or not Mead's account records the 'exact' words spoken by Sherland, Stuteville in Suffolk came into possession of intelligence about parliamentary speeches as detailed as any managed to capture on paper who were writing in the House as Sherland spoke. Bolstering further his intelligence-gathering credentials, Mead had obtained a copy of Sir John Coke's message to the Commons from Charles I on 12 April that he copied verbatim into the letter, describing it as a 'startling message'—no doubt because Charles threatened to bring a premature end to the session. Mead also described the tone of the House after Coke's speech, calling it 'sad and silent' before he gave Stuteville a lengthy rendition of Sir Francis Nethersole's account of his dreams about sheep and pastures, which caused much mirth in the Commons. After more parliamentary news from Monday 14 and Tuesday 15 April, the letter closed with a lengthy postscript updating Stuteville about news that had recently arrived in Cambridge.

Mead's communication with Stuteville comprised more than just his passing on the news that came into Cambridge, be it orally or by letter. Mead collected and copied parliamentary separates either into the text of his letter or as an enclosure. In 1621 he sent on a catalogue of the acts passed by both Houses in the first sitting, mistakenly though telling Stuteville that these had been sent to the King to be ratified.[67] Later in the Parliament he included a copy of Sir Edward Cecil's speech on the defense of the kingdom.[68] Mead too obtained a copy of the Earl of Arundel's submission to the Lords for his quarrel with Lord Spencer, when he demeaned Spencer's ancestry,[69] but he forbore from sending it, as he thought that Stuteville would have received it already from his friend, the MP and diarist Sir Thomas Holland.[70] Throughout the 1620s Mead continued to supply Stuteville with separates, including the Earl of Bristol's petition to the Lords in 1626, and both the King and Lord Keeper's opening addresses to the 1628 Parliament.[71] For the duration of the 1628 Parliament, as political tension heated up, Mead was busy collecting the increasing number of separates inundating Cambridge from London and forwarding them on to Dalham.[72]

Mead provided more than just daily parliamentary news and manuscript separates to Stuteville. As David Randall has noted, Mead 'assimilated [printed] corantos into his sociable newswriting with remarkable speed.'[73] Following his practice in dealing with manuscript separates, Mead sometimes copied the corantos into his letters or enclosed them, creating what Randall has termed 'mixed media.'[74] Mead turned to this practice in the 1620s with parliamentary material in the instances that it became available. In 1621 he promised to obtain a printed copy of the King's opening speech: '[We] expect that the whole speech printed should come down today: if it doth you shall have it on Tuesday sent to Newmarket.'[75] He also forwarded the King's speech in 1628 along with the Duke of Buckingham's speech on Parliament and subsidies before the Privy Council, both of which were printed. It was Buckingham's speech that led John Selden to complain that the counsels of Parliament were being laid on stalls.[76]

Even with Mead's deployment of 'mixed media' from his skills learnt in reading and forwarding corantos, the flow of information was so great that he was unable to cope with the sheer quantities of incoming material. Mead was therefore forced to sift and select what he deemed relevant information. It became physically impossible for him to copy and transmit everything he received. On 29 March 1628, Mead informed Stuteville that while he had a copy of the Speaker's opening oration he had not transcribed it, as 'it was long and nothing but complements and straines.'[77] Neither did he bother with the Lord Keeper's answer, 'which contained nothing but a repetition and an approbation of what the Speaker sayd before.'[78] On occasion also, Mead was short a clerk to assist him, which again limited the amount of information he could forward on in a timely manner.[79] His letter of 26 April 1628 opens, '[W]hat news we received on Saturday, you shall find inclosed and w[i]th it the Kings speech on Monday before. I saw also the Keepers preamble and the petition for unbilleting of souldiers but because they were long and I had no scribe to write them I have not furnished you with them, And alas what delight could you find in reading them.'[80] However, he occasionally admitted to his faults as a correspondent. In 1621 he informed Stuteville, '[S]ince my last I saw a copie of the 5 particulars of the petition of the Parliament for the better execution of laws against Jesuits, Priests, Recusants. I was too lazie to copie it out but the marrow is this.'[81]

The detail of the interest and information available exceeded parliamentary reporting before the 1620s. News traveled into the countryside not only in the form of bare-bones accounts of speeches and decisions but also in tandem with copies of the actual speeches and intimate details of the mood of the House and the reception of parliamentary discourse. Mead's letter of 22 April 1626, which he copied off a letter from London written by an MP, contained within it news about the Commons proceedings against the Arminian King's chaplain, Richard Montagu. He mentioned the two-hour oration by John Pym delivered 'so well and fully that the most admired and Montagues friends were amazed. The effect was that not one man spake in the house but in detestation of him and his best friends were observed to leave the House, before the question came.'[82] News, like parliamentary diaries, had shifted from dry, formalized renditions of set pieces to a vibrant world of tone that captured what had happening in the chambers of Parliament. The news that Mead reported after the commitment of Digges and Eliot in 1626 refers to MPs 'sadly communicating' to one another in Westminster Hall.[83] Even the arrival in Parliament of Buckingham and Digby in 1626 was deemed newsworthy especially as Buckingham turned up in an 'old coach' and Digby on his own horse looking 'brave and rich with cloth of gold' and eight other horsemen in attendance.[84]

Mead was not Stuteville's only source of information. Sir Simonds D'Ewes also set up a regular correspondence, on one occasion claiming that his letter from Sir William Spring in London contained 'moore parliament newes then Mr Meades.'[85] Like Mead, D'Ewes sent separates into Suffolk he obtained from Parliament along with general news of parliamentary proceedings.[86] By 11 May 1626, news of Parliament and foreign affairs flooded into D'Ewes's residence at such a rate that he told Stuteville that no longer did his correspondence deserve to be called a letter but should be renamed a coranto:[87] 'London, like Africa, *semper aliquid novi parens.'*[88]

The Mead/D'Ewes to Stuteville correspondence was of course only one spoke in the wheel of a national social network of information and communication. The Mead to Stuteville correspondence is the most extensive extant communication, but it was by no means an isolated instance. In 1626 Matthew Hutton, MP for Richmond, wrote a series of newsletters to his father, Sir Timothy Hutton. Although only one survives, he promised 'a weekly account of our parliamentary proceedings.'[89] Another MP who set up a regular correspondence on parliamentary news was Thomas Meautys, who sat for Cambridge. His letters to his cousin, Lady Anne Bacon, concentrate mainly on the charges against Buckingham. Given that Buckingham was Meautys's patron, it is hardly surprising that his letters reveal a flattering portrait of the Duke and strong support for the government. Despite his previous experience as an MP in 1621 and 1625, Meautys misinterpreted the mood of the House right from the outset. 'Our Parliament falls not as yet upon the main of business, it being but early days with us and many members absent. Only Sir Edward Coke's election has been disabled and is like to be determined against him with few days, and is he and the rest of his fellow sheriffs be excluded (as it conceived they will), we shall have a tame House, only the King will master his own ends without much ado.'[90] As late as 19 May Meautys saw Buckingham's case as 'not desperate' and thought on 8 June that the Duke 'has this day made his answer to out charge against him, an ingenuous and clear answer and very satisfactory, as is conceived to all indifferent [unbiased] ears.'[91]

Another series of correspondence between the Millington brothers, John and Gilbert, reveals the extent to which the news about Parliament spread throughout London and beyond. John, from his lowly position as purveyor of the King's wine cellar, kept up a regular correspondence with his brother in Nottingham. His early intelligence of the Commons activity was sufficient that among other proceedings he could identify Rudyerd's speech on ministers on 10 February and Eliot's questioning of the King's finances later that day. His report arrived in sufficient detail to note Sir George Goring's affront at Eliot's use of the word 'courtier' to imply 'faction.'[92] Even later in the Parliament, when Millington was confined to his bed with an 'ague,' he was able to send parliamentary business to his brother, as he put it, 'shaking out the news that I have.'[93] Millington clearly had more than just a source within Parliament; he was able to obtain documents as well. As he commented, 'I have not had time to copy things of Parliament out, nor almost to get news, but thus the world wags.'[94] Millington's final letters of May and June were again full of parliamentary news, especially Digby's charges against Buckingham. Highlighting John's access to parliamentary documents, he noted that 'Digby's answer is almost 3 hundred sheets long on paper, therefore requires some time to work out. You shall have all the whole materials of the House for your retiredness to work upon in the meantime.'[95] Millington seems to have had no difficulty getting hold of the proceedings and sending them to his brother in the country.

The inveterate letter-writer and correspondent, Sir Francis Nethersole, received a myriad of letters from his friend Sir Benjamin Rudyerd. Nethersole who had previously been returned for Parliament in 1624 and 1625, and himself an avid parliamentary newsletter writer, was unsuccessful in obtaining a seat in 1626 despite Rudyerd's intervention with his patron, the Earl of Pembroke. He was thus left reliant on Rudyerd for his news. Rudyerd proved to be a worthy correspondent and apprised Nethersole of all the relevant parliamentary affairs. Rudyerd not only provided a detailed running commentary but also enclosed copies of the major parliamentary speeches and documents, including what was possibly his own intervention on 23 March, in which he reminded the House that war meant opening their purses to finance intervention against Spain.[96] Throughout the Parliament, Rudyerd wrote in a despondent tone about its success. As early as 19 March he informed Nethersole (after enclosing 'all that has hitherto been done [in] Parliament.') that 'whereof you must not expect many particulars so far off, the points being so dangerous as we dare not speak freely among ourselves.'[97] 'The storms of the Parliament have been very high,' he noted on 6 April, and on 2 June, '[W]hat will issue of this Parliament, God knows.'[98] But throughout the Parliament, in every letter to Nethersole, Rudyerd enclosed separates of parliamentary activity.

Francis Staresmore, who had been elected MP for Leicestershire in 1626 on the interest of his patron, Henry Hastings, Earl of Huntington, also kept up a semiregular correspondence of parliamentary news. His extant letters provide Huntington with all the Parliament news, from MPs coming to town late, a list of bills read, Dr. Turner's charges against Buckingham, and Bristol's petition to be admitted to the Lords.[99]

Framlingham Gawdy, a well-established member of the Norfolk gentry, kept his wife informed of parliamentary events during his long career as an MP (1614–26, April and November 1640). In 1621, he kept her abreast of the news about the disgrace of the notorious monopolist Sir Giles Mompesson, and in 1626 let her know about their cousin, Clement Coke, and his ill-judged speech in which he complained that he 'had rather suffer by a foreign enemy than at home?' He passed on further news about the Earl of Arundel's imprisonment and enclosed a copy of Samuel Turner's attack on Buckingham.[100] Despite being pricked as a sheriff and thus being ineligible to stand in the 1628 Parliament, Gawdy did not lack for news of the Parliament. From his friend, the MP for King's Lynn, John Hare, he received a book of all the names of the MPs and peers as well as news of parliamentary business.[101] Another friend and MP who corresponded regularly with him during the 1628 Parliament was Edmund Moundeford, whose seat at Thetford he owed to Gawdy's influence.[102] Moundeford was not recorded as speaking in the Parliament or as being appointed to any committees but he certainly attended, as his letters to Gawdy illustrate. On 14 April he told Gawdy that 'four' subsidies had been agreed to and that he had been with the members of the Commons to deliver the petition on billeted soldiers to the King, but 'what answer we shall have is not known. Our House proceeds not with the calm it did; God grant a good end.'[103] On 25 April, Moundeford's pessimism had increased: '[S]uch is the stay of all our business in the Upper House that I can write you no proceedings. We have daily feared our period such is the division in the Lords.'[104] By 5 May he considered that little had been achieved when he again wrote to Gawdy: 'I am sorry to be a messenger of sad tidings; the fears of an ill ending of this Parliament are now grown so great as they command belief. Our last day is appointed tomorrow sevennight and we are as far from ending our work as when we began.'[105]

Another to benefit from information provided by his electoral client was Sir John Coke. As the main government speaker in 1628, Coke had been responsible for trying to force the government agenda for money through the Commons as well as to defend the King. Valiantly but ineffectively, he had attempted to stem the rising tide of anger in the House. However, the dire situation of the English fleet at La Rochelle meant that urgent naval preparations required Coke's presence in Portsmouth. Coke may have been away from the Commons, but he continued to receive parliamentary news. His client, Thomas Alured, who sat for Hedon, updated him on the Petition of Right debates, the Commons' attacks on Arminianism, and the unresolved matter of Tunnage and Poundage.[106] Coke's fellow secretary, Lord Conway, also kept him apprised of parliamentary news.[107] Coke had earlier tried to block the circulation of parliamentary documents, with no success. The propositions concerning the navy, introduced into the Commons on 26 March, were met with a speech by Christopher Wandesford in which he suggested that everyone in the House should circulate a transcription to their friends in the countryside. Coke requested that if copies were made, 'confine them only to parliament men.'[108] Illustrating the extent to which MPs now viewed parliamentary documents not as matters of secrecy to be kept *arcana imperii*, member after member rejected Coke's suggestion. Sir John Strangeways summed up the mood of the House: 'I am not of the opinion that these propositions should be only confined to parliament. We have left behind us in the country as wise men as any we have here. Shall we not make use of their advice?'[109]

Letters were on one hand personal and on the other proliferated and were widely circulated among the dense networks of communication defined by clientage, family, and locality in early modern England. Sir Simonds D'Ewes's news from London wound its way around East Anglia as it was copied and passed on; he asked Sir Martin Stuteville: 'Let me entreate yow Sir when Sir William Spring shall returne yow the Oxford title, that yow would send it to Mr [Joseph] Meade and desire him from mee to lend it to Mr Beeston of St Johns and to John Scott of Cambridge who hath sent to mee to desire it of mee. I have sent you the worke of two afternoons in Parliament, by which yow may guesse what the whole would bee [and] send them to Sir William Spring to view.'[110] D'Ewes, though, was occasionally concerned about the sensitive nature of his parliamentary reporting. When he informed Stuteville of Charles's visit to the House of Lords to complain that Sir Dudley Digges's comparison of Buckingham to Sejanus implied that the King must be the tyrannical Tiberius, D'Ewes asked his friend 'to keepe to your selfe as your owne by separating this halfe sheete and burning itt or concealing it, though ther bee nothing in it unlawfull or unfit to bee saied.'[111] Aware perhaps that intelligence from Parliament was potentially dangerous, Mead was careful to protect his sources. Often the names of MPs who provided information, whether by letter or in person, remain largely anonymous in the newsletters and were referred to as a 'parliament man' or 'my author.' Mead too was aware that threats had been made against Sir Robert Cotton for using his library to research parliamentary precedents.[112]

It was not only the provincial gentry who received the news of Parliament but also Charles's sister, Elizabeth Queen of Bohemia. Sir Francis Nethersole, who sat in Parliament as an MP for Corfe Castle, kept up a regular and lengthy correspondence with Elizabeth. Like those circulating among the gentry, Nethersole's letters mix a measure of the atmosphere of the Parliament, with daily snippets of news and copies of the important speeches and parliamentary documents. For instance, on 14 April 1628, noting that he was continuing on from his previous missive, Nethersole opened with the news that after much apprehension that Parliament would be dissolved without conducting any business, the mood at Westminster was significantly improved. Coke's speech at the joint conference with the Lords on the liberties of subjects was briefly mentioned, Nethersole reflected on the tone of the speech, which was delivered 'with some mixture of mirth . . . which served to make the Lords merry.' He promised Elizabeth a copy of the speech and other proceedings with his next letter. The letter continued with daily news of parliamentary activity for the week and an enclosure of the King's answer to both houses' petition on religion.[113] Elizabeth gained further intelligence and also received parliamentary news from another letter writer, the MP for Hastings, Sir John Ashburnham.[114] She could scarcely have been better informed if she was in London.

News of Parliament was also transmitted into the European capitals through the dispatches of resident ambassadors in England. Amerigo Salvetti, the Tuscan resident in London, sent detailed letters back to Florence on parliamentary affairs. He attended the opening ceremony in 1625, noting the details of the King's opening speech as well as the Lord Keeper's. With a wry sense of humor, he was amused that the French ambassador and his other countrymen at the opening were unaware that prayers were said before the King spoke, and did not have 'time to escape' the Protestant ceremony.[115] Salvetti concentrated his news on matters of religion and finance, especially parliamentary attacks on Catholics and the progress of the subsidy bills. Despite the fact he had fled London for Richmond and was soon to go farther afield to escape the plague in London, Salvetti's intelligence was sufficient to enable reports from the Oxford session as well, from which he described in detail the King's opening address. His parliamentary news continued from his temporary lodgings in Huntington, where he described the dissolution of Parliament and the disgruntlement at this course of action felt by the members of Parliament and the populace at large.[116]

Salvetti continued his correspondence in 1626, sending back the articles on Dr. Turner's charges against Buckingham as well as detailed information on the proceedings and temper of the Parliament. At the beginning of the Parliament Salvetti astutely referred to the 'opposing' demands of Charles's desire for subsidies and the Commons' investigation into war expenditure, noting that 'it will be difficult to induce Parliament to do anything in one direction without concessions in the other.'[117] Salvetti often included quotes from the King's speeches and obtained information from both Houses, dividing his reports into sections on the Lords and Commons. The attacks on Buckingham provided a ready source of news for Salvetti as he attempted to convey not just the proceedings but also the tone of the proceedings. His letter of 8 May comments that 'the arraignment of the Duke of Buckingham occupies the exclusive attention of the House of Commons. The excitement grows daily as new and important complaints are brought forward.'[118] Salvetti too managed to lay his hands on parliamentary documents, copying out into his missive of 29 May the article of charges brought by the Earl of Bristol against Buckingham.[119] Parliament increasingly occupied Salvetti's attention, and he complained on 12 June that 'the adjournment of Parliament for eight days for Whitsuntide holidays has caused some dearth of matter to write about this week.'[120] But at the resumption his letters again filled with parliamentary news, copying documents and reporting speeches.[121]

The third Caroline Parliament (1628) again brought Salvetti much to write about. He closely followed the preparations, noting the ascendancy in the elections of 'the Puritanical party' in the Commons and frequently sending detailed reports back to Tuscany.[122] In his dispatch of 17 April Salvetti included the points made by Sir John Coke on 5 April regarding the war and copied in full the petition against Catholics that the Parliament presented to Charles on 10 April. He also gave a full text of the King's reply and continued his in-depth and knowledgeable reports.[123]

Similar communication throughout the 1620s also came from the Venetian ambassadors, Girolamo Lando, Alvise Valaresso, and Alvise Contarini. Although Lando had difficulty obtaining the King's opening speech in 1621, intelligence of parliamentary affairs was not in short supply, and the letter later notes, 'I could fill many sheets of every despatch with the events which are happening daily in this Parliament.'[124] Throughout the 1620s regular reports were sent back to Venice detailing parliamentary activity, often enclosing copies of speeches and other proceedings. In the first week of the 1628 Parliament, Contarini wrote about events in both Houses and enclosed the King's speech at the opening.[125] On 16 April he set a separate of the King's wartime proposals to Parliament.[126] Among other documents he also obtained the printed version of Buckingham's speech on parliamentary affairs, a copy of the Petition of Right, and the two answers that Charles gave to the Petition. Contarini was sufficiently well informed to report the details of votes in Parliament and the 'mood' of the Houses as they debated religion and the subsidies. Thus by the end of the 1620s, parliamentary speeches, votes, and documents were no longer the preserve of a selected few, but openly discussed and disseminated in the country at large and in the capitals of foreign powers.

~

The last 1620s Caroline Parliament marked a watershed in the reporting of parliamentary news. Mead was not the only one to realize the importance of the debates in the Houses and shift his writing to a daily format. In May 1628 one anonymous newsletter writer laid out his missive in a daily fashion reporting the events of Parliament, and around the court as well, as news from abroad for each day.[127] Similarly, Christopher Lewkenor's weekly missives to Henry Percy, Earl of Northumberland, took the form of a diurnal report, summarizing speeches, naming speakers and the general business of the House in great detail.[128] Separates too multiplied. Sir Richard Grosvenor, one of the Knights of the Shire for Cheshire, as well as keeping a daily account of the session, deliberately set out to obtain as many separates as he could from the 1629. The Parliament began on 20 January, and Grosvenor, who did not arrive until 5 February, already listed twelve different separates available from the opening messages to his answer to the Commons on its petition for a fast. Already available were the most important salvos in the Commons—speeches on 26 January by Kirton on the religious troubles of the kingdom and Eliot on proceeding slowly with the subsidy bill before other issues had been addressed.[129] Grosvenor also obtained Francis Rous's stirring speech on 27 January concerning religious liberty.[130] To this list he added the King's message to Parliament (23 January), his speech (24 January), the Commons Apology of 30 January, and the 'profession touching religion' (29 January).[131] The dominance of religious issues in the session is clear from both Grosvenor's scribbled notes in his diary and on the separates he so assiduously sought: Sir John's Coke declaration about the Jesuit College at Clerkenwell, three different pieces on the anti-Calvinist, John Cosin, another two on Cosin's friend the Arminian, Richard Montague, and a letter to the universities about Arminians.[132] The second major issue of the session, Tunnage and Poundage, was also reflected in Grosvenor's collection, as he wanted to obtain three separates on this matter.

The collection of such a number of separates was not a cheap undertaking and speaks to Grosvenor's interest in the business at hand. One of

Sir Robert Cotton's speeches was for sale for 2 shillings, the lengthy Lord Keeper's speech was 4 shillings and 6 pence, while other speeches and documents varied between 8 shillings and just under 2 shillings. Clearly, a substantial collection such as Grosvenor's could run into a hefty financial outlay,[133] although in some cases it is possible that documents were freely distributed rather than needing to be paid for. On 5 May 1628, the Speaker's message to the King and his response on the liberties of the subject were ordered by the House to 'be given out jointly together, and not singly, by the Clerk with speed.'[134]

As John Rous noted in his news diary in 1628, 'Having condescended, if it were not now a happie parliament, the sinne was theirs, he was free: when I was writing hereof Mr Pratte brought this. The Kings majesties message to the House of Commons, June 6, 1628.'[135] Through the efforts of scriveners such as Ralph Starkey and the clerks of both Houses, these documents were put forth with increasing frequency as tensions between the Crown and Parliament dominated the news of the day. By the time of the last early Caroline Parliament, separates could be obtained for virtually every important speech or document. The extent to which parliamentary material was available and obtainable had reached new heights. On everyday separates of the most important speeches, orders and other parliamentary activities were copied and circulated for sale. It was now the preserve of diarists and newsletter writers to report not only daily proceedings but the daily speeches as well. What was available for sale and laid on the stalls was the daily proceedings of Parliament.

The form of political communication changed, coming with an immediacy that paralleled but in many ways surpassed the development of the newspaper that required the transmission of information from abroad. By the end of Parliament, Mead and his circle of confidants had obtained all the relevant news from Parliament. Well-informed, provisioned with separates and other parliamentary documents, there was little information they did not know or could not obtain. On occasion, information arrived more slowly, but eventually it *did* arrive. It was not necessary to be in Parliament to know what was happening. By 1629 living in the country with sources of intelligence was sufficient. From 1621 to 1629, news spread from Parliament through the countryside at a rate and in detail that far surpassed Parliament before the 1620s. As Richard Cust noted, this flow of information served to polarize the nation and emphasize the differences between Parliament and the Crown. But it also served another purpose—namely, turning Par-

liament into the focal point and placing it at the center of the political nation.

The correspondence of the gentry on parliamentary matters reached new
intensity as the 1620s wore on. Parliament was the fulcrum around which
the governing class and Crown argued, fought over and debated the fiscal state of the country, the liberties of the subject, religion, war, and control over government ministers. Accustomed by now to the free flow of
information from printed coranto, access to and interest in parliamentary
news exploded. Meeting the 'newsy' needs of the countryside were those
engaged in the process: MPs who wrote frequently and at length to their
friends and relatives, professional newsletter writers who seized upon the
most dramatic news of the day, antiquarians, and avid collectors of information. Despite occasional delays in the post, news of Parliament and separates of parliamentary activity were easy to come by. Newsletters regularly
enclosed the work of scribes who copied parliamentary speeches, and some
printed works found their way into the marketplace and from thence into
the country. The secrets of Parliament were not only laid on the stalls but
also were purchased and disseminated at an unprecedented rate. Thus by
1629, the tide of paper flooding into Parliament had been surpassed by the
flood of paper out of it. Legislative activity was largely abandoned and lobbying had mainly ceased. MPs aware of the dissemination of proceedings
now came with copies ready to be displayed to the world outside of the
chambers. Parliament had become the news, and that news was now a great
deal more public.

Permeable Boundaries

Setting the Stage:
Parliament and the Chambers

If the walls of Parliament had been made more permeable by the flow of information from inside the chambers to the countryside at large, then so too were the boundaries porous to those members of the public who had business in the chambers and committee rooms or who simply wanted to witness the political nation at work. Although contemporary writers on Parliament as well as its membership often professed to the need to keep the speeches and decisions made in the chambers secret from those who haunted the rooms and corridors of Westminster Palace, in reality strict confidentiality was a measure enforced only during times of political crisis. Just as the torrent of parliamentary writings flowed out of the chambers in newsletters, separates, and journals, so too paper increasingly poured in during the 1620s. The transmission of information between Parliament and the people was not just paper traffic, however; it was also the coming and going of a diverse array of persons with business in Parliament. Lobbyists and petitioners, in particular, stalked the environs to distribute their wares and speak to members of Parliament and peers. Parliament functioned in the immediate vicinity of nonmembers and might be clearly observed by those who walked through the Palace of Westminster.[1]

≈

The opening of Parliament was always a dramatic occasion of public ritual and ceremony, and the Palace became a hive of activity. Supervised by the Lord Chamberlain and the Office of Works, within the Palace of Westminster workers delivered wall-hangings and furniture to both Houses, windows were repaired and canopies erected to keep out the sun. Canvas,

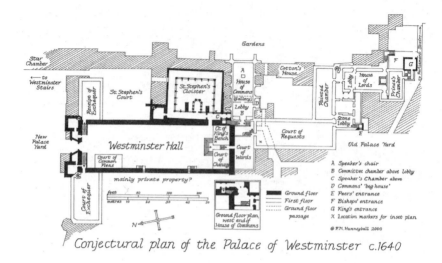

Conjectural plan of the Palace of Westminster c.1640

wool, and hay were purchased to remake the seats in the Lords, and benches were repaired and constructed in the Commons. Supplies of stationery, fire tongs, and wood were purchased, and curtains were hung in order to accommodate the six hundred or so people who would make the Palace of Westminster their daily workplace while Parliament was in session.[2]

Befitting the assembly of the governing body of the realm, preparations were both elaborate and expensive. In the mid-1560s, Sir Thomas Smith described the Lords Chamber as 'richly tapessed and hanged, a princely and royal throne as appertaineth to a king.'[3] As Alasdair Hawkyard and Maria Hayward have noted, among these tapestries were four illustrating the founding of Rome in the *Story of Romulus and Remus* that Henry VIII had purchased in 1529 and seemed to be moved to Parliament whenever it was in session.[4] The removal of furniture and decorative items from royal palaces and storehouses was part of the preparation for any Parliament. In 1628 furnishings arrived at Parliament from the Tower, Whitehall, Windsor, and Oatlands. Rich tapestries were hung in the Houses and forty ells of canvas purchased as a sunshade for the large window in the Commons.[5] The cloth of state, 'worked with gold,' was placed behind the throne in the Lords, pillows comforted the seats of officers of state, and as customary, the chamber was bedecked with crimson tape secured with copper nails. The Speaker's dining room was furnished with ten 'turkey' carpets, and the room was decorated with tapestries depicting the myth of Diana and Actaeon.[6]

Throughout Parliament, the Crown was also responsible for the diets of privy councillors and the legal assistants in the Lords. As Elizabeth Read Foster has estimated, this came to somewhere in the region of £1605 in 1628. A further £21 10s. provided for the regular cleaning and sweeping of the chambers, £323 9s. 3d. in repairs and furnishings from the Office of Works, while the Wardrobe contributed furnishings worth £150 17s. The fees of officers added nearly £400 and messengers somewhere in the region of £70. In total, the recoverable costs of the Parliament ran to a substantial £2,565 15s. 9d. But missing from these fragmentary accounts are the costs of stationery (£147 10s. in 1610); printing (amount unknown); the royal barge (£550 in 1621 and £620 in 1640); and the care and repair of robes (£170 7s. 12d. in 1626). The royal robes themselves were resplendent; £617 7s. 8d. was spent on garments for James and Prince Henry in 1603, and no doubt Charles's robe in 1625 was an equally fine piece of apparel.

Calling a Parliament and keeping it in session was an expensive business. On the opening day, in a public procession, the monarch and the court paraded past 'the presse of the people,' who were held back by newly erected railings in streets that had been repaved and swept clean. Onlookers rented rooms and houses with the best view, many of which were decorated with tapestries especially for the occasion. Starting from Whitehall or St. James's Palace, the procession wound its way to Westminster Abbey and from there across Old Palace Yard to the Houses of Parliament. Heralds clad in their distinctive livery marshaled the procession, and everyone was ranked according to status and relationship to the monarch. Those farthest away were the trumpeters and messengers. Following them came the administrative clerks, the royal judges, and the privy councillors, who were commoners. Arrayed in their Parliament robes, the nobility came next in order of precedence, and then the senior officers of state carrying the monarch's regalia of office. At the apex of the procession, the monarch rode or was carried in a chair of state surrounded by members of the Royal Guard. The arrival of the procession at Westminster Palace, in theory, marked the end of the public ceremony as the King moved inside to give his opening address to the Parliament assembled in the Lords, and the Houses retired to their chambers to debate matters of state ostensibly in secret.[7] In 1604, however, the process went awry.

The opening of the first Parliament of James's reign was already marred by a precedence dispute between the French and Spanish ambassadors over which of them was the senior foreign diplomat. James, unwilling to commit to an early decision, played each one off against the other.[8] As a result, that year no ambassadors at all were invited to witness the King's speech. Instead, James rented them houses along the route of the procession.[9] It was an inauspicious start to the first Parliament of a new reign. Things deteriorated further inside the Upper House when the King addressed the peers. James taxed the patience of those present with a speech lasting nearly an hour, and the Lords failed to send a messenger to the Commons to call them to attend the ceremony. As a result, most of the Lower House continued to wait in their own chamber and missed the oration. Although some old Parliament hands had succeeded in getting into the Lords, an over-zealous Royal Guard, Brian Tash, compounded the debacle by keeping the doors firmly shut and by pushing and insulting the MP Sir Herbert Croft as he sought admittance.[10]

The main cause of this problem lay in the crush of people who had jammed into the Lords to hear the first speech to Parliament of their new King. Before he began his speech, James had asked whether the Commons were present and had been assured that they were. In fact, the majority of those inside the House were interested members of the public who had simply turned up to hear James speak. As the clerk noted in the Commons Journal, '[T]he Error was discovered to grow by the Intrusion of sundry Gentlemen, his Majesty's Servants, and others (no Members of Parliament) into the Higher House, during the time of this his Majesty's Speech, who were taken for the Commons; and thereby his Majesty was induced to direct his Speech, as if the whole House of Commons had been present, and heard him.'[11] James's first Parliament had opened with a public invasion.[12]

This problem of nonmembers crowding in on the opening ceremony did not go away. It happened again in 1614, when the Lords was so full 'with strangers' that there was not enough room for the Commons.[13] Nor had matters improved by the opening of the next Parliament in 1621 in which the Lords again neglected to send for the Lower House, and during the King's speech 'many which were not of the [Lower] House stayed to get in . . . and so many of the old parliament men were kept out.'[14] The division of the opening of Parliament into public and private components was a failure, at least in the reign of James I.

It has recently been suggested by Oliver Arnold that the 'Commons, as a corporate body, vigorously sought to prevent the development of a *popular* audience to their proceedings and punished members for speaking of Parliament's business in public.'[15] Thus he argues that Parliament operated in a cone of silence, where 'nearly everything MPs did was "hid and secret."'[16] But this reveals a fundamental misapprehension about the architecture, physical space, and institutional context of the Palace of Westminster. St. Stephen's Chapel, the meeting place of the Commons since the mid-sixteenth century, and the House of Lords were both nestled in a complex of public buildings.[17] As the plan indicates (see illustration), the chambers themselves were surrounded by the judicial apparatus of early modern England. Within Westminster Hall, the three main courts, King's Bench, Chancery, and Common Pleas, operated during the law terms. Off the North end of the Hall, the Court of Exchequer was found in an adjacent structure, while the Court of Wards was separated from the Commons only by the lobby to the Lower House and a passageway. Between the two Houses, the Court of Requests provided a well-traveled path between the Commons and Lords. The courts remained in session hearing cases and conducting business while the Parliament was sitting, and members of Parliament who were lawyers scurried between both venues. As one commentator noted in 1572, one sure way to delay legislation in the Commons was to 'appoint lawyers in terme time' to the committee, as they were too busy with their legal business to attend the committee meetings.[18] The judicial business of the nation brought into Westminster Hall and the surrounding area plaintiffs, defendants, law clerks, legal students taking notes on trials, and interested onlookers, creating a busy and very public and crowded space along one of the main thoroughfares through which MPs walked to their chamber. As Thomas Nash commented in 1594, '[A] man can scarce breath' in the Hall.[19] Westminster Hall also housed booksellers and vendors as well as scriveners and possibly hawkers.[20] Furthermore, it seems to have been something of a tourist attraction, and was one of the recommended stops for those visiting London.[21] The immediate vicinity also contained private dwellings. Not the least of these was Sir Robert Cotton's house, which occupied part of the land between the two chambers.[22] Parliament thus debated matters of state surrounded by the continual to-ing and fro-ing of members of the public going about their daily affairs in the law courts, buying goods in Westminster Hall, or eating and drinking in the venues off Old Palace Yard.[23]

Also open to the public were the lobbies off both Houses. Here the sergeant at arms and doorkeepers worked in conjunction with clerks and messengers. Members of the public arrived to deliver petitions, read committee lists posted to the doors,[24] or attend, if summoned to either House. The assistants to the Clerk of the Commons worked on tables in the lobby, copying parliamentary documents and receiving petitions.[25] There seems to have been little effort made to limit the attendance of interested onlookers, let alone those who had business with Parliament. One perennial problem in the lobbies and the stairs leading off them was that many people congregated there, especially the servants and coachmen of peers and MPs.

The area surrounding the Palace housed the notoriously riotous taverns of Heaven, Hell, and Purgatory, and in the bustling environs the noise became so loud that in 1642 a chain was hung across the entry to Old Palace Yard to limit unnecessary traffic.[26] Further disturbances arose from the crowds gathered around the Yard and congregated in the doorways that gave access to the House of Commons. The press of people around the doors and stairways, often the staff of MPs and peers, often caused trouble. In 1581 in response to the 'lewd disorder and outrage' of several pages and serving-men that had taken place on the stairs in Westminster Hall, which MPs traversed to gain access to the Commons, the Warden of the Fleet was to station two men there to ensure no repeat of such behavior.[27] The stairs remained a focal point for pages fond of trouble. In 1601 the MP Sir Francis Hastings was threatened with being thrown down the stairs, and in 1606 Henry Yelverton informed the Commons of further abuse by pages in the same area.[28] John Pym complained in 1621 of a fight between the servants of two MPs that had taken place in Westminster Hall and disrupted the sitting of King's Bench. This was, Pym thought, 'the reason of dissorder the Coachmen and footemen upon the stayres.'[29] This in turn led Sir William Spencer to recall that there was an 'old order that the Warden of the Fleet should be commanded to cause two of his men to stand upon the stairs to see that there be no such misdemenors done.'[30] Trouble too was found next to the peers' entrance when an order was given in 1624 for a tavern run by George Whitchair to be closed while Parliament was in session. In this instance, the 'idle' coachmen, led by the drivers of the Duke of Buckingham, Lord Keeper Williams, and the Earls of Pembroke and Bridgwater, had formed a Company of Coachmen complete with officers, a book of orders, and the paraphernalia of office (rods, staffs). This the House of Lords found unacceptable, and gave orders that it be closed down.[31] But perhaps the most notorious incident occurred in the depths of the 1610 winter when a clerk holding the coat of the Speaker (Sir Edward Phelips) was violently assaulted and relieved of the said item. This led to a mass brawl between servants of various MPs and pages from the House of Lords and the theft of more coats. The clothes were recovered at the nearby Prince's Arms tavern, where they had been pawned by pages from the House of Lords who could not pay their bill for drink.[32] The lobbies were ordered cleared only in times of high political crisis or if crowds in the vicinity became too noisy.[33]

The changing role of Parliament in the early Stuart period also led to increased numbers of people in proximity to the chambers. The revival of the judicial role of the Lords in 1621 drew petitioners, witnesses, and counsel to Parliament to argue their cases. In the Commons, the rise of standing committees in the 1620s for Justice, Trade, and Grievances also heard witnesses and received documents pertaining to the cases before them. What also must have led to crowding around the environs of the Palace was the Commons' desire to move their committee business closer to St. Stephens Chapel. As the House in the 1620s became a more self-aware body, so too it moved its business nearer the actual chamber. The Commons had only one room outside the chambers over which it had a propriety right—namely, the committee chamber above the lobby. Therefore, committees met in the courts around the Palace or as far away as the Middle Temple and Lincoln's Inn Halls. In 1604 the most often used venues were Middle Temple Hall and the Exchequer Chamber. During the 1620s, however, there was a noticeable shift in committee meeting spaces to rooms closer by. In 1624, for example, only four committees were appointed to meet at the Middle Temple, as opposed to fifty-nine in 1604. The Courts of Westminster, especially Wards, Star Chamber, and the Exchequer, now dominated the meeting places. The effect of this was not only a more efficient process, as members had less distance to travel to meetings, but also an increase in the number of people present around the chambers to attend committees.[34]

These myriad groups of parliamentary attendees were by and large present on official business either of their own volition or summoned by the Lords or Commons. That they had a reason to be around Parliament should not detract from the point that more and more people interacted with Parliament. These individuals and a wide range of persons from all ranks of the social order, from servants and victuallers to legal counsel, were thus afforded proximity to the chambers and through their presence could learn what was happening inside. That it was possible to hear speeches and discussions in Parliament from the lobbies is clear, even on those occasions when the doors were closed.[35] Furthermore, there is little evidence that the Commons, at least, attempted to restrict access to the lobbies, and so it was possible for members of the public to loiter there and hear the debates. On 2 April 1628, Philip Parsons, an Oxford scholar, was called into the House after it was noticed by Sir Francis Stuart that he had spent the last hour standing in full view in the doorway listening to the debate on supply. The House interrupted its proceedings to call Parsons in, and a subcommittee examined him later that afternoon.[36] Parsons was discharged without penalty the following day after pleading ignorance of his fault. He had heard that he could present a grievance that day and had waited for the opportunity.[37] It is possible, however, that Parsons had other motives and may have sought to listen on behalf of his patron, Bishop William Laud, who in June was condemned as an Arminian in the Commons Remonstrance. Parsons dedicated his Arcadian Latin comedy, *Atalanta*, to Laud, who was his head of college in Oxford, and in 1633 Laud nominated him for the position of head of Hart Hall, Oxford.[38] Significantly, though, it was an hour before Parsons was noticed standing in the doorway, and clearly, in the continual movement of members and messengers in and out of the House, it took some time before eavesdroppers could be identified. Later in the session, another Oxfordshire gentlemen, Robert Barbour, was also caught listening in the doorway, and he too pleaded ignorance of the Commons' rules on secrecy; after he was vouched for by two MPs, he too was pardoned without punishment.[39] No doubt discovering these eavesdroppers was made more difficult too by members themselves, who had a propensity to loiter in the doorway rather than taking their seats in the chamber.[40]

Even regulating those who sat in the House was difficult. The Commons suffered from a perennial problem of strangers actually entering the House and listening to debates. In a chamber of more than 450 members, many of whom were not well known lawyers, courtiers, or prominent Parliament men, identifying who was an MP and who was not was a difficult task. On 28 November 1584, Richard Robinson, a skinner by trade, sat in the House for two hours before he was discovered.[41] Likewise, on 3 March 1593, John Legg, a servant of the Earl of Northumberland, spent the 'greater part of this Forenoon' listing to debates in the Commons.[42] For all those incidents in which interlopers were apprehended, many more may have gone unnoticed. As John Hooker noted in 1572, '[No] manner of person being not one of the Parlement house: ought to enter or come within the house, as long as the sitting is there: upon pain of imprisonment or suche other punishment, as by the house shalbe ordered and adjudged.'[43] In practice, however, the Commons took a lenient tone with strangers found in the House and only rarely imposed a sentence of brief imprisonment.[44] In most instances the House merely ordered the offenders to take the oaths of allegiance and supremacy before releasing them with a stern admonition to keep secret what they had heard. Even Mr. Bulkeley, who in 1614 had lied his way into the Commons, telling the sergeant that he was an MP, was imprisoned only briefly.[45]

Members too complained how the business of the Commons was echoed in the streets, as Sir Robert Cecil informed the House in 1601 during the contentious monopolies investigation:

> I ffeare we are not secret amonge our selves. Then muste I needes give yow this for a ffuture caution, that whatsoever is subject to a publique expectatcion cannot be good. Whie, Parleament matters are ordinarye talke in the streetes. I have hearde my self, being in my coache, these words spoaken alowde: 'God prosper those that further the overthrowe of these monopolies.'[46]

In 1606 Sir Robert Johnson complained that as he had walked through the streets he had been subject to the 'turbulent clamour and outcry of certain women against him . . . for speaking against the Bill touching Wherrymen and Watermen.'[47] In response, the House asked the Speaker to write to the Middlesex justices of the peace, but that was the extent of the action taken. These complaints highlight how the deliberations of Parliament were not *arcana imperii*, and, as I have argued elsewhere, '[T]his was not a closed world where entry was strictly enforced, information was limited and the elite gathered.'[48]

Having determined that Parliament operated in a space open to members of the general public (whether they were engaged with Parliament or not), the following two chapters look at how Parliament became the focal point for lobbying interests and the recipient of printed material in the 1620s. Lobbying and its by-product, the newly emerging engagement of Parliament with printed materials, flooded Westminster with people lobbying for and against legislation, and distributing printed briefs at the door of the chambers. The 1604 Parliament opened with a public invasion; the 1620s Parliaments closed with nonmembers handing out printed material at the doors of the House.

CHAPTER FIVE

Open Doors:
Pressure Groups and Lobbying

Sir John Mablisten of the Order of St. John of Jerusalem was dismayed at the Order's prospects of securing favorable legislation in 1532: 'As to the matters which you wish preferred at this Parliament, my Lord [Sir William Weston, Prior of the Knights of St. John] does what he can. Yf we had money inoughe I suppose sum of them might be brought to passe: and without grete plenty therof nothing here passythe.'[1] Mablisten had an inside source, the prior's younger brother, Sir Richard Weston, represented Berkshire in the Reformation Parliament.[2] But the Knights had run into the reality of private legislation—it was a vastly expensive project, often totaling hundreds of pounds. Everyone surrounding Westminster needed to be paid, lobbied, bribed, entertained, and wined and dined. Petitions needed to be drawn, clerks, speakers, and officials paid, MPs and Lords favorable to the specific interest had to be found, representatives sent to London, and lawyers hired and placed on retainers. When Sir John Mill found himself elected to Parliament for Southampton in 1529, one of his main tasks was to obtain an act of Parliament remitting an excess fee-farm of 40 shillings that the town paid to the King every year. Mill was successful in this enterprise, and 22 Henry VIII cap. 20 was enacted in 1531 after a town petition the previous year. In order to secure its passage, Mill paid the Clerk of the Parliament 40s. and his deputy 10s. to write it onto the Parliament Roll, and Ralph Pexall £4 11s. 8d. for recording it in Chancery. Mill also solicited powerful figures to assist his enterprise. The Duke of Suffolk, Charles Brandon, and Sir Henry Guildford (privy councillor and Comptroller of the Household) both received fees, as did the barons of the Exchequer. A gift worth more than £7 was also given to Mary Fitzwilliam, the wife of the treasurer of the King's Household and privy councillor, Sir William Fitzwilliam, 'because her husband was very good in helping the town to the new Act.'[3] The deep pockets of Southampton had succeeded, but many others failed. Money was not the sole route to success in Parliament, but little could be done without it. Towns, individuals, and companies all sought to exploit the legislative sovereignty of Parliament in order to further their aims. And as Parliament grew to dominate the political scene in the 1620s, so lobbying became more sophisticated. Furthermore, the establishment of new procedural devices in the Lords and Commons, especially the permanent standing committees of the 1620s, opened up new avenues through which petitioners could seek redress.

Typically the lobbying of Parliament has been assessed in terms of whether or not legislation was enacted as a result.[4] But lobbying cannot simply be measured by results. In the competitive, highly pressurized atmosphere of early modern Parliaments, securing even the attention of the Houses to a proposed measure required administrative and organizational acumen in a way that cannot be grasped if we focus only on the legislative results instead of on the practice itself. Lobbying was a necessary managerial skill in order to get the attention of Parliament in a marketplace of competing pressure groups and the manifold legislative desires of private individuals. It was not only that bills needed the assistance provided by lobbyists, friends in the chamber, and parliamentary officials favorable to the cause in order to proceed through the system, but money and skillful maneuvering were also vital to their having a hearing at all. Even the experience, financial clout, and organization of London and its interest groups rarely succeeded in pushing legislation through to enactment. Successful lobbying could and did mean achieving a place on the parliamentary agenda. Private interest bills that created factions were rarely ensured of an uncontested passage through the Houses, and it was certainly easier to delay or defeat a bill than it was to enact one. For this reason it is necessary to measure whatever modicum of 'success' there might be over a period of time rather than one session. Both pressure groups and individuals were clearly aware of this process, repeatedly sponsoring and lobbying for legislation from Parliament to Parliament, often for more than a decade, or, in some cases—for example, the Great Yarmouth versus Lowestoft fishing dispute and Carew Raleigh's estate bill—for in excess of thirty years.[5] It was important to keep up the pressure even if individual pieces of legislation did not pass in a parliamentary session, at least until the late 1620s, when matters of state forced some private interests out of legislative activity and into new ways of interacting with Parliament.

This chapter, then, is based upon two premises—(1) that sophisticated lobbying tactics were a necessity in order for pressure groups to *promote* their legislation onto the parliamentary agenda; and (2) that any success at all needs to be construed over a long period of time. Therefore the effectiveness of lobbying and private interests cannot be measured by the success of legislation alone.

~

The market in which these competing groups sought legislative attention was a 'point of contact' between the governing class and the monarchy.[6] But Parliament was also a place where conflicting interest groups confronted one another. The Crown was primarily interested in supply, while Parliament sought to delay the passage of subsidy bills until their grievances had been heard and answered. The Privy Council and individual members sponsored legislation of interest to the Commonweal, and Parliament increasingly became embroiled in great matters of state, hearing legal cases and impeachment proceedings. Into this volatile mix, individuals and pressure groups sought to manage their parliamentary business and fight for a place upon an ever more crowded agenda. Parliament required, as Michael Graves brilliantly put it, 'the mixed managerial arts of surveillance, canvassing, persuasion, propaganda and opposition.'[7] The introduction of a bill to Parliament was in many ways a relatively simple proceeding. Most employed legal counsel to draft the measure, and from there a bill could be introduced by a member from the floor of the House or given directly to the Speaker.[8] The issue, however, was not getting the bill into Parliament but navigating the procedures to maximize its chances of being enacted as statute law. This required money, friends inside the chambers, the attention of parliamentary officials, legal assistance, and a fair share of good fortune.

Private legislation 'offered to individuals a definitive settlement of particular problems and thus extended the usefulness of Parliament beyond the concerns of the great agglomerates of [Crown], Church and commonwealth.'[9] But the introduction of private legislation also hindered the passage of public bills advocated by the government. Thomas Norton, the quintessential Elizabethan Parliament-man, warned of the dangers, for private bills 'ever be egerlie followed and make factions.'[10] Norton's solution was to appoint a committee to examine all legislation and advance those of most benefit to the Commonweal. The early Stuart author of 'Policies in Parliaments' offered similar advice as to the importance of public versus private: '[G]enerall bills ar to be passed before private. Private bills ar commonly reade in the morning when the howse is not full, or at tymes of leasure.'[11] For some, though, even this relegation of private matters to quieter periods in the House was not enough. The representative body of the realm was too important to concern itself with such private issues. As Sir Henry Poole opined: '[It] is unworthy the greatnes of the Howse to take care of the paveing of Streetes.'[12] Poole's pomposity was quickly shouted down by factional interests; Parliament was a place not only for great matters of state but also for small matters of local and individual concern.

However, Parliament served as only one forum available to interest groups, and because of its infrequent, short meetings and expense, it was not necessarily the forum of first resort. Often, pressure groups took advantage of the calling of Parliament to shift their requests and lobbying from local authorities, courts, and the Privy Council to the national arena. But despite the difficulties of successfully managing legislation in Parliament, it offered the great benefit of sovereign legislative authority, and, for an additional fee, the enrollment of private legislation on the sessional statute roll, which was printed and distributed throughout the nation.[13] None of this, however, came cheaply.

The parliamentary system of early modern England ran on the traditional administrative structure—small annual salaries and material perks supplemented by fees from petitioners, MPs, and others conducting business in Parliament. One of the most lucrative offices was the Clerk of the Parliament. Receiving an annual stipend of £40, irrespective of whether Parliament was in session, the clerk also received a fee for every stage a private bill reached in the three-reading procedure and was among the first on every petitioners' list for an *ex gratia* payment to ease business. His supplementary rewards also included the right to claim his desk at the end of each Parliament. His counterpart in the Lower House, the Underclerk of the Parliament, had a stipend of £10 per annum. The Speaker of the Commons was paid £100 for each parliamentary session, but like the Speaker in the Lords (the Lord Chancellor), he received most of his income through fees for private bills and other gifts.[14] The position was extremely lucrative. Before the first reading of any private bill in the Commons, the Speaker claimed a fee of £5.[15] In the busy legislative session of 1624, seventy-five private bills received at least one reading (potentially £375).[16] Every subsequent stage of procedure further lined the pockets of the Speaker and the clerk. Bills that were written or amended by the clerk were charged per line, at a rate which doubled during late Elizabethan parliaments, from 1d. per ten lines to possibly over 2d.[17] When a bill was engrossed, the charge in 1624 was 3s. 4d. per skin.[18] The clerk also received a payment at the start of the session for every MP who took the oath and shared with the sergeant a fee for every prisoner brought into the House.[19] Participating also in this largesse were the sergeants at arms in both Houses, the yeoman usher in the Lords, grooms, messengers, doorkeepers, and porters. Those with a vested interest in frequent parliamentary business, such as the Corporation of London, often paid retainers to officials over and above the standard fees.[20] Because the Speaker largely determined the order of business and because of the pressure of time in congested parliamentary sessions, the favor of the Speaker and to a lesser extent, the clerk, 'amounted to life or death' for a bill.[21] Without complete accounts it is not possible to discover the amount the Clerk of the Parliaments received, but in 1649 the office was estimated to be worth £500 per annum.[22]

This fee structure was too steep for some interest groups, who pleaded poverty. The Fruiterers Company of London asked for the assistance of the two Knights of the Shire for Kent in 1624, Sir Edwin Sandys and Sir Nicholas Tufton, to procure a bill to halt the importation of cherries and other fruit from Holland but informed them they had no money to prefer a bill.[23] Perhaps unsurprisingly, no Fruiterers' bill was read in 1624. Others tried to avoid charges altogether. Sir Edward Cecil most likely sought election in 1624 in order to manage a naturalization bill for his children. Aware, however, that fees were due for every person so named in the bill, Cecil was the likely mover of a more general bill that sought to naturalize children of soldiers whose fathers had been 'ymployed in the warres of the United Provinces.'[24] The bill failed to move past a first reading and received an 'honorable burial.'[25] Numerous practical and legal objections were raised, but there was never any doubt that a measure that would have removed a significant source of income from parliamentary officials was doomed to failure. Cecil then reverted to introducing a specific bill for his children (and those of other military commanders). Although a similar measure had passed both Houses three years earlier, only to fail through the dissolution of Parliament, Cecil's bill never made it past a first reading.[26] Whether he or the others did not pay the fees, or whether parliamentary officials were sufficiently annoyed at Cecil's attempt to rob them of their rightful dues, is unclear.

Others attempted to delay their payments until success was at hand. Justice Walmesley asked the Clerk of the Parliaments, Robert Bowyer, to do what he could to further the bill against 'Barwicke,' for which he would be 'paid what I said if the bill is enacted.'[27] The sheer complexity of navigating what appears to be a superficially simple administrative system is evident in all the parliamentary lobbying and petitioning that went on in early modern England.

The buzz that surrounded the rumors of a new Parliament being called immediately heightened the activities of those eager to appropriate it for their own purposes. The first and most obvious avenue was to ensure that MPs were elected who were sympathetic to the cause, or in many cases, parties thereof. Towns made sure their MPs were well informed of their interests and whatever legislation or action they required. Carpetbaggers soliciting a place passionately offered to safeguard the interests of their prospective constituency and to serve without fee or remuneration. Letters were sent back and forth from Westminster, and parliamentary proceedings were collected and dispatched to the countryside. Aldermen and town officials often traveled to Westminster to assist and advise their MPs and report back to the locale. MPs too sought election to Parliament to pursue their own private initiatives. For Thomas Barfoot in 1604, his decision to stand for election at Melcombe Regis was in order to secure the passage of legislation to secure his house as the new rectory for a resident clergyman in the town.[28] Roland Egerton, after having found himself libeled by his cousin, Edward Egerton, in 1621, decided to stand for Parliament in 1624 in order to head off further potential legislation,[29] while John Evelyn sought to defend his monopoly of the saltpeter trade by securing election to the Commons in 1628 and once there preferring a bill favorable to his saltpeter interest.[30] Sir John Catcher in 1621 secured his election at Truro, where his brother was an alderman, to protect his consortium's interest the West Country tin industry.[31] His election came none too soon, as the London Pewterers introduced legislation to thwart Catcher. As it happened, Catcher was able to remain silent, as the Pewterers ran into opposition from the powerful Duchy of Cornwall lobby, who succeeded in having the bill rejected at the first reading.[32]

A bill to limit the legal fees in Courts of Record (a perennial complaint) was introduced by Sir John Parker, who held a grant that gave him 1s. for every pleading in Chancery. Parker probably utilized his friends to secure a seat in 1604 at East Looe so he could prosecute a bill against the Six Clerks. He wrote to Sir Robert Cecil to elicit his support, but nothing came of it until he introduced his bill in the second session. Despite speaking enthusiastically in its favor, the bill failed to move beyond the committee stage. Parker tried again in the same session with a similar lack of success. Undaunted, he drafted another bill in the third session, complaining of 'the infinite charge and mischief falling daily upon the subject by the length, width and wasteful writings of copies in sundry offices towards the law.' The issue rumbled on into the fourth session, and another bill was introduced, probably by Parker. The Six Clerks of Chancery solicited help from an MP, Sir John Leveson. In this instance, the Six Clerks lobbied Leveson, who had been appointed to the bill committee. Nicholas Roberts, a Chancery Clerk, penned various objections against the bill and hoped Leveson would oppose it and to 'labour as many of your good friends as you can, to concur with you in the same opinion.'[33]

Sir John Acland most likely stood in a by-election in 1607 for a Knight of the Shire for Devon because he wished to promote a bill to reassign the revenues of Cutton prebend to fund a preacher and schoolmaster in his own parish.[34] Although the bill passed the Commons, possibly with support from Acland's good friend, the Exeter parliamentary manager and MP John Prowse, it stalled in committee in the Lords despite Acland's securing the backing of the Bishop of Exeter. Acland tried a slightly different strategy three years later, turning his private interest measure into one that appeared to be a public bill. Acland's bill for the better maintenance of husbandry by employing apprentices was designed to support the charitable grants that he had already made, and in his will he specifically set up two hundred apprenticeships in Devon in accordance with the terms of the statute, 'which was made and provided by my special means and endeavours.' Acland had managed to turn private legislation into public, and unlike Sir Edward Cecil, achieved his aim and avoided the fees for private bills and factional interests.

For private interests seeking time in Parliament, careful preparation was necessary. The most efficient corporate organization for a forthcoming Parliament was that of the various London lobbies.[35] Both the Corporation of London, livery companies, and other London-based groups meticulously prepared themselves for parliamentary sessions. In 1624, following their customary practice, the city met before Parliament; it was

> thought fitt and so ordered by this Court, that the knights and burgesses
> for the Cittie of London shall sufficiently informe themselves what already
> hath binn propounded and answered, for and against this Cittie at the last
> parliament and from tyme to tyme advise and consider with Sir Thomas
> Bennett, Sir Edward Barnham . . . Alderman William Gore, Mr Comon
> Serieant and Mr Stone what is fitt and requisitt to be propounded for and in
> the behalfe of this Cittie.

London even went so far as to provide them with an assistant for the duration of the Parliament.[36] London, though, certainly did not have it all its own
way. The Corporation often had conflicts of interest with livery companies
and other London groups that looked to Parliament, and those companies
fought among themselves.[37] Throughout medieval Parliaments, those of the
Tudors, and into the Jacobean sessions, London formed by far the largest
corporate interest group, often clogging the parliamentary agenda. As early
as 1572, the city's own Remembrancer, Thomas Norton, advised that the way
to keep parliamentary sessions short was to abridge 'the bills of occupation,
mysteries and companies and specially the bills of London.'[38]

London had long been the most important lobbying interest in Parliament. Throughout the fifteenth century, as its economic power increased
and the livery companies' wealth and influence grew, the city and its con-
stituents increasingly turned to Parliament for redress of grievances and to
promote their own agenda.[39] In this they were helped by their own MPs,
who in many cases were members of companies themselves. In 1453, for example, two of London's MPs were Mercers, and the Company wasted little
time in devising a bill for the Parliament.[40] Nor were they slow to realize
the value of soliciting friends and gift-giving. In 1433 the Brewers gave eight
bushels of malt to 'divers persones of the parlement,' and the Mercers paid
the MP John Whittoksmead 6s. 8d. to work for them during the 1455 Parliament.[41] By the reign of Henry VIII, London had a well-tested structure and
organization for dealing with Parliament.[42]

By the mid-sixteenth century, the London lobbies were even harder at
work in organization. On a bill regarding strangers working in corporate
towns, a note was circulated to companies, possibly by the Corporation:

> there is xv companies on sundry occupacions conteyned in the statute whereof
> yours be one, and to consider thereof in the meane tyme every companie hath
> one booke,[43] and to be at St Peters church over against the crosse in cheape
> on Sunday next at one of the clocke and there to meete together two of every
> company to gyve advise howe this bill shalbe redd in the parliament howse.[44]

For virtually every Parliament London established a standing committee to deal with parliamentary business, communicated with its MPs which bills to promote and which to oppose. The city attempted to regulate the legislation that companies introduced and often worked against its own companies which sought to evade Aldermanic supervision. When the Artizan Clothworkers of London preferred a bill in 1624 that would have forced every person involved in clothworking to serve an apprenticeship with the Company, the Corporation quickly asked the London MPs 'to use there indeavor and best intants to suppresse the said act.'[45] The London MPs subsequently attended every committee meeting on the bill, successfully delaying its passage until time ran out.[46]

Other large cities, such as York, Norwich, Hull, Exeter, and Bristol also meticulously prepared for Parliament. York in particular often had very ambitious parliamentary aims and detailed instructions for its members. In the first Jacobean Parliament, the city campaigned to alter the course of the River Ouse, secure an abatement of taxes, and halt any suggestion that tithes in the city should be changed, while six York companies (butchers, cordwainers, pewterers, tanners, tapissers, and vintners) all wished bills passed on their behalf.[47] No doubt aware of the difficulties in securing private legislation, the complete failure of all these measures in the first Jacobean Parliament did not diminish York's enthusiasm, and in 1614 its members were instructed to proceed on the Ouse bill again, as well as the measures for tithes, vintners, and a new bill to restrict London merchants selling their wares north of the Trent River. Unfazed again by failure, the Ouse bill became a staple of Parliaments in the 1620s, as did other legislation promoted by the city. York, then, an experienced lobbying group, was very well aware of the difficulties in securing factional legislation and continued to press its case from Parliament to Parliament, playing the long game in the hopes of eventual success.

Norwich too kept a close watch on parliamentary affairs. The city actively encouraged the passage of an act in 1610 to regulate the wool industry and examined the possibility of submitting legislation regulating their worsted weaving trade in 1621. A measure hostile to corporation interests introduced by ministers in the city was easily defeated by an alliance of the Norwich MP, John Pettus, and the city's High Steward, Sir Henry Hobart, in 1606, ably assisted by a Norwich representative sent to Westminster to help with the matter.[48] Norwich interest groups, for example, the Dornicks Weavers, also sponsored legislation, attempting without success to incorporate their company in 1610, 1621, and 1624.[49] Totnes was also mindful of potential parliamentary activity. Afraid that the split that had developed in the town over the 1596 charter would spill over into Parliament, both MPs attended every day as 'many threats given out against us for many matters, but we can hear none read yet. When they come I doubt not we will answer them.'[50]

The interests of towns and corporations that made up the majority of private legislation were normally doomed to failure despite their active lobbying and parliamentary management. London's powerful Corporation and experience in lobbying ensured that it had some success, but bills that privileged one locality, despite money, support, and logistics from the country often ran into other factional interests or were not deemed sufficiently important by the Houses to find time on the packed parliamentary agenda. However, London was not the only powerful lobby group. The Duchy of Cornwall, long an important player in electoral patronage, utilized Parliament for legislative aims as well. In the early 1620s the Duchy lobby certainly benefited from a royal presence in Parliament. Prince Charles's attendance in the Lords 'coincided' with legislation introduced on his behalf and managed by him through the Lords and his officials in the Commons.[51] Although largely successful in his legislative endeavors and packing of committees with his servants, even such a powerful interest was not 100 percent guaranteed of success. Despite the fact that he advanced £22 of his own money toward the bill to enfranchise Durham, and one of the projected new constituencies was the 'Prince's town' of Barnard Castle, the bill met opposition in 1621 and was vetoed in 1624 by his father, who thought it unnecessary to add more constituencies when 'ye have manie burgesses that come to Parliament from burroughes quite decayed as from ould Sarum where there is nothing but Conies.'[52] Charles had even less success with a bill to restrict brewing on Tothill Street in Westminster. Apparently, Charles was fed up with the smell that emanated from the brewers and drifted into his palace at St. James. Despite his personal interest in the bill and message to the Commons that it was 'specially commended by the Prince,' the Lower House, concerned at the disruption to livelihoods in the area, declined to pass the bill.[53] Even for Charles, Parliament needed to be managed and paid for. Two bills introduced in 1624 for assuring his estates cost him more than £100 in fees alone.[54]

Charles had the advantage of sitting in Parliament; others were forced to rely on friends or paid advocates. 'Before a man meane to move a matter in the house tis a good course to acquaint some of his friends thearwithall and to desire them to second him, espetially such men as are gratious with the house.'[55] Having friends in Parliament offered a chance to keep abreast of parliamentary proceedings and receive due notification of any business that might affect a company or town. Two avenues were widely utilized to provide quick information about business in Parliament: first, payments to officials, and second, gratuities to those in attendance at Westminster as well as retainers to MPs. The London Fishmongers' Company kept Sir Robert Wroth, a stalwart of the House since 1563, on a retainer. 'A forward man' in the Company's business, he assisted the Fishmongers in parliamentary legislation throughout the late Elizabethan period, receiving both money and 'half a C of lings' for his efforts.[56] Those who held official positions, especially legal offices, were in high demand for their advice. The Vintners' Company in 1604 employed the lawyer and MP for Reading, Francis Moore, as well as the London MP, Nicholas Fuller, and London's Recorder, Sir Henry Montague, for their advice on alehouse legislation.[57] Fuller and Montague sold their services elsewhere as well. The Blacksmiths' Company paid Fuller to draft their bill in 1604/5, and Montague for his counsel on the measure.[58] The Merchant Tailors followed suit, as did the Tilers and Bricklayers.[59] The outlay on parliamentary bills was often substantive. Montague was reimbursed £300 'towards the chardges disbursed in obteyninge an acte of p[ar]liament' to secure lands held by the Grocers' Company in 1606–7.[60] Montague also worked for the Carpenters and Fuller for the Coopers.[61] The Cappers in presenting their 1604 bill for the continuance of the Capper Trade asked Sir Edward Hoby for his 'best meanes, furtherance and voice at this present parliament to revive the Act.'[62]

Most who sought to introduce legislation made sure that they had good counsel. Lawyers were required to draft briefs and present the case at committee meetings, but counsel within the House was also vital. William Fleetwood recalled, 'I remember a bill against vynters, which was dasht here, afterwards I and a company were had to a tavern by the vynters and had good chere and came in the after noone and revued it and it paste. I remember Mr Horsey said it was a good bill.'[63] His recollection of the Vintners bill of 1566 was somewhat shaky. In fact the bill had been passed on a somewhat less than sober Saturday afternoon, before it was rejected the following Monday.[64] Nevertheless, Fleetwood's anecdote emphasizes not only the extent of lobbying but also how important it was to have 'friends' within the House itself. Heywood Townshend spoke against the bill of 'Llandonerer,' as he had been given a note against the bill by an acquaintance he trusted at the Inner Temple.[65] Indeed, it is even possible that certain counselors came to specialize in arguing cases before Parliament.[66] The House was in general inclined to help those of its members who introduced uncontroversial legislation. For example, Sir Robert Cecil made a special plea for Sir Anthony Cooke's bill to be read in 1593, and although 'the House being redy to departe,' stayed until the bill had been read and passed.[67]

The dispersal of information was dependent on the intimacy of contact between parliamentary officials and those sponsoring or watching Parliament at work. Access was power, and some, like the Carpenters' Company, managed their lobbying brilliantly. In 1621 the Company paid the usual fees to Parliament officials for the progress of a bill concerning building through the Commons. Not content to rest with the standard fees, they sent a delegation to the house of the Speaker, Sir Thomas Richardson, easing their access through a payment to his doorkeeper. A clerk from the Lord Mayor's office was employed to monitor when committee meetings would be held, and an assistant to the Recorder of London watched proceedings as well. Lawyers and other clerks were placed on the payroll. The solicitor-general, Sir Robert Heath, was consulted, and 'dynner and drinking at the Clerk of the Parliament's house, the Forest and the Globe' added to the cost. The parliamentary doorkeeper was paid off, as was the Clerk of the Parliament's assistant and 'a drinking' with the Speaker's clerk cost a further 2s. 9d. Further payments to counsel, the Solicitor's bag-carrier and chamber-keeper, the Recorder's chamber-keeper, dinner with Heath, fees to the sergeant at arms, Richardson's cook, three MPs, and Lord Arundel all occurred *before* their bill had even reached Parliament. A nocturnal visit to the Speaker before the bill was read in Parliament added 2s. 4d. to the process, and 11s. more was given to the Speaker's chief clerk to remind the Speaker to proceed with the bill in the morning. Then the Carpenters ramped up their lobbying—multiple dinners with MPs, the doorkeepers, recorders', sergeants', clerks', speakers', and solicitors' men, as well as boathire, copies of the bill and breviates; all added additional charges to their cause. In total, the Carpenters spent more than £50 preparing a bill that failed to proceed past a first reading.[68]

The bitter dispute between the Grocers and Apothecaries in 1621 highlights the importance of legal counsel and monitoring parliamentary proceedings. Concerned that the Apothecaries would move against them in Parliament, the Grocers paid John Wright, the Clerk of the Parliament, 22s.

as a retainer to warn them of any moves by their rivals. Wright's clerk received 11s. to remind his superior of the Grocers' business. When indeed the Apothecaries showed their hand, the Grocers employed one Mr. Pheasant to draft a counterpetition. Pheasant, Mr. Stone, London's solicitor, Mr. Mosse, Sir Robert Heath (solicitor-general), and Wright as Clerk of the Commons were all paid for their advice on the petition. The lines quickly became blurred between official responsibilities and outright 'corruption' when John Wright's eponymous son, who was his deputy in the House, was paid to 'prepare, read and *expedite* the peticion in Parliament.'[69] Two sergeants-at-law were employed to attend the parliamentary hearings, sundry other payments were made for copies of documents, and a coach was hired to take Sir Thomas Middleton to Parliament about the petition.[70] In 1624 Sutton Hospital, in order to move their bill forward when the committees did not have a meeting scheduled, paid the Recorder of London, Sir Heneage Finch, the expensive rate of £10 for several motions to have their bill given a committee time. Despite the high cost, which did not include the 20s. to the recorder's servant at the same time, the payment at least had the desired outcome, as the committee met on 11 April.[71]

Knowing whom to lobby was also a key element, and obtaining accurate information about who sat in Parliament and who was a committee member allowed those with a vested interest to maximize their chances of success. Although it was possible to discover the names of committee members and dates of meetings from where they were posted in the Commons lobby, many interested parties obtained their own copies.[72] In the 1597–98 Parliament the Coopers of London kept track of committee members in both the Lords and Commons, paying 12d. for the Lower House's names and 4s. for those in the Upper House. Again with their legislation in 1601 and 1604, they sought out committee lists.[73] So too did other London interest groups. For example, the Vintners Company obtained names in 1604, the Tilers and Bricklayers in 1605–6, the Grocers in 1621, and the Governors of Sutton's Hospital in 1628.[74] John Prowse, the Exeter MP, who was charged in 1610 with managing the town's bill to build a new weir, obtained lists for the committees in both the Lords and Commons at the high cost of 7s. 6d.[75] So too did interested parties purchase the names of all members of the Lords and Commons.[76] The Curriers in 1587 spent 10s. on such a list.[77] Although the lists of MPs, peers, and committees were clearly useful documents, times and places of meetings changed so frequently that pressure groups needed a physical presence around the chambers to pass on the latest information. The extent to which this lobbying was effective depended heavily on public access to Parliament and its members.

Gift-giving was an important element of prosecuting a case through Parliament. For the Coopers, wine was the gift of choice. In 1597–98 the Speaker of the Commons, Sir Christopher Yelverton, and the sergeant-at-arms received hogsheads, while in 1604 23s. 2d. was spent on wine 'to one of the P[ar]liament house.' Another unspecified person received a rundlet of canary wine, and even the Clerk of the Parliament's horsekeeper was engaged by the Company. The Coopers also spent 33s. 4d. on hypocras (heated, spiced wine) for the House of Lords, possibly even throwing a catered event for them. Roger Pedley, the lobbyist for the Southampton Corporation in 1607, also provided the Lords with food and drink when their bill was passing through the Upper House,[78] as did the Corporation of Exeter in 1610.[79] The Vintners were unsurprisingly also offering gifts of wine. In 1621, included in the Company's outlay of £32 19s. 11d. spent fighting the patent that forced them to buy wine from French merchants, were two hogsheads of claret to Sir Thomas Richardson, the Speaker, and one each to two influential MPs, Sir Henry Marten and Sir Robert Heath.[80]

Towns and individuals offered gifts as well and, as might be expected, London was the most organized in this regard. In 1624, the Speaker, Sir Thomas Crew, received £10 for 'the favoures and respect shewed unto this Cittie.'[81] Bristol sent butts of sack to the Commons' Speaker,[82] while Lord Saye and Sele gave Robert Bowyer, Clerk of the Parliament, a piece of venison in 1610.[83] George Byng, MP for Dover in 1604, was ordered by the town 'to invite certain of the burgesses of the Parliament he shall think meet to a dinner or a supper, thereby rather to encourage them to be friendly to us touching the continuation of the Statute of Tonnage, and what money he shall thereby disburse to be allowed out of the treasure of the town.'[84] The Guestling of the Cinque Ports presented Sir Edward Phelips, the Commons' Speaker, with 24s. worth of fish in 1604,[85] and the Tilers and Bricklayers bestowed a thirteen-and-a-half-pound sugar loaf on their counsel and the MP, Nicholas Fuller.[86] They also gave the Speaker's wife a sugar loaf while recognizing the extraordinary efforts of the Company page, who received a new pair of shoes 'in respect of his travels he took in the business.'[87]

MPs could also benefit from their parliamentary actions. Grateful constituencies supplemented their parliamentary wages to MPs by the occasional gift. Sir Thomas Waller, MP for Dover in 1604, received half a tun of wine and a large sugar loaf for his wife because of his efforts in helping secure the passage of a bill beneficial to the town's interests.[88] John Prowse, who managed Exeter's parliamentary business in the Commons from 1604 to 1624, received a bonus of £20 for his work in the 1606–7 session.[89]

There existed a fine line between payments to officials and MPs and what might be perceived as outright corruption. In 1604, the notorious patent abuser William Tipper was accused of taking a bribe of £100 to ensure that a bill for the true making of felts and hats would pass through Parliament. Tipper was alleged to have taken the money to bribe MPs. Nicholas Fuller, MP for London and himself the recipient of many a payment for 'assisting' with legislation and other parliamentary matters, told the Commons that he had been informed that Tipper had been paid 'for following and procuring passage to this bill.'[90] Tipper denied these accusations, and the matter faded from view. What seems to have concerned the House in this allegation of corruption is twofold. Tipper's own odious patents made him a target of grievances. This, in combination with the fact that rumors were circulating in London that the £100 was to corrupt MPs, meant that the House acted to preserve its own reputation. The admixture of 'corruption' with the theoretically *arcana imperii* proceedings of Parliament was explosive. Some years before, the MP Arthur Hall had drawn the ire of the Commons by his allegation of the inherent corruption in the body:

> To turne the Cat in the panne and to be a hirelyng, or a penny-boy for any particuler person, to have clientes in matters of Parliament, is token of too muche vilitie . . . . What should I write of this most filthie, unnatural, and servile vice, whiche shall for a fewe angels make you pleade as partially in parliament as in any other court, not regarding your countrey but the jinks in your pocket.[91]

Hall had compounded his offense by printing his attack on the Commons and was subsequently expelled from the House he described as full of 'drye-handed men, [who] can not well tende the penning and copying out of lawes, without a little moystnyng.'[92] Hall was not the only one to complain about the propensity of MPs, and especially lawyers, to forward private interests in exchange for a fee: 'private bills are usually drawn by counselors of law not being of the House, and sometimes by those of the House, and that for their fees; which, howsoever it hath by divers been held to be lawful, yet cannot be but very inconvenient, seeing afterwards they are to be judges in the same case.'[93]

Very occasionally, the Commons actually attempted at least to identify those who had a vested financial interest in legislation. On the 1621 Free Trade bill it was moved 'whether the burgesses, free of companies, should have voice at committee.'[94] In the end the House agreed that everyone had the right to speak but that they should identify themselves as members of a trading company before they spoke. As Sir Robert Phelips moralistically rejoiced, '[No] man be presumed to bringe hether private affections.'[95] It is unlikely that many in the House would have agreed with him.

Although Parliament was a financial boon for clerks and officials, perhaps no group benefited more than scriveners and those who controlled access to parliamentary records needing to be copied. Parliament voraciously consumed paper, distributing it to officials, MPs, and all who had an interest in the session. William Hakewill noted how it was customary for those who introduced bills to draft a breviate for the use of the clerk and Speaker.[96] In 1576, the Brewers paid 13s. 4d. for notes to distribute to their 'friends' in Parliament, 'for answering unto such bills as was exhibited into the Parliament House against us.'[97] Exeter Corporation in 1610 spent £1 on breviates 'to deliver abroad,'[98] a sum dwarfed by the 44s. the Brewers spent four years later.[99] In addition to printing their breviates in 1607, the Carpenters obtained ten copies of objections to their bill and made three other payments for copies of parliamentary documents.[100] In 1621 the Company obtained twenty-four copies of its petition for 12s.[101] Breviates cost Sutton's Hospital 20s. in 1628,[102] and Archbishop Abbot paid 3s. 6d. to the clerk for copies of bills in 1614.[103]

The Vintners, always concerned about the amount of legislation concerning alcohol that came into Parliament, made sure that they obtained copies of any bills which might affect their trade. Virtually every constituency that could afford it obtained copies of acts of Parliament that affected them and, more often than not, other matters of parliamentary interest.[104]

Haywood Townshend noted in his 1601 parliamentary diary that the MPs of Devon 'made a ffaction' to defeat the fustian cloth bill.[105] Frequently, those who sought to manipulate the system found themselves outmaneuvered by their well-organized opponents. It was, after all, much easier and less expensive to defeat a measure than to manage one through two Houses of Parliament. Edward Clere, the son of one of the wealthiest land-owners in Norfolk, stood for election in Thetford in 1604, although his candidacy garnered only a few votes.[106] Clere's lack of success was unsurprising given that the family had long been in dispute with the Thetford Corporation over his failure to pay the town rents it was owed from the will of his father-in-law, Sir Richard Fulmerston.[107] Despite his failure at the polls, Clere advanced a bill in Parliament to protect his interests. Clere, however, found it difficult to manage the bill from prison, where he was sent after accusations of sheltering a seminary priest, and the Thetford MPs along with their Norfolk allies easily quashed the measure.[108] In 1610, Thetford retaliated against Clere, introducing its own legislation after securing the support of its patron, the Earl of Northampton. Although Northampton pleaded with parliamentary officials to consider the bill without paying the standard fees, the Corporation had agreed to meet the costs of the measure, dispatched its legal counsel to London along with a burgess, and employed a London lawyer, Mr. Gerrard, to represent it. Clere too, despite his continued incarceration, hired a lawyer and was allowed to attend the committee meeting on the bill in the Lords. However, Northampton's patronage as well as the influence of Norfolk MPs favorable to the measure saw the bill enacted.[109]

The city of Westminster effectively used its connections with royal officials and Parliament-men to shepherd through Parliament in 1585 an act concerning its governance.[110] The measure was controversial because it involved a clash of interests between the authority of townspeople and the jurisdiction of the Dean and Chapter of Westminster.[111] The impetus for the bill came from the parishioners of St. Margaret's Church, also the church of the House of Commons, and the cost of the measure was to be borne by the townspeople of St. Margaret's.[112] Westminster's High Steward, William Lord Burghley, and their MPs, Robert Cecil (Burghley's son) and Sir Thomas Knyvett, were enlisted to help. The bill, supported by Westminster's MPs and Burghley's clients in the Commons, including Recorder Fleetwood,[113] passed without controversy in the Commons but ran into substantial difficulty in the Lords. By the time it reached the Upper House, the Dean and Chapter of Westminster belatedly realized that their authority was under threat:

> Whereas some of the inhabytantes of the cittie of Westminster did exhibite a bill into the parliament for the alteration of the government of the said cittie, which bill beinge passed the lower house unwyttinge unto us, it pleased the lordes of the higher howse, upon oure humble petition, to graunte unto us a certen proviso in the said bill for the preservinge of oure liberties and pryvledges, which proviso they delivered unto us to be considered of by oure learned counsel.[114]

Although a scant 200 yards from Parliament, the Dean and Chapter had failed to keep abreast of parliamentary activity. Behind their backs, the Westminster inhabitants worked hard to secure their bill. Both Westminster MPs received a marzipan at Christmas, the Commons bill committee was treated to dinner, and wine and cakes were sent to MPs while the bill itself was drafted by a servant of Burghley's.[115] But the Dean and Chapter lobbied effectively in the Lords and succeeded in limiting the degree to which their jurisdiction would be diminished.[116]

Lowestoft also found it difficult to defeat the powerful Norfolk MP lobby. The subject of fishing not surprisingly dominated Yarmouth's interest in Parliament during the period, as it had for many centuries before in the form of its long-running dispute with Lowestoft over fishing rights. The history of the dispute is well documented and illustrates a continual fight, utilizing the forum of Parliament, to gain superiority.[117] Since the reign of King John, Yarmouth had the right to collect tolls and customs from ships off-loading near its haven. By an act in 1357, Yarmouth's authority was deemed to extend seven 'lewes' from the haven.[118] Collection of duties within this area was particularly important during the annual herring fair but was complicated by the continual silting of the mouth of the haven, resulting in the need to cut new passages. That in turn, led more boats to anchor in the calm waters of what was known as the Kirkley Road—an area over which Yarmouth and Lowestoft disputed jurisdiction. After much dispute and the revoking and regranting of Yarmouth's charter—seven times in ten years (1376–86)—Yarmouth solved its problems by cutting a new haven, thus rendering the Kirkley Road less important.[119] However, the matter again flared up during Elizabeth's reign, and, after years of debate before the Privy Council and in Parliament, Yarmouth succeeded in having its privileges confirmed by Parliament in 1581 and 1597–98.[120]

Despite this success, the Yarmouth Corporation was not content to rest on its achievements and in 1608 was granted a new charter by James I.[121] Yarmouth claimed that it was 'the only place where your Majesty's subjects of Scotland often resort [and] usually touch in their voyages to the Low Countries, France and Spain.'[122] Yarmouth also noted that the cost of maintaining the haven was more than £500 per annum and that new privileges were required in order to finance these works. It confirmed the town's privileges, but, more important, Yarmouth was granted the admiralty rights between Easton Ness and Winton Ness, a distance of over fourteen leagues and one that positioned Lowestoft under the authority of its Norfolk rival.[123] The Lord Admiral and Yarmouth's High Steward, the Earl of Nottingham, seem to have been the guiding force in London behind the granting of the charter. Nottingham gave up his admiralty rights over Yarmouth to James I, who in turn passed them over to Yarmouth.[124] This action was clearly regarded by Lowestoft as a resumption of hostilities, and the town drafted a bill to be introduced in the next session of Parliament. Yarmouth's endorsed copy of the bill survives among their records. The draft legislation was very similar to the bill placed before the Commons by Lowestoft in 1597–98 and if enacted, would have narrowed Yarmouth's jurisdiction to a boundary seven *miles* from Crane Quay.[125] This placed both Lowestoft and the Kirkley Road (still important as a safe anchorage) outside Yarmouth's jurisdiction. Yarmouth immediately went onto the offensive after the bill's first reading on 26 February.[126] On 5 March the Corporation sent two aldermen to London to assist its MPs and prepare a number of documents illustrating the bill's faults.[127] The Corporation complained that the measurement adopted by Lowestoft should have been seven *leagues* from the *mouth* of the haven and not seven *miles* from *Crane Quay*.[128] The bill, in effect, limited Yarmouth's authority by one-and-a-half miles. Other objections to the bill included factual errors in the measure relating to the terms of charters and the length of the herring fair. Yarmouth, and particularly one of its MPs, Thomas Damet, who had led the opposition to Lowestoft's Elizabethan attacks, were not above denigrating Lowestoft as 'a town of small importance to [the] state.' It was not an incorporated town and paid no fee farm to the King. Moreover, its inhabitants were poor 'by their idleness.'[129] Damet went so far as to mention that Lowestoft had succumbed during Ket's rebellion and was rescued and Ket beaten only because of Yarmouth's intervention.[130] Damet and his Yarmouth allies emerged triumphant again in their ongoing battle with their southern neighbor. The bill stalled in committee and no more was heard of the matter in 1610;[131] although Lowestoft may have drafted legislation again in 1621, little is known of its proceeding.[132]

As Lowestoft discovered to its repeated cost, lobbying did not ensure legislative success or even favorable opinions toward the cause. Interest groups needed money and required friends at Westminster, but there was a limit to what lobbying could buy, particularly when faced with powerful lobbies and mobilization of opposition within the House. One London company discovered this to its perennial cost. Since the reign of Henry VIII, the Armourers had drafted bills to Parliament to delineate the craft

of armory and the right of search. In 1569 the Armourers gained approval
of a new set of Company ordinances, in the process offering substantial
gifts to those involved. The ordinances affirmed their right to search for
those who made guns, axes, knives, swords, armor, and crossbows. This,
however, soon brought them into conflict with the Blacksmiths' Company,
who had also confirmed their right to search for exactly the same items—a
right given to them by the same few officials who had approved the Armourers' ordinances. Faced with this discrepancy and also in dispute with
London gunmakers, who were seeking incorporation as a separate company, the Armourers decided to utilize the ultimate legislative sovereignty
of an Act of Parliament to shore up their position. As soon as Parliament
assembled in 1581, the Armourers acted. A bill was drafted and advice taken
from London's Remembrancer, Thomas Norton. The Armourers then approached the Lord Chancellor, who read and amended the measure before
personally recommending it to the Commons' Speaker, John Popham. A
'holle afternoone' was spent explaining the necessity of the bill to Popham,
who, convinced of its merits, made his own amendments and then gave it
a first reading in the Commons.[133] However, given the Queen's propensity
for short parliamentary sessions and her desire to avoid private legislation
that clogged up Parliament's time, Popham was hard pressed to find time
to advance the Armourers' cause: 'Daie by daie we applied Mr Speaker,
and sometimes twise a day'; all the while the Blacksmiths sought to have
the measure rejected, even going so far as to tell the privy councillor and
Northamptonshire MP, Sir Walter Mildmay, that the Armourers had no
skill in producing either weapons or armor. Stung by this, the Master of the
Armourers, Richard Hutton, held an audience with Mildmay in which they
convinced him of their case. With still no proceeding on the bill, the Master
waited outside the Commons for Mildmay and Valentine Dale, a Master
of Requests, and engaged them in conversation. Pleading his case and offering a wager to Dale that the Company could produce the finest armor,
Mildmay offered to 'do the best for it I cane and so enterid the parlament
howsse.'

The Armourers next approached the Queen's Champion and Master of
the Armouries, Sir Henry Lee, who sat for Buckinghamshire. Lee was evidently favorable to their plight, hosting a dinner for various MPs, including
Serjeant Edward Flowerdew, James Dalton,[134] Francis Alford, John Gw-
ynne, and Robert Bainbridge. As time went on, the Armourers kept in close
contact with the Speaker, who claimed that the press of official business had

prevented him from offering the bill for a second reading. Although when the Speaker offered to have the bill read, the Armourers begged him to stay the matter, as 'our frendes that could speak to the bill could not be ther.' For the following week the Armourers haunted Westminster every day until finally Popham, leaving the House on Saturday, approached the Master and promised to read the bill on Monday. At least nine MPs pledged to attend on Monday to support the bill before disaster struck—the Queen demanded passage of her legislation, which occupied the entire day. The Armourers, realizing the degree to which the Queen and the government were orchestrating the parliamentary agenda, next approached the matter through the Queen's parliamentary manager, Sir Christopher Hatton. Although Hatton promised to 'move hir maiestie of it,' and suggested that it could be dealt with by the Council instead of Parliament, Hatton, the court, and the Queen soon became embroiled in the entertainment of the French ambassadors and the negotiations surrounding Elizabeth's proposed marriage to Francois, Duc d'Alençon. The route through Hatton, though, was clearly a promising avenue, at least on the surface. His influence with the Queen and power as a parliamentary manager was such that the Mayor of Weymouth and Melcombe Regis, Thomas Howard, disgustedly wrote back to the town, '[F]or when I should have bestowed chargeable sums of money in framing bills, in rewarding them that should speak favourably in them, . . . then I should look for a hard passage of the bill, by reason that Sir Christopher Hatton . . . would work much against it, and surely would overthrow it when it should come to her Majesty's hands.'[135]

The Armourers paid heavily for their utter failure—more than £19 for a first reading. William Fleetwood, the Recorder, benefited the most, charging £2 for his counsel, although many participated in the Company's largesse. Finding out the membership of the Commons cost them 7s. 6d., and a copy of the bill 17s. Wining and dining MPs at the Paul's Head on at least nine separate occasions added to their costs, as did providing boat hire on 4 March to transport three MPs to Parliament in the company of the Master. Payments to doorkeepers, servants of the sergeant at arms, a dinner with the Clothworkers, who also had a bill before Parliament, and 2s. to Sir Henry Lee's man added to the bill. Lee himself received a lamb and two capons for his pains, and another burgess was provided with a pair of gauntlets. Undaunted by this expenditure and sure of their rights, the Armourers again introduced their measure in 1584 and subsequent Parliaments, with an equal lack of success.[136]

Other groups, like the Woodmongers in their bitter dispute with the Wharfingers, lobbied Parliament by using their friends at Westminster to pack committees in their favor.[137] When the Wharfingers introduced a bill that would have limited the Woodmongers' ability to sell licenses for carting in London, the Woodmongers printed two documents for distribution to interested MPs and members of the Grievances Committee. Copies of these were sent to the Whitchurch MP and evident friend of the Company, Sir Thomas Jervoise. The Woodmongers endorsed their document to Jervoise:

> Sir there is a bill put in by certaine fellows that call themselves wharfengers against the Master and Wardens of the Companie of Woodmongers which hath byn once read already and if it should be put to Comittees at the second readinge we desire you to be one and alsoe to nominate Sir Thomas Edmonds, Sir Baptist Hickes, Sir Robert Knowles, Sir Dudly Dudly [*sic*] Diggs, Sir Roberte Heathe his majesties solicitor, Sir Thomas Lowe, Mr Roberte Bateman, Mr William Towerson, Mr John Angell, Mr Roberte Bacon the Citties remembrer, Mr Richard Diggs with Mr John Pymm and all the rest of the Cittie burgesses which have heard the examinacion already of the said business or anie other of this honorable house whom you please to nominate.[138]

The lobbying technique of seeking to pack committees and find MPs favorable to a cause was hardly a new development. Lowestoft in 1598 had 'openlie in the howse canvassed for voices,'[139] and in 1576 the Clothiers circulated MPs with a leaflet:

> The clothiers humbly desireth your honourable presence and assistance by two of the clock at the committee of the bill which Sir Henry Poole, knight, preferred unto the honourable House for Gloucestershire, Wiltshire, Somerset and other counties; and that you will be well pleased to consider the equity therein desired, which is only to reform the common abuses and deceits used in wool and yarn, with some other things very necessary to the good state of clothing within this kingdom. The penalties therein contained are very small and the benefit of them only to the use of the poor, without any cheating or profit to any partie . . . the committee is in the Star Chamber.[140]

Pressure groups haunted the doors of Parliament, and their presence did not go unnoticed; nor their employment of parliamentary officials.[141] During the lengthy dispute in Parliament between the Curriers and the Cordwainers, Sir Henry Mildmay observed somewhat sarcastically, '[H]ere be the showmakers crying and following ready to pull their bill out of my hande. I pray yow, Mr Speaker, let the sergeant call them in, he knows them, they be his clyentes.'[142] But not all private interests created factions. Some types of measures designed to benefit individuals aroused little opposition. This was particularly true of bills that naturalized aliens as English citizens. In 1624, for example, of the seventeen naturalization bills in Parliament, twelve became statutes. Of those that failed, one for a merchant, Philip Jacobson, was vetoed by James, as he feared a loss of customs revenue. The failure of other measures is more likely to have been because of a lack of parliamentary time or the payment of fees rather than any hostility to the measures.[143]

While legislative sovereignty was the ideal solution, pressure groups and individuals increasingly turned to petitioning Parliament as well. Although there was no drop in private legislative initiatives in 1621, there was substantial increase in petitions exhibited in Parliament. As David Zaret noted '[No] communicative practice for sending messages from the periphery to the center had greater legitimacy than petitioning.'[144] For centuries the traditional method for redress of grievances in Parliament was through petitioning, as is clearly illustrated by the more than sixteen thousand petitions introduced to Parliament between 1200 and 1500. However, petitioning as a legislative implement was gradually replaced during the late fifteenth and early sixteenth centuries by procedure by bill. But with the establishment in the early seventeenth century of standing committees in the House of Commons, petitioning came back into vogue.[145] The appointment of standing committees for trade and courts of justice in 1621, in addition to those already in existence (Grievances and Privileges/Returns), presented another avenue of possible redress for those who saw Parliament as the means to an end.[146] It was in many ways a watershed in contact between Parliament and those outside the chambers, opening up a new line of communication and one fundamentally simpler and less expensive. Those who utilized this method may not have gained the legislative authority of statute, but the Commons soon proved itself to be an effective force in the condemnation of the general ills of the commonwealth. Petitioners were not slow to react to this new development, often using it in conjunction with the more traditional procedure by bill.

The impetus for these committees came from the economic depression into which England had sunk, in alliance with the increasing number of monopolistic patents that plagued the commonwealth.[147] The Commons' investigations, and opening up and entertaining the submission of grievances to these committees, opened the floodgates. With committees chaired by the powerful triumvirate of Sir Edward Coke (Grievances), Sir Lionel Cranfield (Trade), and Sir Robert Phelips (Justice),[148] patents were called in and investigated. By 12 March, more than eighty grievance petitions were in the hands of the committee.[149] While the House also proceeded by bill, petitioners rushed to take advantage of these committees. Both the Wharfingers and Woodmongers, already involved in a legislative dispute, also shifted their confrontation to Parliament. Both as well, taking their cues from the antimonopolistic atmosphere of the House, condemned each other's activities as monopolies grievous to the commonweal.[150] From the Glasiers of London, to the Masters in Chancery, the Merchant Adventurers, and those opposed to the Welsh wool staple, the Grievances Committee worked tirelessly to hear and catalogue grievances. Those who sought remedies for particular ills attempted to ensure that sufficient copies were available, either in scribal or printed format, for all committee members to have one. Apart from the usefulness of information contained in the petitions, they seemed also to have served a useful function as handy pieces of paper for MPs to jot notes on, whether in the House or committee.[151]

The establishment of these standing committees and the efficient development of a relatively easy (and inexpensive) procedural system no doubt encouraged petitioners to submit their grievances and forced a response from those complained about. The House quickly adopted its procedures for hearing private bill legislation, calling witnesses and counsel before it. 'They investigated facts, pronounced a judgment and made some efforts to execute that judgment.'[152] Furthermore, and unlike most legislative action, the actions of Commons were effective. In some instances, such as the Monopolies bill, legislative action went hand in hand with the actions of the Grievances Committee. Legislation also sprang out of particular grievances—for example, the concerns over the maintenance of Dungeness and Wintertonness lighthouses by Trinity House.[153] But as Sir Edward Coke noted, '[S]ince there are so many grievances here in the House complained of . . . as that we cannot make Laws against them all, that we should have a petition made to the King, beseeching his Majesty to be pleased by a Proclamation or otherwise to decry or make void the same.'[154] Duly, the most egregious of patents were included in the Grievances' petition to the King at the end of the session, and many were condemned by proclamation on 10 July 1621.[155]

As the Commons expanded its powers and actively solicited cases and grievances and thereby deliberately intensified lobbying, so too did the House of Lords step outside the walls of its chamber and more into the public light. The revival of the judicial authority of the Lords in 1621, coupled with the fact that petitioners and their counsel on legislation also lobbied the Lords, moved the Upper House more and more into the public eye. Although the most dramatic rejuvenation of the appellate jurisdiction of the Lords was impeachment, the acceptance of the petition of Edward Ewer to review a ruling against him in King's Bench opened a floodgate. At least 30 petitions were presented to the Lords in 1621, 62 in 1624, rising to 133 in 1626.[156] The Lords rapidly developed a standing committee for petitions supporting the peers named with the House's legal assistants. Like any other court, the Lords called witnesses, copied briefs, ensured that petitioners and defendants had legal counsel, and issued rulings. While the Ewer case was actually referred to the House by the King, as the numbers of cases indicate, petitioners quickly turned to the Lords. Some of those, such as George Morgan, were already petitioners to Parliament in other forms as well. Morgan, in fact, had introduced legislation and petitioned the grievance committee before he won a hearing through his approach to the Lords.[157] Others, such as John Johnson, who was engaged in a King's Bench suit with Sir Giles Mompesson, took advantage of Parliament's attack on Mompesson in 1621 to petition the Lords in his favor—a petition they quickly rejected after investigating Johnson's claims.[158] The Lords' restoration of its function as a court increased the desirability of Parliament as an avenue for redress of grievances. In a similar fashion to the Commons' addition of standing committees, the Lords Committee on Petitions became an increasingly important part of the House's business and substantially increased the numbers of those who attended the Upper House and lobbied it.

The Lords' establishment of this committee also had another side effect, a dramatic increase in the number of women petitioners. Traditionally, women had not utilized Parliament as a venue for redress of grievances. Only very rarely did private legislation directly concern women, and equally rare were women's petitions to the House of Commons.[159] But the Lords Committee provided an opportunity for women to have their legal grievances heard. In 1626, seventeen petitions by women were heard or scheduled for discussion, or 13 percent of all petitions submitted.[160] A similar pattern is found in 1628, when twelve of ninety petitions were from women.[161] Many of the petitions involved the recovery of debts or the establishment of titles and rights of individual women after their husbands had died. The complaints ranged from Dorothy Browne's claim to lands from which she and her mother-in-law had been forcibly ejected to a mass petition from the wives of two thousand mariners in captivity in Sallee, Morocco. As James Hart has noted, the desire for legal redress of women 'appear[s] to have been the product of changing legal doctrine; specifically of the notion—only just evolving in Chancery—that a woman had the right to sue in equity in order to establish certain propriety rights in marriage.'[162] How this may have influenced women who petitioned Parliament is unclear, but for whatever reason, women felt more able to press their case in the highest court in the land during the 1620s than they had before, and this was a direct result of the Lords standing committee on petitions.

∼

Parliament was failing as a legislative avenue for private measures. In some ways, perhaps not so much for individuals, there appears to have been a certain weariness among pressure groups at the perennial expense and failure of legislation. Parliamentary sovereignty of legislation was effective only if it was actually possible to get that legislation enacted. As Conrad Russell famously noted, '[P]arliamentary success in arousing public expectation was equaled only by their failure to satisfy it.'[163] By the time the 1621 Parliament opened there had been an eleven-year span since any legislation had been enacted. Both private and public measures flooded into the chambers, leading the Exeter MP, Nicholas Duck, to advise his constituency not to present a bill to build a new grammar school: '[To] move yet in the parlement yet would bee but a hassard to expend mony upon a douptfull event, for the parlement is possessed with many petitions and billes, and yf everi daye wear a weeke, yet would bee time little yenoufe to determine them, and many will come short of ther expectation.'[164] While for private individuals the Parliaments of 1621 and 1624 provided lengthy opportunities for the introduction of bills, London had virtually abandoned attempts at legislation. Some companies—for example, the Woodmongers and Apothecaries referred to earlier—continued their legislative quest, but the Corporation did not. Like its Elizabethan forbears, in the first Jacobean Parliament of 1604–10 London promoted a substantial number of bills to further its own interests: for example, seven in 1604 and 1605–6, and six in 1610. But in the 1620s the city made little effort to promote bills. They offered their support for the Butter and Cheese measure sponsored by the London cheesemongers in 1621 and 1624, but that was all. In the 1625 and 1628 Parliaments London was conspicuous by its total absence, and only one bill was introduced in 1626. The Corporation records provide no clue as to why the city deserted Parliament, but it is quite possible that they had decided that cost and lack of success made it a fruitless exercise.

Practical considerations no doubt played a role in the lack of private legislation, subsequent to 1624 as well. Few were interested in being in proximity to possible plague victims in London in 1625, and fewer still in traveling to Oxford for the abortive continued sitting. The 1626 Parliament was concerned primarily with matters of high state, and legislation was very much an afterthought. Once again, legislative matters largely took a back seat in 1628–29 as grievances and the Petition of Right dominated the agenda. While a select few continued to introduce legislation between 1625 and 1629, a high proportion of the private measures examined by Parliament in those years were uncontroversial bills for naturalization, or measures concerning peers. Private matters lost out to matters of state. In this atmosphere of high politics seemingly triumphing over private measures, lobbyists and members of pressure groups who stalked the halls and rooms of Westminster Palace adapted their strategies to cope. One avenue that seemed to offer promise was print.

CHAPTER SIX

Shifting Stages: The Emergence of Parliamentary Print Culture

In 1572 the town of Shrewsbury submitted a handwritten petition to Parliament to repeal legislation enacted in 1567; it was one of a few dozen petitions.[1] By the 1620s hundreds of printed petitions rolled off the presses, some in print runs exceeding four hundred and intended for distribution to all MPs and peers. Parliament had become a marketplace for print. MPs, peers, and the public could purchase the sermons preached at the opening of Parliament, the names of their colleagues sitting in Parliament along with woodcut representations of the Houses in session, lengthy petitions to Parliament on such subjects as the re-edification of St. Paul's Cathedral, the trials and tribulations of one Benjamin Crokey, or the dire economic problems in the leather trade. In addition, the speeches of the King to Parliament, verse broadsides, and illustrations of major parliamentary events were also printed for sale to those interested in matters of state. MPs and peers, however, did not purchase the vast majority of printed material that they accumulated over the course of a Parliament in the 1620s—it was distributed to them by lobbyists, parliamentary agents, individual petitioners, and London companies. That this material was prolific can be seen by the collection of one anonymous individual, probably a member of the 1621 Commons' Grievances Committee, who received more than sixty printed petitions.[2] These separates, usually one quarto sheet, were the most available form of printed parliamentary documents and also the most controversial.

This chapter will demonstrate the process of vigorous engagement and exchange between Parliament and what can probably be best described, *avant la lettre*, as public opinion in print. Furthermore, the political contestation of early modern England can be seen to lie not just between Parliament and the Crown but also between the realm of public discourse outside the Commons and the Commons itself.

～

The transition from a parliamentary scribal culture to one of print is not a 1640's story of steady progress and the sudden dominance of the printed page. Harold Love and Arthur Marotti are only the latest to have argued that as 'late as the early seventeenth century, the activities of the law and Parliament were conducted with hardly any recourse to the printed word.'[3] However there was a substantial amount of parliamentary printed material prior to the 1640s—it was a large and extraordinarily significant component of the discourse produced by those who, on the inside, sought to govern and legislate, and on the outside, sought to influence Parliament. Through the promulgation of statutes, Parliament and print had been linked since as early as 1484.[4] And from 1510 it became an official enterprise with the King's printer. As Geoffrey Elton notes, '[W]hat had started as the application of the new technology to the serving of a much older lawyers' market for acts of Parliament came to be part of the government's running of parliamentary affairs.'[5] By the early Stuart period it was customary for the public acts to be printed and sent out to the shires in batches of five hundred copies each, although for quasi-public acts, such as those for Westminster, only fifty copies were made.[6]

Proclamations also established a link between Parliament and print. It was customary for prorogations and dissolutions to be announced by a printed proclamation circulated throughout the country, which detailed not only the dates of Parliament's closing but also often the monarch's reasons for sending the members of the Commons and Lords home.[7] The proclamation that dissolved the 1621 Parliament commenced with a lecture on the right of the monarch to call and close Parliament at the King's discretion, before James outlined 'some especiall proceedings mooving Us to this resolution.'[8] Often too, the business of the Parliament was reflected and explained in royal proclamations,[9] and the Crown attempted to ensure the caliber of members of Parliament through issuing proclamations that suggested the fitness of those who were to be elected.[10] Statutes and proclamations were the long-established and official side of parliamentary print culture but increasingly became only one shrinking proportion of an exponentially expanding printed milieu.

PRINTED PRAYERS

Parliament established a further presence in the literate print-reading nation through the medium of prayers and sermons. As early as 1585 a specific 'Prayer to be used in the Parliament Only' was printed by the royal and parliamentary printer, Christopher Barker.[11] The purpose of the printing remains unclear, as there is no indication that it was to be sold, and both the title and content make clear that this was a prayer read at the start of Parliament every day. It may indeed simply have been published in order to illustrate the Parliament working as a unified and orderly body:

> And sith it has pleased thee to govern this Realm by ordinary assembling the three estates of the same: our humble prayer is, that thou wilt graff in us good minds to conceive, free liberty to speak, and on all sides a ready and quiet consent to such wholesome laws and Statutes, as may declare us to be thy people, and this Realm to be prosperously ruled by thy good guiding and defence.

This appeal to the benevolence of Elizabeth does not seem to have been repeated in the subsequent Parliaments. Nevertheless, the parliamentary prayer or sermon fitted into a common genre of printing liturgical works concerning particular events. Prayers were printed and issued every year on the day of the accession of Elizabeth, James, and Charles.[12] Under Elizabeth, even the French King was remembered in state-sanctioned printed prayers during the Huguenot crisis, while both the Gowrie Conspiracy and Gunpowder Plot were remembered annually in James's reign.[13] The occasion of a Parliament was also an opportunity to take advantage of the increased visibility and name recognition. In 1604, John Smith published a tract under the title *An heavenly Act of Parliament . . .'* that bears no relationship to Parliament other than the opportunistic borrowing of 'Act' and its parliamentary connotations.[14]

The printing of prayers concerning Parliament was revived under James when Robert Barker, the King's printer,[15] published 'Prayers for the Parliament' in 1604.[16] This was followed two years later by a Prayer for the Commons' Speaker, Sir Edward Phelips.[17] But like so much parliamentary printing, the 1620s saw a much greater use of the medium. James Ussher, later Archbishop of Armagh, preached the traditional opening sermon before the Commons in the parliamentary church, St. Margaret's, Westminster. The sermon was entered in the Stationer's Register the following month and put forth into print by John Bartlett.[18] Bartlett, sensing a market in the conjunction of a popular preacher, Ussher, and the national (newsworthy) event of a Parliament, dominated the admittedly small trade in parliamentary sermons during the 1620s. Ussher's sermon was reissued in 1624 and again in a revised edition in 1631. Bartlett was also responsible for the publication of Isaac Bargrave's opening sermon to the Commons in 1624.[19] In this instance though, the Commons itself ordered the publication and appointed Sir Arthur Ingram and Sir Edward Villiers to suggest Bargrave go into print.[20] In 1625 William Laud's opening sermon was available in print, while Humphrey Sydenham prepared one for the general fast in August but, because of the dissolution of Parliament, he preached it at St. Mary's Oxford instead.[21] The following year Laud's sermon preached on 6 February at the start of the Parliament was in print.[22] By 1628–29 the parliamentary sermons had become so popular that the public was able to buy the fast sermon preached before the Commons by John Harris (the resident preacher at St. Margaret's), and another by Jeremiah Dyke.[23] The Lords' fast sermons, preached by Joseph Hall, Bishop of Exeter, and John Davenant, Bishop of Salisbury, were both sold, along with William Laud's opening sermon to Parliament and John Williams' sermon to the Lords on 6 April.[24] All these were ordered to be printed by the Lords. Perhaps, though, in a sign of increasingly fraught times, the occasional printing of a fast sermon in the 1620s had given way by 1641 to a prayer appeal to the public with the printing of *A Divine Prayer necessary to be used every day in each particular family, during the time of this present Parliament*.[25]

VERSE

If prayer fitted naturally with Parliament, then so did addresses to the political nation in verse. John Dee seems to have been the first to capitalize on this method to make a specific point.[26] Dee, who had been (in his opinion) continually slandered for more than fifty years, petitioned both the King and Parliament in 1604 for relief. Dee's work, *The Letter . . . apologeticall,* was a reprint of his 1599 printed petition to Elizabeth, but he added a verse to Parliament and the King asking for an Act against Slander to be passed in 1604.[27] As he commented, this would enable him to clear his name from being accounted 'a companion of the helhounds, and a caller and conjuror of wicked spirits.'[28] Dee even went so far as to offer to stand trial to clear his name. The verse itself to the Commons opened with a standard petitionary supplication:

> The Honor due unto you all,
> And reverence, to you each one,
> I do first yeeld most speciall;
> Grant me this time, to hear my mone.

Four stanzas later Dee presented a solution to his ills:

> And so your* Act, with Honor great,
> All ages will hereafter prayse:
> And trueth, that sitts in Heavenly seat,
> Will, in like case, your Comforts rayse
>
> *An Act generall against Sclaunder, and a speciall penall Order for John Dee his case.[29]

Dee's eloquent complaint went unanswered, and there is no evidence that the Commons considered a bill on slander. Similar misfortune befell the next poet to address a verse to the Commons, John Taylor the water-poet, in 1621. In this instance Taylor's address, *The Subjects Joy for the Parliament*, did not make specific demands on Parliament's time. Also, unlike Dee's, the poem was an elaborate production with an engraving of King James and a highly stylized if crude portal surrounding the text. It was also printed to be sold.[30] The verse itself was a panegyric which suggested that God originally dispensed laws in the form of a Parliament:

> That the Almighty, did long since ordaine
> Lawes, that should our rebellious wils restaine.
> And from that Parlament, of highest Heaven
> A Statute, and an Ordinance was given.

However, Taylor may have written the verse to present his company, the Watermen, in a favorable light and well disposed toward Parliament, especially as it was pressing the Parliament to enact legislation that the Company had introduced and supported this with a printed petition.[31] Taylor not only penned this verse but also took full advantage of the calling of Parliament to dedicate his *Superbiae Flagellum* (1621) to Sir Thomas Richardson, the Speaker of the House of Commons, and referenced Parliament again in *Taylors Goose* (1621).[32] Ben Jonson, a denizen of Westminster, also took note of Parliament, penning an epigram entitled 'To the Parliament':

> There's reason good, that you good lawes should make:
> Men's manners ne're were viler, for your sake.[33]

These few examples reflect verses addressed to Parliament or specifically about the institution, but Parliament was also more obliquely and problematically represented in many satires. The early Jacobean years saw the rise of a coterie of wits, such as the MPs Christopher Brooke, John Hoskyns, and Richard Martin, who were part of the early-seventeenth-century literary circle that convened on occasion in the *Mitre* and *Mermaid* taverns and who were associated with the prefatory poetical outpourings of the popular *Coryats Crudities* (1611).[34] Although much of their 'output' was verbal or in manuscript circulation (the 'Parliament Fart' verses), this group also intersected with printed satires on government and Parliament. As Michelle O'Callaghan noted, '[P]rint became one of the primary modes whereby the citizen poet participated in the commonwealth and transformed the concept of counsel, extending it from an elite body of magistrates within court to the relationship between a writer and his readers within a public sphere.'[35] In and around the 1614 Parliament, this burst of literary energy in print manifested itself in George Wither's *Abuses Stript, and Whipt* (1613) and *The Shepherds Hunting* (1614), Brooke's *The ghost of Richard the third* (1614), and William Browne's *The Shepheards Pipe* (1614), to which Wither and Brooke both contributed eclogues.[36]

Wither's thinly veiled (and later admitted) critique of the Earl of Northampton as an 'evil counsellor' had most likely been the cause of his imprisonment in the Marshalsea, where he had resided since shortly after the Parliament opened. It may too have been the popularity of Wither's essays that convinced Northampton to act as *Abuses* went through five editions in 1613 and a pirated copy appeared in early 1614.[37] Wither was not the only one of this group to feel the anger of the state, as Hoskyns found himself imprisoned for his rash speeches at the end of the Addled Parliament. Brooke, who had walked a tightrope during the Parliament while advocating the impositions bill and straying into the realm of the King's prerogative powers, turned to print as well. His study of tyranny in *The ghost* ties in with his experience, and the experiences of his fellow MPs and literary friends, of the impositions debates of 1610 and 1614 and the limits of royal authority. Throughout the 1620s, Brooke continued this theme of printed and manuscript poetic engagement with parliamentary issues and royal policy in his *Poem on the late massacre in Virginia* (1622) and 'A funeral elegy for Sir Arthur Chichester.'[38]

Wither also continued to pen printed political satire involving Parliament and public politics in the 1620s. In his *Motto* (1621), Wither specifically addressed the monopolies debates in Parliament and the charges against

Viscount St. Alban, Francis Bacon:

> *I care not* when there comes a *Parliament:*
> For I am no Proiector, who invent
> New *Monopolies*, or such *Suites*, as Those,
> Who, wickedly pretending goodly showes,
> *Abuses* to reforme; engender more:
> And farre lesse tollerable, than before.
> Abusing *Prince*, and *State*, and *Common-weale*;
> Their (just deservrd) beggaries to heale:
> Or, that their ill-got profit, may advance,
> To some Great Place, their Pride, and Ignorance.
> Nor by Extortion, nor thorugh Bribery,
> To any Seat of Iustice, climb'd am I.[39]

Wither's verses on Bacon and matters of state fell under the rubric of the Bacon-penned proclamation against 'lavish and licentious speech,' and after his examination by the Privy Council he was again imprisoned.[40]

Wither's fellow satirist, Richard Braithwaite, who had copied the style of *Abuses Stript* in *A Strappado for the Devil* (1615),[41] similarly addressed the 1621 Parliament in verse, although with more circumspection. In his work *Times Curtaine*, Braithwaite included a verse prayer to the Parliament but in a tone laudatory to James as the head of state and Parliament:

> It is thy *fruitfull vine*, may it increase
> Vnto thy glory (Lord) and Syon peace,
> That ravenous Wolfe or subtill Fox nere may
> Breake in by force and steale her Grapes away.
> And for asmuch Confusion needes must breede
> Where *members* doe subsist without a *heade*,
> Blesse our Drad Soueraigne, Lord, blesse him, that He
> Both in himselfe and his Posteritie,
> May stere, support, and guide the sterne of State,
> That *Others* eying vs, may wonder at
> The blessed peace and freedome we obtaine
> Vnder so wise and good a Soueraigne.
> And may *Hee* ever haue one of his owne
> (if' t be thy pleasure) to sit on this Throne,
> This peacefull Ile to solace and secure,
> So long as Sunne or Moone shall ere endure.
> lesse the most prudent Councell of this Land,
> Lord in their Consultations haue a hand;
> May Thou and they in Iudgement still consent,

But specially th'*High house of Parlament*,
Which by thy will and prouidence divine,
To right the State,'s assembled at this time.
Lord be amongst them, that whats'ere they doome,
May be to th'Weale and Peace of Christendome.
May popular Opinion never draw them,
May loue to God and Good-men overaw them:
May all their *Acts* bee a continued Story,
To further and advance thy sacred glory:
May *Prince* be pleas'd, *State* eas'd, and men with men
Liue here in Loue, and rest in peace: Amen.[42]

Ballads, woodcuts, and engravings too depicted Parliament and events in the chamber. In 1621 the fall of the notorious monopolist Sir Giles Mompesson was illustrated in an elaborate folio engraving of three panels entitled *The Description of Giles Mompesson late Knight censured by Parliament: The 17th of March A⁰ 1620*.[43] The stories inscribed in the engraving represent Mompesson's extortion of money from innkeepers, his escape from the custody of the sergeant at arms (Edward Grimston), and finally his miserable, poverty-stricken, and crippled life in exile in France, where he is invited to wander the countryside with two the notorious 'villians' of the early sixteenth century, Richard Empson and Edmund Dudley. Mompesson's story is told in rhyming couplets across the top of the panels, and a general coda (also in rhyming couplets) warning against monopolistic practices spans the bottom of the illustration. The centrality and necessity of Parliament to rooting out corruption is reflected in the verse. Mompesson would have continued his activities unhindered without a Parliament:

> Oppression sore hee used where hee went
> As yet not thinking of a Parliament
> But Parliament once call'd then Giles was brought
> Unto account, contrary to his thought.

Text within the illustration also indicates the role of Parliament in bringing down Empson and Dudley:

> In first yere of Kinge Henry last
> By Parliament to death they past.

Mompesson was not the only monopolist punished by the 1621 Parliament to find himself for sale on the streets. Sir Francis Michell, who was degraded from his recently acquired knighthood, fined £1,000, and imprisoned for his role in the notorious alehouses, and gold and silver thread patents, was reviled in a two-part ballad, *The Deserved Downfall*, to the tune of *The humming of the Drone*.[44] Although Michell is not specifically named, the full title can refer only to him: *The Deserved Downfall of a Corrupted Conscience degraded from all Authority and title of Knighthood, censured in the high Court of Parliament, and executed at the Kings Bench barre upon the 20 day of June last. 1621, in the presence of foure great Peeres of this Kingdome.*

Parliament too was the 'hero' in a 1624 engraving, *The Travels of Time*, which illustrates the failure of the pope to reconvert England to Catholicism and repeal the penal laws against Catholics after the breakdown of the negotiations for the marriage of Prince Charles to the Infanta of Spain. The figure of 'Policie' hovers over a basket of eggs and the related character, 'Politicke,' who is scheming on behalf of Catholics, rues the day Parliament was called:

> Then came a Parliament, whose weighty stroake
> Found out my nest, and all my Eggs they broke.[45]

Despite the literary tenor of these few examples, most poetic forms associated with Parliament were scribally produced libels. What is clear that events in Parliament and its actions spilled over into the world of cheap print in verse, further publicizing Parliament as a panacea for the nation's ills and as an integral part of political life.

LISTS AND REPRESENTATIVES

As we have seen from the earlier discussions on lobbying, knowing upon whom to rely or whom to bribe was an important tool of parliamentary management—the names of members of the Commons and the Lords was obviously crucial to this process. Further evidence of the parliamentary print proliferation in the 1620s can be found in the printed lists of MPs and peers that were available for sale from at least 1624. Although manuscript lists of MPs had been available before 1624, the last Jacobean Parliament seems to have been the first one in which the names of all MPs were published and put up for sale in shops.[46] Two editions were produced that not only listed the MPs and their constituencies but also gave a catalogue of those entitled to be summoned to the Upper House and those who attended Parliament in an official capacity, such as the legal assistants and the officers of the Houses (Clerk of the Parliament, yeoman usher, and so forth).[47] Individual peers were not, however, listed either by names or title. The Commons listing was a sophisticated analysis of both the 1621 and 1624 Parliaments laid out in two columns showing whether the member had sat in the earlier Parliament and for what constituency.

The compiler of the list was Edward Grimston, the House of Commons' sergeant at arms, who clearly saw the opportunity to make money from the sale of the document as well as a chance to advance his own condition.[48] The sergeant was the officer of the Commons entrusted with ensuring that the names of members were entered in the official register, and thus Grimston was in the ideal position to provide exact and up-to-date information. The preface to the second edition was dedicated to John St. Amand, MP, for Stamford, Lincolnshire.[49] Grimston noted that St. Amand could 'informe your knowledge' of both current and past members and hoped that St. Amand would 'keepe this Collection by you.'[50]

Despite continuing as sergeant in the new reign, Grimston did not enter the market again, but he spawned an imitator in Thomas Walkley, a bookseller who was to control much of the material relating to Parliament in the late 1620s and early 1640s.[51] Walkley had a long association with political publishing and the parliamentary world. From his shop, the Eagle and Child, in Westminster's shopping emporium, Britain's Burse, he was perfectly situated to cater to the pamphlet-buying habits of members of Parliament and peers. Furthermore, as Zachary Lesser has noted, Walkley's early publications, 'plays like *Othello* and *A King and no King* could be understood by contemporaries to be closely engaged with the concerns of the House of Commons and the Privy Council, functioning at the intersection of multiple and disputed visions of the state and authority.'[52] Walkley was also closely associated with the prominent member of Parliament and courtier, Sir Henry Neville, to whom he dedicated Fletcher and Beaumont's *A King and no King*.[53]

Walkley's 1625 parliamentary list was modeled on Grimston's, although he deleted the section on the House of Lords. The list provided the reader with the names of members of Parliament from 1621, 1624, and 1625, annotated with numbers that ranged from one to three beside each member to illustrate their parliamentary experience in the 1620s.[54] This procedure was abandoned for the 1626 Parliament when only a single list was printed, but it also included for the first time the names of those in the Upper House.[55] By 1628, in a clearly flourishing market, Walkley continually revised and

updated his lists, 'very much enlarged' as he noted for those who had purchased early copies.[56] In 1628, Walkley also printed a *Catalogue of the Lords*,
which listed all the peers summoned to the Parliament. This publication,
however, met with some displeasure in the Upper House, and Walkley was
called to the bar for printing the names 'very falsely.' Despite producing a
warrant for the printing Walkley was 'sharply reprehended.' The books were
ordered to be burned and he was forbidden to print any similar material
without the authorization of the Earl Marshal (Thomas Howard, Earl of
Arundel), the official responsible for heraldic matters.[57] Despite this order,
Walkley's efforts continued in 1640 when he produced two tracts, one detailing the names of those called to the Lords and a separate pamphlet on
the Commons for both the Short and Long Parliaments.[58]

Simple printed lists were not the only tracts to come onto the market,
nor was the Parliament the only subject. In 1628 it was possible to buy the
names of all the sheriffs in England and Wales, while the members of the
1624 Upper and Lower Houses of Convocation of Canterbury were listed
in a single sheet broadside surrounding woodcuts of both Houses in session.[59] No similar visual representation survives for Parliament until 1628,
when two single sheets were printed for Henry Gosson with the names of
the peers and Commons arrayed around woodcuts of the Houses in session.[60] The prominence of the sergeant in the foreground of the picture
suggests a continuing link (or homage) to Grimston.

As Grimston noted in 1624, these documents were valuable as an aide-
memoire for members and no doubt peers as well. But their availability in
the marketplace also suggests a wider audience. As with so much of this
material, it is not possible either to establish print runs or to determine just
how widely they were circulated. Nevertheless, the lists were clearly part of
the flourishing print activity concerning Parliament in the 1620s, and their
continuing runs from 1624 to 1640 and beyond suggest that it was a profitable enterprise. This can be further determined from Walkley's four editions
in 1628 and the competition from the two sheets produced by Gosson. Also
suggestive of sales outside the parliamentary chambers are the four Walkley
editions. Lists were continually updated by hand by their owners as the
Commons membership changed through by-elections, contested returns,
and expulsions.[61] For those in the Commons or Lords wanting updated
information, this method would have been sufficient, but for those outside
and not in everyday communication with the Commons, the most updated
printed version would have been of greater use. The changes between the

editions were significant. The first edition was rushed into print before all the returns had reached Westminster—late returns ensured that the second edition had sixteen additions to the Commons membership, while the voters of Tavistock were probably relieved to find that their member in the second edition was John Pym, not John Pyne—likewise those at Poole, who in the second edition could call upon Pyne, not Pym, for assistance. By the printing of the fourth 'much enlarged' edition, an even greater number of double returns and contested elections had been resolved. One copy of the 1628 list of members of the Lords shows that it could be used for more than just lobbying purposes. Annotated with 'n,' 'C,' or 'A' next to the names of each bishop, it indicates 'how each divine stood on the crucial religious question: Arminian, Calvinist or neutral.'[62]

PRINTED SPEECHES

The matter of printed speeches was much more controversial than simply publishing lists of members' names. As the proceedings of Parliament were supposedly *arcana imperii,* the publication of speeches was certainly a breach of custom and potentially a dangerous development. Of course, some parliamentary speeches were printed, but these were, for the most part, confined to the addresses made by the monarch at the opening or closing of Parliament or on some particular occasion of state. Even this royal printing of parliamentary proceedings was primarily a Jacobean innovation. The examples from Elizabeth's reign, such as the printing of the 1601 Golden Speech, are rare.[63] Apart from 1601 the only parliamentary proceedings that seem to be extant are from the 1586 Parliament, when the royal printer, no doubt in accordance with Elizabeth's wishes, printed a pamphlet that contained the major parliamentary addresses to be sent to Robert Dudley, Earl of Leicester, in the Netherlands.[64] The use of parliamentary printing, in this instance, enabled the Queen to shift some of the pressure for the execution of Mary Queen of Scots and to share the blame with Parliament, the 'body of the whole realm.' Thus the publication was a case of pressing political need over-ruling any idea that speeches in Parliament were secret.[65]

If the Mary Queen of Scots pamphlet and the Golden Speech paved the way for the printing of royal (parliamentary) speeches, then the Stuart dynasty was quick to provide information on the new King. His opening address to Parliament in 1604 was published in London by the royal printer, Robert Barker, and simultaneously issued under the imprint of Thomas Finlason in Edinburgh.[66] No stranger to print, James exploited the medium throughout his reign. The Gunpowder Plot provided fresh impetus for the sale of royal speeches and for making the image of the monarch, while occasional parliamentary reversals were met with James's printed explanations. The interested public could purchase his speeches from the end of the 1606–7 session of Parliament on why the Union project had stalled and on the collapse of the Great Contract negotiations in 1610.[67] Reasons for dissolutions and prorogations, justification for often unpopular actions, and information formed the basis of the royal parliamentary speeches throughout the 1620s as the Crown sought to publicize its side of parliamentary activity.[68] Complaints were made in the 1628 Commons about the printing of royal speeches and that of the Duke of Buckingham's report to the King on the progress of the subsidy bill. As John Selden noted, '[S]hall the counsels of parliament be laid on stalls.'[69] But this one-sided print 'discourse' was effectively challenged that year when two major speeches rejecting the Lords' position on the Petition of Right were printed, one by John Glanville and another by Sir Henry Marten.[70] Benjamin Rudyerd, who would become one of the most printed parliamentarians of the early 1640s, also found a voice in print that year. However, the nature of Rudyerd's involvement—if any—with the tract *Sir Beniamin Ruddierd's speech in behalfe of the Cleargy* (Oxford, 1628) is not known, and it was probably the printer who added the biblical quotation at the end: 'Some were perswaded with the things that were spoken, and some beleeved not.'[71] These few pamphlets hardly challenged the royal monopoly of printing parliamentary proceedings, but they were significant precursors of their 1640s counterparts.[72] Speeches and debate, slower than other parliamentary tracts, were nonetheless moving from a scribal culture to a printed one.

PETITIONS, PAMPHLETS, AND BROADSIDES

The largest category of unofficial printed material relating to early modern Parliaments is that of petitions submitted by individuals, companies, corporations, and boroughs. As we saw in the previous chapter, petitioning Parliament was by now a long-established tradition. David Zaret in his *Origins of Democratic Culture* has linked the worlds of petitioning and print in the early 1640s,[73] but the impact of printed petitions on Parliament started much earlier. Zaret's claim that 'petitions to Parliament were not held to violate contemporary norms of secrecy and privilege because petitionary rhetoric portrayed grievance as an apolitical flow of information on local conditions to the political center'[74] is correct, at least for scribal petitions. But what if those petitions were printed, fly-posted, distributed to MPs and peers, and available for anyone to buy? As we shall see, by the 1620s the traditional forms and nature of petitioning had been blurred with appeals to the public and dissemination of information.

While printed petitioning was a characteristic of both the 1620s and 1640s, it is important to distinguish between them. Both Zaret and Anthony Fletcher before him have examined the mass petitioning of Parliament in the 1640s, both through the physical impact on the center of hundreds of people attending the chamber to present a petition and the collection of thousands of signatures to one petition.[75] Fletcher and Zaret see this as a 'petitioning movement.' By early 1642, when thirty-eight out of forty counties in England sent printed petitions to Westminster inscribed with thousands of signatures, the process was highly organized and politically motivated. It is also the case that the majority of these petitions concerned matters of Commonweal interest, 'Root and Branch' reform of the church, appeals for the removal of royal servants, and complaints about prerogative taxation. However, it is a mistake to see these as having no antecedents and to link the novelty of print with petitioning.[76] Petitions before 1640 may have been less polemical and elaborate and not a part of a well-organized nationwide propaganda campaign,[77] but the link between Parliament, print, and petitions was established before the opening of the Short Parliament in April 1640.

The majority of printed petitions from the 1620s that were designed to be sold were in pamphlet form.[78] Unsurprisingly, a number were written by religious polemicists, who took advantage of the captive audience provided by a Parliament in session to address their work to that body. This form of political pamphleteering had been employed during the Marprelate controversy with *An Admonition to Parliament* (1572) and was picked up early in James's reign in publications from the presses of William Jones and Gabriel Powel.[79] A post–Gunpowder Plot Parliament provided the opportunity for 'Philopatris' (lover of country) to produce a forty-five-page anti-Catholic tract formed in the style of a 'humble petition' addressed to Parliament.[80] But these early pamphlets do not seem to have spawned imitators until the late 1620s, when heightened religious tensions in the Church brought about a ferocious attack on the prelacy by the arch-Puritan Alexander Leighton.[81] Leighton's address to Parliament was suffused with optimism that Parliament could act as a 'Panacaean or cure-all Court.' The preface spoke of Parliament's past successes, probably referring to the Petition of Right, and expressed optimism about its ability to serve as the 'eyes, eares, and hands to our Soveraigne.'[82]

Parliament was also subject to lengthy petitions on usury, St. Paul's Church, Leather, Debt, the East India Company, and Wotton-upon-Edge grammar school. The latter provides a clear insight into how print, Parliament, and the book-buying public were linked by the 1620s, as printed material addressed to the Commons and Lords rolled off the presses and into the hands of peers and MPs at a remarkable rate. Benjamin Crokey had long been in a legal dispute over land belonging to Wotton-under-Edge grammar school in Gloucestershire that he claimed had been appropriated by his kinsman John Smyth of Nibley.[83] Learning of Crokey's design to submit a bill to Parliament in 1621, Smyth managed to secure election to Parliament as a burgess for Midhurst, Sussex, in order to block the bill.[84] Crokey responded by printing a one-page breviate of the bill for distribution to the Commons and Lords and by petitioning both Houses as well.[85] Smyth's position in the Commons appears to have stymied Crokey's attempts in the Lower House, and when he managed to get the Lords to set up a commission to inquire into the case, Smyth instigated proceedings that saw him imprisoned for debt, thus delaying the inquiry.[86] Foiled in Parliament and the law courts, Crokey went public when the 1625 Parliament met. Taking advantage of Smyth's absence from Parliament, Crokey printed a sixty-four-page tract addressed to Parliament that outlined his case and supported his introduction of legislation.[87] Not without a sense of humor, or perhaps a realistic appraisal of the (il)literacy of the Upper House, he advised the Lords 'that in respect of its tediousnes . . . to leave the reading thereof to yo[ur] secretaries.' Crokey not only offered his tract to Parliament but also attempted to gather public support by spending £9 to print four hundred copies for sale. Despite an order by the House of Lords in 1624, which prohibited printing petitions to Parliament, Crokey probably would have escaped censure were it not for his polemical style. Crokey was later prosecuted in Star Chamber for publishing the work and was found to have libeled not only Smyth but also the late King James, Lord Chancellor Ellesmere, Lord Keeper Williams, and the Archbishop of Canterbury.[88]

Perhaps deterred by his impending Star Chamber trial, Crokey refrained from expressing himself again in print until 1640. The death of Smyth the same year, and no doubt the loosening of controls on printing, encouraged Crokey to renew his attack, and printed pamphlets were addressed to Parliament in 1640, 1645, and 1647.[89]

The prosecution of Crokey does not reveal an outright hostility toward petitioning Parliament in print, and Crokey was not criticized for this; his censure was based upon the libelous content of the pamphlet. Nevertheless, his subsequent absence from the printed medium suggests not only that had he failed in his objective but also that he was wary of repeating his foray into print, given his forthcoming Star Chamber censure. Smyth was careful not to get caught in the same trap, and his eighty-one-page petition to Parliament in 1626 defending himself against Crokey's pamphlet was written in longhand by his secretary.[90]

Crokey's failure was not unusual. The success rate of printed parliamentary pamphlets that promoted a specific legislative agenda was minuscule. Indeed, it is possible that one of the purposes of printing pamphlets for sale was to increase public pressure on Parliament to influence an otherwise reluctant body to tackle precisely the issues raised in the petition. In Crokey's case he needed to fight against a sitting member with important gentry connections. The group of Leathersellers who printed a twenty-seven-page pamphlet and single sheet broadside in 1629 did not have the support of their own London Company.[91] The East India Company had fared no better the year before.[92] Henry Farley's pamphlet on the need for repairs to the fabric of St. Paul's Cathedral deliberately tried to whip up public opinion and pressure Parliament and the commissioners appointed for repair by James I in 1620.[93] It was first issued in 1616, and Farley, like many of his fellow petitioners, took the opportunity of a Parliament to change his general plea to one that was specifically addressed to Parliament. As the title noted, it was 'intended for the view of that most high and Honorable Court [Parliament], and generally for all such as beare good will to the restoring estate of the said Church.'[94] As with the religious polemicists, there is a sense that Parliament provides a new and captive audience—that it is a public body worth addressing over and above any notion of a legislative outcome.

The campaign for St. Paul's may have been an individual enterprise on the part of Farley, but if one pamphlet is to be believed, thousands of poor prisoners were petitioning for their relief from debt. It is unclear where the specific impetus for debt relief petitions and legislation originated. However, it was certainly an organized campaign. Before June 1621 a bill was submitted to Parliament for the relief of indebted prisoners.[95] Accompanying the bill was a single-page printed petition praising the worthiness of the Commons and begging relief from prisoners in King's Bench, the Fleet, and other prisons. The petition's author claimed that thirty-five hundred people resided in the squalor of London's fifteen prisons—and the prisoners were not only 'most miserable' but also 'most loyall' subjects.[96] Particular praise was even lavished on one of the senior members of the Commons, Sir Edward Coke, for his remarks on debt relief. But the author did not let the matter rest solely with a single-page petition to Parliament. A fifty-six-page pamphlet was also produced with a lengthy discourse on imprisonment for debt.[97] However, neither short nor long petition swayed the Commons, and the bill failed to receive a first reading. Another attempt was made in 1624, when the bill and a single-page petition were again introduced, but they too met with abject failure.[98]

The sole legislative success story was the usury petition.[99] By 1621 and the publication by Sir Thomas Culpepper of *A Tract against usurie. Presented to the High Court of Parliament*, usury had metamorphosed from a predominately religious issue to a secular one.[100] Culpepper's tract and its arguments for the economic advantage in lowering the interest rate from 10 to 8 percent struck the right note in a Parliament concerned with the economic plight of England. The arguments in the debate followed closely along the lines written by Culpepper, and one of the most prominent members in 1621, Edward Alford, owned a copy that he annotated.[101] However, Culpepper did not so much persuade Parliament to his point of view by printing the pamphlet as provide ready-made arguments in favor of a subject already widely discussed in Parliament.[102]

These petitions, which were specifically 'public documents,'[103] differ from their 1640s counterparts in a number of ways. The petitions were important as propaganda, 'at least in the minimal sense that contemporaries valued them as devices to influence the opinions of persons within and outside Parliament. Second, petitions are an indicator of opinions; that is, they have some connection to debates in civil society and not merely literary inventions foisted upon an unsuspecting public.'[104] However, they were not politicized, nor did they form part of a movement or campaign. Furthermore, their utility was confined to either a select group or an individual, whether that was the pugnacious Crokey or 'thousands' of prisoners. Nonpartisan and generally uncontroversial, the pamphlets form part of a change in early modern communicative practice in relation to Parliament. It is myopic to see print only in relation to the success of specific legislative outcomes. Print was disseminated with a legislative *terminus ad quem* but also a more general aim, the power of dissemination itself. The inherent vox populi aspect of the pamphlets presents us with an early modern sense of what ought to constitute democratic representation. Print in this instance was thus important for its discursive power rather than the legislative outcome per se.

BROADSIDES

That some petitions were available for purchase and made specific public, political points should not blind us to the fact that the majority of petitions were printed by individuals and companies to ensure that they reached the wider audience *inside* Parliament. In contrast to those that were written in order to be sold, broadside petitions were printed as a means to reach those in Parliament who would decide the fate of specific grievances or pieces of legislation. They also offered an inexpensive and efficient way to counter the arguments of opposing parties. Cheap print, in this instance, revolutionized parliamentary business, moving arguments from a primarily oral and scribal tradition to a printed one.

Parliament had always been a legislative marketplace, but by 1621 it was in danger of failing to fulfill one of its prime purposes—the enactment of legislation for the benefit of the commonweal, individuals, and towns. The failure to pass any legislation in the final session of the 1604 Parliament and the dissolution of the Addled Parliament (1614) left a backlog of grievances and a need for better and different techniques of management. In part, this new challenge for the petitioner was met by the impact of the printed word. For the 1620s, more than 130 broadsides survive. That is in stark contrast to the fewer than five broadsides that date from before 1621. As might be expected, the one segment of society that was at the forefront of this parliamentary innovation was the London companies. The companies had long been the most sophisticated and organized lobbying group,[105] and they were no strangers to the printed medium. In 1604, after obtaining a proclamation in their favor, the Woolmen printed five hundred copies for distribution, while both the Grocers and Blacksmiths printed thousands of copies of their apprentices' oaths.[106] The Stationers themselves printed a petition in 1604, probably addressed either to Parliament or to the Corporation of London.[107] Thus, it is unsurprising that a London company, the Carpenters, produced the earliest surviving printed broadside petition to Parliament, in 1593.[108] Despite the early efforts of the Carpenters, the medium was slow to catch on, probably because the old ways of scribal petitioning and in-house management were adequate methods. Only two other broadside petitions can definitely be linked to parliaments before 1621. The Carpenters turned to print again in 1607, and the Tilers and Bricklayers fought their nemesis, the Plasterers, through print in 1614.[109]

Edward Egerton best summed up the reasons for turning to print, 'to avoyde the excessive greate charge w[hi]ch . . . [he] should have byn put unto if the said Brevyatts should have byn written, he dyd cause them to be printed (as manye others of his ma[jes]ties subiects w[hi]ch had the like suits and Bills dependeinge in parlyamente did).'[110] Egerton's breviates were distributed to members of Parliament by his solicitor, George Tarling, and fly-posted around the New Exchange and 'on divers other posts and gates within the cities of London and Westminster.'[111]

Egerton was not exaggerating the actions of his fellow petitioners, as print exploded into the 1621 Parliament. More than sixty petitions and breviates still survive from that Parliament alone. Over a third of these are either from London companies or relate to London matters, such as the London commissioners of buildings who had invoked the ire of the 'thousands of poor distressed carpenters, bricklayers, smiths, plasterers, glasiers, painters and other handicraft men' by pulling down buildings and prohibiting building in wood.[112] The clerks of the Customs' House complained about the new office of the Clerk of the Bills in a printed brief and a petition, appending nearly three hundred signatures from themselves and aggrieved merchants.[113] This type of mass petitioning foreshadowing the 1640s was unusual, although occasionally companies combined together to defeat an opponent. The Bookbinders, Painters, and Cutlers joined forces to criticize the new company of Goldbeaters, who they claimed had dramatically raised the price of gold foliate since their incorporation in 1619.[114] Two separate sheets were printed, a brief of their petition and an abstract of grievances. Each company also submitted its own petition against the bill.[115] The Commons Grievances Committee thus had five broadsides against the Goldbeaters and the Goldbeaters' printed answer.[116] The committee was not short of information or printed material. The cause was heard on 27 April, condemned in the Commons on 2 May, and the grant was annulled by proclamation in July.[117] Encouraged by their success the Bookbinders also submitted a broadside to the 1624 Parliament condemning George Wither's patent printing the Hymns of the Church with every Psalm book.[118]

Cooperation between London companies was the exception rather than the norm, and most spent their money on printing broadsides against each other. The Wharfingers and Woodmongers engaged in a long war of attrition starting (in Parliament) in 1621,[119] while the Grocers and Apothecaries,[120] and Barber-surgeons and Physicians,[121] fought each other in print as well. The Felt-makers asked for a 'severe law' against those who imported felts and hats manufactured abroad,[122] while the Free Butchers of London mounted a successful campaign in alliance with the London MPs to kill off a bill for free grazing of cattle in London.[123] Naturally, the Stationers' Company also printed its petitions. In 1621, 1624, and 1629 it printed single-sided responses to the printing patent held by Martin Boisloré, Roger Wood, and Thomas Symcocke, despite the fact the patentees held the sole right to print on single-sided paper.[124]

If companies were not engaged in a broadside war against each other, they turned their attentions to the myriad of patents that had been issued by the King. The Hot-pressers attacked Sir George Douglas's grant for using the hot press, complaining of how the Recorder of London, Sir Robert Heath, imprisoned their members despite a clear conflict of interest—he was Douglas's lawyer.[125] The Dyers considered their trade to be harmed by Sir Thomas Compton's patent for importing logwood. In addition to a bill they also introduced a petition and a printed breviate.[126] The Merchant Staplers continued their perennial request for a Free Trade act (and a restoration of their powers);[127] the alnager patent held by the Duke of Lennox provoked the ire of a group of London merchants;[128] and the Muscovy Company grant was the subject of a broadside listing reasons it should be suppressed.[129] The London companies took no time at all to adopt the new strategy of turning to print and the flexibility it provided to produce more than one document for circulation.

Away from London, others were quick to seize on the benefits of the new medium. An innkeeper in Wiltshire,[130] two parsons squabbling over the rectory and living of Stalbridge, Gloucestershire,[131] the town of Great Yarmouth, Norfolk,[132] the parishioners of Winwick, Lancashire,[133] the Tewkesbury Corporation,[134] and the Drapers of Shrewsbury all petitioned in print.[135] Still others brought their Chancery cases or other legal grievances in print to Parliament. Printed petitions were employed not only by wealthy corporations or organizations but by individuals as well. Lady Elizabeth Dale printed details of her dispute with the East India Company,[136] as did William Deye of Eye, Suffolk, who complained about a popish schoolmaster, Simon Dormer.[137] Griswell Rogers protested her treatment at the hands of Sir Arthur Ingram via the printing press,[138] and the manor of Sundrish in Kent formed the basis of a clash between Thomas Browker and George Fouch and Nicholas Streete.[139]

The cost of such petitions was certainly greater than introducing a single scribal petition, but given the possibility of swift parliamentary intervention balanced against the employment of legal counsel and preparation of multiple documents for a lengthy Chancery trial, it had the potential to be money well spent. The ability of print to reach a much wider audience also influenced the decision to turn away from scribal publication. In 1641 Robert Jager, the agent of the cinque port Sandwich, informed the corporation that 'he had put forth to print that every man of the House might have one' Sandwich's argument to be exempt from the subsidy.[140] Crokey likewise claimed that he had printed 400 copies of his petition so that he could provide everyone in Parliament with a copy.[141] Certainly this was the intention of the Tilers and Bricklayers Company, who paid 10 shillings to print breviates in 1614, probably about 300 sheets in total. In 1621 they spent 11 shillings initially and later another 5 shillings on 150 further copies.[142] The Butchers Company in 1624 printed their reasons against a bill for free grazing of cattle and spent 20 shillings on copies.[143] Merton College too printed its breviates in 1626, paying 13 shillings and 4 pence to produce breviates of the college's bill to confirm possession of the manor of Maldon, Surrey.[144] George Wither claimed that while he had intended to print 3,000 copies of a scurrilous tract against the Stationers entitled *The Schollers Purgatory*, these were meant for distribution only to members of Parliament, Convocation, and the King and Prince Charles. Wither's print run would have given each person three or four copies each, a point not lost on the Court of High Commission looking into the matter.[145]

Unlike the lengthy printed pamphlets, most of these flimsy petitions survive in only one or two copies. The survival rate of sixteenth-century broadside ballads has been estimated at 1 in 10,000 copies, and although the rate jumps higher for newsbooks after 1620, these were more substantial tracts.[146] These types of print were not recorded in the Stationers' Register, and it is impossible to recover the exact numbers. However, through the collection in the Guildhall Library, and to a lesser extent those at the Society of Antiquaries and in the British Library, tentative suggestions can be made for 1621. The bulk of the Guildhall Library collection consists of more than sixty petitions submitted to the Commons in 1621. From the contemporary endorsements these appear to have been in the possession of one Parliament-man, probably a member of the Grievances Committee. When we consider these alongside the copies in Edward Alford's papers at the British Library and the Lemon Collection at the Society of Antiquaries, the figure jumps to over seventy.[147] Unfortunately, the 1621 member remains anonymous, and no other substantial collection exists for the rest of the 1620s. It would be surprising if, after this first explosion of parliamentary print, the medium did not continue to be exploited. The remaining petitions from the 1620s, more than sixty individual items, suggest that this was the case, and that a much greater number were printed but have been lost. In contrast, those parliamentary pamphlets that were printed for sale are extant in multiple copies. At least twelve copies of the debtors' petition survive, along with eleven copies of the East India petition and the same number of the Leathersellers' pamphlet.

If cheap print offered the ability for parliamentary petitioners to get their case across to the broadest possible audience, then it also offered unparalleled flexibility to react to changing circumstances. Print provided an opportunity to mobilize allies, publicize a cause, and form new alliances between Parliament's vested interests. In 1609 Richard Bowdler was one of a group of patentees who were given the grant to farm the alum works. Their factor at Middleburgh was George Morgan, who raised loans on their behalf worth over £22,000. The farm collapsed in 1612, Bowdler obtained a royal protection against his creditors, and Morgan was left to discharge the debt. Cross bills were launched in Chancery by Morgan and Bowdler in 1616–17, and both produced bills introduced in the 1621 Parliament as well as printed breviates.[148] This was but the start of a paper war. Bowdler attacked Morgan's bill in *A declaration of especiall untruths,* while Morgan accused Bowdler of using Parliament as an excuse to delay the case in Chancery.[149] Morgan also produced a detailed breakdown of the monies owed to him.[150] No solution was forthcoming in 1621, and the presses rolled back into action when the 1624 Parliament opened. Morgan printed another breviate of his bill and amended the financial breakdown broadside.[151] Although he claimed success in four days of hearing the case during May 1624, the Parliament ended before a ruling could be published.[152] Undaunted, Morgan submitted a bill to the 1625 Parliament and another printed breviate but was again thwarted by the dissolution of Parliament.[153] Morgan had no better luck in 1626, after which the matter disappears from the records.[154] Throughout the dispute both Morgan and (to a lesser extent) Bowdler attempted to provide the Commons with the most up-to-date information and to publicize their arguments as widely as possible inside St. Stephen's Chapel. And they did so through print. This was cheap print for an elite audience.

In the absence of contemporary comments, it is impossible to gauge the direct impact of this form of cheap print on the success or failure of petitions or legislation. No member of Parliament conveniently scribbled in his diary that he had supported the legislation after reading a printed brief on the bill. But that it became so widespread and popular in so short a period of time does at least suggest that petitioners quickly assumed its usefulness and rushed into print themselves. Neither, as we have seen, were petitioners necessarily put off by failure at the first attempt. The London companies kept printers in business Parliament after Parliament, and the examples of George Morgan and the debt prisoners suggest that they considered the money spent on printing worthwhile. Nevertheless, there was some disquiet shown over this new method of petitioning. The experienced Parliament-man Sir James Perrot complained about Paul Bassano's printed brief in 1621. He considered it 'inconvenyent to have breifes delivered to us before the cause be heard as it was in this cause of Bassanoes in print,' but Sir Edward Coke regarded the matter as a joke and looked forward to receiving a counterpetition—'I would never take the breviate of one syde, unless I might have bothe. Ile keep my eares open for both parties, I love to come even,' he commented.[155] Perrot was not the only member to receive the petition that day; Edward Alford found his copy useful for taking notes of the debates the same day.[156]

More serious opposition arose in 1624. On 5 April the Lords ordered the Stationers' Company 'not to printe any petic[i]on or briefes to the p[ar]liam[en]t.'[157] The effect of this is impossible to judge, for 1624 at least, but there may have been a limited tailing off of printed petitions in the early Caroline Parliaments. They by no means disappeared, but the numbers that survive are diminished from 1621 and 1624. That may be due to the exigencies of collecting and survival, but printers may alternatively have been wary of incurring the ire of Parliament and the Stationers' Company. George Morgan's broadsides in 1624 and 1625 were partly printed sheets with numerous blanks filled in by hand. In the earlier instance it appears that the printer was unwilling to name either the Lord Keeper in the document or Sir Edward Leech, whom Williams had appointed to arbitrate the matter. Morgan had objected to Leech, considering that he favored Bowdler and the other defendants. Whenever the Lord Keeper or Leech was mentioned a blank was left in the document and their names were written in by hand.[158] In 1625 the printer took further precautions, leaving Morgan to complete the title, 'A *Breefe of* [Morgans Bill in Parliamt].'[159] The printer too was no doubt wary of what had happened to one of Morgan's early printed briefs used in the Chancery case. Williams had ordered the collection of all the copies, which were then brought into the court and burned by the Warden of the Fleet.[160]

Lord Deyncourt also fell afoul of a Lord Keeper, this time Lord Thomas Coventry in 1629. Deyncourt handed Coventry a printed brief of his Chancery case as they both entered Parliament on the morning of 5 February 1629. Coventry immediately took offense at the impugning of his name and the court in the brief and brought it to the attention of the House. Deyncourt pleaded his innocence, but Coventry was not convinced: '[F]inding a brief when there is neither Bill nor Petition exhibited in this House against the decree, the Lord Keeper said he could do no less than declare the same to this House, lest, the brief being printed and divulged, his silence might be an argument of Faultiness.'[161] As the investigation proceeded, it became clear that Deyncourt's counsel, David Waterhouse, had suggested printing the document and that they had drafted it together. Waterhouse and the printer, Felix Kingston, were summoned before the Lords. Appearing at the bar of the House the following day, Waterhouse laid the blame squarely on Deyncourt's shoulders, denying any wrongdoing. His plea carried little weight with the Lords, however, and he was sent to the Fleet. Kingston fared somewhat better. Arguing that he had repeatedly refused to print the petition, he had agreed to do so only because Deyncourt was a peer and that he had assured him that it would not be presented to Parliament. With a stern warning not to print such petitions again, Kingston was dismissed.[162] Deyncourt's position worsened on 12 February. In a day devoted almost entirely to hearing the particulars of the original Chancery case and Deyncourt's subsequent actions, the House threw the proverbial book at him. Deyncourt did not help his own cause by absenting himself at the start of the day, and momentum quickly swung against him. The House confirmed the Chancery decree against Deyncourt, removed his right of parliamentary privileges, and ordered that he pay damages. His failure to pay would result in imprisonment in the Fleet. Humbled and thoroughly defeated, Deyncourt agreed to these terms.[163]

Deyncourt's was the only petition excluded in such a manner, and Kingston the only printer admonished. The Lords certainly did not have to look far to find other printed petitions, and despite their order of 1624, they seemed happy to receive them, provided no member of the House was impugned and the correct procedure of petitioning or proceeding by legislation was followed. For example, Thomas Russell in 1626 took advantage of the Parliament to promote his new process for the manufacture of saltpeter using lime, urine, and earth. Russell printed a petition in folio asking that Parliament sanction his process and approve a stock issue of £20,000 to advance his venture.[164] In the Lords, and especially in the committee on the safety and defense of the kingdom, Russell's proposal received enthusiastic support. With the nation at war, fluctuating saltpeter prices on the Continent, and the tantalizing prospect of an English source, the Lords even agreed to introduce legislation in a subsequent Parliament if Russell could deliver on his promise.[165] Shortly after the Parliament ended Russell received a royal grant to make saltpeter, and a proclamation was issued to that effect as well.[166]

The other concern in the Deyncourt case, and probably others, was the degree to which the broadsides were distributed outside of Parliament. For members of the Commons and peers to receive petitions such as Russell's (and many others) was one matter; for the wider public to discuss openly the proceedings of Parliament (or Chancery cases) was quite another. So we should be cautious in attributing fault to the medium in this case. The probable reason for the 1624 clampdown on printed briefs seems to be the sheer number of documents being distributed to members of both houses; the difference is one of scale. Small quantities of scribal petitions were unlikely to circulate widely beyond the walls of Westminster Palace. On the other hand, hundreds of printed petitions, even if not intended for wider distribution, certainly held the potential for fly-posting and greater public awareness of parliamentary proceedings. Nevertheless, regulations on print were not widely enforced, and the rule may well have been imposed so it *could* be enforced rather than so it *would* be. Certainly, the Lords was more troubled by these matters than the Commons. That is unsurprising. Many of the petitions concerned ongoing cases in Chancery or decisions under appeal from there. The presence of the Lord Chancellor in the Upper House and real or perceived criticism of his actions (and those of other law officers) meant the House was prickly about public criticism.

Most petitioners and printers followed a standardized form of address to their audience in the Lords and Commons. The page was unadulterated by scrollwork or bordering, and often the only difference between petitions addressed to the Upper House came through a substitution of 'Lords' for 'Commons' in the title. But the superior social standing of the Lords did not always go unrecognized. Erasmus Record added a decorative scroll at the top of his petition to the Upper House. In all other respects it was the same as that produced for the Commons.[167] Record's attitude was unusual, and, no doubt mindful of printing costs, most refrained from extraneous decoration, relying either on no decoration or pre-existing stock images.[168]

Not all petitioners adopted the standard typeface.[169] The most unusual aspect of some of these documents is the use of a form of civilité type, almost indistinguishable from a hand-written manuscript.[170] The first surviving instance of this relating to Parliament is a petition introduced in 1593 from the London Carpenters. This was a single printed sheet, looking like perfectly formed secretary hand, complaining about interlopers in their trade. The Stationers' Company presented the most dramatic example of this font in their condemnation of Martin Boisloré's printing grant in 1621.[171]

Because virtually none of the broadsides bear a printer's mark, it is difficult to establish who controlled the parliamentary trade. But it is possible to build a picture of the broadside business from the few names we have and their relationship with Boisloré, Symcocke, and Wood. Since 1619, Boisloré and his assignees had held the patent for printing on a single side of sheets of paper.[172] This had been a profitable trade that was closely guarded and parceled out between some senior members of the Company. Play bills were controlled by William Jaggard, apprentice indentures by Humphrey Lownes, and briefs for casualties by Thomas Purfoot. The Company, led by Lownes as Master, may also have been truthful in stating that much of this work was sent out to the poorest printers to provide them with financial assistance. The Stationers appealed to the King and an inquiry was set up. Taking the opportunity of Parliament, which was sitting in 1621, the Stationers printed their petition (theoretically this right remained with Boisloré), but the Company 'circumvented' the patent by printing in civilité, making it appear as if it was handwritten.[173] The patentees, Boisloré et al., also distributed printed petitions around Parliament.[174] However, the existence of the grant does not seem to have stopped a number of well-known printers from producing broadsides. Boisloré's patent may account for the fact that so few carried a printer's mark, but certainly William Stansby, William Jones, Jaggard, and Lownes were involved in the trade.[175] Symcocke and Wood may have parceled out for printing the majority of these petitions, and that would account for the large number in 1621, the first Parliament after the patent was issued. Overall, the list of printers producing material concerning events in Parliament or for Parliament consumption includes most of those heavily involved in the political cheap book trade. To those above we can add those who plied the trade in lists of members and catalogues of the nobility, Henry Gosson, Augustine Matthews, and the bookseller Thomas Walkley, who sold an enormous range of political material.

The Stationers also probably encouraged a printed petition against George Wood's grant for printing on linen cloth,[176] suspecting correctly that he would not confine himself to printing only on linen but use his press for paper books. The Company gained the support of the Corporation of London in condemning the patent. While it was not revoked, like the Boisloré grant, a royal proclamation allowed those aggrieved to take remedy by Common Law.[177]

SHIFTING STAGES

The culmination of parliamentary printing before 1640 was the Petition of Right in 1628. The role of the petition in the development of Parliament and publishing was that the order to print it was issued by the Lords with the recommendation of the Commons. The two houses of Parliament, for so long the consumers of print, became the instigators.[178] The matter of the petition has been thoroughly explored elsewhere and requires little telling here. In many ways, the petition simply resembled any other statute, and it was published by the royal printer in the customary fashion. Its printing before the session ended, however, was novel, as was the extraneous material appended to the first print run by the King. By now, the Commons and Lords had already adopted the techniques of publicity. They ordered printed sermons delivered to each House, although this remained firmly in their control and much less controversial than relying on the King and his printer. Charles, after having assented to the petition on 7 June 1628 and agreed to its publication, recalled the fifteen hundred copies already printed, which were 'made waste paper.' He altered the wording to reflect his original unfavorable answer to the Commons and added his own spin: '[S]ince I see that even the House of Commons begins already to make false constructions of what I granted in your petition lest it be worse interpreted in the country I will now make a declaration concerning the true intent thereof.'[179] In this instance, the Crown's hold on print and greater experience in utilizing the medium had stymied the first forays of the Commons and Lords into political print culture. But the idea of responding to the Crown in print was now available to the Houses of Parliament. The growing importance of the public dimension of political debate helped foster tension between the Parliament, or at least parts of the Houses, and the Crown, and led to the beginnings of the battle for control of the print domain that became central in the 1640s.

The Crown through statutes and proclamations had long been the 'parliamentary printer.' James, in particular, had seen print's ideological and political benefits and utilized it from above. Apart from the Crown, though, it was initially those who sued for power, the petitioners and the public, who utilized the medium, rather than those who held power and brokered it, the Lords and Commons. But print crossed these boundaries, gradually becoming in the 1620s an ever-increasing part of normal parliamentary activity. Parliament also became a business opportunity and a chance for profit for cheap print publishers and booksellers, as well as for those inside Parliament, such as Edward Grimston. New patterns of profit motive and public interest emerged in the printed lists of members, sermons, verse addresses, and speeches as Parliament increasingly became a recipient of print. Here, importantly, what is at issue is not Parliament's promulgation of power in print—that is, Parliament does not simply mimic and usurp the earlier royal prerogative of print, merely disseminating its edicts in declamatory fashion. Rather, what is at stake is Parliament's new status as the site of exchange, negotiation, and contestation, enacted via the print medium. Not so much the origin of print in this network of exchange, Parliament was rather the locus of these enactments. Parliament was becoming a center of power in this period, and nowhere is this more evident in the tide of print publication that swept through the institution in the 1620s.

There remains an erroneous idea in much recent scholarship that print plus Parliament equals the 1640s.[180] In fact, the two were inextricably intertwined before then, and what occurred in the 1640s was an adaptation of techniques and practices already in place. Those members of the public in 1628 who wandered the aisles of Saint Paul's Cathedral, frequented the New Exchange, or browsed through the bookshops on Fleet Street could not only hear parliamentary news and business, they could also buy it in print. The relationship between print and Parliament had shifted, and with it the focus, from the royal stage to the public one in the theater of state.

Conclusion

Sir John Eliot's incarceration in the Tower after the 1629 Parliament ended with his death from tuberculosis in November 1632.[1] Unforgiven by Charles, and unrepentant, this 'viper' was interred in the Tower because his family were refused permission to convey his body back to his native Cornwall. Still languishing within the Tower walls were two of his fellow 'snakes,' Benjamin Valentine, who had helped hold the Speaker in his chair, and William Strode, who had frequently and vociferously called for Eliot's paper to be read on 2 March 1629. That day Strode had also insulted the Speaker and impugned Charles, 'that we may not be turned of[f] like scattered sheepe, as we were at the end of the last Session, and have a scorne put upon us in print; but that we may leave something behind us.'[2] Neither was released until shortly before the Short Parliament opened.

Eliot, Strode, and Valentine may have reflected the feelings of many MPs at the dissolution of a Parliament in which neither the vexed issues of religious innovation nor a statutory confirmation of Tunnage and Poundage had been resolved. In fact, all that had been gained was but a vote of subsidies and Charles's deceitful answer to the Petition of Right. It would, however, be anachronistic to suggest that the nine MPs that Charles blamed for the failure of the session represented the attitudes and actions of all members. Nevertheless, Eliot in particular can in some respects be seen as typifying what a Parliament-man could (or had) become by the end of the 1620s. Eliot's parliamentary career started in 1614, when he was elected MP for St. Germans, Cornwall, a borough in which he had substantial landholdings. His first parliamentary session, though, was spent—like that of the vast majority of his fellow MPs—in silence, at least as far as the record indicates.[3]

Eliot's parliamentary career did not resume until the mid-1620s. It is not known whether he stood for election in 1621, but three years later he secured a seat at Newport in Cornwall. Much had of course changed in the intervening ten years. The outbreak of the Thirty Years' War pitted Protestant Europe against Catholic Europe in outright hostilities, a rival power base centered around Prince Charles had emerged to challenge the influence of the aging King, and a new favorite, the Duke of Buckingham, dominated the political scene. For Eliot, now a vice admiral of Devon and a client of Buckingham, Parliament provided a stage on which he could find his voice. It was on 27 February, just over a week into the session, that in the words of Paul Hunneyball, Eliot staged his 'first great *coup de théâtre*.'[4] Eliot embarked upon a lengthy, and much misliked, defense of the liberties of the Commons. His speech, evidently well prepared in advance, propelled into the open the idea of petitioning the King for a specific confirmation of the Commons' liberties and privileges, the exact situation that had caused the King to tear angrily the protestation from the Commons Journal in 1621 and that most MPs wanted buried, at least for the moment. Eliot also called for a general oath of secrecy to be imposed upon MPs, so that 'his Majestie would reject the Whispers of our enemies, or not beleeve them: for t'is those that feare our Parliaments that traduce them, & in the report deforme the priviledges of this place according to theire owne intentions.'[5] Eliot's controversial opening to the Parliament came to little, and the matter was shunted off to committee and away from the floor of the House.[6]

However, Eliot's contribution in 1624 was largely in keeping with the anti-Hapsburg agenda of his patron and the 'patriot coalition.' A fervent supporter of war against Spain and in favor of the impeachment of Lionel Cranfield, the Earl of Middlesex, Eliot's intervention resembled those of many in the House eager to press England into a more aggressive foreign policy.[7] If, despite the occasional misstep, Eliot can be said to have found his feet on the national stage in 1624, then the early Caroline Parliaments witnessed his turn from playing a minor role to being among the leading actors.

In 1625, Eliot was again elected for Newport, and although he was not the most vocal contributor, his interventions were both powerful and significant, especially on 23 June, in a lengthy oration against recusants.[8] Despite his increasing distrust of royal demands for financial assistance, Eliot

largely backed the government agenda and attempted to negotiate a com-
promise between the Crown and Buckingham's call for further subsidies
over and above the two already granted in the first session. Eliot's distaste
for the additional request for supply was evident, but he continued in the
belief that Parliament was necessary to the financing and conduct of the war
when he called for a winter session to continue the discussions.[9] By the time
the 1626 Parliament assembled, Eliot, now the MP for St. Germans, had de-
cisively broken with his patron Buckingham over the disastrous war effort
and the Duke's advancement of more favored clients, especially Sir John
Coke. In total, Eliot gave more than a hundred speeches as he mounted a
vehement attack on Buckingham. Eliot's vitriolic rhetoric throughout the
Parliament eventually pushed Charles over the edge, and after he had delivered a stinging indictment of Buckingham before the Lords on 10 May in
which he compared Buckingham to Sejanus, Eliot was arrested and held in
custody for over a week.[10]

The following year saw Eliot in prison yet again, this time as one of
those who refused to contribute to the Forced Loan. These two spells of
imprisonment did little to dispel Eliot's ardor for the new Parliament to
which he was elected as a Knight of the Shire for Cornwall. In 1626 Eliot's
target was Buckingham and his focus was on ministerial responsibility. Two
years later Eliot returned to the powers of Parliament, arbitrary imprisonment and the redress of grievances. Eliot gave a staggeringly high number
of speeches—172—during the Parliament (1628–29), ranging (as usual by
now) from short, sharp interventions to powerful rhetoric.[11] In his 'great'
speech of 3 June after Charles's dismissive answer to the Petition of Right
the day before, Eliot launched into a series of dangers faced by the kingdom
and called for a Remonstrance to be delivered to Charles. This may have
been the start of debate on a Remonstrance, but the speech was in many
ways the culmination of Eliot's ideas developed over his parliamentary career. Always concerned about the parliamentary liberties of the Commons,
Eliot started by reminding his audience that they sat as the King's Great
Council before he moved on to specific grievances—the increasingly dangerous religious atmosphere as popery crept into the Church, the disastrous military campaigns, and the porous financial position of the Crown.
No doubt remembering his own imprisonment(s), Eliot continued, '[F]or
the oppression of the subject, which as I remember is the next particular
I proposed, that needs no demonstration; the whole kingdom is proof.'[12]
These dangers he thought were like 'that Trojan horse brought in to sur-

prise us.[13] Eliot's speech on 3 June was a tour de force of adversarial rhetoric played out a national stage.

If Eliot embodied many the aspects of parliamentary speech in the 1620s, a mix of powerful adversarial rhetoric, along with the occasional misstep of failing to read the mood of the House,[14] and short, sharp intervention in debate, then in other ways as well he can be seen as an early Stuart Parliament-man. Although he does not appear to have kept a diary of every session, his memoirs written in the Tower, *Negotium Posterorum*, focus upon Parliament. As the editors of *Proceedings in Parliament 1625* noted, Eliot's work differs from most parliamentary diaries offering 'a connoisseur's view of oratorical effect and effectiveness of the speakers he reports on, and with an orator's instinct he caressingly picks up their rhetorical flourishes.'[15] Eliot, too, like many of his fellow MPs, kept copies of his own speeches and numerous parliamentary separates, from the King's addresses to Parliament to the widely circulated speech of Sir Henry Marten in 1628.[16] In addition, in *Negotium*, Eliot compiled his report of 1625 from copies of the Commons Journals and the Committee Book.[17] Again, utilizing by now a widespread practice, Eliot relied on the parliamentary diaries and compilations of others, in particular the 1625 diary of Sir John Pym, which was also possessed by the Earl of Bedford as well as Eliot's friend and correspondent while in the Tower, Richard Knightly, and Oliver St. John.[18]

No one MP among the 1,782 who sat in the early Stuart Commons could ever embody all the differing aspects of the political and material culture of Parliaments described in this book, which is primarily a study of the institution rather than the individual actors, and Eliot was not involved in lobbying (at least not in the practical ways noted in Chapter Five), nor were his speeches published until 1641, when his oration of 29 January 1629 against Arminianism was printed.[19] But for a powerful adversarial rhetorician, a noisy perturber of the peace, diarist, and collector of parliamentary material, Parliament was the theater in which Eliot stood prominently, controversially, center stage.

Although recent work has de-emphasized the relationship between Parliament and the theater,[20] this book has demonstrated that the two institutions constitute structurally analogous configurations of issues and audience in the post-Reformation public sphere. The foreign policy of England in the 1620s and its relationship to Spain were debated at length in the chambers and played out on the stage in *A Game at Chess*, the most popular production of the 1620s.[21] In 1628, only a fortnight before his assassination, the Duke of Buckingham sponsored and attended a revival of Shakespeare's *Henry VIII* at the Globe as a means of rebuilding his political reputation and popularity as a wrongly maligned favorite.[22] Through the lists of MPs and peers, the *dramatis personae* of Parliament in the 1620s were for sale in the bookshops of London, and, mimicking the techniques of memorialization from which many play texts found their way into print, auditors copied, disseminated, printed, and sold the words coming from the stages of Parliament. An audience convened around the doors and during high moments of political drama, such as the trial in Westminster Hall of the Gunpowder plotters in 1605, that audience even had to pay for their seats.[23] Parliament had become the *Theater of State*.

The decade of this transformation was the 1620s. No doubt, the frequency of meetings (eight sessions in nine years) helped establish an institutional memory, but the decade also marked a watershed in the way that Parliament operated. Opening in 1621 with the revival of the House of Lords as a judicial tribunal, the resumption of the process of impeachment provided an avenue for those in Parliament to attack government ministers. They did so successfully in 1621 with the fall of Lord Chancellor Bacon, and in 1624, in a campaign orchestrated by the Duke of Buckingham, with Lord Treasurer Cranfield.[24] As Buckingham found to his cost, however, impeachment was a double-edged sword, and after his fall from public favor in the mid-1620s, he became the target of impeachment proceedings that ultimately led to the failure and dissolution of the 1626 Parliament. These were very public matters that cut to the very heart of royal government. But the judicial process was taken a step further in 1621 with the trial of the notorious projector, Sir Giles Mompesson. Amid growing condemnation in the country at large at the egregious grants of monopoly patents, the Commons levied charges against one of its own; Mompesson had been elected as an MP for Great Bedwyn. However, Mompesson 'shed a faire paire of heeles'[25] and fled to France rather than wait around for his punishment when the Commons sent a lengthy list of offenses to the Lords, who, acting in their capacity as the highest court in the land, imposed a £10,000 fine and ordered him imprisoned for life. Parliament's attack on Mompesson quickly became a very public event, illustrated in an elaborate engraving for sale under the title *The description of Giles Mompesson late Knight censured by Parliament*.[26] Falling from grace the same year and also humiliated in print, Sir Francis Michell likewise fell afoul of the Commons' investigation into patent abuses. Michell was roundly condemned in a printed ballad while he, along with Mompesson and Bacon, all found themselves the scurrilous talk of the town and the subject of various libels.[27] In 1621 then, Parliament was already the focus of gossip and news, as its deliberations and judgments lay in the bookshops of London.

Away from high matters of state, the Lords judicature filtered down into the general population as the Upper House once again resumed the role of an appellate court, a process that had lain dormant since 1589.[28] Although the Lords formally accepted only twelve cases in 1621 (another sixteen were received), the practical effect of this was that Parliament was made more public as it started to serve a wider constituency—namely, those with appeal claims from the lower courts, their counsel, witnesses, and opponents. The popularity of this process is reflected in the 400 percent increase in cases in 1624 and its continuing rise throughout the 1620s.

If the Lords in 1621 took on more business, then so too did the Commons. The grievances of the nation played out not only in the flood of legislation that arrived in the Commons but also in how the Lower House handled grievances. This was in part due to the crisis over monopolies. Encouraged by the Commons' investigation into royal grants of monopoly, many who petitioned parliament for relief mounted a two-pronged strategy, submitting legislation as well as a petition to the Grievances Committee.[29] This had the effect of increasing the number of people who viewed Parliament as a remedy for individual, local and national grievances, and thus those who stalked the corridors of power around the chambers. Along with the scribes who wrote out breviates, legislation, and petitions to Parliament, printers churned out hundreds of copies of documents addressed to Parliament, some for sale and others to be distributed to MPs and peers at the doors of the chambers. The social milieu of Parliament filled the lodgings in Westminster and London, while MPs dined and discussed parliamentary business in the taverns and inns of the metropolis.[30] Families and servants traveled with many MPs, using the opportunity of being in London to shop and meet friends and relatives. Parliament also provided a social occasion for MPs themselves, be it through meeting other MPs who were friends and relatives, or socializing together. Parliament had taken over both Westminster and London.

The 1621 Parliament ended in acrimony as James tore the words and deliberations of the Commons from their official journal with his own hands.[31] But this act of physical destruction could erase neither the collective memory nor the copies of the Protestation in circulation. While the

1621 Parliament was remarkably inefficient in solving the legislative necessities of the nation (a matter partly remedied by its successor three years
later), it had nonetheless opened up new avenues of debate and redress,
which Parliament showed no signs of wanting to close as the 1620s wore
on. This pattern of engagement continued and intensified in the course
of the decade. As the foreign policy debates of the early 1620s turned into
war against the European superpowers, France and Spain, after Charles I's
succession to the throne in 1625, so Parliament found itself financing defeat
instead of victory and agonizing over the causes of that ignominy. Adding
to the immediacy and intensity of the debate, a vocal part of the governing
class, and one well-represented in Parliament, feared a shift toward a more
tolerant policy toward Catholicism and the rise of Arminianism within
royal and clerical circles. The foreign policy crisis, the conduct of the war,
and religious debates brought into sharp focus the constitutional powers
of the monarchy and the rights and liberties of Parliament. Debates that
took place in Parliament and were circulated, read, and then copied in the
country, enhancing the reach and intensity of the post-Reformation public
sphere and the centrality of Parliament to that sphere.

By 1629, the flow of information from the center to the periphery was
uncontrolled and uncontrollable—at least while Parliament was sitting.
However, the last Parliament of the 1620s was dissolved by proclamation
on 2 March 1629,[32] and on 27 March another proclamation was issued 'for
suppressing of false rumours touching Parliament.'[33] Yet even such temporary stops in the flow of information now constituted news to be reported.
As one letter writer informed Sir Simonds D'Ewes, 'I having taken the liberty of silence which you pleased to graunt I shall certify you what newes
wee have though it be not much; for the Proclamation (you know) stopps
our mouths for talking of Parliament.'[34] The 'giddy-headed multitude,' or
at least those not imprisoned by Charles, had returned to their homes in
the country, carrying with them printed and scribal accounts from the Parliament.[35] With the dissolution, Charles ushered in what would become
the eleven years of 'personal rule,' in which he governed England without
recourse to Parliament. But it was too late. By then, Parliament had turned
into the focal point of the political nation and in doing so had moved from
being an institutional event into an institution, albeit it one that could still
be dissolved at the whim of the monarch. It had developed to an extraordinary degree an institutional memory that was not eradicated by this enforced hiatus.

Conrad Russell placed the blame for the personal rule and the lack of Parliaments between 1629 and 1640 squarely on the failure of Parliament to fulfill one of its primary roles, providing finance for the Crown.[36] This, however, is only part of the story. More important, the Crown dispensed with Parliament because it was too powerful and too popular. Parliament had become the center of the post-Reformation public sphere. As Peter Lake and Steven Pincus have argued, '[T]he quantitative expansion of the public sphere in England's early modern period necessarily meant that an increasingly wide array of people was brought within the nexus of political communication.'[37] This book has argued for the creation of this public sphere in the 1620s, and yet it is a story for which the past is not, perhaps, prologue. Many of the elements of Parliament we are familiar with from the early 1640s, arguments between a section of the governing class and courtiers, the circulation and printing of parliamentary speeches, the importance of petitioning, the involvement of the wider political nation and a dissemination of parliamentary ideas and documents, were simply picked up and expanded from their counterparts twenty years earlier. We can see this as well in the multitude and circulation of parliamentary diaries and in the popularity of what Richard Cust has termed 'the public man'—the most popular of actors in the chambers whose speeches everyone recorded and purchased, as well as in note-taking and the daily reporting of business from inside the chambers.[38] Crucially, however, in the 1620s these devices were employed to publicize and manipulate those *inside* the chambers. This is in stark contrast to the postrevolutionary public sphere of the 1640s that manipulated and sought to control public opinion at large, especially after the breakdown of state censorship in the early 1640s. Parliaments in the 1640s were the recipients of mass petitions from the countryside, they were involved in a printed war of words, and they sustained propaganda campaigns—the factors that distinguished Parliament in 1641–42 from its antecedents and emerged as a breakdown in the relationship between segments of the governing class and the Crown that led to civil war and the establishment of Parliament as the executive. The difference between the 1620s and 1640s, then, is more than simply one of scale. But Parliament in the 1620s did inaugurate an institutional dynamic that, as it would again twenty years later, take on a public life of its own.

REFERENCE MATTER

Abbreviations

Add.	Additional Manuscript, British Library
BIHR	*Bulletin of the Institute of Historical Research*
APC	*Acts of the Privy Council*
BL	British Library, London
CJ	*Journals of the House of Commons*
CLRO	Corporation of London Record Office
CRO	County Record Office
CSP Dom.	*Calendar of State Papers Domestic*
CSP Ven.	*Calendar of State Papers Venetian*
GL	Guildhall Library, London
HJ	*Historical Journal*
HLQ	*Huntington Library Quarterly*
HLRO	House of Lords Record Office (Parliamentary Archives)
HMC	*Historical Manuscripts Commission*
HR	*Historical Research*
HPT	History of Parliament Trust
JBS	*Journal of British Studies*
KSRL	Kenneth Spencer Research Library, Kansas
LJ	*Journals of the House of Lords*
LPL	Lambeth Palace Library
ODNB	*Oxford Dictionary of National Biography*
PH	*Parliamentary History*
RO	Record Office
TNA	The National Archives, London
TRHS	*Transactions of the Royal Historical Society*

Notes

INTRODUCTION

1. *The Proceeding of the parliament being this day related to the King* . . . (London, 1628), *STC* 24739; Robert C. Johnson, Mary Frear Keeler, Maija Jansson Cole, and William B. Bidwell, eds., *Commons Debates and Lords Proceedings 1628* (6 vols., New Haven, 1977–83), II, pp. 411–12, 416.

2. On the idea of Parliament as a 'point of contact,' see G. R. Elton, 'Tudor Government, the Points of Contact, 1: Parliament,' *Transactions of the Royal Historical Society* (5th ser., 24, 1974), pp. 183–200; Kevin Sharpe, 'Crown, Parliament and Locality: Government and Communication in Early Stuart England,' *English Historical Review* (101, 1986), pp. 321–50; and Robert Tittler, 'Elizabethan Towns and the "Points of Contact,"' *Parliamentary History* (8, 2, 1989), pp. 275–88.

3. Vernon F. Snow, ed., *Parliament in Elizabethan England: John Hooker's Order and Usage* (New Haven, 1977), p. 163.

4. On popularity, see Thomas Cogswell, 'The People's Love: The Duke of Buckingham and Popularity,' in Thomas Cogswell, Richard Cust, and Peter Lake, eds., *Politics, Religion and Popularity in Early Stuart Britain: Essays in Honour of Conrad Russell* (Cambridge, 2002), pp. 211–34; Cogswell, 'The Politics of Propaganda: Charles I and the People in the 1620s,' *Journal of British Studies* (29, 3, 1990), pp. 187–215; Cogswell, 'John Felton, Popular Political Culture, and the Assassination of the Duke of Buckingham,' *HJ* (49, 2, 2006), pp. 357–85; Thomas Cogswell and Peter Lake, 'Buckingham Does the Globe: *Henry VIII* and the Politics of Popularity in the 1620s,' *Shakespeare Quarterly* (60, 3, 2009), pp. 253–78; Richard Cust, 'Charles I and Popularity,' in Cogswell, Cust, and Lake, *Politics, Religion and Popularity in Early Stuart Britain*, pp. 235–58; Cust, '"Patriots" and "Popular" Spirits: Narratives of Conflict in Early Stuart Politics,' in Nicholas Tyacke, ed., *The English Revolution c.1590–1720: Politics, Religion and Communities* (Manchester, 2007), pp. 43–61; Joad Raymond, 'Describing Popularity in Early Modern England,' *HLQ* (67, 1, 2004),

pp. 101–29; Paul E. J. Hammer, 'The Smiling Crocodile: The Earl of Essex and Late-Elizabethan Popularity,' in Peter Lake and Steven Pincus, eds., *The Politics of the Public Sphere in Early Modern England* (Manchester, 2007), pp. 95–115; and Peter Lake, 'The Politics of "Popularity" and the Public Sphere: The Monarchial Republic of Elizabeth I Defends Itself,' in Lake and Pincus, *Politics of the Public Sphere*, pp. 59–94.

5. Alastair Bellany, *The Politics of Court Scandal in Early Modern England* (Cambridge, 2002); Tom Cogswell, *The Blessed Revolution: English Politics and the Coming of War* (Cambridge, 1989); Richard Cust, '"Patriots" and "Popular" Spirits: Narratives of Conflict in Early Stuart Politics,' in Tyacke, *The English Revolution*, pp. 43–61; Cust, *The Forced Loan and English Politics 1626–1628* (Oxford, 1987); Cust, 'News and Politics in Early Seventeenth-Century England,' in Margo Todd, ed., *Reformation to Revolution: Politics and Religion in Early Modern England* (London and New York: Routledge, 1995), pp. 232–51.

6. J. E. Neale, *The Elizabethan House of Commons* (London, 1949); Wallace Notestein and Frances Helen Relf, eds., *Commons Debates for 1629* (Minneapolis, 1921).

7. The major work on the 1620s Parliaments remains Conrad Russell, *Parliaments and English Politics 1621–1629* (Oxford, 1979). On individual Parliaments, see Robert Zaller, *The Parliament of 1621: A Study in Constitutional Conflict* (Berkeley, 1971); Robert E. Ruigh, *The Parliament of 1624: Politics and Foreign Policy* (Cambridge, MA, 1971); Cogswell, *Blessed Revolution*; and Chris R. Kyle, '*Lex Loquens*: Legislation in the Parliament of 1624' (Ph.D. diss., Auckland University, 1994). See also David L. Smith, *The Stuart Parliaments, 1603–1689* (London, 1999); Elizabeth Read Foster, *The House of Lords, 1603–1649* (Chapel Hill, NC, 1983); Cust, *Forced Loan*; David Colclough, *Freedom of Speech in Early Stuart England* (Cambridge, 2005), ch. 3; Oliver Arnold, *The Third Citizen: Shakespeare's Theater of the Early Modern House of Commons* (Baltimore, 2007); James S. Hart, *Justice upon Petition: The House of Lords and the Reformation of Justice 1621–1675* (London, 1991); Conrad Russell, *Unrevolutionary England 1603–1642* (London, 1990); L. J. Reeve, *Charles I and the Road to Personal Rule* (Cambridge, 1989); Kevin Sharpe, ed., *Faction and Parliament: Essays on Early Stuart History* (Oxford, 1978); Sharpe, *The Personal Rule of Charles I* (New Haven, 1992), part I; Chris R. Kyle and Jason Peacey, eds., *Parliament at Work: Parliamentary Committees, Political Power and Public Access in Early Modern England* (Woodbridge, 2002); Derek Hirst, *The Representative of the People?: Voters and Voting under the Early Stuarts* (Cambridge, 1975); Mark Kishlansky, *Parliamentary Selection: Social and Political Choice in Early Modern England* (Cambridge, 1986); Robert Zaller, *The Discourse of Legitimacy in Early Modern England* (Stanford, 2007), ch. 7; and George Yerby, *People and Parliament: Representative Rights and the English Revolution* (Basingstoke, 2008).

8. On the 1640s, see Jason Peacey, *Politicians and Pamphleteers: Propaganda during the English Civil Wars and Interregnum* (Aldershot, 2004). On the events leading up to these developments, see, in particular, David Cressy, *England on Edge: Crisis*

and Revolution 1640–1642 (Oxford, 2006); David Scott, *Politics and War in the Three Stuart Kingdoms, 1637–1642* (Basingstoke, 2003); Conrad Russell, *The Causes of the English Civil War: The Ford Lectures delivered at the University of Oxford, 1987–1988* (Oxford, 1990); and Russell, *The Fall of the British Monarchies* (Oxford, 1991).

9. This delineation between the early Stuart Parliaments and the 1640s is most apparent in Smith, *Stuart Parliaments,* which also treats the Short Parliament of 1640 as a part of the 'Early Stuart Parliaments.'

10. Peter Lake and Steven Pincus, 'Rethinking the Public Sphere in Early Modern England,' in Lake and Pincus, eds., *The Politics of the Public Sphere in Early Modern England* (Manchester, 2007), pp. 1–30. See also David Zaret, *Origins of Democratic Culture: Printing, Petitions and the Public Sphere in Early-Modern England* (Princeton, 2000); Zaret, 'Petitioning Places and the Credibility of Opinion in the Public Sphere in Seventeenth-Century England,' in Beat A. Kümin, ed., *Political Space in Pre-Industrial Europe* (Farnham, 2009), pp. 175–96; Harold Love, *Scribal Publication in Seventeenth Century England* (Oxford, 1993); Alexandra Halasz, *The Marketplace of Print: Pamphlets and the Public Sphere in Early Modern England* (Cambridge, 1997); Conal Condren, 'Public, Private and the Idea of the Public Sphere in Early Modern England,' *Intellectual History Review* (19, 1, 2009), pp. 15–28; and Anthony Milton, 'Marketing a Massacre: Amboyna, the East India Company and the Public Sphere in Early Modern England,' in Lake and Pincus, *Politics of the Public Sphere,* pp. 168–90.

11. Lake and Pincus, *Politics of the Public Sphere,* p. 9.

12. S. T. Bindoff, ed., *The House of Commons 1509–1558* (3 vols., London, 1982); P. W. Hasler, ed., *The House of Commons 1558–1603* (3 vols., London, 1981); Andrew Thrush and J. P. Ferris, eds., *The House of Commons, 1604–1629* (6 vols., Cambridge, 2010); B. D. Henning, ed., *The House of Commons 1660–1690* (3 vols., London, 1983). Volumes in progress include 1640–1660 under the editorship of Stephen Roberts. See also Williams M. Mitchell, *The Rise of the Revolutionary Party in the English House of Commons 1603–1629* (New York, 1957); and David Harris Willson, *The Privy Councillors in the House of Commons, 1604–1629* (New York, 1971).

13. Peter Mack, *Elizabethan Rhetoric: Theory and Practice* (Cambridge, 2002), p. 215.

14. *LJ,* IV, p. 43.

15. M. F. Keeler, 'The Emergence of Standing Committees for Privileges and Returns,' *PH* (1, 1982), pp. 25–46; Russell, *Parliaments and English Politics,* pp. 38–41; Foster, *House of Lords,* pp. 111–16; Sheila Lambert, 'Procedure in the House of Commons in the Early Stuart Period,' *English Historical Review* (95, 1980), pp. 759–60.

16. Keith Thomas, 'The Place of Laughter in Tudor and Stuart England,' *Times Literary Supplement,* 21 January 1977, pp. 77–81; Quentin Skinner, 'Why Does Laughter Matter to Philosophy?' Passmore Lecture, Australian National University, December 2000. See also Sammy Basu, "'A Little Discourse *Pro & Con*": Levelling Laughter and Its Puritan Criticism.' *International Review of Social History, Supplement* (15, 2007), pp. 95–113.

17. There is very little work on the concept of silence in Tudor and Stuart England. For an analysis of the use of silence in drama, see Christina Luckyj, *A Moving Rhetoricke: Gender and Silence in Early Modern England* (Manchester, 2002).

18. See, for example, his 1624 diaries, BL, Add. 26639; Northamptonshire County Record Office, Finch-Hatton MS. 50.

19. Wiltshire CRO, unnumbered MS.

20. Wallace Notestein, Frances Helen Relf, and Hartley Simpson, eds., *Commons Debates 1621* (7 vols., New Haven, 1935); Thomas Tyrwhitt, ed., *Proceedings and Debates in the House of Commons in 1620 and 1621 by Edward Nicholas* (2 vols., Oxford, 1766). Proceedings and diaries have been published for all the early Stuart Parliaments except 1624. See Chris R. Kyle, ed., *Parliament, Politics and Elections, 1604–1648* (Camden Society, 5th ser., 17, 2001); David Harris Willson, ed., *The Parliamentary Diary of Robert Bowyer 1606–1607* (New York, 1971); Elizabeth Read Foster, ed., *Proceedings in Parliament 1610* (2 vols., New Haven, 1966); Maija Jansson, ed., *Proceedings in Parliament 1614* (Philadelphia, 1988); Maija Jansson and William B. Bidwell, eds., *Proceedings in Parliament 1625* (New Haven, 1987); William B. Bidwell and Maija Jansson, eds., *Proceedings in Parliament 1626* (4 vols., New Haven, 1991–96); Johnson, Cole, Keeler, and Bidwell, eds., *Commons Debates and Lords Proceedings 1628* (6 vols., New Haven, 1977–83); and Notestein and Relf, eds., *Commons Debates for 1629*. For other individual diaries, see Lady Evangeline De Villiers, 'The Hastings Journal of the Parliament of 1621,' *Camden Miscellany XX* (Camden, 3rd ser., 1953); Samuel Rawson Gardiner, ed., *Parliamentary Debates in 1610* (Camden, old ser., 81, 1862); Gardiner, ed., *Notes of the Debates in the House of Lords . . . 1621* (Camden, old ser., 103, 1870); Gardiner, *Notes of the Debates in the House of Lords . . . 1624 and 1626* (Camden, new ser., 24, 1879); David R. Ransome, ed., 'The Parliamentary Papers of Nicholas Ferrar, 1624,' *Camden Miscellany XXXIII* (Camden, 5th ser., 7, 1996); Christopher Thompson, ed., *The Holles Account of Proceedings in the House of Commons in 1624* (Orsett, Essex, 1985); and Thompson, ed., *Sir Nathaniel Rich's Diary of Proceedings in the House of Commons in 1624* (Orsett, Essex, 1985).

21. Cust, 'News and Politics in Early Seventeenth Century England,' pp. 60–90; Fritz Levy, 'How Information Spread amongst the Gentry, 1550–1640,' *JBS* (21, 1982), pp. 11–34; Notestein and Relf, *Commons Debates for 1629*, Introduction.

22. See Joad Raymond, *The Invention of the Newspaper* (Oxford, 1996), pp. 100–108, 130–33.

23. See John Norden's description of the city in 1592 in William Benchley Rye, *England as Seen by Foreigners* (reprint New York, 1967), pp. 93–97.

24. David M. Dean, 'Parliament, Privy Council, and Local Politics in Elizabethan England: The Yarmouth-Lowestoft Fishing Dispute,' *Albion* (22, 1990), pp. 39–64; Dean, 'London Lobbies and Parliament: The Case of the Brewers and Coopers in the Parliament of 1593,' *Parliamentary History* (8, 1989), pp. 341–65; Dean, 'Public or Private? London, Leather and Legislation in Elizabethan England,' *HJ* (31, 1988), pp. 525–48; Dean, 'Pressure Groups and Lobbies in the Elizabethan and Early Jacobean Parliaments,' *Parliaments, Estates and Representation* (11, 1991), pp.

139–52; Ian Archer, 'The London Lobbies in the Sixteenth Century,' *HJ* (31, 1988), pp. 17–44; Edwin Green, 'The Vintners' Lobby, 1552–1568,' *Guildhall Studies in London History* (1, 2, 1974), pp. 47–58.

25. See Chris R. Kyle, 'From Broadside to Pamphlet: Print and Parliament in the Late 1620s,' *PH* (26, 1, 2007), pp. 17–29.

26. James F. Larkin, ed., *Stuart Royal Proclamations, Volume II, Royal Proclamations of King Charles I 1625–1646* (Oxford, 1983), nos. 108, 110.

1. 'FITTEST SPEECH': RHETORIC AND DEBATE

1. William B. Bidwell and Maija Jansson, eds., *Proceedings in Parliament 1626* (New Haven, 1992), II, p. 308.

2. Robert C. Johnson, Mary Frear Keeler, Maija Jansson Cole, and William B. Bidwell, eds., *Commons Debates and Lords Proceedings 1628* (New Haven, 1977), III, p. 542.

3. Elizabeth Read Foster, 'Speaking in the House of Commons,' *BIHR* (43, 1970), p. 52.

4. I am grateful for the comments of Markku Peltonen and Tom Cogswell on this chapter.

5. Mary Dewar, ed., *De Republica Anglorum by Sir Thomas Smith* (Cambridge, 1982), p. 82.

6. Foster, 'Speaking in the House of Commons,' p. 52.

7. Dewar, *De Republica Anglorum*, pp. 82–83.

8. Elizabeth Read Foster, *The House of Lords 1603–1649* (Chapel Hill, 1983), pp. 25–26; *HMC House of Lords*, X, pp. 1–11.

9. Vernon F. Snow, ed., *Parliament in Elizabethan England: John Hooker's Order and Usage* (New Haven, 1977), p. 151.

10. On freedom of speech in early Stuart Parliaments, see David Colclough, *Freedom of Speech in Early Stuart England* (Cambridge, 2005), pp. 120–95; Harold Hulme, 'The Winning of Freedom of Speech by the House of Commons,' *American Historical Review* (61, 4, 1956), pp. 825–53; J. E. Neale, 'The Commons Privilege of Free Speech in Parliament,' in R. W. Seton-Watson, ed., *Tudor Studies presented to . . . Albert Frederick Pollard* (London, 1924), pp. 257–86; J. H. Hexter, 'Introduction,' in Hexter, ed., *Parliament and Liberty from the Reign of Elizabeth to the English Civil War* (Stanford, 1992), pp. 1–19; and Christopher Thompson, *The Debate on Freedom of Speech in the House of Commons in February 1621* (Orsett, 1985).

11. Dewar, *De Republica Anglorum*, p. 166.

12. Peter Mack, *Elizabethan Rhetoric: Theory and Practice* (Cambridge, 2002), p. 23.

13. Ibid., p. 13.

14. Bruce R. Smith, *The Acoustic World of Early Modern England* (Chicago, 1999), p. 248.

15. See Chapter Five for the impact of lobbying by interest groups.

16. Johnson, Keeler, Cole, and Bidwell, *Commons Debates and Lords Proceedings 1628*, IV, p. 232.

17. Carleton's speech was given on 30 April 1607, and Wingfield's comment was the following day (1 May). David Harris Willson, ed., *The Parliamentary Diary of Robert Bowyer* (New York, 1971), pp. 278–80, 284.

18. Mack, *Elizabethan Rhetoric*, p. 217.

19. *CJ*, I, p. 743.

20. See below, pp. 65, 68, 76, 77.

21. Catherine Strateman Sims, 'The Speaker of the House of Commons: An Early Seventeenth Century Tractate,' *American Historical Review* (45, 1, 1939), pp. 90–95.

22. Quoted in J. E. Neale, *The Elizabethan House of Commons* (London, 1949), p. 355.

23. Ibid., pp. 354–55; *HMC Rep. IX*, II, p. 373.

24. *HMC Finch*, I, pp. 43–44.

25. Snow, *Parliament in Elizabethan England*, p. 165.

26. *CJ*, I, p. 541.

27. D. H. Willson, *The Privy Councillors in the House of Commons, 1604–1629* (Minneapolis, 1940), pp. 217–25; Ian H. C. Fraser, 'The Agitation in the Commons, 2 March 1629, and the Interrogation of the Leaders of the Anti-Court Group,' *BIHR* (30, 1957), pp. 86–95.

28. A 1628 compilation of parliamentary materials refers to it as both 'The Speakers Excusatory Speech' and 'The Speakers Progression.' Exeter College Library, Oxford, MS 100, vol. 1, f. 303.

29. In 1604, however, a lack of organization led to 'some silence' after the question was asked, and when Sir Edward Phelips's name was finally mentioned, other names were also called out or 'muttered,' as the clerk wrote in his journal. *CJ*, I, p. 141.

30. T. E. Hartley, *Proceedings in the Parliaments of Elizabeth I* (Leicester, 1995), III, p. 282. This is a description of the procedure carried out in 1601.

31. Mack, *Elizabethan Rhetoric*, esp. p. 36.

32. Pisander was an Athenian citizen who opposed Athenian democracy in 412/411 BCE, seeking help from the Persian king and the recall of Alcibiades to lead the Athenian military forces. At this time he proposed abolishing the democracy, which led to the short-lived oligarchic 'Rule of the 400.' Robert B. Strassler, ed., *The Landmark Thucydides* (New York, 1996), 8.49.1, 8.53.1–3. He was accused by Aristophanes of seeking office out of personal greed. Aristophanes, *Lysistrata*, ed. and trans. Jeffrey Henderson (Loeb Classical Library, 179, Cambridge MA, 2000), ll, pp. 490–91. I am grateful to Craige Champion for his assistance with this reference.

33. *CJ*, I, pp. 146–47.

34. Simon Healy, 'Debates in the House of Commons, 1604–1607,' in Chris R.

Kyle, ed., *Parliament, Politics and Elections, 1604–1648* (Camden Society, 5th ser., 17, Cambridge, 2002), p. 53.

35. P. W. Hasler, ed., *The House of Commons 1558–1603* (London, 1981), I, p. 422. For Bell's speech, see Hartley, *Proceedings in the Parliaments of Elizabeth I,* I, pp. 339–41. Cambridge University Library, MS ff. 5.14 (*Lewd Pasquil*).

36. Bidwell and Jansson, *Proceedings in Parliament 1626,* I, p. 30.

37. William Lenthall, *Mr Speaker his Speech to his Majestie in the High Court of Parliament, the fifth of November, 1640* (London, 1640), sig. A2, *STC* 15462.3.

38. Ibid., sig. A4.

39. Hartley, *Proceedings in the Parliaments of Elizabeth I,* II, pp. 474, 475.

40. I am grateful to Markku Peltonen for his assistance with this passage. For a clear and succinct discussion of commonplaces, see Mack, *Elizabethan Rhetoric,* pp. 43–44.

41. Hartley, *Proceedings in the Parliaments of Elizabeth I,* II, p. 480.

42. Ibid., III, p. 223 (my italics).

43. Ibid., p. 144.

44. Ibid., p. 310.

45. Ibid., p. 368.

46. Stanford E. Lehmberg, *The Reformation Parliament, 1529–1536* (Cambridge, 1970), p. 171.

47. Ibid., pp. 196–97.

48. Hartley, *Proceedings in the Parliaments of Elizabeth I,* I, p. 410; II, p. 115.

49. Wallace Notestein, Frances Helen Relf, and Hartley Simpson, eds., *Commons Debates 1621* (New Haven, 1935), II, p. 95.

50. Ibid., pp. 21, 70.

51. See below, Chapter Three. On the use of rhetoric more broadly in Parliament, see Markku Peltonen, *Rhetoric, Politics and Popularity in Pre-revolutionary England* (forthcoming).

52. Hartley, *Proceedings in the Parliaments of Elizabeth I,* III, p. 432.

53. Ibid., p. 486 (17 December 1601).

54. Hasler, *HPT 1558–1603,* I, p. 98.

55. Figures calculated from Johnson, Keeler, Cole, and Bidwell, *Commons Debates and Lords Proceedings 1628.*

56. Catherine Strateman Sims, ed., '"Policies in Parliaments": An Early Seventeenth Century Tractate on House of Commons Procedure,' *HLQ* (15, 1, 1951), p. 47.

57. Healy, 'Debates in the House of Commons, 1604–1607,' p. 58.

58. Maija Jansson, ed., *Proceedings in Parliament 1614* (Philadelphia, 1988), p. 191. It is not evident who the clerk thought was above Bacon in the eloquence stakes.

59. Maija Jansson and William B. Bidwell, eds., *Proceedings in Parliament 1625* (New Haven, 1987), p. 516.

60. Ibid., p. 539.

61. Elizabeth Read Foster, ed., *Proceedings in Parliament 1610* (New Haven, 1966), II, p. 92.

62. *CJ*, I, p. 172.

63. Robert C. Johnson, Mary Frear Keeler, Maija Jansson Cole, and William B. Bidwell, eds., *Commons Debates and Lords Proceedings 1628* (6 vols., New Haven, 1977–83), II, p. 374, VI, p. 183; *CJ*, I, p. 881.

64. BL, Add. 30197, f. 6.

65. Jansson, *Proceedings in Parliament 1614*, p. 107.

66. Purveyance was the disputed prerogative right of the monarch to buy household supplies at below market rates. See Pauline Croft, 'Parliament, Purveyance and the City of London, 1559–1608,' *Parliamentary History* (4, 1985), pp. 9–34; Eric Lindquist, 'The King, the People and the House of Commons: The Problem of Early Jacobean Purveyance,' *HJ* (31, 3, 1988), pp. 549–70; and Lindquist, 'Supplement: The Bills against Purveyors,' *PH* (4, 1985), pp. 35–43.

67. *CJ*, I, pp. 162, 226, 396, 399, 406; Healy, 'Debates in the House of Commons, 1604–1607,' p. 63.

68. Andrew Thrush and J. P. Ferris, eds., *The House of Commons 1604–1629* (6 vols., Cambridge, 2010), Sir George Chaworth.

69. Clarke was referring to Sir Edward Coke's attack on Buckingham the previous day. Clarke was a client of Buckingham. Jansson and Bidwell, *Proceedings in Parliament 1625*, pp. 413, 418.

70. Ibid., p. 426.

71. Thomas Tyrwhitt, ed., *Proceedings and Debates in the House of Commons in 1620 and 1621 by Edward Nicholas* (2 vols., Oxford, 1766), I, p. 45; *CJ*, I, p. 521.

72. Notestein, Relf, and Simpson, *Commons Debates 1621*, IV, p. 53. Nicholas also mentions that Sheppard accused Earle of being a 'perturbator of the Peace,' adding 'and a Puritan.'

73. Ibid.

74. E. S. De Beer, ed., *The Diary and Correspondence of John Evelyn* (London, 1889), IV, p. 303.

75. See Chapter Two.

76. BL, Add. 34218, f. 21v.

77. Letter, possibly from Christopher Brooke, to John Donne. Sir Toby Matthew, *A collection of letters, made by Sr Tobie Mathews Kt. With a character of the most excellent lady, Lucy, Countesse of Carleile: by the same author. To which are added many letters of his own, to severall persons of honour, who were contemporary with him* (London, 1660), p. 293. See also P. B. Whitt, 'New Light on Sir William Cornwallis,' *Review of English Studies* (8, 30, 1932), pp. 155–69.

78. Lehmberg, *Reformation Parliament*, p. 125.

79. Hartley, *Proceedings in the Parliaments of Elizabeth I*, I, p. 202.

80. Willson, *The Parliamentary Diary of Robert Bowyer*, p. 1.

81. *CJ*, II, p. 8.

82. Willson, *The Parliamentary Diary of Robert Bowyer*, p. 7.

83. Ibid., p. 61.

84. Notestein, Relf, and Simpson, *Commons Debates 1621*, IV, p. 439. Quoted in Conrad Russell, *Unrevolutionary England, 1603–1642* (London, 1990), p. 68.

85. Willson, *The Parliamentary Diary of Robert Bowyer*, pp. 279–80.

86. See below, p. 29.

87. Sir James Perrot speaking: 5 May 1604; *CJ*, I, p. 199.

88. Sir Francis Goodwin: 15 April 1606: *CJ*, I, p. 298.

89. Ibid., p. 536.

90. Hartley, *Proceedings in the Parliaments of Elizabeth I*, I, pp. 34–35. Quoted in Mack, *Elizabethan Rhetoric*, p. 220 n. 16.

91. Neale, *Elizabethan House of Commons*, p. 404.

92. Dewar, *De Republica Anglorum*, p. 166 n. 56.

93. *CJ*, I, p. 358.

94. Ibid. For the entire speech, see pp. 357–63.

95. Jansson, *Proceedings in Parliament 1614*, p. 327.

96. Folger Shakespeare Library, V.b.189, p. 70.

97. Tyrwhitt, *Edward Nicholas, Proceedings and Debates in the House of Commons*, II, p. 219.

98. Foster, 'Speaking in the Commons,' p. 55 n. 2.

99. I am grateful to Peter Stallybrass for a discussion of this matter.

100. Hartley, *Proceedings in the Parliaments of Elizabeth I*, I, p. 344.

101. Willson, *The Parliamentary Diary of Robert Bowyer*, p. 345. I am grateful to Andrew Thrush for this reference.

102. Jansson and Bidwell, *Proceedings in Parliament 1625*, p. 507.

103. Hartley, *Proceedings in the Parliaments of Elizabeth I*, I, p. 223.

104. Ibid., p. 312.

105. Quoted in Neale, *Elizabethan House of Commons*, p. 411.

106. Quoted in ibid., p. 410.

107. Hartley, *Proceedings in the Parliaments of Elizabeth I*, II, p. 109.

108. On the writing of diaries and recording of notes in the chamber, see Chapter Three.

109. Willson, *The Parliamentary Diary of Robert Bowyer*, p. 246.

110. Wallace Notestein, *The Winning of the Initiative by the House of Commons* (London, 1924).

111. Sheila Lambert, 'Procedure in the House of Commons during the Early Stuart Period,' *English Historical Review* (95, 377, 1980), pp. 759–73.

112. Foster, *Proceedings in Parliament 1610*, II, p. 320.

113. Johnson, Keeler, Cole, and Bidwell, *Commons Debates and Lords Proceedings 1628*, I, p. 16.

114. Ibid., III, pp. 268–97.

115. J. E. Neale, *Elizabeth I and Her Parliaments* (London, reprint 1969), II, pp. 384–93.

116.   Croft, 'Parliament, Purveyance and the City of London,' pp. 9–34.

117.   David L. Smith, *The Stuart Parliaments, 1603–1689* (London, 1999), pp. 101–9; Pauline Croft, 'Free Trade and the House of Commons, 1605–6,' *Economic History Review* (2nd ser., 28, 1, 1975), pp. 17–27; Croft, 'Parliamentary Preparations, September 1605: Robert Cecil, Earl of Salisbury on Free Trade and Monopolies,' *Parliamentary History* (6, 1987), pp. 127–32; Robert Ashton, 'The Parliamentary Agitation for Free Trade in the Opening Years of James I, *Past and Present* (38, 1967), pp. 40–55; Ashton, 'Jacobean Free Trade Again,' *Past and Present* (43, 1969), pp. 151–57.

118.   On the 1614 parliament, see Linda Levy Peck, *Northampton, Patronage and Policy at the Court of James I* (London, 1982); Conrad Russell, *The Addled Parliament of 1614: The Limits of Revision* (Stenton Lectures, Reading, 1991); and Thomas L. Moir, *The Addled Parliament of 1614* (Oxford, 1958).

119.   Wallace Notestein, *The House of Commons 1604–1610* (New Haven, 1971), p. 503.

120.   The best general survey of the decade remains Conrad Russell, *Parliaments and English Politics, 1621–1629* (Oxford, 1979). See also Thomas Cogswell, *The Blessed Revolution: English Politics and the Coming of War 1621–1624* (Cambridge, 1989); and Richard Cust, *The Forced Loan and English Politics 1626–1628* (Oxford, 1987).

121.   Michael A. R. Graves, 'The Management of the Elizabethan House of Commons: The Council's Men-of-Business,' *Parliamentary History* (2, 1983), pp. 11–38; Graves, 'Thomas Norton the Parliament Man: An Elizabethan MP, 1559–1581,' *HJ* (23, 1980), pp. 17–35; Graves, 'Elizabethan Men of Business Reconsidered,' in S. M. Jack and B. A. Masters, eds., *Protestants, Property, Puritans: Godly People Revisited, Parergon* (XIV, 1996), pp. 111–27.

122.   Neale, *Elizabeth I and Her Parliaments*, II, pp. 325–432.

123.   See Willson, *The Privy Councillors in the House of Commons*, esp. pp. 92–101, 205–46. Michael Graves has made the point that the councillors later in Elizabeth's reign, such as Sir John Fortescue, Sir William Knollys, and Sir Robert Cecil, were no match for her earlier group of advisors: Sir Christopher Hatton, Sir William Cecil, Sir Walter Mildmay, and Sir Francis Walsingham. Graves, 'Managing Elizabethan Parliaments,' in D. M. Dean and N. L. Jones, eds., *The Parliaments of Elizabethan England* (Oxford, 1990), p. 47.

124.   Quoted in Richard Cust, 'Charles I and Popularity,' in Thomas Cogswell, Richard Cust, and Peter Lake, eds., *Politics, Religion and Popularity in Early Stuart Britain* (Cambridge, 2002), p. 237.

125.   Bidwell and Jansson, *Proceedings in Parliament 1626*, II, p. 395.

126.   Foster, *Proceedings in Parliament 1610*, I, p. 278.

127.   Ibid., p. 279.

128.   Russell, *Parliaments and English Politics*, p. 143.

129.   *LJ*, IV, p. 43.

130.   Sir Henry Hobart. See Foster, *Proceedings in Parliament 1610*, II, p. 198.

131.   Mack, *Elizabethan Rhetoric*, p. 60.

2. AUDIENCE REACTIONS: THE NOISE OF POLITICS

1. Ben Jonson, *Epicoene*, 3.2.

2. Jesus, Fray Francisco de. *El hecho de los tratados matrimonio pretendidio porel principe de Gales con la serenissima infante de España Maria, yomado desde sus principios para demostración de la verdad, y ajustado con los papeles orignales desde consta por el maestro F. Franciso de Jesus, predicador de rey nuestro señor. Narrative of the Spanish marriage treaty. Ed. S. R. Gardiner* (Camden Society, old ser., 101, 1869), p. 288.

3. See above, pp. 33–34.

4. Keith Thomas, *Religion and the Decline of Magic* (London, 1971), p. 192; Sir Simonds D'Ewes, *The Journals of all the Parliaments During the Reign of Queen Elizabeth* (London, 1682), p. 651.

5. E. M. Simpson and G. R. Potter, eds., *The Sermons of John Donne* (10 vols., Berkeley 1962), X, p. 132. Quoted in John Craig, 'Psalms, Groans and Dogwhippers: The Soundscape of Worship in the English Parish Church, 1547–1642,' in Will Coster and Andrew Spicer, eds., *Sacred Space in Early Modern Europe* (Cambridge, 2005), p. 112.

6. John Earle, *Micro-cosmographie* (London, 1628), sigs. I11r–K1r, *STC* 7440. Quoted in Emily Cockayne, *Hubbub: Filth, Noise and Stench in England, 1600–1770* (New Haven, 2007), p. 121. Earle thought the political talk of St. Paul's was much greater than that which occurred in Parliament. Earle, *Micro-cosmographie*.

7. Quoted in Andrew Gurr, *Playgoing in Shakespeare's London* (Cambridge, 1987), p. 45.

8. Ibid. See John Lyly, *Campaspe, played before the Queenes maiestie on newyeares day at night, by her Maiesties children, and the children of Paules* (London, 1584), prologue Sig A3v, *STC 17048a*; Lyly, *Midas Plaied before the Queenes Maiestie upon Twelfe day at night, by the Children of Paules* (London, 1592), prologue Sig A2v, *STC 17083*.

9. Gurr, *Playgoing in Shakespeare's London*, p. 91.

10. Thomas Dekker, *The dead tearme. Or, Westminsters complaint for long vacations and short termes. Written in manner of a dialogue betweene the two cityes London and Westminster* (London, 1608), n.p., *STC* 6496.

11. I am grateful to Paul Hunneyball for his estimate of the distances involved.

12. For a more detailed description of the public space in which Parliament operated, see Part Three, below.

13. *Manuscripts of the House of Lords* (12 vols., new ser., London, 1900–1977), 10, 6, p. 11.

14. *LJ*, III, p. 52.

15. T. E. Hartley, *Proceedings in the Parliaments of Elizabeth I* (Leicester, 1995), I, p. 495.

16. Ibid., III, p. 308 (2 November 1601).

17. Chris R. Kyle and Jason Peacey, '"Under cover of so much coming and going": Public Access to Parliament and the Political Process in Early Modern England,' in Kyle and Peacey, eds., *Parliament at Work: Parliamentary Committees, Po-*

litical Power and Public Access in Early Modern England (Woodbridge, 2002), pp. 14–15.

18. Hartley, *Proceedings in the Parliaments of Elizabeth I*, II, p. 103.

19. Ibid., III, p. 173.

20. Ibid., p. 62. Knowledgeable members also managed the same feat in 1601. Ibid., pp. 298–99.

21. Ibid., p. 62.

22. Ibid., p. 299; D'Ewes, *Journals of all the Parliaments*, p. 621.

23. *CJ*, I, p. 141.

24. Arnold Hunt, *The Art of Hearing: Preachers and the Audiences in Early Modern England* (Cambridge, 2010), p. 111. I am grateful to Dr. Hunt for sharing his work with me in advance of publication.

25. Hartley, *Proceedings in the Parliaments of Elizabeth I*, II, p. 37.

26. D'Ewes, *Journals of all the Parliaments*, p. 346.

27. David Harris Willson, ed., *The Parliamentary Diary of Robert Bowyer 1606–1607* (New York, 1971), p. 377.

28. Hartley, *Proceedings in the Parliaments of Elizabeth I*, II, p. 124.

29. Ibid., III, p. 106.

30. "Noisy disturbance" (*OED*).

31. Hartley, *Proceedings in the Parliaments of Elizabeth I*, III, p. 358.

32. Keith Thomas, 'The Place of Laughter in Tudor and Stuart England,' *Times Literary Supplement*, 21 January 1977, p. 77.

33. Thomas Wilson (1554) ff. 74v, 75. Quoted in Quentin Skinner, 'Why Does Laughter Matter to Philosophy?' Passmore Lecture, Australian National University, December 2000, p. 2.

34. Ibid., p. 3.

35. D'Ewes, *Journals of all the Parliaments*, p. 678.

36. Conrad Russell, *Parliaments and English Politics, 1621–1629* (Oxford, 1979), p. 29.

37. Hartley, *Proceedings in the Parliaments of Elizabeth I*, II, p. 125 (n.d. but 1585).

38. Ibid., III, pp. 354–55.

39. Quoted in David Cressy, *Dangerous Talk: Scandalous, Seditious, and Treasonable Speech in Pre-Modern England* (Oxford, 2010), p. 104.

40. Russell, *Parliaments and English Politics*, 117; Cressy, *Dangerous Talk*, p. 105.

41. *LJ*, III, p. 134; see also N. E. McClure, ed., *The Letters of John Chamberlain* (2 vols., Philadelphia, 1939), II, p. 377.

42. Hartley, *Proceedings in the Parliaments of Elizabeth I*, III, p. 327 (7 November 1601).

43. Folger Shakespeare Library, V.b.189, p. 70.

44. Hartley, *Proceedings in the Parliaments of Elizabeth I*, III, p. 485.

45. Ibid., p. 117 (9 March 1593).

46. Ibid., p. 328 (7 November 1601).

47. *Facetiae: Musarum Deliciae . . . and Wit Restor'd* (2 vols., London, 1817), I, p. xviii.

48. Willson, *The Parliamentary Diary of Robert Bowyer,* pp. 213–14; *LJ*, II, p. 483.

49. Crooke as a King's sergeant attended the Lords as a legal assistant and as such often bore the responsibility of conveying messages from the Lords to the Commons.

50. Willson, *The Parliamentary Diary of Robert Bowyer*, p. 213 n. 1.

51. Michelle O'Callaghan, *The English Wits: Literature and Sociability in Early Modern England* (Cambridge, 2007), pp. 86–87; Sir Edward Conway's version of the poem adds the stanza.

Ned Jones Dick Martyn, Hopkins [*sic*], & Brooke.

The fower compilers of this booke,.
Fower of like witte, fower of like arte.
And all fower not worth a farte.
BL, Add MS. 23299 f. 17v.

52. I. A. Shapiro, 'The Mermaid Club,' *Modern Language Review* (45, 1, 1950), pp. 6–17.

53. Sir John Mennes, *Musarum Deliciae* (London, 1655); Sir Benjamin Rudyerd, *Le Prince d'Amour* (London, 1660); Thomas D'Urfey, *Wit and Mirth: or Pills to Purge Melancholy* (London, 1699).

54. Michelle O'Callaghan, 'Performing Politics: The Circulation of the Parliament Fart,' *HLQ* (69, 1, 2006), p. 126.

55. BL, Add. MS. 4149, f. 213.

56. John Aubrey, *Aubrey's Brief Lives*, ed. Oliver Lawson Dick (Ann Arbor, MI, 1957, reprint Jaffrey, NH, 1999), p. 307.

57. This reference has echoes of the occasion on 19 May 1641, when laths cracked in the Commons' gallery, causing panic and MPs to flee the House; it was even claimed that powder had been smelled. Maija Jansson, ed., *Proceedings of the Long Parliament: House of Commons* (vol. IV, Rochester, 2003), pp. 459–60, 469, 470. I am grateful to Ben Coates and Paul Hunneyball for helping me track down this reference.

58. Quoted from https://www.earlystuartlibels.net ll, 158–63. On silence, see below, pp. 47–50.

59. Mennes, *Musarum Deliciae*, p. 72. Other versions often have quite different endings. As the editors of earlystuartlibels.net noted, the Parliament Fart 'proved to be one of the most malleable poems of the period.'

60. Ibid., p. 67. On Pigott, see Thrush and Ferris, *HPT 1604–1629*.

61. Christina Luckyj, *A Moving Rhetoricke: Gender and Silence in Early Modern England* (Manchester, 2002), p. 39.

62. Roskell, Clark, and Rawcliffe, *HPT 1386–1421*, I, pp. 158–59.
63. Bindoff, *HPT 1509–58*, II, p. 573.
64. *CJ*, I, p. 76; D'Ewes, *Journals of all the Parliaments*, p. 128.
65. Healy, 'Debates in the House of Commons, 1604–1607,' p. 123.
66. Robert C. Johnson, Mary Frear Keeler, Maija Jansson Cole, and William B. Bidwell, eds., *Commons Debates and Lords Proceedings 1628* (6 vols., New Haven, 1977–83), IV, p. 68. 'Light troubles speak; the weighty are struck dumb,' from Seneca, *Hippolytus (Phaedra)*, 607, ibid., IV, Supl. Glossary, pp. 485. See also Russell, *Parliaments and English Politics*, 377–79. Note that the date Russell gives for this speech is incorrect.
67. Johnson, Keeler, Cole, and Bidwell, *Commons Debates and Lords Proceedings 1628*, IV, pp. 114, 118, 123, 129.
68. Ibid., IV, pp. 114, 123.
69. Hartley, *Proceedings in the Parliaments of Elizabeth I*, III, p. 331 n. 498, quoting Stowe, p. 359.
70. Hartley, *Proceedings in the Parliaments of Elizabeth I*, III, pp. 330, 331, and 498 n.
71. Ibid., p. 333.
72. J. E. Neale, *The Elizabethan House of Commons* (London, 1949), pp. 354–55.
73. Hartley, *Proceedings in the Parliaments of Elizabeth I*, III, p. 301.
74. *CJ*, I, pp. 139–40.
75. Maija Jansson, ed., *Proceedings in Parliament 1614* (Philadelphia, 1988), p. 276.
76. Ibid., p. 278; McClure, *The Letters of John Chamberlain*, I, p. 531. Martin, who had sat in Parliament in 1601 and 1604, had a reputation as a forthright parliamentary speaker, and as one with a 'slipperie tongue.' McClure, p. 425; Hasler, *HPT 1559–1603*, III, pp. 22–23.
77. Hartley, *Proceedings in the Parliaments of Elizabeth I*, III, p. 377.
78. Ibid., p. 476.
79. Healy, 'Debates in the House of Commons, 1604–1607,' p. 129.
80. *CJ*, I, p. 335.
81. Ibid. However aptly politic the Commons' reasoning and response was, it should be noted that the general view of silence in the early modern period was that it signified consent. See Morris Palmer Tilley, *Elizabethan Proverb Lore in Lyly's Euphues and in Pettie's Petite Pallace with Parallels from Shakespeare* (New York, 1926), pp. 274–75.
82. Johnson, Keeler, Cole, and Bidwell, *Commons Debates and Lords Proceedings 1628*, III, p. 557.
83. *ODNB*; Arthur Hall, *A letter sent by F. A toyching the proceedings in a private quarell and unkindnesse between Arthur Hall, and Melchisedech Mallerie gentleman, to his very friene L.B. being in Italie. With an admonition to the father of F.A. to him being a burgesse of the Parliament, for his better behaviour therein* (London, 1573), sig. Aiv, *STC* 12629.

84. Hartley, *Proceedings in the Parliaments of Elizabeth I*, I, p. 326.

85. Ibid., p. 357.

86. See Chapter One, on speech.

87. Hartley, *Proceedings in the Parliaments of Elizabeth I*, II, p. 124.

88. Ibid., III, p. 47.

89. Ibid., p. 238.

90. Ruth Spalding, ed., *The Diary of Bulstrode Whitelocke 1605–1675* (Records of Social and Economic History, new ser. XIII, Oxford, 1990), p. 53.

91. Healy, 'Debates in the House of Commons, 1604–1607,' p. 57.

92. *CJ*, I, p. 423.

93. Jansson, *Proceedings in Parliament 1614*, pp. 150, 157 (5 May).

94. Elizabeth Read Foster, 'Speaking in the House of Commons,' *BIHR* (43, 1970), p. 52.

95. *CJ*, I, p. 209.

96. William B. Bidwell and Maija Jansson, *Proceedings in Parliament 1626* (New Haven, 1992), II, p. 262.

97. *CJ*, I, p. 841.

98. BL, Harleian 390, f. 410.

99. Johnson, Keeler, Cole, and Bidwell, *Commons Debates and Lords Proceedings 1628*, iv. p, 113 nn. 1, 2.

100. BL, Harleian 390, f. 10.

101. Hartley, *Proceedings in the Parliaments of Elizabeth I*, III, p. 370.

102. Ibid., II, p. 53.

103. See Part III, pp. 111–12.

104. Wallace Notestein and Frances Helen Relf, *Commons Debates for 1629* (Minneapolis, 1921), p. 254.

105. Ian H. C. Fraser, 'Agitation in the Commons, 2 March 1629, and the Interrogation of the Leaders of the Anti-Court Group,' *BIHR* (30, 1957), p. 91.

106. I am very grateful for discussions on Eliot with Paul Hunneyball.

107. Jansson, *Proceedings in Parliament 1614*, p. 148. John Chamberlain reported 'the truth is yt shold seeme by theyre carriage, and by that I have heard from some of them, that there was never knowne a more disorderly house, and that yt was many times more like a cockpit then a grave counsaile, and many sat there that were more fit to have ben among roaring boyes then in that assemblie.' McClure, *The Letters of John Chamberlain*, I, p. 538.

108. Croft's reference to a cockpit is ambivalent. He could have been referring to the cockpit of a theater, to which the Commons was sometimes compared (see Chapter One, pp. 1–2), or to a site in which cock-fighting took place. *OED*. In both venues noise was a constant part of the experience of the audience. In 1625 when the Parliament met in the Divinity School in Oxford University, an observer described the construction of the seating in the chamber as done 'in manner of a cockpit.' Corpus Christi College, Oxford University, MS 257, f. 131. I am grateful to Jason Peacey for this reference.

3. SWIFT PENS: RECORDING PARLIAMENT

1. BL, Add. 53726, f. 22v.

2. Vernon F. Snow, ed., *Parliament in Elizabethan England: John Hooker's Order and Usage* (New Haven, 1977), p. 187.

3. See Chapter Four, on manuscript news.

4. Bodleian Library, MS Dep.e.468.

5. On Nicholas, see Wallace Notestein and Frances Helen Relf, eds., *Commons Debates for 1629* (Minneapolis, 1921), pp. lxi–lxiii.

6. Alford's notes are scattered throughout his papers in the BL, See, for example, Harleian 6803, ff. 6v, 12v, 13v. Grosvenor's diary is printed in Robert C. Johnson, Mary Frear Keeler, Maija Jansson Cole, and William B. Bidwell, eds., *Commons Debates and Lords Proceedings 1628* (6 vols., New Haven, 1977–83).

7. William Hakewill, *The Manner How Statutes are Enacted in Parliament by Passing of Bills* (London, 1641), p. 23.

8. J. E. Neale, 'The Commons' Journal of the Tudor Period,' *Transactions of the Royal Historical Society* (4th ser., 3, 1920), pp. 136–70; Sheila Lambert, 'The Clerks and Records of the House of Commons, 1600–1640,' *BIHR* (43, 1970), pp. 215–31.

9. Elizabeth Read Foster, 'Staging a Parliament in Early Stuart England,' in Peter Clark, Alan G. G. Smith, and Nicholas Tyacke, eds., *The English Commonwealth 1547–1640* (Leicester, 1979), p. 138. Only fragmentary accounts survive before 1640. In November 1605, the Clerk of the Commons, Ralph Ewens, received £21 14s. 2d. for parliamentary supplies, The National Archives, E403/2725, f. 140. In 1614 the clerk was reimbursed £94 18s., Foster, 'Staging a Parliament in Early Stuart England,' p. 138. It should be noted, however, that this total included £50 2s. for 2,512 proclamations on various matters and 20s. for bibles for James and Anne of Denmark. The accounts appear to be the initial costs of getting ready for Parliament rather than the total cost of paper and supplies consumed during the session. See also HLRO Braye (Osborn) 55, no. 90, where the accounts note the delivery of four reams of fine paper and four reams of coarse and 'more from tyme to tyme as there shalbe cause.'

10. Foster, 'Staging a Parliament in Early Stuart England,' p. 139.

11. HLRO, Braye 54 no. 41; 55 no. 90.

12. The clerk read out the morning prayers each day from the Book of Common Prayer. *CJ*, I, pp. 150, 266; Paulet Diary, f. 32. In 1614 the prayers for the Parliament were included with the Book of Common Prayer. HLRO, Braye (Osborn), p. 54, no. 40.

13. Foster, 'Staging a Parliament in Early Stuart England,' p. 138.

14. Ibid.

15. TNA, AO 3/1276, Box 2.

16. The Lords Journal probably developed sometime in the fifteenth century, and fragments survive from 1449, 1453, and 1461. Michael A. R. Graves, *The Tudor Parliaments: Crown, Lords and Commons, 1485–1603* (London, 1985), p. 44.

17. For example, in 1626 separate books survive for the register of petitions, answers to petitions, a catalogue of the petitions, and a register of proceedings on bills. The clerk also drew up a daily agenda paper. HLRO, Main Papers, 6 February 1626, 23 February 1626.

18. See Chapter Five, on lobbying.

19. TNA, C66/1649.

20. For further details of Bowyer's parliamentary career, see Chris Kyle, 'Robert Bowyer,' in Andrew Thrush and J. P. Ferris, eds., *The House of Commons, 1604–1629* (6 vols., Cambridge, 2010).

21. 'Bowyer,' Thrush and Ferris, *HPT 1604–1629*; HLRO, Braye 61; Inner Temple Library, Petyt MS 537/8.

22. Petyt 537/1. Quoted in Elizabeth Read Foster, ed., *Proceedings in Parliament 1610* (2 vols., New Haven, 1966), I, p. xxvi.

23. Ibid., p. xxv.

24. HLRO, Main Papers, 29 January, 6 March, 20 May 1610. The Dean and Ashe bill was enacted as 7 James I OA 43.

25. Ibid. 5 March, 6 July 1610; 7 James I OA 19, 42.

26. Ibid. 15 March, 14 June 1610. I have not been able to find the bill to which Walmesley referred.

27. Ibid. 22 March, 16 June, 29 June 1610. Respectively, 7 James I OA 35, 62, 41. On Bath's interest in the River Tow bill, see TNA, SP 14/19/75–77.

28. *LJ*, II, pp. 562, 575.

29. Inner Temple, Petyt 537/38, ff. 172–73.

30. The oath had been instituted in 1610, but Elsynge was the first to actually take it. Maurice F. Bond, 'The Clerks of the Parliaments, 1509–1953,' *English Historical Review* (73, 1, 1958), pp. 79–80; *LJ*, III, pp. 59–60; HLRO, Main Papers, 21 March 1621.

31. Elizabeth Read Foster, 'The Painful Labour of Mr Elsyng,' *Transactions of the American Philosophical Society* (new ser., 62, 8, 1972).

32. James S. Hart, *Justice upon Petition: The House of Lords and the Reformation of Justice 1621–1675* (London, 1991), pp. 9–12, 16.

33. Johnson, Keeler, Cole, and Bidwell, *Commons Debates and Lords Proceedings 1628*, V, p. 186.

34. There are a couple of reasons for this supposition. First, we know D'Ewes was active in the 1620s compiling his diary from the Elizabethan journals. Second, D'Ewes, although not an MP in 1624, wrote a diary of the Parliament that is heavily based upon the Commons Journal (BL, Harleian 159). These factors together at least open the possibility that D'Ewes had obtained the original journals that were subsequently lost.

35. Lambert, 'The Clerks and Records of the House of Commons,' pp. 16–17; David Harris Willson, ed., *The Parliamentary Diary of Robert Bowyer 1606–1607* (New York, 1971), p. 344.

36. *CJ*, I, p. 390.

37. Foster, *Proceedings in Parliament 1610*, II, pp. 3–4.

38. *APC*, VI, pp. 108–10; TNA, SP 14/124/83; Robert Zaller, *The Parliament of 1621: A Study in Constitutional Conflict* (Berkeley, 1971), p. 185.

39. G. Roberts, ed., *Diary of Walter Yonge esq., Justice of the Peace and MP for Honiton . . . 1604–1628* (Camden Society, 41, 1848), p. 41.

40. Johnson, Keeler, Cole, and Bidwell, *Commons Debates and Lords Proceedings 1628*, II, p. 512.

41. Foster, *Proceedings in Parliament 1610*, I, p. xxxvii.

42. Andrew Thrush, 'The House of Lords' Record Repository and the Clerk of the Parliaments' House: A Tudor Achievement,' *Parliamentary History* (21, 3, 2002), pp. 367–73.

43. Foster, 'The Painful Labour of Mr Elsyng,' pp. 23–24.

44. Samuel Rawson Gardiner, ed., *Notes of the Debates in the House of Lords . . . 1621* (Camden, old ser., 103, 1870), pp. 73–74.

45. *LJ*, III, p. 74.

46. Victoria and Albert Museum, W.16:1, 2–1995; w.9–1947; W.12–1955; W.4–1911; W.4–1919.

47. An example of the table book in use is Renold Elstracke, *The Portracture of Sir Thomas Overbury*, 1615–16, Society of Antiquaries. See also the cover of Alastair Bellany, *The Politics of Court Scandal in Early Modern England: News Culture and the Overbury Affair, 1603–1660* (Cambridge, 2002).

48. On the auditory conditions in the House, see Chapter Four.

49. Inner Temple, Petyt MS 538/7, f. 227.

50. *CJ*, I, p. 382.

51. Foster, *Proceedings in Parliament 1610*, I, p. lxviii.

52. BL, Harleian 354, f. 2.

53. Foster, *Proceedings in Parliament 1610*, II, p. 331.

54. *CJ*, I, p. 352. Holt may have taken a diary of the session that no longer survives. Later in the session, the clerk failed to get an accurate account of Holt's report on a joint conference and noted in the margin of the journal, '[R]emember to enquire for his notes.' Ibid., p. 1032.

55. Peter Stallybrass, Roger Chartier, J. Franklin Mowery, and Heather Wolfe, 'Hamlet's Tables and the Technologies of Writing in Renaissance England,' *Shakespeare Quarterly* (55, 2004), pp. 379–419. I am grateful to Peter Stallybrass for many illuminating hours spent discussing table books.

56. See, for example, BL, Harleian 6800, f. 397v; 6803, ff. 6v; 13v, 19v.

57. Wallace Notestein, Frances Helen Relf, and Hartley Simpson, eds., *Commons Debates 1621* (New Haven, 1935), VII, p. 628.

58. TNA, AO3/1088/1, pt.1, f. 2; 1246/Box 2, unf.

59. Michael Mendle, 'News and the Pamphlet Culture of Mid-Seventeenth Century England,' in Brendan Dooley and Sabrina Baron, eds., *The Politics of Infor-*

mation in Early Modern Europe (London, 2001), pp. 63–67. I am grateful to Michael Mendle for his assistance on this subject.

60. Frances Henderson, 'Reading, and Writing, the Text of the Putney Debates,' in Michael Mendle, ed., *The Putney Debates of 1647: The Army, The Levellers and the English State* (Cambridge, 2001), p. 46.

61. For an example of Nicholas's system, see the illustrations in Notestein and Relf, *Commons Debates for 1629*, between pp. 106 and 107.

62. BL, Harleian 2104, ff. 269–81 (Whitby); Johnson, Keeler, Cole, and Bidwell, *Commons Debates and Lords Proceedings 1628*, I, pp. 32–33.

63. BL, Add. 53726, f. 22v.

64. Ibid., Harleian 159.

65. James Orchard Halliwell, ed., *The Autobiography and Correspondence of Sir Simonds D'Ewes, Bart., during the reigns of James I and Charles I* (2 vols., London, 1845), I, p. 280.

66. Johnson, Keeler, Cole, and Bidwell, *Commons Debates and Lords Proceedings 1628*, I, p. 26.

67. See, for example, his notes on 22 February on proclamations, which sum the arguments up in a paragraph. The notes in the 'X' diary on the same matter run to four pages. Notestein, Relf, and Simpson, *Commons Debates 1621*, V, p. 484; II, pp. 118–122.

68. Ibid., I, p. 29.

69. I am grateful to the staff of the 1604–1629 section of the History of Parliament Trust for their advice on this matter, esp. Andrew Thrush, Paul Hunneyball, Simon Healy, and Ben Coates.

70. The diary continues into the 1620s, covering the Parliaments of 1621, 1624, and 1625.

71. University of Nottingham, Portland MSS, MS A, ff. 17v-80 (Holles); The Rich diary is now lost. See Maija Jansson, ed., *Proceedings in Parliament 1614* (Philadelphia, 1988), pp. xlvi–xlvii.

72. Lowther (1624, 1626, 1628, 1629); Holland (1621, 1624); Rich (1614–28); Pym (1621–25); Dyott (1624, 1625); Grosvenor (1626, 1628).

73. HLRO, HL/CL/JO/1/12, p. 14. See also BRY/73, a record of the proceedings between 12 and 25 February in Wright's hand.

74. Ibid., HL/CL/JO/1/13.

75. TNA, SP 14/166.

76. BL, Harleian 6799, ff. 131–33.

77. Ibid., Add. 26639, ff. 1–37v.

78. Northamptonshire RO, Finch-Hatton 50.

79. See above, pp. 65, 203 n. 34.

80. BL, Harleian 159, ff. 59–136v.

81. David R. Ransome, ed., 'The Parliamentary Papers of Nicholas Ferrar, 1624,' *Camden Miscellany* XXXIII (5th ser., 7, 33 (1996), pp. 5–104.

82. BL, Add. 18597.

83. Ibid., Harleian 6383, ff. 80v-141.

84. Respectively, Hampshire RO, Jervoise Papers, unnumbered MS; Staffordshire RO, 661/11/1/2.

85. Holland's notes are in two books. Bodleian, Tanner 392 and Rawlinson D1100.

86. Harvard University, Houghton Library, MS English 980. Quotation from f. 234.

87. John Hawarde, *Les Reportes del in Camera Stellata, 1593–1609* (London, 1894).

88. Wiltshire RO, Ailesbury MSS, Hawarde Diary, 1624. Hawarde also compiled a diary for 1621 although only the proceedings of the second sitting are extant. Ibid., Hawarde Diary, 1621.

89. BL, Add. 46191.

90. KSRL, MS E237, ff. 93–114.

91. Bodleian, Rawlinson D723, ff. 84v-90v.

92. Ibid., B151, ff. 58–70, 103v.

93. *CJ*, I, p. 597. Sir Christopher Hildyard, William Nyell, Sir Thomas Riddell, Sir Edwin Sandys, John Guy, Sir Robert Payne, Sir Edward Giles, Sir Edward Coke, Sir Henry Anderson, William Towerson, and John Whitson.

94. Thomas Tyrwhitt, ed., *Proceedings and Debates in the House of Commons in 1620 and 1621 by Edward Nicholas* (2 vols., Oxford, 1766), I, p. 353.

95. Notestein, Relf, and Simpson, *Commons Debates 1621*, I, p. 66. Belasyse was one of the diarists who gravitated toward writing the words of *eminences grises* in the House, esp. Coke, Sandys, Sir Nathaniel Rich, Edward Alford, William Noy, Sir Robert Phelips, and William Hakewill.

96. Ibid., V, pp. 114–15.

97. Ibid., p. 355.

98. Ibid., II, p. 332.

99. Ibid., IV, pp. 275–76.

100. Ibid., p. 302 (Stowe 366).

101. The author of the dairy followed this debate very closely, recording sixteen more speeches than the next most prolific reporter. Normally, however, the author lagged behind other diarists in numbers of speeches. See the analysis in Johnson, Keeler, Cole, and Bidwell, *Commons Debates and Lords Proceedings 1628*, I, p. 24.

102. Ibid., p. 307.

103. The quotation is from Harleian 2313. Johnson, Keeler, Cole, and Bidwell, *Commons Debates and Lords Proceedings 1628*, II, p. 315.

104. Ibid., IV, 44.

105. Ibid., IV, 48–49. In the midst of the dispute Sir William Bulstrode remembered that a Cambridge alumnus bribed the clerk with 5s. to place his University first in a bill. See also Willson, *The Parliamentary Diary of Robert Bowyer*, pp. 55–56.

106.   Montagu was elected in 1621 and sat in the Lower House in the first sitting that year.

107.   This is printed in Chris R. Kyle, ed., *Parliament, Politics and Elections 1604–1648* (Camden Society, 5th ser., 17, Cambridge, 2001), pp. 52–103, 122–47.

108.   Johnson, Keeler, Cole, and Bidwell, *Commons Debates and Lords Proceedings 1628*, V, pp. 162–65.

109.   Ibid., pp. 210–14.

110.   BL, Add. 78652 (Evelyn Papers).

111.   Ibid., 26637.

112.   Notestein, Relf, and Simpson, *Commons Debates 1621*, IV, p. 308 n. b.

113.   *CJ*, I, p. 861.

4. PROCREATIVE PENS: DISSEMINATING NEWS FROM PARLIAMENT

1.   BL, Harleian 383, ff. 13–14.

2.   See, in particular, F. J. Levy, 'How Information Spread amongst the Gentry, 1550–1640,' *JBS* (21, 2, 1982), pp. 11–32; Richard Cust, 'News and Politics in Early Seventeenth Century England,' *Past and Present* 112 (1986), pp. 60–90; Michael Frearson, 'The Distribution and Readership of London Corantos in the 1620s,' in Robin Myers and Michael Harris, eds., *Serials and Their Readers* (Wincester, 1993), pp. 1–25; Jason Scott-Warren, 'News, Sociability and Bookbuying in Early Modern London: The Letters of Sir Thomas Cornwallis,' *Library* (7, 1, 2000), pp. 381–402; James Daybell, '"Suche newes as on the Quenes hye wayes we have mett": The News and Intelligence Networks of Elizabeth Talbot, Countess of Shrewsbury,' in Daybell, ed., *Women and Politics in Early Modern England, 1450–1700* (Aldershot, 2004), pp. 114–31; Sabrina Baron, 'Manuscript News/Printed News: The Two Faces of Dissemination in Early Seventeenth-century England,' in Sabrina Baron and Brendan Dooley, eds., *The Politics of Information in Early Modern Europe* (London, 2001), pp. 41–56; Ian Atherton, 'The Itch Grown a Disease: Manuscript Transmission of News in the Seventeenth Century,' *Prose Studies* (21, 2, 1998), pp. 39–65; and Fritz Levy, *The Decorum of News*, *Prose Studies* (21, 2, 1998), pp. 12–38.

3.   Thomas Fuller, *Ephemeris Parliamentaria* (London, 1654), ¶¶ v.

4.   *The New Tydings out of Italie*, George Vessler, to be sold by Petrus Keerius dwelling in Calvert Street (Amsterdam, 1620), BL, C.55.1.2, *STC* 18507.1.

5.   On the early history of English corantos, see Joad Raymond, *The Invention of the Newspaper* (Oxford, 1996), Introduction; Chris R. Kyle and Jason Peacey, 'Introduction,' in *Breaking News: Renaissance Journalism and the Birth of the Newspaper* (Folger Shakespeare Library, University of Washington Press, Seattle, 2008), pp. 12–14; Matthias A. Shaaber, *Some Forerunners of the Newspaper in England, 1476–1622* (Philadelphia, 1929), pp. 311–17; Joseph Frank, *The Beginnings of the English Newspaper, 1620–1660* (Cambridge, MA, 1961), ch. 1; Frederick Seaton Siebert, *Freedom of the Press in England 1476–1776: The Rise and Decline of Government Control* (Urbana,

1965), pp. 147–56; Folke Dahl, *A Bibliography of English Corantos and Periodical News-books* (Boston, 1977); and Sheila Lambert, 'Coranto Printing in England: The First Newsbooks,' *Journal of Newspaper and Periodical History* (8, 1992), pp. 1–33.

6.   Thomas Scott, *Vox Populi. Or, Newes from Spayne* (London, 1620), STC 22100.8. On Scott, see Simon Adams, 'Captain Thomas Gainsford, the "Vox Spiritus" and the *Vox Populi*,' *BIHR* (49, 1976), pp. 141–44; and Peter Lake, 'Constitutional Consensus and Puritan Opposition in the 1620s: Thomas Scott and the Spanish Match,' *HJ* (25, 1982), pp. 805–25. After *Vox Populi* was suppressed, copies continued to circulate in manuscript form. See, for example, Folger Shakespeare Library, V.a.310.

7.   James F. Larkin and Paul Hughes, *Stuart Royal Proclamations* (Oxford, 1973), pp. 495–96.

8.   James Spedding, R. L. Ellis, and D. D. Heath, eds., *The Works of Francis Bacon* (14 vols., London, 1857–74), *Life and Letters*, VII, p. 152.

9.   *CSP Ven. 1619–21*, p. 577.

10.   N. E. McClure, ed., *The Letters of John Chamberlain* (2 vols., Philadelphia, 1939), II, p. 338.

11.   Larkin and Hughes, *Stuart Royal Proclamations*, pp. 493–95.

12.   Spedding, Ellis, and Heath, *The Works of Francis Bacon*, VII, p. 126.

13.   BL, Harleian 7000, f. 27.

14.   Ibid. 389, ff. 14–15v.

15.   Wallace Notestein and Frances Helen Relf, *Commons Debates for 1629* (Minneapolis, 1921), p. xx.

16.   Cust, 'News and Politics in Early Seventeenth Century England,' p. 63; see, for example, Brian Cave's commonplace book of 1621 documents. Folger Shakespeare Library, V.a.402.

17.   Levy, 'How Information Spread amongst the Gentry,' p. 23 esp.

18.   See G. R. Elton, *The Parliament of England 1559–1581* (Cambridge, 1986); Michael A. R. Graves, *The Tudor Parliaments: Crown, Lords and Commons, 1485–1603* (London, 1985); and David M. Dean, *Law-Making and Society in Late Elizabethan England* (Cambridge, 1996).

19.   For the Elizabethan diaries, see T. E. Hartley, *Proceedings in the Parliaments of Elizabeth I* (3 vols., Leicester, 1981–95).

20.   Chris R. Kyle, '*Lex Loquens*: Legislation in the Parliament of 1624' (unpublished Ph.D. diss., University of Auckland, 1994); Thomas Cogswell, *The Blessed Revolution: English Politics and the Coming of War, 1621–1624* (Cambridge, 1989).

21.   See Chapter Five, on lobbying.

22.   Andrew Thrush and J. P. Ferris, eds., *The House of Commons, 1604–1629* (6 vols., Cambridge, 2010), Exeter.

23.   Thrush and Ferris, *HPT 1604–1629*, Exeter.

24.   Somerset RO, D/B/bw 1609. I am grateful to Paul Hunneyball for this reference.

25. Norfolk RO (Norwich), Y/C/19/5, f. 296.

26. Thrush and Ferris, *HPT 1604–1629*, Bristol.

27. Norfolk RO (Norwich), Y/C19/5, f. 77; Y/C36/7/2. On the long and bitter dispute between Yarmouth and Lowestoft, see David M. Dean, 'Parliament, Privy Council and Local Politics in Elizabethan England: The Yarmouth-Lowestoft Fishing Dispute,' *Albion* (22, 1, 1990), pp. 39–64.

28. Thrush and Ferris, *HPT 1604–1629*, Hull. I am grateful to Simon Healy for a discussion of Hull's parliamentary interests and regular communication with Westminster.

29. Levy, 'How Information Spread amongst the Gentry,' pp. 20–21.

30. Quoted in William Powell, *John Pory, 1572–1636: The Life and Letters of a Man of Many Parts* (Chapel Hill, 1977), p. 26.

31. For a full list of Pory's correspondents, see Baron, 'Manuscript News/Printed News,' p. 56 n. 32.

32. Ibid., p. 45.

33. McClure, *The Letters of John Chamberlain*, I, p. 8. Backhouse served as an MP from 1604 to 1610 and in 1614; Borlase (1604–10, 1614); Carleton (1604–10, 1626); Edmondes (1601, 1604–10, 1621, 1624, 1625, 1626, 1628); Lytton (1586, 1597, 1604–10); Savile (1604–10, 1614, 1629); Wallop (1597, 1601, 1614, 1621, 1624, 1625, 1626, 1628, April 1640, November 1640); Winwood (1614).

34. Levy, 'How Information Spread amongst the Gentry,' p. 21.

35. William B. Bidwell and Maija Jansson, eds., *Proceedings in Parliament 1626* (4 vols., New Haven, 1991–96), IV, pp. 260–62.

36. The letter is now missing.

37. Bidwell and Jansson, *Proceedings in Parliament 1626*, II, pp. 12, 13.

38. Ibid., IV, p. 269.

39. On the development of these printed catalogues, see Chapter Six. Edward Grimston, *The Order and Manner of the Sitting of the Lords . . . and also the Names of the Knights for Counties, Citizens, Burgesses for the Boroughs . . .* (London, 1626), *STC* 7742–46.

40. Thomas Birch, *The Court and Times of Charles I* (2 vols., London, 1848), I, p. 85.

41. Ibid.; Bidwell and Jansson, *Proceedings in Parliament 1626*, IV, p. 270.

42. Birch, *Court and Times Charles I*, I, pp. 89–90.

43. Bidwell and Jansson, *Proceedings in Parliament 1626*, IV, p. 274.

44. Ibid., pp. 275–77.

45. Birch, *Court and Times Charles I*, I, p. 92.

46. Ibid., p. 93.

47. Bidwell and Jansson, *Proceedings in Parliament 1626*, IV, pp. 277–78; Exodus 14, 24, 25.

48. Birch, *Court and Times Charles I*, I, p. 93.

49. Ibid., p. 97: 22 April.

50.　Ibid.

51.　Ibid., p. 99; Bidwell and Jansson, *Proceedings in Parliament 1626*, I, pp. 328–29.

52.　Birch, *Court and Times Charles I*, I, p. 102.

53.　Ibid., p. 103; Bidwell and Jansson, *Proceedings in Parliament 1626*, I, p. 305, III, pp. 192–93. For the full charges, see *Proceedings in Parliament 1626*, I, pp. 408–10. As the editors of that work note, the text of the charges was circulated widely as a separate, and it is possible that Mead had access to this. See BL, Add. 22474, ff. 207–50; Cornell University Library, MS H83, ff. 56–167v; and National Library of Scotland, Gordon-Cummings Papers, Deposit 175, Box 80.

54.　Birch, *Court and Times Charles I*, I, pp. 103–4.

55.　Ibid., pp. 107–9; Bidwell and Jansson, *Proceedings in Parliament 1626*, IV, p. 291.

56.　Birch, *Court and Times Charles I*, I, pp. 109–110; Bidwell and Jansson, *Proceedings in Parliament 1626*, IV, pp. 292–93. Mead described the Commons as 'wonderfully exasperated.'

57.　*LJ*, III, p. 682.

58.　Birch, *Court and Times Charles I*, I, p. 112.

59.　Conrad Russell, *Parliaments and English Politics, 1621–1629* (Oxford, 1979), pp. 343–44.

60.　Robert C. Johnson, Mary Frear Keeler, Maija Jansson Cole, and William B. Bidwell, eds., *Commons Debates and Lords Proceedings 1628* (6 vols., New Haven, 1977–83), II, p. 58.

61.　BL, Harleian 390, f. 404.

62.　Johnson, Keeler, Cole, and Bidwell, *Commons Debates and Lords Proceedings 1628*, VI, p. 183; Birch, *Court and Times Charles I*, I, pp. 342–46. Birch omits this opening sentence.

63.　Johnson, Keeler, Cole, and Bidwell, *Commons Debates and Lords Proceedings 1628*, VI, p. 183.

64.　John Morrill, 'Reconstructing the History of Early Stuart Parliaments,' *Archives* (21, 1994), pp. 67–72; Morrill, 'Paying One's D'Ewes,' *Parliamentary History* (xiv, 1995), pp. 179–86; Morrill, 'Getting over D'Ewes,' *Parliamentary History* (xv, 1996), pp. 221–30. On the debate about the accuracy of words recorded by members in Parliament and how historians should use these sources, see also J. H. Hexter, 'Parliament under the Lens,' *British Studies Monitor* (III, 1972–73), pp. 4–15; Hexter, 'Quoting the Commons, 1604–1642,' in DeLloyd J. Guth and John W. McKenna, eds., *Tudor Rule and Revolution* (Cambridge, 1992), pp. 369–91; Maija Jansson, 'Dues Paid,' *Parliamentary History* (xv, 1996), pp. 215–20; and Chris R. Kyle, 'Introduction,' in Chris R. Kyle, ed., *Parliament, Politics and Elections 1604–1648* (Camden Society, 5th ser., 17, Cambridge, 2001), pp. 4–6.

65.　Johnson, Keeler, Cole, and Bidwell, *Commons Debates and Lords Proceedings 1628*, II, p. 385.

66. Ibid., pp. 388, 392.

67. BL, Harleian 389, ff. 45–46v. Although both Houses had passed forty-nine bills that were ready for royal approval, they were never submitted to the King. The following week, Mead realized that his intelligence had been lacking and informed Stuteville that only the two subsidy acts had been passed. Ibid., ff. 48–49v.

68. Ibid., f. 67-v.

69. Elizabeth Read Foster, *The House of Lords, 1603–1649* (Chapel Hill, NC, 1983), p. 24.

70. BL, Harleian 389, f. 95.

71. Ibid., 390, ff. 48, 367v, 370.

72. See, for example, the Earl of Warwick's speech in the Lords of 21 April, Benjamin Rudyerd's speech of 28 April, and various verbatim speeches on 10 May. Ibid., ff. 393v, 394–95, 401–2.

73. David Randall, 'Joseph Mead, Novellante: News, Sociability and Credibility in Early Stuart England,' *Journal of British Studies* (45, 2, 2006), p. 304.

74. Ibid., p. 305.

75. BL, Harleian 389, f. 14.

76. Ibid. 390, ff. 380, 382–85.

77. Ibid., f. 370.

78. Ibid., f. 370.

79. See, for example, ibid. 390, ff. 388v, 396.

80. Ibid., f. 396.

81. Ibid. 389, f. 30.

82. Ibid. 390, f. 45-v.

83. Ibid., f. 56v.

84. Ibid., f. 53.

85. Ibid. 383, f. 59-v. 7 May 1628.

86. For example, ibid., ff. 31–32, 11 May 1626.

87. Birch, *Court and Times Charles I*, I, p. 100.

88. Quoting from Pliny the Elder, *Historia Naturalis*, VIII, p. 42. I am very grateful to Samantha Herrick for her assistance with this reference.

89. Quoted in Bidwell and Jansson, *Proceedings in Parliament 1626*, IV, pp. 259–60.

90. Ibid., p. 294.

91. Ibid., pp. 295, 296.

92. Ibid., pp. 302–3.

93. Ibid., p. 303.

94. Ibid.

95. Ibid., p. 305.

96. Ibid., p. 308; II, pp. 350–51.

97. Ibid., IV, p. 307.

98. Ibid., pp. 308, 310.

99.   Ibid, pp. 317–21.

100.   Norfolk RO (Norwich), MC2/92, pp. 7–10.

101.   Johnson, Keeler, Cole, and Bidwell, *Commons Debates and Lords Proceedings 1628*, IV, p. 204.

102.   Thrush and Ferris, *HPT 1604–1629*, Edmund Moundeford.

103.   BL, Egerton 2715, f. 437; C. R. Manning, 'News-Letters from Sir Edmund Moundeford, Knt., M.P., to Framlingham Gawdy, Esq., 1627–1633,' *Norfolk Archaeology* (V, 1859), p. 64. The correct number of subsidies voted was five. The Egerton ms. clearly notes four. The editor of *Norf. Arch.* has mistranscribed the number as five.

104.   BL, Egerton 2715, f. 362.

105.   Ibid. f. 439.

106.   *HMC Cowper*, I, pp. 348, 350–53.

107.   Johnson, Keeler, Cole, and Bidwell, *Commons Debates and Lords Proceedings 1628*, IV, pp. 211–13.

108.   Ibid., p. 129.

109.   Ibid.

110.   BL, Harleian 383, f. 26, March 1625.

111.   Ibid., f. 32, 11 May 1626.

112.   Birch, *Court and Times Charles I*, I, p. 98: 28 April.

113.   Johnson, Keeler, Cole, and Bidwell, *Commons Debates and Lords Proceedings 1628*, VI, pp. 189–92.

114.   Ibid., pp. 209–10.

115.   *HMC 11th Report, Appendix I*, p. 23.

116.   Ibid., pp. 25–31.

117.   Ibid., p. 50.

118.   Ibid., p. 61.

119.   Ibid., pp. 66–68.

120.   Ibid., p. 70.

121.   Ibid., pp. 70–76.

122.   Ibid., p. 142.

123.   Ibid., pp. 145–49.

124.   *CSP Ven. 1619–21*, p. 577.

125.   Ibid. *1628–29*, no. 58, 5 April.

126.   Ibid., no. 77.

127.   Johnson, Keeler, Cole, and Bidwell, *Commons Debates and Lords Proceedings 1628*, VI, pp. 174–75.

128.   Ibid., pp. 177–81. As the editors note, while only one newsletter is extant, Lewkenor had promised to write weekly. Ibid., p. 181 n. 4.

129.   For the speeches of Kirton and Eliot, see Notestein and Relf, *Commons Debates for 1629*, pp. 14–15, 108.

130.   Ibid., p. 14. At least seventeen copies of this separate are extant. Ibid., p.

271. It was printed in 1641 as *A Religious and Worthy Speech spoken by Mr Rous in Parliament* (London).

131. Notestein and Relf, *Commons Debates for 1629*, p. 173.

132. Ibid.

133. Ibid., pp. xxxiii–xxxiv; Inner Temple Library, Petyt MS 538/18, ff. 19, 56.

134. Johnson, Keeler, Cole, and Bidwell, *Commons Debates and Lords Proceedings 1628*, III, p. 265. In contrast in 1624, the clerk was requested to make available the text of the King's answer on the Spanish threat so members could copy it out themselves. *CJ*, I, p. 679.

135. Mary Anne Everett Green, *Diary of John Rous incumbent of Santon Downham, Suffolk, from 1625–1642* (Camden Society, old ser., 66, 1856), p. 16.

PART III: PERMEABLE BOUNDARIES

1. This introduction is based in part upon the fuller accounts concerning Parliament and public space in Chris R. Kyle, 'Parliament and the Palace of Westminster: An Exploration of Public Space in the Early Seventeenth Century,' in Clyve Jones and Sean Kelsey, eds., *Housing Parliament: Dublin, Edinburgh and Westminster, Parliament History* (21, 2, 2002), pp. 85–98; Chris R. Kyle and Jason Peacey, '"Under cover of so much coming and going": Public Access to Parliament and the Political Process in Early Modern England,' in Kyle and Peacey, eds., *Parliament at Work: Parliamentary Committees, Political Power and Public Access in Early Modern England* (Woodbridge, 2002), pp. 1–23.

2. For an examination of all the costs and changes to the building in preparation for a parliamentary session, see Elizabeth Read Foster, 'Staging a Parliament in Early Stuart England,' in Peter Clark, Alan G. G. Smith, and Nicholas Tyacke, eds., *The English Commonwealth 1547–1640* (Leicester, 1979), pp. 129–46, 239–48.

3. Sir Thomas Smith, *De Republica Anglorum*, ed. Mary Dewar (Cambridge, 1982), p. 80. Similar comments were made frequently by travelers and ambassadors. See, for example, G. B. Harrison and R. A. Jones, eds., *De Maisse: A Journal of All that was Accomplished by Monsieur de Maisse, Ambassador in England from King Henry IV to Queen Elizabeth Anno Domini 1597* (London, 1931), p. 38; and Gottfried von Bülow, trans., 'Journey through England and Scotland made by Lupold von Wedel in the Years 1584 and 1585,' *Transactions of the Royal Historical Society* (new ser., 9, 1895), p. 261.

4. Alasdair Hawkyard and Maria Hayward, 'The Dressing and Trimming of the Parliament Chamber, 1509–1558,' *Parliamentary History* (29, 2, 2010), p. 230. As they note, *Romulus and Remus* was particularly apt, as the brothers restored civil order and overcame the tyrant Amulius. See also Thomas P. Campbell, *Henry VIII and the Art of Majesty: Tapestries at the Tudor Court* (New Haven, 2007), pp. 195–98, 306.

5. Foster, 'Staging a Parliament,' p. 135.

6. Ibid.; TNA, LC5/132, p. 11.

7. David M. Dean, 'Image and Ritual in the Tudor Parliaments,' in Dale Hoak, ed., *Tudor Political Culture* (Cambridge, 1995), pp. 243–71. For the procession and opening of the 1614 Parliament, see Maija Jansson, ed., *Proceedings in Parliament 1614* (Philadelphia, 1988), pp. 3–10.

8. R. Brown, G. Cavendish-Bentick, et al., eds., *Calendar of State Papers relating to English Affairs in the Archives of Venice, and in other libraries of Northern Italy* (38 vols, London, 1864–1947), X (1603–1607), p. 10, no. 204. At a jousting tournament on Saturday, 3 April, both ambassadors were given boxes opposite the royal stand—the French ambassador was seated on the right, the Spanish ambassador on the left, and sandwiched between them was Nicolo Molin. As he commented, '[T]his has given rise to endless discussion. Some say that, as France was placed on the right hand, his was the post of honour, others that, as the Spanish box had the best view, it was the place of honour.'

9. *CSP Ven.*, p. 140, Ambassador Nicolo Molin to the Doge and Senate, 7 April 1604.

10. *CJ*, I, pp. 139–41; Simon Healy, 'Debates in the House of Commons, 1604–1607,' in Chris R. Kyle, ed., *Parliament, Politics and Elections, 1604–1648*, Camden 5th ser., 17 (Cambridge, 2001), pp. 22, 42, 52–53.

11. *CJ*, I, p. 141.

12. As a result of this intrusion of the public, James repeated his opening speech the following day, this time in the presence of the Commons, which ordered a copy to be entered into the Commons Journal. As Sir Edward Montagu noted, the King 'satisfie[d] the greefe of the house.' Healy, 'Debates in the House of Commons, 1604–1607,' p. 53.

13. Maija Jansson, ed., *Proceedings in Parliament 1614* (Philadelphia, 1988), p. 12.

14. Wallace Notestein, Frances Helen Relf, and Hartley Simpson, eds., *Commons Debates 1621* (7 vols., New Haven, 1935), II, pp. 1–2 n. 1. In 1625 the Lords appointed the Lord Chamberlain and Earl Marshal to vet those who entered to hear the King's speech. Maija Jansson and William B. Bidwell, eds., *Proceedings in Parliament 1625* (New Haven, 1987), p. 191. This process seems to have put an end to public invasions of the opening ceremony, but it not solve the problem of the Lords' neglect in calling for the Commons to attend. See Bidwell and Jansson, eds., *Proceedings in Parliament 1626* (4 vols., New Haven, 1991–96), I, p. 25; and BL, Harleian 390, f. 13v. Joseph Mead to Sir Martin Stuteville. In 1628 the Commons took umbrage that a messenger, Mr. Crane, rather than Black Rod, had been sent to inform them to attend the Upper House. Robert C. Johnson, William B. Bidwell, Maija Jansson Cole, and Mary Frear Keeler, eds., *Commons Debates and Lords Proceedings 1628* (6 vols., New Haven, 1977–83), II, p. 12.

15. Oliver Arnold, *The Third Citizen: Shakespeare's Theater and the Early Modern House of Commons* (Baltimore, 2007), p. 57. See also Arnold, 'Absorption and Representation: Mapping England in the Early Modern House of Commons,' in Andrew Gordon and Bernhard Klein, eds., *Literature, Mapping and the Politics of Space in Early Modern Britain* (Cambridge, 2001), pp. 15–34.

16. Arnold, *Third Citizen*, p. 18. For the development of this idea in the reign of Charles II, see Annabel Patterson, *The Long Parliament of Charles II* (New Haven, 2008).

17. On St. Stephen's Chapel, see Alasdair Hawkyard, 'From Painted Chamber to St. Stephen's Chapel: The Meeting Places of the House of Commons at Westminster until 1603,' in Clyve Jones and Sean Kelsey, eds., *Housing Parliament: Dublin, Edinburgh and Westminster, Parliamentary History*, 21, 1 (2002), pp. 62–84.

18. BL, Harleian 253, ff. 33v, 34v-5. The most notorious culprit was the Recorder of London, William Fleetwood. In 1585 he complained to the Commons about the poor attendance in the chamber, as many members were 'at the bars in her Majesties Courts attending their clients causes, and neglecting the service of the House.' Later that day Fleetwood himself was found pleading a case in Common Pleas while Parliament remained in session. Sir Simonds D'Ewes, *A Compleat Journal of the Votes, Speeches and Debates, Both of the House of Lords and House of Commons throughout the whole reign of Queen Elizabeth* (London, 1682), p. 347. On the chronic absenteeism from committee meetings, see Chris R. Kyle, '"It will be a Scandal to show what we have done with such a number": House of Commons Attendance Lists, 1606–1628,' in Kyle, *Parliament, Politics and Elections, 1604–1648*, pp. 179–235.

19. Thomas Nash, *The Terrors of the Night* (London, 1594), sig. B4.

20. Kyle and Peacey, *Parliament at Work*, p. 5.

21. M. Exwood and H. L. Lehman, eds., *The Journal of William Schellinks' Travels in England 1660–1663* (Camden Society, 5th ser., 1, London, 1993), p. 59; *Les Voyages de Monsieur de Moncoys* (4 vols., Paris, 1695), II, pp. 65–66.

22. On Cotton's house, see Colin G. C. Tite, *The Manuscript Library of Sir Robert Cotton* (London, 1994), pp. 81–85.

23. On the drinking establishments in this area, see below, pp. 114–15.

24. Jansson, *Proceedings in Parliament 1614*, pp. 99, 101; Notestein, Relf, and Simpson, *Commons Debates 1621*, II, p. 32.

25. Vernon F. Snow, ed., *Parliament in Elizabethan England: John Hooker's Order and Usage* (New Haven, 1977), p. 164; *CJ*, I, p. 205, 10 May 1604.

26. Foster, 'Staging a Parliament,' p. 131.

27. Sir Simonds D'Ewes, *The Journals of all the Parliaments During the Reign of Queen Elizabeth* (London, 1682), pp. 290–91.

28. T. E. Hartley, *Proceedings in the Parliaments of Elizabeth I* (3 vols., Leicester, 1981–95), III, pp. 327, 449; *CJ*, I, pp. 258, 259.

29. Notestein, Relf, and Simpson, *Commons Debates 1621*, IV, pp. 28–29; *The English Reports* (178 vols., Edinburgh, 1930–32), LXXIII, pp. 415–16: 2 Dyer Rep. 188; ibid., LXXVII, p. 1349: 12 Coke Rep. 71, I, pp. 403, 404.

30. Notestein, Relf, and Simpson, *Commons Debates 1621*, II, p. 41.

31. HLRO, Main Papers, 25 June 1625; *LJ*, III, p. 446. However, the tavern remained open during the 1625 Parliament.

32. *CJ*, I, pp. 403, 404.

33. See, for example, the order made by the Commons on 6 June 1628 at the

height of the debates on the liberties of the people and the Petition of Right: 'the outward door to be kept shut and attended, and the room to be kept clear,' Johnson, Keeler, Cole, and Bidwell, *Commons Debates and Lords Proceedings 1628*, IV, p. 138.

34. For further details on committee meetings and venues, see Chris R. Kyle, 'Attendance, Apathy and Order?': Parliamentary Committees in Early Stuart England,' in Kyle and Peacey, *Parliament at Work*, esp. pp. 48–49.

35. R. Latham and W. Matthews, eds., *The Dairy of Samuel Pepys* (11 vols., London, 1970–83), III, pp. 60–61.

36. Johnson, Keeler, Cole, and Bidwell, *Commons Debates and Lords Proceedings 1628*, II, pp. 244, 262, 265, 271.

37. Ibid., II, p. 275.

38. *ODNB*. sub. Philip Parsons.

39. Johnson, Keeler, Cole, and Bidwell, *Commons Debates and Lords Proceedings 1628*, III, pp. 368, 376.

40. On 6 February 1621 Sir Francis Barrington commented that 'all ought to take their places, for otherwise some may come that are strangers that may relate these things to others.' Notestein, Relf, and Simpson, *Commons Debates 1621*, II, p. 32. This was in relation to a number of MPs standing in the doorway. *CJ*, I, p. 511. That the problem continued is evident from the imposition of a fine of 12d. made on 9 February on 'whosoever standeth in the entry.' *CJ*, I, p. 515.

41. D'Ewes, *Journals of all the Parliaments During the Reign of Queen Elizabeth*, p. 334; Hartley, *Proceedings in the Parliaments of Elizabeth I*, II, p. 66.

42. D'Ewes, *Journals of all the Parliaments During the Reign of Queen Elizabeth*, p. 486. The House was packed on 3 March, as a division reveals a staggeringly high turnout of 434 members that probably accounts for why Legg was able to go unnoticed for so long. Hartley, *Proceedings in the Parliaments of Elizabeth I*, III, pp. 95–96.

43. Snow, *Parliament in Elizabethan England*, p. 186.

44. See, for example, Robinson, who in 1584 spent four nights in custody. D'Ewes, *Journals of all the Parliaments During the Reign of Queen Elizabeth,*, p. 334.

45. Bulkeley was actually a servant of Sir Anthony Dyott, who sat for Lichfield, and had come to 'see the fashions.' Jansson, *Proceedings in Parliament 1614*, pp. 237, 244.

46. Hartley, *Proceedings in the Parliaments of Elizabeth I*, III, p. 398.

47. *CJ*, I, p. 348, 5 March 1607.

48. Chris R. Kyle, 'Parliament and the Palace of Westminster: An Exploration of Public Space in the Early Seventeenth Century,' in Clyve Jones and Sean Kelsey, eds., *Housing Parliament: Dublin, Edinburgh and Westminster, Parliamentary History* (21, 2, 2002), p. 90.

5. OPEN DOORS: PRESSURE GROUPS AND LOBBYING

1. *Letters and Papers, Foreign and Domestic, Henry VIII* (21 vols., London, 1862–1932), VII, pp. 370–71; TNA, SP 1/69, f. 95.

2. Bindoff, *HPT 1509–1558*, Sir Richard Weston.

3. Ibid. *1509–1558*, John Mill, Sir William Fitzwilliam, Sir Henry Guildford.

4. David M. Dean, 'Parliament, Privy Council, and Local Politics in Elizabethan England: The Yarmouth-Lowestoft Fishing Dispute,' *Albion* (22, 1990), pp. 39–64; Dean, 'London Lobbies and Parliament: The Case of the Brewers and Coopers in the Parliament of 1593,' *Parliamentary History* (8, 1989), pp. 341–65; Dean, 'Public or Private? London, Leather and Legislation in Elizabethan England,' *HJ* (31, 1988), pp. 525–48; Dean, 'Pressure Groups and Lobbies in the Elizabethan and Early Jacobean Parliaments,' *Parliaments, Estates and Representation* (11, 1991), pp. 139–52; Ian Archer, 'The London Lobbies in the Sixteenth Century,' *HJ*, 31 (1988), pp. 17–44; Edwin Green, 'The Vintners' Lobby, 1552–1568,' *Guildhall Studies in London History* (1, 2, 1974), pp. 47–58.

5. See below, pp. 136–37.

6. G. R. Elton, 'Tudor Government. The Points of Contact. I. Parliament,' *Transactions of the Royal Historical Society* (5th ser., xxiv, 1974), pp. 183–200; Robert Tittler, 'Elizabethan Towns and the "Points of Contact": Parliament,' *PH* (8, 2, 1989), pp. 275–88.

7. Michael A. R. Graves, 'Managing Elizabethan Parliaments,' in D. M. Dean and N. L. Jones, eds., *The Parliaments of Elizabethan England* (Oxford, 1990), p. 38.

8. David Dean, *Lawmaking and Society in Late Elizabethan England* (Cambridge, 1996), p. 7.

9. G. R. Elton, *The Parliament of England, 1559–1581* (Cambridge, 1986), p. 303.

10. BL, Harleian 253, f. 34; Michael A. R. Graves, *Thomas Norton: The Parliament Man* (Oxford, 1994).

11. Catherine Strateman Sims, ed., '"Policies in Parliaments": An Early Seventeenth Century Tractate on House of Commons Procedure,' *HLQ* (15, 1, 1951), p. 49.

12. Wallace Notestein, Frances Helen Relf, and Hartley Simpson, eds., *Commons Debates 1621* (7 vols., New Haven, 1935), IV, p. 306.

13. For an example of this, see below, pp. 135, 221 n. 110.

14. Elizabeth Read Foster, 'Staging a Parliament in Early Stuart England,' in Peter Clark, A. G. R. Smith, Nicholas Tyacke, eds., *The English Commonwealth, 1547–1640* (Leicester, 1979), pp. 140–41.

15. If the bill concerned more than one individual, the Speaker was entitled to claim £5 from each individual.

16. Chris R. Kyle, '*Lex Loquens*: Legislation in the Parliament of 1624' (unpublished Ph.D. diss., University of Auckland, 1994), pp. 529–34.

17.   J. E. Neale, *The Elizabethan House of Commons* (London, 1949), p. 326.

18.   Ibid., p. 327 n.1. This could add up to a substantial fee. One of the longest private bills in the 1620s was the assurance of the manor of Newlangport to Martin Lumley (HLRO, OA 21 James I cap. 58), which ran to five membranes at sixty-four lines per membrane, or 16s. 8d. in total.

19.   *CJ*, I, p. 167; Robert C. Johnson, Mary Frear Keeler, Maija Jansson Cole, and William B. Bidwell, eds., *Commons Debates and Lords Proceedings 1628* (6 vols., New Haven, 1977–83), III, p. 208.

20.   Neale, *The Elizabethan House of Commons*, p. 324.

21.   Ibid., p. 325.

22.   Maurice Bond, 'The Clerks of the Parliaments, 1509–1953,' *English Historical Review* (73, 1958), p. 80; see HLRO, Braye 55 no. 86.

23.   BL, Add. 33924, f. 32v.

24.   HLRO, Main Papers, 12 March 1624; Hawarde Diary, 12 March 1624.

25.   D'Ewes Diary 1624, f. 83v. For the objections to the bill, see Pym Diary 1624, f. 27. A similar bill in 1566 also met its fate at the first reading. Elton, *Parliament of England, 1559–1581*, p. 310.

26.   *CJ*, I, pp. 588, 593, 605, 762; *LJ*, III, pp. 113, 118, 139; HLRO, Main Papers, 12 April 1624.

27.   HLRO, Main Papers, 15 March, 14 June 1610. I have not been able to find the bill to which Walmesley referred.

28.   Andrew Thrush and J. P. Ferris, eds., *The House of Commons, 1604–1629* (6 vols., Cambridge, 2010), Thomas Barfoot.

29.   On the Egerton's dispute and printing of documents, see Chapter Six, p. 164.

30.   Thrush and Ferris, *HPT 1604–1629*, John Evelyn.

31.   I am grateful to Paul Hunneyball for the information on Catcher.

32.   *CJ*, I, p. 619–20; Thomas Tyrwhitt, ed., *Proceedings and Debates in the House of Commons in 1620 and 1621 by Edward Nicholas* (Oxford, 1766), II, p. 64; Notestein, Relf, and Simpson, *Commons Debates 1621*, VI, p. 154.

33.   TNA, C173/2, bundle 1. I am grateful to Andrew Thrush for this reference.

34.   I am grateful to Paul Hunneyball for the information on Acland.

35.   Archer, 'The London Lobbies in the Later Sixteenth Century,' pp. 17–44.

36.   CLRO, Repertories, 38, f. 61b.

37.   Dean, 'London Lobbies and Parliament'; Chris R. Kyle, 'Parliament and the Politics of Carting in Early Stuart London,' *London Journal* (21, 2, 2002), pp. 1–11; Graves, 'Managing Elizabethan Parliaments,' pp. 53–54.

38.   BL, Harleian 253, ff. 33v, 34v.

39.   A substantial and important body of literature now exists on London lobbying in the fifteenth century. See Matthew Davies, 'Lobbying Parliament: The London Companies in the Fifteenth Century,' *Parliamentary History* (23, 2004), pp. 136–48; Hannes Kleineke, 'Lobbying and Access: The Canons of Windsor and the

Matter of the Poor Knights in the Parliament of 1485,' *Parliamentary History* (25, 2, 2006), pp. 145–59; Carole Rawcliffe, 'Parliament and the Settlement of Disputes by Arbitration in the Later Middle Ages,' *Parliamentary History* (9, 1990), pp. 316–42; and Caroline Barron, 'London and Parliament in the Lancastrian Period,' *Parliamentary History* (9, 1990), pp. 343–67.

40. Davies, 'Lobbying Parliament,' p. 143.

41. Ibid., pp. 140, 141.

42. Helen Miller, 'London and Parliament in the Reign of Henry VIII,' *BIHR* (35, 1962), pp. 128–49.

43. The term refers to a copy of the bill.

44. GL, MS 19629. This copy was sent to the Masons Company.

45. CLRO, Rep., 38, f. 117b.

46. HLRO, Main Papers, 15 April 1624. A similar fate befell a bill introduced by the Butchers Company that London also ordered its MPs to halt. CLRO, Rep., 38, f. 115; HLRO, Main Papers, 19 April 1624; *CJ*, I, p. 770; Chris R. Kyle, ed., *Parliament, Politics and Elections, 1604–1648* (Camden 5th ser., 17, Cambridge, 2001), pp. 215–16; Kyle, 'Parliamentary Committees in Early Stuart England,' in Kyle and Jason Peacey, eds., *Parliament at Work: Parliamentary Committees, Political Power and Public Access in Early Modern England* (Woodbridge, 2002), pp. 51–53.

47. Thrush and Ferris, *HPT 1604–1629*, York.

48. Bodleian, Tanner 290, f. 102; *CJ*, I, pp. 261, 267; Francis Blomefield, *Topographical History of Norfolk* (5 vols., Fersfield, 1739–75), III, pp. 361–62; Norfolk RO (Norwich), Assembly Book 1585–1613, f. 322v.

49. *CJ*, I, pp. 424, 619, 768, 769; Notestein, Relf, and Simpson, *Commons Debates 1621*, V, p. 374; VI, p. 154; D'Ewes Diary 1624, f. 110; Holland II Diary 1624, f. 37; Earle Diary 1624, f. 147v.

50. Devon RO, Totnes Borough Records, 1579A/10/13. Quoted in David Dean, 'Locality and Parliament: The Legislative Activities of Devon MPs,' in Todd Gray, Margery Rowe, and Audrey Erskine, eds., *Tudor and Stuart Devon: The Common Estate and Government* (Exeter, 1992), p. 80.

51. For detailed information, see Chris R. Kyle, 'Prince Charles in the Parliaments of 1621 and 1624,' *HJ* (41, 3, 1998), pp. 603–14. On Duchy electioneering, see Paul Hunneyball, 'Prince Charles's Council as Electoral Agent 1620–1624,' *PH* (23, 2004), pp. 316–35.

52. BL, Harleian 159, f. 133r-v.

53. Ibid., Add. 26639, f. 35; *CJ*, I, pp. 701, 705, 715, 786, 790, 798; *LJ*, III, pp. 269, 342, 362–63; TNA, SP 14/165/34.

54. Duchy of Cornwall RO, Warrants and Letters 1623–6, f. 87v; Acts of the Council 1624, f. 44. 21 James I caps. 46, 47.

55. Sims, 'Policies in Parliaments,' p. 47.

56. GL, 5570/1, Fishmongers' Minutes, pp. 181, 297, 314.

57. Ibid., 15333/2, Vintners Company Account Book, p. 359.

58. Ibid., 2883/3, Blacksmiths Account Book, p. 92.

59. Ibid., 34048/8, p. 463; 34049/9, unf., Merchant Tailors Account Books; 3054/1, unf., Tilers and Bricklayers Account Book.

60. Ibid., 11571/9, Grocers Company Account Book, f. 30v.

61. Ibid., 4326/6, unf., Carpenters Account Book; 5606/2, f. 298v, Coopers Account Book.

62. National Library of Scotland, Adv. MS, 34.2.15 f. 71. Reference from Andrew Thrush.

63. Recorder Fleetwood speaking. T. E. Hartley, *Proceedings in the Parliaments of Elizabeth I* (Leicester, 1995), III, p. 116.

64. Green, 'The Vintners' Lobby, 1552–1568,' pp. 54–55.

65. Hartley, *Proceedings in the Parliaments of Elizabeth I*, III, p. 414.

66. The editors of *Commons Debates 1621* suggest that because Sir Thomas Ireland, Sir Lawrence Hyde, and Mr Holt 'so frequently appear before the House or its committees it may be assumed that they have developed a particular practice in pleading cases' in Parliament. Notestein, Relf, and Simpson, *Commons Debates 1621*, II, p. 50 n. 23.

67. Hartley, *Proceedings in the Parliaments of Elizabeth I*, III, p. 148.

68. GL, 4326/6, Carpenters Account Book 1592–1622, ff. 567–68; *CJ*, I, p. 619.

69. My italics.

70. GL, 11571/10, Grocers Account Book, ff. 444v-45v.

71. London Metropolitan Archives, Sutton Hospital, ACC/1876/G/01/10/4. The doorkeeper of the Court of Wards Committee Chamber also received a 'reward' of 12d.

72. *CJ*, I, p. 468; Notestein, Relf, and Simpson, *Commons Debates 1621*, II, p. 32.

73. GL, 5606/2, ff. 239, 270, 298v.

74. Ibid., 15333/2 Vintners Account Book, p. 359; 3054/1, unf, Tilers and Bricklayers Account Book; GL, 11571/10 Grocers Account Book, f. 445; London Metropolitan Archives, Sutton Hospital, ACC/1876/G/01/10/5. I am grateful to Andrew Thrush for suggesting that I examine the Sutton Hospital records.

75. Devon RO, Exeter Corporation Archive, B 1/6, f. 207. I am grateful to Paul Hunneyball for this reference.

76. See also Chapter Six for the printing of these documents during the 1620s, pp. 154–57.

77. Dean, 'Public or Private,' p. 537.

78. Southampton City Archives, SC5/2/2, f. 112v. I am grateful to Andrew Thrush for this reference.

79. Devon RO, Exeter Corporation Archive, B 1/6, p. 207.

80. GL, 15333/3, Vintners Account Book, unf.

81. CLRO, Rep. 38, f. 129b.

82. Thrush and Ferris, *HPT 1604–1629*, Bristol.

83. HLRO, Main Papers, 20 May 1610.

84. Thrush and Ferris, *HPT 1604–1629*, George Byng.

85. Felix Hull, ed., *A Calendar of the White and Black Books of the Cinque Ports, 1432–1955* (London, 1966), p. 379.

86. GL, 3054/1, unf. Tilers and Bricklayers Account Book.

87. Ibid.

88. BL, Add. 29623, f. 5; *CJ*, I, p. 994.

89. *HMC Exeter*, p. 321.

90. *CJ*, I, p. 199.

91. Arthur Hall, *A letter sent by F.A. touchyng the proceedings in a private quarell and unkindnesse betweene Arthur Hall, and Melchisedech Mallerie* . . . (London, 1576), p. 100, *STC* 12629.

92. Ibid., p. 101; Hartley, *Proceedings in the Parliaments of Elizabeth I*, I, p. 508; J. E. Neale, *Elizabeth I and Her Parliaments, 1559–1581* (London, 1953), pp. 407–10.

93. BL, Add. 36856 f. 30b.

94. *CJ*, I, p. 595.

95. Notestein, Relf, and Simpson, *Commons Debates 1621*, V, p. 110.

96. William Hakewill, *The Manner How Statutes are Enacted in Parliament by Passing of Bills* (1641), p. 11.

97. Dean, 'Public or Private,' p. 546.

98. Devon RO, B 1/5, f. 207.

99. GL, 5442/5, Brewers Account Book, unf.

100. Ibid., 4326/6, Carpenters Account Book, unf.

101. Ibid., 4326/7, f. 86.

102. LMA, ACC/1876/G/01/10/5.

103. Lambeth Palace Library, MS 1730, f. 10v, Archbishop Abbot's Account Book.

104. See Chapter Four, on manuscript news.

105. Hartley, *Proceedings in the Parliaments of Elizabeth I*, III, p. 450.

106. Thetford Town Council, King's House, T/C1/3, pp. 2–3; Norfolk RO (Norwich), Hare of Stow Bardolph 61357, f. 36.

107. Hasler, *HPT 1558–1603* (Edward Clere); Blomefield, *Topographical History of Norfolk*, II, p. 128.

108. TNA, SP 14/19/107; *HMC Hatfield*, 18, pp. 386–87; *CJ*, I, pp. 258, 259, 278.

109. *HMC Hatfield*, 17, pp. 531–32; HLRO, Main Papers, 22 March 1610; Coke, *8th Report*, Thetford School case (1610); 1 Equity Case Abridged 100 in *English Reports*, 21, pp. 909–10; *LJ*, II, pp. 598, 600, 603, 604; *CJ*, I, pp. 435, 438, 440, 442, 443; Thetford Town Council, T/C1/3, pp. 29–30. The measure was enacted as 7 James I cap. 11.

110. 27 Eliz. I O.A. 47. The city also paid to have the bill enrolled as a public act, and so it appeared on the Parliament Roll. Dean, *Lawmaking and Society in Late Elizabethan England*, p. 254.

111.   J. F. Merritt, *The Social World of Early Modern Westminster* (Manchester, 2005), p. 88.

112.   A plaque listing the names of those who contributed to the cost of the bill was placed in St. Margaret's Westminster Archive Centre, E5 (1587–88), f. 26v; E2413, ff. 6–8.

113.   Fleetwood's notes on the bill, BL, Lansdowne 43/74, ff. 178v-79v.

114.   C. S. Knighton, ed., *Acts of the Dean and Chapter of Westminster, 1543–1609* (Westminster Abbey Record Series, vol. II, no. 376). Quoted in Merritt, *Social World of Early Modern Westminster,* p. 89.

115.   Westminster Archive Centre, E2413, ff. 6–7.

116.   For the objections of the Dean and Chapter drafted by their counsel, Mr. Vale, TNA, SP 12/177/27.

117.   Dean, 'Parliament, Privy Council, and Local Politics in Elizabethan England,' pp. 39–64; Robert Tittler, 'The English Fishing Industry in the Sixteenth Century, the Case of Great Yarmouth,' *Albion* (9, 1977), pp. 40–60; A. Saul, 'The Herring Industry at Great Yarmouth,' *Norfolk Archaeology* (38, 1981), pp. 33–43.

118.   A *lewe* was French for the Latin *leuca,* or league in English.

119.   Roskell, Clark, and Rawcliffe, *HPT* 1386–1421, Great Yarmouth constituency article.

120.   Dean, 'Parliament, Privy Council, and Local Politics in Elizabethan England,' p. 58.

121.   Norfolk RO (Norwich), Y/C18/4, ff. 67–76v.

122.   Ibid. Y/C18/4, f. 66v. James's brother-in-law, King Christian of Denmark, landed at Yarmouth during his visit to England in 1606. Ibid. C19/5, f. 52.

123.   The rights also extended seven leagues out to sea. This section is based in part on my constituency article in Thrush and Ferris, *HPT 1604–1629,* Great Yarmouth.

124.   Norfolk RO (Norwich), Y/C19/5, f. 66r-v.

125.   Ibid. Y/C36/7/2.

126.   *CJ,* I, p. 400.

127.   Norfolk RO (Norwich), Y/C19/5, f. 77.

128.   The exact location of Crane Quay is unclear.

129.   Ibid. Y/C36/7/2, 21, 25; BL, Harleian 6838, ff. 230v-1, 243; Suffolk RO (Lowestoft), M18/06/1, ff. 42v-54v. Lowestoft spent £54 on the introduction and passage of the bill. Ibid. f. 68v.

130.   He also noted that Yarmouth still displayed the Lowestoft ordnance that Ket had captured and used to besiege Yarmouth.

131.   *CJ,* I, p. 410.

132.   Norfolk RO (Norwich), Y/C20/1, f. 12v.

133.   GL, 12071/2, Armourers Company Minute Books, pp. 412–15; Hartley, *Proceedings in the Parliaments of Elizabeth I,* I, p. 530; *CJ,* I, p. 121.

134.   Dalton had previously spoken in the 1556–57 Parliament in behalf of the Ar-

mourers, for which he received three 'ryals' of gold. GL, 12071/2, Armourers Company Minute Books, pp. 151, 161.

135.   *HMC 5th Rep.,* p. 597.

136.   GL, 12605/2, Armourers Company Renter Warden's Account Book, ff. 24v-25v, f. 38v; Claude Blair, 'The Armourers' Bill of 1581: The making of Arms and Armour in Sixteenth-Century London,' *Journal of the Arms and Armour Society* (XII, 1. 1986), pp. 42–44.

137.   Chris R. Kyle, 'Parliament and the Politics of Carting in Early Stuart London,' *London Journal* (27, 2, 2002), pp. 1–11.

138.   Hampshire RO, Jervoise Papers, TD 540, Scrapbook, unf.

139.   Dean, 'Parliament, Privy Council, and Local Politics in Elizabethan England,' p. 40.

140.   TNA, SP 12/107/48. Quoted in Neale, *The Elizabethan House of Commons,* p. 377.

141.   For details on public access to Parliament, see Chapter Five; and Chris R. Kyle and Jason Peacey, '"Under Cover of so much coming and going": Public Access to Parliament and the Political Process in Early Modern England,' in Kyle and Peacey, eds., *Parliament at Work: Parliamentary Committees, Political Power and Public Access in Early Modern England* (Woodbridge, 2002), pp. 1–23.

142.   Quoted in Dean, 'Public or Private,' p. 534.

143.   Kyle, 'Lex Loquens,' pp. 435–41.

144.   David Zaret, *Origins of Democratic Culture: Printing, Petitions and the Public Sphere* (Princeton, 2000), p. 81; see also R. W. Hoyle, 'Petitioning as Popular Politics in Sixteenth-Century England,' *Historical Research* (75, 190, 2002), pp. 365–83.

145.   As Zaret points out, petitioning had not disappeared from the realm of political discourse. Zaret, *Origins of Democratic Culture,* pp. 81–83.

146.   On standing committees, see Sheila Lambert, 'Procedure in the House of Commons in the Early Stuart Period,' *English Historical Review* (95, 1980), pp. 775–77; J. F. Jameson, 'The Origin of the Standing Committee in American Legislative Bodies,' *Political Science Quarterly* (9, 1894), pp. 246–67; and Mary Frear Keeler, 'The Emergence of Standing Committee for Privileges and Returns,' *PH* (1, 1982), pp. 25–46.

147.   On monopolies, see Elizabeth Read Foster, 'The Procedure of the House of Commons against Patents and Monopolies, 1621–1624,' in W. A. Aiken and B. D. Henning, eds., *Conflict in Stuart England: Essays in Honour of Wallace Notestein* (London, 1960), pp. 57–85; and Chris R. Kyle, '"But a New Button to an Old Coat": The Enactment of the Statute of Monopolies, 21 James I cap. 3,' *Journal of Legal History* (19, 3, 1998), pp. 203–23.

148.   Phelips was appointed chair of the committee on 12 March after the previous chair, Sir Edward Sackville, had pleaded illness. *CJ,* I. p. 549.

149.   Ibid., p. 550.

150.   Kyle, 'Parliament and the Politics of Carting,' pp. 20–21.

151. For example, see Edward Alford's notes on various petitions and bills in BL, Harleian 6803, ff. 6v, 12v, 13v, 19v, 26, 43, 53–4v, 110v, 179v.

152. Foster, 'The Procedure of the House of Commons against Patents and Monopolies,' p. 75.

153. See Notestein, Relf, and Simpson, *Commons Debates 1621*, VII, pp. 395–402.

154. Tyrwhitt, *Proceedings and Debates in the House of Commons*, II, p. 115.

155. James F. Larkin and Paul Hughes, *Stuart Royal Proclamations* (Oxford, 1973), I, no. 217.

156. James S. Hart, *Justice upon Petition: The House of Lords and the Reformation of Justice 1621–1675* (London, 1991), pp. 16–17.

157. See Chapter Six, pp. 167–69; HLRO, Main Papers, 24 March 1626.

158. Hart, *Justice upon Petition*, p. 37; *LJ*, III, p. 157.

159. Of those that did interact with Parliament, Joan Thomas, 'a poore distressed and oppressed Widdow,' clearly saw Parliament as a legitimate avenue of redress for women. She printed her petition to Parliament noting herself 'a part of that great Common body which you represent.' BL, Coke Papers, Add. 69917, f. 74. See also Notestein, Relf, and Simpson, *Commons Debates 1621*, IV, p. 140.

160. William B. Bidwell and Maija Jansson, eds., *Proceedings in Parliament 1626* (4 vols., New Haven, 1991–96), IV, pp. 127–31. The official register of petitions received by the Lords list ninety in total. This number varies slightly from the official catalogue of petitions received, which totals ninety-five. HLRO, Main Papers, 6 February 1626, 23 February 1626.

161. Calculated from Johnson, Keeler, Cole, and Bidwell, *Commons Debates and Lords Proceedings*, VI, pp. 19–25.

162. Hart, *Justice upon Petition*, p. 109.

163. Conrad Russell, *Parliaments and English Politics 1621–1629* (Oxford, 1979), p. 37.

164. *Historical Manuscripts Commission: Report of the Records of the City of Exeter* (London, 1916), pp. 137–38.

6. SHIFTING STAGES: THE EMERGENCE OF
PARLIAMENTARY PRINT CULTURE

1. *Manuscripts of the House of Lords* (vol. XI, new ser. London, 1962), p. 15.

2. GL, Broadside collection. For a fuller discussion of these separates, see below, pp. 164–70.

3. Harold Love and Arthur Marotti, 'Manuscript Transmission and Circulation,' in David Loewenstein and Janel Mueller, eds., *The Cambridge History of Early Modern Literature* (Cambridge, 2002), p. 55.

4. G. R. Elton, 'The Sessional Printing of Statutes, 1484–1547' in E. W. Ives, R. J. Knecht, and J. J. Scarisbrick, eds., *Wealth and Power in Tudor England: Essays Presented to S. T. Bindoff* (London, 1978), p. 68. See also J. H. Beale, *A Bibliography of Early English Lawbooks* (Cambridge, MA, 1926).

5. Elton, 'Sessional Printing of Statutes.' p. 76.

6. On the printing of acts and proclamations, see BL, Add. MS 5756, ff. 135, pp. 138, 139.

7. See Rudolph W. Heinze 'Proclamations and Parliamentary Protest, 1539–1610,' in Delloyd J. Guth and John W. McKenna, eds., *Tudor Rule and Revolution* (Cambridge, 1982), pp. 237–59.

8. James F. Larkin and Paul Hughes, *Stuart Royal Proclamations* (Oxford, 1973), no. 223.

9. See, for example, the monopolies proclamations of 1601 and 1621. Paul Hughes and James F. Larkin, *Tudor Royal Proclamations* (3 vols., New Haven, 1964–69), III, no. 812; Larkin and Hughes, *Stuart Royal Proclamations*, no. 217.

10. Larkin and Hughes, *Stuart Royal Proclamations*, no. 33.

11. William Keating Clay, ed., *Liturgical Services: Liturgies and Occasional Forms of Prayer set forth in the Reign of Queen Elizabeth* (Cambridge, 1847), p. 582. I am grateful to Dympna Callaghan for this reference.

12. See, for example, *A fourme of prayer, with thankes gevyng, to be used every yeere, the 17 of November beyng the day of the queenes maiesties entrie to her raigne* (London, 1576), *STC* 16479; *A fourme of prayer . . .* (London, 1604), *STC* 16483; and *A forme of prayer . . . to be used the 27 of March. Being the day of His Highnesse entry to this kingdome* (London, 1626), *STC* 16485.

13. *A prayer used in the queenes maiesties house and chappell, for the prosperitie of the French King assayled by rebels 21 Aug. An. 1590* (London, 1590), *STC* 16523.7; *A fourme of prayer . . . every fift of August: Being the day of his Highnesse happy deliverance from the traiterous and bloody attempt of the Earle of Gowry* (London, 1623), *STC* 16492; *Prayers and thanksgiving . . . from the most traiterous and bloody intended massacre by gunpowder* (London, 1606), *STC* 16494.

14. *An heavenly Act of Parliament* (London, 1604), *STC* 98.

15. Robert was the eldest son of the Queen's printer, Christopher Barker. H. R. Plomer, *A Dictionary of the Booksellers and Printers Who Were at Work in England, Scotland and Ireland from 1641–1667* (London, 1907), pp. 13–14.

16. BL, C.25.m.11; Society of Antiquaries Broadside 176.

17. BL, C.25.e.14.

18. *Stationers Register*, vol. 4, 13; *A Sermon preached before the Commons House of Parliament in St Margarets Church at Westminster, the 18 of February 1620 by James Ussher*, London, 1621, *STC* 24553.5.

19. *A Sermon Preached before the Honorable Assembly of Knights, Cittizens and Burgesses of the Lower House of Parliament: February the last. 1623* (London, 1624), *STC* 1415. Bargrave's attack on recusants and Church 'dissemblers' apparently drew the ire of James I. BL, Lansdowne 985, no. 9, f. 36. See also Thomas Cogswell, *The Blessed Revolution: English Politics and the Coming of War, 1621–1624* (Cambridge, 1989), pp. 169–70.

20. *CJ*, I, pp. 675, 722, 726. I am grateful to Andrew Thrush for these references.

21.   William Laud, *A Sermon preached before his Majestie, on Sunday XIX of June, at Whitehall. Appointed to be preached at the opening of the Parliament. By the Bishop of S. Davids* (London, 1625), *STC* 15302; Humphrey Sydenham, *Moses and Aaron or the Affinitie of Ciuill and Ecclesiasticke Power. A Sermon intended for the Parliament held at Oxon, August 7 1625. But by reason of the sudden and unhappy dissolution, then, not preach't, but since upon occasion, was; at St Maries in Oxford* . . . (London, 1626), *STC* 23568. John Preston's sermon at the general fast was printed in 1634. Lincoln's Inn Library, Pamphlet Collection no. 194, *STC* 20262, John Preston, *The Saints Qualification* . . . (London, 1634), pp. 264–305.

22.   William Laud, *A Sermon preached On Munday, the sixt of February at Westminster: At the opening of the Parliament. By the Bishop of S: Davids* (London, 1625), *STC* 15304.

23.   In 1625 Bargrave was paid £10 for his opening sermon. Westminster City Archives, E.14 Parish accounts, St. Margarets, Westminster n.f. I am grateful to Andrew Thrush for this reference. John Harris, *The Destruction of Sodome: A Sermon preached at a publicke Fast, before the honourable Assembly of the Commons House of Parliament. A Sermon preached at the publicke fast* . . . *by Ier. Dyke* (London, 1629), *STC* 12806.

24.   Joseph Hall, *One of the sermons preach't to the Lords* (London, 1629), *STC* 12692; John Davenant, *One of the sermons preached at Westminster* (London, 1628), *STC* 6299, 6300; William Laud, *A sermon preached on Munday* . . . *at the opening of Parliament* (London, 1628), *STC* 15305, 15305.5; John Williams, *A sermon preached in the collegiat church of S. Peter* (London, 1628), *STC* 25729.

25.   Folger Shakespeare Library, 202868.

26.   See, though, Barnfield's *Affectionate Shepheard* in 1594, which specifically refers to acts of Parliament. Richard Barnfield, *The Affectionate Shepheard, Containing the Complaint of Daphnis for the love of Ganymede* (London, 1594), sig. Fv, *STC* 1480.

27.   William H. Sherman, *John Dee: The Politics of Reading and Writing in the English Renaissance* (Amherst, 1995), p. 19. I am grateful to Bill Sherman for a discussion of this document.

28.   Henry English's translation of Euclid. *ODNB*, sub. John Dee.

29.   At least six copies of this survive, suggesting a wide audience. All the extant copies contain both the verse to Parliament and the letter to the King, suggesting that they were distributed together. Bodleian, 4⁰.S.2, 7a, b; Ashmole 133 (3, 4); Corpus Christi College, Oxford, Φ.A.1.10 (38, 39); Huntington Library, RB 41808–9; Folger Shakespeare Library, *STC* 6461, 6465. See also *STC* 6460.

30.   The colophon reads: Printed by E. Allde for H. G. and are to be sold by Edw. Wright, *STC* 23795.7.

31.   GL, Broadside 16.39, *STC* 16787.

32.   John Taylor, *Superbiae Flagellum, or, The Whip of Pride* (London, 1621), *STC* 23796. A variant edition is dedicated to Edward Seymour, Earl of Hertford; Taylor, *Taylors Goose* (London, 1621), *STC* 23799.

33.   Ben Jonson, *Workes* (London, 1616), p. 775, *STC* 14751.

34.   On this topic, see in particular Michelle O'Callaghan, *The 'shepheards nation':
Jacobean Spenserians and Early Stuart Political Culture* (Oxford, 2000); O'Callaghan,
The English Wits: Literature and Sociability in Early Modern England (Cambridge,
2007); O'Callaghan, '"Now thou may'st speak freely"': Entering the Public Sphere
in 1614,' in Stephen Clucas and Rosalind Davies, eds., *The Crisis of 1614 and the Addled
Parliament* (Aldershot, 2003), pp. 63–79; O'Callaghan, 'Literary Commonwealths:
A 1614 Print Community, *The Shepheards Pipe* and *The Shepherds Hunting*,' *Seventeenth Century* (13, 2, 1998), pp. 103–23; O'Callaghan, '"Talking Politics": Tyranny,
Parliament, and Christopher Brooke's *The Ghost of Richard the Third* (1614),' *HJ* (41,
1, 1998), pp. 97–120; and O'Callaghan, 'Tavern Societies, the Inns of Court, and the
Culture of Conviviality in Early Seventeenth-century England,' in Adam Smyth,
ed., *A Pleasing Sinne: Drink and Conviviality in Seventeenth-century England*, Studies
in Renaissance Literature (14, Cambridge, 2004), pp. 37–51. See also Andrew McRae,
Literature, Satire and the Early Stuart State (Cambridge, 2004).

35.   O'Callaghan, *'Shepheards Nation,'* p. 162.

36.   Respectively, *STC* 25891.5; 25922; 3830; 3917.

37.   O'Callaghan, 'Now thou may'st speak freely,' p. 69, *STC* 3830.5; BL, Egerton
2405.

38.   O'Callaghan, 'Talking Politics,' p. 101.

39.   George Wither, *Wither's motto* (London, 1621), sig. D8, *STC* 25927. Quoted
in O'Callaghan, *'Shepheards Nation,'* p. 193.

40.   *CSP Dom. 1619–1623*, p. 268, 27 June 1621; *APC 1619–21*, p. 408. See also J.
Milton French, 'George Wither in Prison,' *Proceedings of the Modern Language Association* (45, 4, 1930), p. 960. French claims Wither was examined by the House of
Lords on 27 June, but Parliament had been adjourned on 4 June so that is not possible.

41.   *STC* 3588.

42.   Richard Braithwaite, *Times Curtaine Drawne or the Anatomie of Vanitie. With
other choice poems, entitled; Health from Helicon* (London, 1621), *A Prayer to the High
Court of Heaven, for the High Court of Parliament now assembled*, *STC* 3589.

43.   *STC* 18003.9. I am grateful to the Society of Antiquaries Library and the Folger Shakespeare Library for letting me examine their copies of this engraving. For
a further description of the engraving, see Helen Pierce, *Unseemly Pictures: Graphic
Satire and Politics in Early Modern England* (New Haven, 2008), pp. 69–77.

44.   Pepys Library, Magdalene College, Cambridge, Pepys 1.142–43. Part one is
discussed and reproduced in Pierce, *Unseemly Pictures,* p. 79.

45.   Society of Antiquaries 229, *STC* 8726.

46.   For a list of MPs in the 1601 Parliament, see Inner Temple Library, Petyt
MS 537/16, ff. 513–24. For the 1604–10 Parliament, see Folger Shakespeare Library,
V.a.589. Through internal evidence it is possible to date the list to February/March
1610. It may have been sold by William James, a servant of the Norwich bookseller
Thomas Ollyett. I am grateful to Georgianna Ziegler for her assistance with this

document. See also lists in TNA, SP 14/7/82:II; BL, Add. 38139; and Harleian 158. A 1614 manuscript list is at the Huntington Library, Hastings MS, HA Parliament 1 (6), Oversized Parliament Box, reprinted in Maija Jansson, ed., *Proceedings in Parliament 1614* (Philadelphia, 1988). Lists for 1621 include BL, Hargrave MS 311 pp. 459–503; Huntington Library, Hastings MS, HA Parliament Box 2 (9). I am grateful to Paul Hunneyball for the Hargrave reference.

47. That there were two editions can be determined from the addition of a preface to the second version as well as a slightly different typeface and decorative bordering. Edward Grimston, *The Order and Manner of Sitting of the Lords spirituall and temporall . . . Also the names of the Knights for the Counties, Citizens, Burgesses for the Buroughes* (London, 1624), STC 7742, 7743.

48. Grimston clearly played upon his position. See his translation from French of a work by Jean Guillemard, *A Combat betwixt Man and Death* (London, 1621), notes 'translated into English by Edw. Grimeston Sargeant at Armes, attending the Commons House of Parliament,' STC 12495. See also his 1627 translation of Jean François Le Petit's *A Generall Historie of the Netherlands* (London, 1627), STC 12376.

49. Why the dedication was to St. Amand is unclear. There appears to be no obvious connection between Grimston and St. Amand.

50. Grimston, *The Order and Manner of the Sitting of the Lords*.

51. On Walkley, see Zachary Lesser, *Renaissance Drama and the Politics of Publication: Readings in the English Book Trade* (Cambridge, 2004), ch. 5; and Thomas Cogswell, 'The People's Love: The Duke of Buckingham and Popularity,' in Thomas Cogswell, Richard Cust, and Peter Lake, eds., *Politics, Religion and Popularity in Early Stuart Britain* (Cambridge, 2002), pp. 227, 229, 230. Lesser (*Renaissance Drama and the Politics of Publication,* p. 161 n. 12) has suggested that Walkley may have been involved in the publication of one of the two lists from 1624. I am grateful to Zachary Lesser and Tom Cogswell for very helpful discussions of Walkley's role in printing these lists and his career in the 1620s.

52. Lesser, *Renaissance Drama and the Politics of Publication,* p. 157.

53. Ibid., p. 166.

54. *The Names of the knights, citizens, burgesses for the Boroughs . . . for the High Court of Parliament, begun at Westminster the 18 day of June . . . 1625* (London, 1625), STC 7742.

55. Grimston, STC 7744.

56. Only three of these lists seem to survive, of which the first two editions were printed by Augustine Matthews and the fourth by Nicholas Okes: 1st edn. Grimston, *The Order and Manner of Sitting of the Lords . . . And Also the names of the . . . Commons, for this Parliament (London, 1628),* STC 7745; 2nd edn. Grimston, *The Order and Manner of Sitting of the Lords . . . And Also the names of the . . . Commons, for this Parliament. The second impression corrected and much amended (London, 1628),* STC 7746; 4th edn., *Most Exact Catalogue of the Lords . . . And Also the Commons* (London, 1628), STC 7746.3.

57. *LJ*, III, p. 870; Johnson, Keeler, Cole, and Bidwell, *Commons Debates and Lords Proceedings 1628*, V, pp. 684, 685, 686.

58. *A Catalogue of the Lord Spiritual and Temporall of the Higher House of Parliament 1640* (London, 1640), *STC* 7746.6; *Catalogue of the Dukes, marquesses, earles, Viscounts, Bishops, Barons, that sit in this Parliament* (London, November 1640), *STC* 7746.9, 7746.10; *A Catalogue of the Names of the Knights for the Counties, Citizens, Burgesses . . . for the House of Commons, for this Parliament. Begun at Westminster the 13 of Aprill, 1640* (London, 1640), *STC* 7746.7; *A Catalogue . . . for the House of Commons for this Parliament. Begun at Westminster the 3 of November, 1640* (London, 1640).

59. Society of Antiquaries Broadside 290, *The Names of all the high sheriffes of the severall counties, within England Wales, chosen and appoynted for the yeare 1628* (London, 1628); *A Venerable Aspect of both the Houses of Convocation . . .* (London, 1624).

60. *The Manner of the Sitting of the Lords Spirituall and Temporall, as Peeres of the Realme in the Higher House of Parliament . . .* (London, 1628); *The Names of the Knights, Citizens and Burgesses . . . now sitting in Parliament* (London, 1628).

61. See, for example, the 1626 catalogue in the Folger Shakespeare Library, *STC* 7744.

62. Lesser, *Renaissance Drama and the Politics of Publication*, p. 162. For the annotations, see BL, Grimston, *The Order and Manner of Sitting of the Lords,'* 884. i.3.(3), sig. A3v. The copy at the Henry E. Huntington Library (San Marino, California) also shows signs of contemporary annotation that indicate it was used in Parliament.

63. *Her Maiesties most princelie answere* (London, 1601), *STC* 7578.

64. *The Copie of a Letter . . . to Leycester . . .* (London, 1586), *STC* 6052.

65. A French edition of the pamphlet was published the following year (*STC* 6053), thus underlining its role in the national and international propaganda war over Mary Queen of Scots. I am grateful to Paul Hammer for this reference and for a discussion of this matter.

66. *The Kings Maiesties speech . . . on Munday the 19. day of March 1603 being the first day of this present Parliament* (London and Edinburgh, 1604), *STC* 14390, 14390.3 (London), *STC* 14390.7 (Edinburgh).

67. *His Maiesties speech to both the houses of Parliament* (London, 1607), *STC* 14395; *The Kings Maiesties speech to the Lords and Commons* (London, 1610), *STC* 14396, 14396.1, 14396.3, 14396.7.

68. The speeches of James and Charles continued to be published throughout the 1620s.

69. *The Proceeding of the parliament being this day related to the King . . .* (London, 1628), *STC* 24739; Johnson, Keeler, Cole, and Bidwell, *Commons Debates and Lords Proceedings 1628*, II, pp. 411–12, 416.

70. *The Copies of two speeches in Parliament. The one by Iohn Glanvill Esquire. The other by Sir Henry Martin Knight* (London, 1628), *STC* 11904. The two speeches also circulated together in manuscript. For example, see Inner Temple Library, Petyt MS 538/20, ff. 729–42. The volume also contains another separate of Glanville's speech,

ff. 1717–28. In 1621 a speech was printed that had been allegedly delivered by Sir Edward Cecil. In fact the speech was never given in Parliament, although copies were distributed by the 'radical publicist' Thomas Scott, *STC* 22087.

71. Acts 28:24.

72. On the printing of speeches in the early 1640s, see A. D. T. Cromartie, 'The Printing of Parliamentary Speeches November 1640–July 1642,' *HJ* (33, 1, 1990), pp. 23–44; and Sheila Lambert, 'The Beginning of Printing for the House of Commons, 1640–42,' *Library* (6th ser., 3, 1981), pp. 43–61.

73. David Zaret, *Origins of Democratic Culture: Printing, Petitions and the Public Sphere in Early-Modern England* (Princeton, 2000).

74. Ibid., p. 92.

75. Ibid., ch. 8; Anthony Fletcher, *The Outbreak of the English Civil War* (New York,1981), ch. 6, esp. p. 192.

76. See, in particular, Zaret, *Origins of Democratic Culture*, p. 240.

77. I am grateful to Jason Peacey for a discussion of these issues. See his *Politicians and Pamphleteers. Propaganda during the English Civil Wars and Interregnum* (Aldershot, 2004).

78. On pamphlets, see Joad Raymond, *Pamphlets and Pamphleteering in Early Modern Britain* (Cambridge, 2003), ch. 1.

79. *Certaine arguments used to perswade and provoke the most honorable . . . Parliament . . . to promote and advance the sincere ministery of the Gospell* (London, 1606), *STC* 7736; Gabriel Powel, *A Consideration of the deprived and silenced ministers . . . exhibited in their late Supplication unto the . . . Parliament* (London, 1606), *STC* 20142.

80. *An Humble Petition offered to the . . . estates of the present Parliament* (London, 1606), *STC* 19884.

81. Alexander Leighton, *An Appeal to the Parliament; or Sion's Plea against the Prelacie* (Amsterdam, 1629), *STC* 15430. See Robert Zaller, *The Discourse of Legitimacy in Early Modern England* (Stanford, 2007), pp. 641–46; *ODNB*, sub. Leighton.

82. Sig. A.

83. The details of the dispute can be followed in Roland Austin, *Catalogue of the Gloucestershire Collection* (Gloucester, 1928), pp. 737, 872–78.

84. Thrush and Ferris, *HPT 1604–1629*, John Smyth.

85. BL, Harleian MS 6803, ff. 56v-57; GL, Broadside 24.43, *A briefe of a bill . . . in Parliament for the re-establishing of a free grammar schoole in Wotton under Edge* (London, 1621), *STC* 6044a.7. This two-pronged strategy of proceeding both by legislation and petition became increasing common in the 1620s. See, above, Chapter Five, and Chris R. Kyle, 'Parliament and the Politics of Carting in Early Stuart London,' *London Journal* (27, 2, 2002), pp. 4–5.

86. *LJ*, III, pp. 170–71; 173–74.

87. Benjamin Crokey, *To his Sacred Maiestie, the Lords Spiritual and Temporal, and the House of Commons* (London, 1625), *STC* 6045. There is no evidence that

the bill received a first reading in 1625. Maija Jansson and William B. Bidwell, eds., *Proceedings in Parliament 1625* (New Haven, 1987), pp. 634–37.

88.   S. R. Gardiner, ed., *Reports of Cases in the Courts of Star Chamber and High Commission* (Camden, new ser. 39, 1886), pp. 37–40.

89.   *To the Right honourable the higher and lower houses of Parliament, now assembled* (London, 1640), STC 6045.5; *The contents and short brief of this book, which showeth the greatest and crying oppression of injustice* (London, 1645); *To the right honourable the House of Parliament: The humble petition of Benjamin Crookey and Sarah his daughter* (London, 1647).

90.   Austin, *Catalogue of the Gloucestershire Collection*, p. 874.

91.   No record of the petition survives in the Leathersellers' records. *Leather: A Discourse, tendered to the High Court of Parliament* (London, 1629), STC 15344.

92.   *The Petition and Remonstrance of the Governor and Company of Merchants of London trading to the East Indies* (London, 1628), STC 7749. See also STC 7450a.5.

93.   *CSP Dom. 1619–1623*, p. 138.

94.   Henry Farley, *The Complaint of Paules to All Christian Soules* (London, 1616), STC 10688.5; Farley, *St. Paules-Church her bill for the Parliament* (London, 1621), STC 10690.

95.   HLRO, Main Papers, [1621]. In 1614 a petition from the Fleet prisoners was presented to the Archbishop of Canterbury during Parliament. Lambeth Palace Library, MS 1730 f. 10.

96.   TNA, SP 14/160/93; Society of Antiquaries Broadside 213, *To the Kings most excellent Maiestie: the honorable lords, knights and burgesses assembled in Parliament. The humble petition of your maiesties . . . prisoners for debt.* STC 14961.5.

97.   *A petition to the Kings most excellent Maiestie, the Lords spirituall and temporall and Commons now assembled. Wherein is declared the mischiefes and inconveniencies, arising . . . by the imprisoning of mens bodies for debt* (London, 1622 [*sic*]), STC 14428.

98.   *To the most honourable assembly of the Commons House of Parliament. The humble petition of distressed prisoners in the King's Bench . . .* (London, 1624), STC 14961.7; *CJ*, I, pp. 739, 771; Spring f. 121; Hawarde [18 March 1624]. See also the general appeals to public opinion in *The humble petition of the poor prisoners in the loathsome hole of Woodstreete Compter* (London, 1614) (*STC* 25968.5) and the petition from King's Bench prisoners, *To all their good Benefactors and Releevers in or about this Honorable City of London* (London, 1627).

99.   21 James I cap. 17.

100.   Norman L. Jones, *God and the Moneylenders* (Oxford, 1989), pp. 186–98.

101.   BL, Harleian MS 7617, ff. 5–15v.

102.   Similar bills had been debated in 1604, 1605–6, and 1614.

103.   Elizabeth Skerpan, *The Rhetoric of Politics in the English Revolution* (Columbia, MO, 1992), p. 73.

104.   Zaret, *Origins of Democratic Culture*, p. 221.

105.   See above Chapter Five, on lobbying.

106.   GL, MS 11571/10, f. 449 (Grocers), *STC* 16777.16; GL, MS 2883/3, p. 334 (Blacksmiths); GL, MS 6901 unf. (Woolmen).

107.   Society of Antiquaries Broadside 312. This in incorrectly dated 1641, but internal evidence suggests that 1604 is the accurate date, *STC* 16786.3.

108.   See below, p. 171.

109.   GL, 4326/6 unf. 5 February 1607 (Carpenters), *STC* 16768.20; 3054/1 unf. 1614 (Bricklayers).

110.   TNA, STAC 8/128/11 pt. 2 f. 15. I am grateful to Andrew Thrush for this reference. See f. 21 for a copy of the breviate, *STC* 7527.3.

111.   Ibid. f. 20. Egerton's opponent, Sir Roland Egerton, also claimed that the breviates were sold, but that seems unlikely given the subject matter. The private business of two squabbling members of the gentry probably had little appeal for the print-buying public.

112.   Society of Antiquaries Broadside 137; BL, Harleian MS 7614 f. 119, *STC* 16768.22, 16768.24, 16768.26. The commissioners had been appointed by proclamation in 1618. The matter was driven forward by the personal interest of James I. See Larkin and Hughes, *Stuart Royal Proclamations,* nos. 51, 78, 87, 120, 175, 186.

113.   GL, Broadside 24.19; Wallace Notestein, Frances Helen Relf, and Hartley Simpson, eds., *Commons Debates 1621* (New Haven, 1935), VII, pp. 515–19. The patentees of the office were servants and allies of Buckingham. See *Commons Debates 1621*, VII, pp. 347–48, *STC* 16776.4.

114.   Hampshire RO, Jervoise Papers, TD540/Scrapbook, *STC* 16776.6.

115.   Society of Antiquaries Broadside 186, *STC* 16777.14, 16768.8.

116.   Hampshire RO, Jervoise Papers, TD540/Scrapbook; BL, Harleian MS 7608, ff. 420v-21; Society of Antiquaries Broadside 594 (misdated as temp. Charles II).

117.   Notestein, Relf, and Simpson, *Commons Debates 1621,* III, p. 130; VII, p. 372; Larkin and Hughes, *Stuart Royal Proclamations,* no. 217.

118.   Society of Antiquaries Broadside 225, *STC* 16768.10.

119.   Kyle, 'Parliament and the Politics of Carting in Early Stuart London,' pp. 1–11.

120.   BL, Harleian MS 1996 ff. 225v-26, 704.

121.   GL, Broadside 24.35, *STC* 16768.4.

122.   Ibid., Broadside 24.21; Society of Antiquaries Broadside 185, *STC* 16777.6.

123.   Society of Antiquaries Broadside 217; HLRO, Main Papers, 19 April 1624; CLRO, Repertories, 38, f. 115. For the Butcher's expenses in fighting the bill, see GL, 6440/2, ff. 322, 323v, 324.

124.   See below, pp. 171–72, *STC* 3217.5; 1678.6.

125.   BL, Harleian MS, 7614, f. 114; GL, Broadside 24.22, *STC* 16778.2.

126.   Society of Antiquaries Broadsides 181, 187; GL, Broadside 24.18; *CJ*, I, p. 602, *STC* 16777.4.

127. BL, Harleian MS 7617, f. 87, *STC* 16779.4.

128. GL, Broadside 24.32.

129. Ibid., Broadside 24.33, *STC* 18307.3.

130. Ibid., Broadside 23.119, *STC* 18307.3.

131. Society of Antiquaries Broadside 191; GL, Broadside 24.1, *STC* 18114.5.

132. BL, Harleian MS 7608 f. 381, *STC* 26076.5.

133. Ibid., Broadside 23.121; Society of Antiquaries Broadside 250, *STC* 25858.7.

134. Ibid., Broadside 24.36, *STC* 23918.5.

135. Ibid., Broadside 24.30, *STC* 22463.7.

136. Harvard University, Houghton Library, *STC* 6191.5.

137. Bodleian, Rawl. MS B151 f. 16, *STC* 6798.6.

138. Society of Antiquaries Broadside 226, *STC* 21176.5.

139. BL, Harleian 7615, ff. 226v-27, *STC* 3902.5.

140. Center for Kentish Studies, Sa/C4 unbound. I am grateful to Jason Peacey for this reference.

141. Gardiner, *Reports of Cases in the Courts of Star Chamber and High Commission*, p. 39.

142. GL, 3054/1 unf.; Broadside 24.17; Society of Antiquaries Broadside 138.

143. GL, 6440/2, f. 322.

144. Merton College, Oxford, Liber Bursarurum 3.1 ff. 222, 226, *STC* 19049.

145. W. W. Greg, ed., *A Companion to Arber* (Oxford, 1967), pp. 209–10, 230–33; William A. Jackson, ed., *Records of the Stationers' Company 1602–1640* (London, 1957), p. xvi, *STC* 25919.

146. Tessa Watt, *Cheap Print and Popular Piety 1550–1640* (Cambridge, 1991), p. 141; Alastair Bellany, *The Politics of Court Scandal in Early Modern England: News Culture and the Overbury Affair, 1603–1660* (Cambridge, 2002), p. 117.

147. Many of the Alford and Lemon petitions are duplicates of the Guildhall broadsides.

148. GL, Broadside 416, *Richard Bowdler, Plaintif. George Morgan, defendant. This bill . . .* (London, 1621); GL, Broadside 23.122, 123i; TNA, SP 14/120/78 *George Morgan plaintiffe . . .* (London, 1621), *STC* 3432.5, 3432.7, 18102a.2.

149. BL, Harleian MS 6803 f. 119v; GL, Broadside 23.123ii.

150. BL, Harleian MS 7607, ff. 400v-1.

151. Hampshire RO, Jervoise Papers 44M69/G2/21; The Queen's College, Oxford, Sel.b.229 no. 2.

152. BL, Harleian MS 7607, f. 393.

153. Jansson and Bidwell, *Proceedings in Parliament 1625*, 429; BL, Harleian MS 7607, f. 404.

154. William B. Bidwell and Maija Jansson, eds., *Proceedings in Parliament 1626* (4 vols., New Haven, 1991–96), I, pp. 213–14; HLRO, Main Papers, 24 March 1626.

155.   Notestein, Relf, and Simpson, *Commons Debates 1621*, V, p. 88.

156.   BL, Harleian MS 7608, ff. 382v-87v; Another copy of the petition is in the Guildhall collection, Broadside 23.120, *STC* 1545.5.

157.   Jackson, *Records of the Court of Stationers' Company*, p. 166.

158.   Hampshire RO, 44M69/G2/21.

159.   BL, Harleian MS, 7607, f. 404.

160.   Hampshire RO, 44M69/G2/21 (annotated by hand).

161.   *LJ*, IV, p. 20; HLRO, Main Papers, 5 February 1629 (Deyncourt's printed brief).

162.   *LJ*, IV, p. 21, 23; HLRO, Main Papers, 7 February 1629.

163.   *LJ*, IV, pp. 28–29.

164.   Society of Antiquaries 272, *STC* 21460.7.

165.   Bidwell and Jansson, *Proceedings in Parliament 1626*, I, pp. 208–9, 210.

166.   TNA, C66/2340, pt. 17; Larkin, *Stuart Royal Proclamations*, II, pp. 116–20.

167.   GL, Broadsides 24.47, 48; *STC* 20795.3 (Commons), 20795.5 (Lords).

168.   For the use of these items in the Overbury cheap print tracts, see Bellany, *Politics of Court Scandal in Early Modern England*, p. 117.

169.   I am grateful to Peter Beal, Peter Stallybrass, and Sabrina Baron for very helpful discussions of this subject.

170.   Philip Gaskell, *A New Introduction to Bibliography* (Oxford, 1972), p. 17.

171.   GL, Broadside 23.115. For Boisloré's grant and the Stationers' reaction, see GL, Broadside 24.3; and Notestein, Relf, and Simpson, *Commons Debates 1621*, VII, pp. 425–26, 535–39.

172.   The history of this grant and the subsequent dispute has been well documented in Greg, *Companion to Arber*, pp. 59–61, 71–72, 164–75; Jackson, *Records of the Stationers' Company*, pp. xvi–xxii; Notestein, Relf, and Simpson, *Commons Debates 1621*, VII, pp. 535–39.

173.   GL, Broadside 23:115.

174.   Ibid. 24:3, *STC* 3217.5.

175.   Ibid.; Notestein, Relf, and Simpson, *Commons Debates 1621*, VII, pp. 536–38.

176.   Society of Antiquaries, Broadside 222, *The particular grievances of those his maiesties subiects throughout England and Wales, which lye under the pression of George Woods patent for the sole printing upon Linen Cloth*, *STC* 25951.5. See also Jackson, *Records of the Stationers' Company*, pp. 14–16.

177.   Larkin and Hughes, *Stuart Royal Proclamations*, no. 217.

178.   For the debates on the Petition of Right, see Conrad Russell, *Parliaments and English Politics 1621–1629* (Oxford, 1979), pp. 342–84; L. J. Reeve, 'The Legal Status of the Petition of Right,' *HJ* (29, 2, 1986), pp. 257–77; and Elizabeth Read Foster, 'Printing the Petition of Right,' *HLQ* (38, 1974), pp. 81–83.

179.   Quoted in Foster, 'Printing the Petition of Right,' p. 82.

180.   See above, p. 147 n.3.

CONCLUSION

1.   I am grateful to Tom Cogswell, Markku Peltonen, and Paul Hunneyball for the opportunity to discuss Eliot's parliamentary career in the 1620s. On Eliot, see Paul Hunneyball, 'John Eliot,' in Andrew Thrush and J. P. Ferris, eds., *The House of Commons, 1604–1629* (6 vols., Cambridge, 2010); J. N. Ball, 'Sir John Eliot in Parliament, 1624–1629,' in Kevin Sharpe, ed., *Faction and Parliament: Essays on Early Stuart History* (Oxford, 1978), pp. 173–208; Sharpe, 'Sir John Eliot at the 1625 Parliament,' *BIHR*, 28 (1955), pp. 113–27; Harold Hulme, 'The Leadership of Sir John Eliot in the Parliament of 1626,' *Journal of Modern History* (4, 1932), pp. 361–86; Hulme, *The Life of Sir John Eliot, 1592–1632: Struggle for Parliamentary Freedom* (New York, 1957); and J. Forster, *Sir John Eliot: A Biography* (2 vols., London, 1864).

2.   Wallace Notestein and Frances Helen Relf, eds., *Commons Debates for 1629* (Minneapolis, 1921), p. 256.

3.   Maija Jansson, ed., *Proceedings in Parliament, 1614* (Philadelphia, 1988).

4.   Hunneyball, 'John Eliot,' IV, p. 184.

5.   John Eliot, *Negotium Posterorum*, I, p. 138.

6.   *CJ*, I, pp. 719–20; Nicholas Diary 1624, f. 28v.

7.   *HPT, 1604–1629*, IV, pp. 183–86. On the 'patriot coalition,' see Tom Cogswell, *The Blessed Revolution: English Politics and the Coming of War, 1621–1624* (Cambridge, 1989).

8.   Maija Jansson and William B. Bidwell, eds., *Proceedings in Parliament 1625* (New Haven, 1987), pp. 504–6.

9.   *HPT, 1604–1629*, IV, p. 187.

10.   Ibid., pp. 188–93; For Eliot's speech, see William B. Bidwell and Maija Jansson, eds., *Proceedings in Parliament 1626* (4 vols., New Haven, 1991–96), III, pp. 220–24.

11.   Conrad Russell, 'Sir John Eliot,' *ODNB*.

12.   Johnson, Keeler, Cole, and Bidwell, *Commons Debates and Lords Proceedings 1628*, IV, p. 64.

13.   Ibid.

14.   See, for example, his motion concerning the antirecusant petition on 27 April 1624, which was described as 'of some length and curiosity.' Quoted in Thrush and Ferris, *HPT 1604–1629*, IV, p. 184.

15.   Jansson and Bidwell, *Proceedings in Parliament 1625*, p. 17.

16.   See *HMC, 1st Report* (1874), esp. pp. 42–44.

17.   Jansson and Bidwell, *Proceedings in Parliament 1625*, p. 19.

18.   For a detailed analysis of the Pym Diary, see ibid., pp. 11–13, 21.

19.   *Sir John Eliot his grave and learned speech spoken in the High Court of Parliament . . .* (London, 1641). *ESTC* lists thirty extant copies of this publication. See also Notestein and Relf, eds., *Commons Debates for 1629*, pp. 24–28.

20.   See, in particular, Oliver Arnold, *The Third Citizen: Shakespeare's Theater and the Early Modern House of Commons* (Baltimore, 2007), esp. ch. 1.

21. Thomas Cogswell, 'Thomas Middleton and the Court, 1624: *A Game at Chess* in Context,' *HLQ* (47, 1984), pp. 273–88; T. H. Howard-Hill, 'Political Interpretations of Middleton's *Game at Chess* (1624),' *Yearbook of English Studies* (21, 1991).

22. Thomas Cogswell and Peter Lake, 'Buckingham Does the Globe: Henry VIII and the Politics of Popularity in the 1620s,' *Shakespeare Quarterly* (60, 3, 2009), pp. 253–78; Chris R. Kyle, 'Henry VIII, or *All is True*: Shakespeare's "Favorite" Play,' in Laurie Maguire, ed., *How to Do Things with Shakespeare* (Oxford, 2008), pp. 82–100. I am grateful to Peter Lake and Tom Cogswell for showing me a copy of their article in advance of publication.

23. David Harris Willson, ed., *The Parliamentary Diary of Robert Bowyer, 1606–1607* (Minneapolis, 1977), p. 10; *CJ*, I, p. 261.

24. See Colin G. C. Tite, *Impeachment and Parliamentary Judicature in Early Stuart England* (London, 1974); James S. Hart, *Justice upon Petition: The House of Lords and the Reformation of Justice, 1621–1675* (London, 1991); and Menna Prestwich, *Cranfield: Politics and Profits under the Early Stuarts* (Oxford, 1966).

25. N. E. McClure, ed., *The Letters of John Chamberlain* (2 vols., Philadelphia, 1939), II, p. 350.

26. Society of Antiquaries, Lemon 182. See also Helen Pierce, *Unseemly Pictures: Graphic Satire and Politics in Early Modern England* (New Haven, 2008), p. 71. It is likely that Mompesson was the inspiration for the character Sir Giles Overreach in Philip Massinger's play *A New Way to Pay old Debts*. On the effect of political libels on public opinion, see Pauline Croft, 'Libels, Popular Literacy and Public Opinion in Early Modern England,' *Historical Research* (68, 1995), pp. 268–85; and Croft, 'The Reputation of Robert Cecil: Libels, Political Opinion and Popular Awareness in the Early Seventeenth Century,' *Transactions of the Royal Historical Society* (6th ser., I, 1991), pp. 43–69. On early Stuart political libels, see Alastair Bellany, '"Raylinge Rymes and Vaunting Verse": Libellous Politics in Early Stuart England,' in Kevin Sharpe and Peter Lake, eds., *Culture and Politics in Early Stuart England* (London, 1994), pp. 285–310, 367–71; Bellany, 'Libels in Action: Ritual, Subversion and the English Literary Underground,' in Tim Harris, ed., *The Politics of the Excluded, c.1500–1850* (Basingstoke, 2001), pp. 99–124; Bellany, 'The Embarrassment of Libels: Perceptions and Representations of Verse Libeling in Early Stuart England,' in Peter Lake and Steven Pincus, eds., *The Politics of the Public Sphere in Early Modern England*' (Manchester, 2007), pp. 144–67; Bellany, 'Railing Rhymes Revisited: Libels, Scandals and Early Stuart Politics,' *History Compass* (5, 4, 2007), pp. 1136–79; and Thomas Cogswell, 'Underground Verse and the Transformation of Early Stuart Political Culture,' *HLQ* (60, 1998), pp. 303–26.

27. *The Deserved Downfall of a Corrupted Conscience* (London, 1621); BL, Harleian 333, f. 14, Samuel Albyn to John Rawson; BL, Harleian, 389, f. 19v; Bodleian, Tanner 306, ff. 247–8v.

28. Hart, *Justice upon Petition*, p. 15. As Hart points out, this process started with a request from James I, to review the case of Edward Ewer.

29. For a specific example of how this lobbying technique was used, see Chris R. Kyle, 'Parliament and the Politics of Carting in Early Stuart London,' *London Journal* (27, 2, 2002), pp. 1–11.

30. Pauline Croft, 'Capital Life: Members of Parliament Outside the House,' in Thomas Cogswell, Richard Cust, and Peter Lake, eds., *Politics, Religion and Popularity in Early Stuart Britain* (Cambridge, 2002), pp. 65–83. On the difficulties of finding lodgings in London, see Lena Cowen Orlin, 'Temporary Lives in London Lodgings,' in Deborah Harkness and Jean Howard, eds., *The Places and Spaces of Early Modern London*, *HLQ* (71, 1, 2008), pp. 219–42.

31. TNA, SP14/124/83; *APC*, VI, pp. 108–10.

32. Larkin, *Stuart Royal Proclamations*, II, pp. 223–24.

33. Ibid., II, pp. 226–28.

34. BL, Harleian 383, f. 84, 9 April 1629.

35. The phrase 'giddy-headed multitude' comes from a parliamentary libel in circulation after the 1628 Parliament purported to be written by Buckingham. Johnson, Keller, Cole, and Bidwell, *Commons Debates and Lords Proceedings 1628*, VI, p. 244. On the imprisonment of nine MPs after the Parliament ended, see John Reeve, 'The Arguments in King's Bench in 1629 concerning the Imprisonment of John Selden and Other Members of the House of Commons,' *Journal of British Studies* (25, 3, 1986), pp. 264–87.

36. Conrad Russell, *Parliaments and English Politics, 1621–1629* (Oxford, 1979), conclusion.

37. Peter Lake and Steven Pincus, 'Rethinking the Public Sphere,' in Lake and Pincus, eds., *The Politics of the Public Sphere in Early Modern England* (Manchester, 2007), p. 19.

38. Richard Cust, 'The "Public Man" in Late Tudor and Early Stuart England,' in Lake and Pincus, *Politics of the Public Sphere in Early Modern England*, pp. 116–43.

Bibliography

ARCHIVAL MANUSCRIPT SOURCES

Bodleian Library, Oxford

Ashmole 133
Dep.e.468   Parliamentary Diary 1626
Malone 23   Collection of Libels
Rawl. B151   Parliamentary Accounts
Rawl. D.723   Parliamentary Diary 1624
Rawl. D.999   Parliamentary Diary 1621
Rawl. D.1100   Parliamentary Diary of Sir Thomas Holland, 1624
Tanner 290
Tanner 392   Parliamentary Diary of Sir Thomas Holland, 1624

British Library

Add. 4149   Transcripts made by Ralph Starkey
Add. 5756   Political Miscellany
Add. 12191   Papers of Robert Bowyer
Add. 18597   Parliamentary Diary of Sir Walter Earle, 1624
Add. 22474   Parliamentary Diary 1626
Add. 26639   Parliamentary Diary of John Pym, 1624
Add. 29623   Extracts from the Records of Dover
Add. 30197
Add. 33924   Streatfeild Collection, Kent
Add. 34218   Westmoreland Papers
Add. 36856   Procedure of the House of Commons, 1621
Add. 46191   Diary of Sir Nathaniel Rich, 1624
Add. 53726   Whitelocke Manuscripts

Add. 69917	Coke Papers
Add. 71446	Diary of Peter Peake, 1626
Add. 78652	Evelyn Papers
Cotton Titus F.IV	Proceedings in Parliament, 1604–14
Egerton 2715	Gawdy Correspondence, 1605–29
Hargrave 311	Miscellaneous Political Papers
Harl. 158	Catalogue of MPs, 1604–10
Harl. 159	Parliamentary Diary of Sir Simonds D'Ewes, 1624
Harl. 253	Thomas Norton's advices on Parliament
Harl. 354	
Harl. 370	
Harl. 383	D'Ewes Newsletters
Harl. 389	Mead Newsletters
Harl. 390	Mead Newsletters
Harl. 1196	
Harl. 2104	
Harl. 2313	Parliamentary Diary 1628
Harl. 6799	Alford Papers
Harl. 6800	Alford Papers
Harl. 6803	Alford Papers
Harl. 6018	
Harl. 6383	Holles Diary 1624
Harl. 6799	Parliamentary Diary of John Pym, 1624
Harl. 6838	Alford Papers
Harl. 7000	Alford Papers
Harl. 7607	Alford Papers
Harl. 7608	Alford Papers
Harl. 7614	Alford Papers
Harl. 7615	Alford Papers
Harl. 7617	Alford Papers
Lans. 43	Miscellaneous Papers
Stowe 357	Proceedings in Parliament
Stowe 366	Proceedings in Parliament

Cambridge University Library

MS Ff.5.14	Lewd Pasquil

College of Arms

B.1–26	Bowyer MSS
Vincent 40	Bowyer MSS

Cornell University Library

MS H83

Centre for Kentish Studies

Sa/C4

Corporation of London Record Office

Reps 38   Repertories of the Court of Aldermen

Corpus Christi College, Oxford

MS 257

Cumbria Record Office

D.Lons. L2/1   Parliamentary Diary of Sir John Lowther, 1624

Devon Record Office

1579A   Totnes Borough Records
B1/6   Exeter Corporation Archive

Duchy of Cornwall Record Office

Acts of the Council
Warrants and Letters

Exeter College, Oxford

MS 100   Parliamentary Compilation 1628

Folger Shakespeare Library

V.a.310   Vox Populi
V.a.402   Commonplace Book
V.a.539   Catalogue of MPs, 1604–10
V.b.189

Guildhall Library

2883   Blacksmiths Company Accounts
3054   Tilers and Bricklayers Company Accounts
4326   Carpenters Company Accounts
5442   Brewers Company Accounts
5570   Fishmongers Company Minute Books
5606   Coopers Company Accounts
6440   Butchers Company Accounts
6901   Woolmen Company Accounts
11571   Grocers Company Accounts
12071   Armourers Company Accounts
15332–3   Vintners Company Accounts
19629   Masons Company Minutes
34048   Merchant Taylors Accounts

Hampshire Record Office

44/M69   Jervoise Papers
TD/540   Jervoise Scrapbook
Unnumbered MS   Parliamentary Diary of Sir Thomas Jervoise, 1624

Harvard University, Houghton Library

English MS 980 Parliamentary Diary of Sir William Spring, 1624

Henry E. Huntington Library, San Marino

Ellesmere Manuscripts
Hastings Manuscripts

Inner Temple Library

Petyt 537   Parliamentary Papers
Petyt 538   Parliamentary Papers

Kenneth Spencer Research Library, Kansas

MS E237   Parliamentary Account

Lambeth Palace Library

MS 1730   Archbishop Abbot's Accounts

London Metropolitan Archives

ACC 1876   Sutton Hospital Records

Merton College, Oxford

Liber Bursarurum 3.1

National Library of Scotland

Adv. MS 34.2.15
Gordon-Cummings Papers

Norfolk Record Office

Hare of Stow Bardolph
MC2/90
Y/C18   Great Yarmouth Book of Entries
Y/C19   City of Norwich Assembly Books
Y/C20

Northamptonshire Record Office

FH 50   Finch-Hatton MSS

Parliamentary Archives

Braye MSS

House of Lords Committee Books
House of Lords Minute Books
Journals of the House of Commons
Journals of the House of Lords
Main Papers
Main Papers (Parchment)
Original Acts

Somerset Record Office

D/B/bw
DD/PH   Phelips MSS

Southampton City Archives

SC5/2   Southampton Corporation Book of Debts

Staffordshire Record Office

D661//1/1/2   Parliamentary Diary of Richard Dyott, 1624

Suffolk Record Office (Lowestoft)

M18/06   Town Records

The National Archives, Kew

AO3   Office of the King's Works
C66   Chancery, Patent Rolls
C173   Chancery, Six Clerks Office
E351   Exchequer, Pipe Office Accounts
E403   Exchequer of Receipt Rolls
LC5   Lord Chamberlain's Department, Miscellaneous
SP 1   State Papers Domestic, Henry VIII
SP 12   State Papers Domestic, Elizabeth I
SP 14   State Papers Domestic, James I
SP 15   State Papers Domestic, Addenda
SP 16   State Papers Domestic, Charles I
STAC8   Star Chamber Records, James I

Thetford Town Council, King's House

T/C1   Thetford Assembly Records

Trinity College Library, Cambridge

MS 0.2.7   Parliamentary Diary 1614

University of Nottingham Library

Portland MS A

Victoria and Albert Museum

W.1   Writing Box
W.4   Writing Box
W.12   Writing Box
W.16   Writing Box

Westminster Archives Centre

E5   Churchwardens' Accounts, St. Margaret Westminster
E14   Churchwardens' Accounts, St. Margaret Westminster
E2413   Vestry Minutes, St. Margaret Westminster

Wiltshire Record Office

Unnumbered MS   Hawarde Diary 1624

PRINTED PETITIONS AND PAMPHLETS TO PARLIAMENT

A Catalogue . . . for the House of Commons for this Parliament. Begun at Westminster the 3 of November, 1640 (London, 1640).

A Catalogue of the Dukes, Marquesses, Earles, Viscounts, Bishops, Barons, that sit in this Parliament (London, November 1640).

A Catalogue of the Lord Spiritual and Temporall of the Higher House of Parliament 1640 (London, 1640).

A Catalogue of the Names of the Knights for the Counties, Citizens, Burgesses . . . for the House of Commons, for this Parliament. Begun at Westminster the 13 of Aprill, 1640 (London, 1640).

A Divine Prayer necessary to be used every day in each particular family, during the time of this present Parliament (London, 1641).

A petition to the Kings most excellent Maiestie, the Lords spirituall and temporall and Commons now assembled. Wherein is declared the mischiefes and inconveniencies, arising . . . by the imprisoning of mens bodies for debt (London, 1622 [sic]).

Apothecaries Company, *To the Honorable howse of Commons in the high Courte of Parliament assembled* (London, 1621).

A Prayer for the Speaker of the Commons House of Parliament (London, 1606).

A Venerable Aspect of both the Houses of Convocation . . . (London, 1624).

An Heavenly Act of Parliament (London, 1604).

Barber Surgeons Company, *To the most Honourable House of Commons, commonly called, the Lower House of Parliament. The humble petition of the masters or gouernors of the mysterie and comminaltie of barbers and chirurgions of London* (London, 1624).

Bargrave, Isaac, *A Sermon Preached before the . . . Lower House of Parliament* (London, 1624).

Bassano, Paul, *A defence of Paul Bassano the suruiuing patentee, for the importation of fresh salmons and lobsters, &c. by a new inuention, which hee most humbly submitteth to this Honorable house of Parliament* (London, 1621).

Boisloré, Martin, *To the Right Honourable, the house of Commons assembled in Parliament. The humble petition and answere of Marin de Boisloree, Roger Wood, and Thomas Symcock, to the stacioners petition* (London, 1621).

Bookbinders Company, *Binders of bookes in London doe most humbly shew, that whereas George Withers, Gent. hath lately composed a book* (London, 1624).

——. *To the Most Honorable Assembly of the Commons House of Parliament* (London, 1621).

Bowdler, Richard, *A declaration of the especiall vntruths contained in Morgans Bill exhibited in Parliament against Bowd[ler and] Meggs; Iones, and others, with answeres thereunto as hereunder followeth* (London, 1621).

——. *Richard Bowdler, plaintif. George Morgan, defendant. This bill is an humble petition of Richard Bowdler and William Meggs, that a report and decree, thereupon made in the high Court of Chancerie betweene George Morgan and them* (London, 1621).

Brewers Company, *To the honourable House of commons . . . The humble petition of the . . . Company of Brewers in London* (London, 1621).

Browker, Thomas, *An Act for settling and establishing of the Manor of Sundrish, alias Sundridge . . . in the Countie of Kent* (London, 1629).

Butchers Company, *Reasons tendred by the Free Butchers of London against the bill in Parliament to restraine butchers from grazing of cattle* (London, 1624).

Carpenters Company, *Abuse used concerning the heawing, sawing and measuring of timber* (London, 1593).

Cecil, Sir Robert, *La copie d'une lettre inscrite à monseigneur le comte de Lecestre* (London, 1587).

——. *The Copie of a Letter . . . to Leycester . . .* (London, 1586).

Certaine arguments used to perswade and provoke the most honorable . . . Parliament . . . to promote and advance the sincere ministrey of the Gospell (London, 1606).

Clerks of the Customs House, *An Abstract of the grievances of the poore Clerkes of his Maiesties Custom-house, London* (London, 1621).

Crokey, Benjamin, *A briefe of a bill . . . in Parliament for the re-establishing of a free grammar schoole in Wotton under Edge* (London, 1621).

——. *The contents and short brief of this book, which showeth the greatest and crying oppression of injustice* (London, 1645).

——. *To his Sacred Maiestie, the Lords Spiritual and Temporal, and the House of Commons* (London, 1625).

——. *To the Right honourable the higher and lower houses of Parliament, now assembled* (London, 1640).

——. *To the right honourable the House of Parliament: The humble petition of Benjamin Crookey and Sarah his daughter* (London, 1647).

Cutlers, Painters, and Bookbinders Companies, *An Abstract of the grievances . . . concerning the Patent . . . of sole making of Gold and Silver Foliat* (London, 1621).

Dale, Elizabeth, *A briefe of the Lady Dales petition to the Parliament* (London, 1624).

Davenant, John, *One of the sermons preached at Westminster* (London, 1628).

Dee, John, *A Letter, containing a most briefe discourse apologeticall* (London, 1609).

———. *To the Honorable Assemblie of the Commons in the Present Parliament* (London, 1604).

Deye, William, *To the right honourable the knights, citizens and burgesses of the Commons house, . . . The most humble petition of William Deye* (London, 1626).

Dyers Company, *The briefe contents of the bill exhibited against logwood, and abuses in dying* (London, 1621).

———. *To the most honourable assembly of the Commons House of Parliament, the humble petition of the wardens and comminalty of the art or mysterie of Dyers in London* (London, 1621).

Dyke, Jeremiah, *A Sermon preached at the publicke fast . . . by Ier. Dyke* (London, 1629).

Egerton, Edward, *An act to reuerse two seuerall decrees made in the Chancerie, and to restore to Edward Egerton Esquire the possession of certaine mannours and lands taken away from him by force of the said decrees* (London, 1621).

Eliot, John, *Sir John Eliot his grave and learned speech spoken in the High Court of Parliament . . .* (London, 1641).

Elizabeth I, *Her Maiesties most princelie answere* (London, 1601).

Farley, Henry, *St. Paules-Church her bill for the Parliament* (London, 1621).

———. *The Complaint of Paules to All Christian Soules* (London, 1616).

Feltmakers Company, *To the most Honorable Assembly of the Commons House of Parliament. The humble Petition of the Feltmakers . . . for the prohibition of the importation of felts* (London, 1621).

———. *To the right honourable assembly of the Commons House of Parliament. The reasons mouing the hot-pressers to draw themselues into an orderly forme of gouernement under his Maiesties gracious protection* (London, 1621).

Great Yarmouth, *For the selling of herrings in and neere the towne of Yarmouth during the faire* (London, 1621).

Grocers Company, *To the Honorable howse of Commons in the high Courte of Parliament assembled* (London, 1621).

Hall, Joseph, *One of the sermons preach't to the Lords* (London, 1629).

Harris, John, *The Destruction of Sodome: A Sermon preached at a publicke Fast, before the honourable Assembly of the Commons House of Parliament.*

Herbert, Arnold et al., *An Abstract of a Case in Chancerie . . . against Lawrence Lownes* (London, 1624).

James I, *His Maiesties speech to both the houses of Parliament* (London, 1607).

———. *The Kings Maiesties speech . . . on Munday the 19. day of March 1603 being the first day of this present Parliament* (London and Edinburgh, 1604).

———. *The Kings Maiesties speech to the Lords and Commons* (London, 1610).

Laud, William, *A Sermon preached before his Majestie, on Sunday XIX of June, at*

Whitehall. Appointed to be preached at the opening of the Parliament. By the Bishop of S. Davids (London, 1625).

——. *A Sermon preached On Munday, the sixt of February at Westminster: At the opening of the Parliament. By the Bishop of S: Davids* (London, 1625).

——. *A sermon preached on Munday . . . at the opening of Parliament* (London, 1628).

Leather: A Discourse, tendered to the High Court of Parliament (London, 1629).

Leighton, Alexander, *An Appeal to the Parliament; or Sion's Plea against the Prelacie* (Amsterdam, 1629).

Lenthall, Sir William, *Mr Speaker his Speech to his Majestie* (London, 1640).

Merton College, Oxford, *Merton Colledge Case* (London, 1626).

Morgan, George, *A briefe of Morgans bill in Parliament* (London, 1624, 1625, 1626).

——. *George Morgan plaintife; William Megges, Richard Bowdler, William Turner, Thomas Ihones, Sir Iohn Bourcher, William Essington, and Robert Barlow . . . defendants* (London, 1621).

——. *The particulars of . . . 22600. l. sterling, owing the 20 of May 1612. for the allom account* (London, 1621).

Morley, Caleb, *To the most honorable assembly of the Commons House of Parliament a briefe of the petitioners cause* (London, 1621).

Most Exact Catalogue of the Lords . . . And Also the Commons (London, 1628).

Order and Manner of Sitting of the Lords . . . and also the Names of the Knights for Counties . . . (London, 1626).

Order and Manner of Sitting of the Lords . . . and also the Names of the Knights for Counties . . . (London, 1628).

Order and Manner of Sitting of the Lords . . . and also the Names of the Knights for Counties . . . (London, 1624).

Philopatris, *An Humble Petition offered to the . . . estates of the present Parliament* (London, 1606).

Powel, Gabriel, *A Consideration of the deprived and silenced ministers . . . exhibited in their late Supplication unto the . . . Parliament* (London, 1606).

Prayers for the Parliament (London, 1604).

Prayers for the Parliament (London, 1606).

Preston, John, *The Saints Qualification . . .* (London, 1634).

Reasons for the suppressing of the monopolizing patent granted to the Muscovia companie (London, 1621).

Record, Erasmus, *To the most honourable assemblie of the Commons House of Parliament, or to any member of the same. Erasmus Recorde humbly beseecheth this most Honourable Court of Parliament, for the confirmation of a decree in Chancery* (London, 1624).

——. *To the right honorable the Lords spirituall and temporall in this present Parliament assembled. The humble petition of Erasmus Record and Millicent Vaughan widow the administratrix of the goods, chattels and debts of Walter Vaughan deceased* (London, 1624).

Rogers, Griswell, *To the right reuerend and right honorable the Lords spirituall and temporall assembled in vpper House of this most high and honorable session of Parliament an abstract of the grieuances and oppressions done by Sir Arthur Ingram, Knight, and his agents, to Griswell Rogers, widow, and her poore orphan* (London, 1624).

Rous, Francis, *A Religious and Worth Speech spoken by Mr Rowse* (London, 1641).

Rudyerd, Sir Benjamin, *Sir Benjamin Rudierd his speech in behalf of the clergie* (London, 1628).

Russell, Thomas, *To the Kings most Excellent maiestie, the Lords Spirituall and Temporall, and the Commons in this present Parliament assembled* (1626).

Scott, Thomas, *A speech made in the lower house of Parliament, anno 1621. By Sir Edward Cicill Colonell* (London, 1621).

Shrewsbury Drapers, *To the right hon: the Lords Spirituall and Temporall, of the higher House of Parliament. The humble petition of the drapers of the towne of Shrewsbury* (London, 1621).

Starkey, Ralph, *The briefe Contents of Ralph Starkyes Bill, exhibited in Parliament* (London, 1624).

Stationers Company, *To the Honourable House of Commons in this present Parliament assembled. The humble petition of the Company of Stationers of the City of London* (London, 1621).

———. *The Particular grieuances of those His Maiesties subiects throughout England and Wales, which lye vnder the oppression of George Woods patent for the sole printing vpon linnen cloth* (London, 1621).

———. *To the right honourable the house of Commons assembled in Parliament. The humble petition of Thomas Man . . .* (London, 1621).

Sydenham, Humphrey, *Moses and Aaron or the Affinitie of Ciuill and Ecclesiasticke Power. A Sermon intended for the Parliament held at Oxon, August 7 1625. But by reason of the sudden and unhappy dissolution, then, not preach't, but since upon occasion, was; at St Maries in Oxford . . .* (London, 1626).

Symcocke, Thomas, and Roger Wood, *An abstract of His Maiesties letters patents granted, vnto Roger Wood and Thomas Symcocke, for the sole printing of paper and parchment on the one side* (London, 1621).

Taylor, John, *The Subjects Joy for the Parliament* (London, 1641).

Tewkesbury Corporation, *Reasons, why the county of Glocester, ought to ioyne with the towne of Tewkesbury, in repayring of a decayed bridge* (London, 1621).

The Contents of the Water-mans bill into the Parliament house (London, 1621).

The Copies of two speeches in Parliament. The one by Iohn Glanvill Esquire. The other by Sir Henry Martin Knight (London, 1628).

The humble petition of the poor prisoners in the loathsome hole of Woodstreete Compter (London, 1614).

The Manner of the Sitting of the Lords Spirituall and Temporall, as Peeres of the Realme in the Higher House of Parliament . . . (London, 1628).

The Names of all the high sheriffes of the severall counties, within England Wales, chosen and appoynted for the yeare 1628 (London, 1628).

The Names of the Knights, Citizens and Burgesses . . . now sitting in Parliament (London, 1628).

The Names of the knights, citizens, burgesses for the Boroughs . . . for the High Court of Parliament, begun at Westminster the 18 day of June . . . 1625 (London, 1625).

The Petition and Remonstrance of the Governor and Company of Merchants of London trading to the East Indies (London, 1628).

Thomas, Joan, *The Humble Petition of Joane Thomas, a poore distressed and oppressed Widow* (London, c.1624).

Tilers and Bricklayers, *To the most Honourable Assemblie of the High Court of Parliament . . .* (London, 1614).

To all their good Benefactors and Releevers in or about this Honorable City of London (London, 1627).

To the Kings most excellent Maiestie: the honorable lords, knights and burgesses assembled in Parliament. The humble petition of your maiesties . . . prisoners for debt (London, 1621).

To the most honourable assembly of the Commons House of Parliament. The humble petition of distressed prisoners in the King's Bench . . . (London, 1624).

To the right honorable the knights . . . of Parliament. The humble petition of the parishioners of Winwick (London, 1621).

Ussher, James, *A Sermon preached before the Commons House of Parliament in St Margarets Church at Westminster, the 18 of February 1620* (London, 1621).

Villiers, George, *April 4. The Proceeding of Parliament* (London, 1628).

Wharfingers Company, *To the honorable assembly of the Commons house of Parliament, and to the committees, for grieuances of the same house. The humble petition of Edward Hopkins, William Barwell, Iohn Bellamy, Robert Vilet, Iohn Walter, Robert Wright, and other wharfingers in and neere the Cittie of London* (London, 1621).

Williams, John, *A sermon preached in the collegiat church of S. Peter* (London, 1628).

Woodmongers Company, *To the honorable assembly of the Commons house of Parliament, & to the committees for grieuances of the same house: the reasons why the wood-mongers should continue their gouernment of carres and carre-roomes* (London, 1621).

——. *To the honorable assembly of the Commons house of Parliament, and to the committees for grieuances of the same house: the answere of the master, wardens and fellowship of woodmongers, London, to the complaint of some few wharfingers and others, whereof, some are forraine, and some free of the same citie* (London, 1621).

PRINTED PRIMARY SOURCES.

Acts of the Privy Council, ed. John Roche Dascent (London, 1890).

A forme of prayer . . . to be used the 27 of March. Being the day of His Highnesse entry to this kingdome (London, 1626).

A fourme of prayer . . . (London, 1604).

A fourme of prayer . . . every fift of August: Being the day of his Highnesse happy deliverance from the traiterous and bloody attempt of the Earle of Gowry (London, 1623).

A fourme of prayer, with thankes gevyng, to be used every yeere, the 17 of November beyng the day of the queenes maiesties entrie to her raigne (London, 1576).

A prayer used in the queenes maiesties house and chappell, for the prosperitie of the French King assayled by rebels 21 Aug. An. 1590 (London, 1590).

Aubrey, John, *Aubrey's Brief Lives*, ed. Oliver Lawson Dick (Ann Arbor, 1957, reprint Jaffrey, NH, 1999).

Barnfield, Richard, *The Affectionate Shepherd, Containing the Complaint of Daphnis for the love of Ganymede* (London, 1594).

Birch, T. E., ed., *The Court and Times of Charles I* (2 vols., London, 1848).

———. *The Court and Times of James I* (2 vols., London, 1849).

Bourcier, Elisabeth, ed., *The Dairy of Sir Simonds S'Dwes, 1622–1624* (Paris, 1974).

Braithwaite, Richard, *Times Curtaine Drawne or the Anatomie of Vanitie. With other choice poems, entitled; Health from Helicon* (London, 1621).

Bülow, Gottfried von, trans, 'Journey through England and Scotland made by Lupold von Wedel in the Years 1584 and 1585,' *Transactions of the Royal Historical Society* (new ser., 9, 1895).

Calendar of State Papers Domestic, ed. M. A. E. Green et al. (81 vols., London, 1845–1947).

Calendar of State Papers Venetian, ed. H. F. Brown and A. B. Hinde (28 vols., Lonon, 1900–40).

Clay, William Keating, ed., *Liturgical Services: Liturgies and Occasional Forms of Prayer set forth in the Reign of Queen Elizabeth* (Cambridge, 1847).

D'Ewes, Sir Simonds, *A Compleat Journal of the Votes, Speeches and Debates, Both of the House of Lords and House of Commons throughout the whole reign of Queen Elizabeth* (London, 1693).

D'Urfey, Thomas, *Wit and Mirth: or Pills to Purge Melancholy* (London, 1699).

Davis, J. Conway, ed., *Catalogue of Manuscripts in the Library of the Honourable Society of the Inner Temple* (3 vols., London, 1972).

De Beer, E. S., ed., *The Diary and Correspondence of John Evelyn* (London, 1889).

De Villiers, Lady Evangeline, ed., 'The Hastings Journal of the Parliament of 1621,' *Camden Miscellany* XX (Camden, 3rd ser., 1953).

Dekker, Thomas, *The dead tearme. Or, Westminsters complaint for long vacations and short termes. Written in manner of a dialogue betweene the two cityes London and Westminster* (London, 1608).

Dewar, Mary, ed., *De Republica Anglorum by Sir Thomas Smith* (Cambridge, 1982).

Earle, John, *Micro-cosmographie* (London, 1628).

English Reports (178 vols., Edinburgh, 1900–30).

Exwood, M., and H. L. Lehman, eds., *The Journal of William Schellinks' Travels in England 1660–1663* (Camden Society, 5th ser., 1, London, 1993).

Foster, Elizabeth Read, ed., *Proceedings in Parliament 1610* (2 vols., New Haven, 1966).

Fuller, Thomas, *Ephemeris Parliamentaria* (London, 1654).

Gardiner, Samuel Rawson, ed., *Notes of the Debates in the House of Lords . . . 1621* (Camden old ser., 103, 1870).

———. *Notes of the Debates in the House of Lords . . . 1624 and 1626* (Camden new ser., 24, 1879).

———. *Parliamentary Debates in 1610* (Camden old ser., 81, 1862).

Green, Mary Anne Everett, *Diary of John Rous incumbent of Santon Downham, Suffolk, from 1625–1642* (Camden Society, old ser., 66, 1856).

Grimston, Edward, trans., Jean Guillemard, *A Combat betwixt Man and Death* (London, 1621).

———. Jean François Le Petit's *A Generall Historie of the Netherlands* (London, 1627).

Grosart, Alexander B., ed., *An Apology for Socrates and Negotium Posterorum by Sir John Eliot* (2 vols., 1881).

Hakewill, William, *The Manner How Statutes are Enacted in Parliament by Passing of Bills* (London, 1641).

Hall, Arthur, *A letter sent by F.A. touchyng the proceedings in a private quareli and unkindnesse betweene Arthur Hall, and Melchisedech Mallerie . . .* (London, 1576).

Halliwell, J. O., ed., *The Autobiography and Correspondence of Sir Simonds D'Ewes during the Reigns of James I and Charles I* (2 vols., London, 1845).

Hartley, T. E., ed., *Proceedings in the Parliaments of Elizabeth I* (3 vols., Leicester, 1981–95).

Hawarde, John, *Les Reportes del in Camera Stellata, 1593–1609* (London, 1894).

Henderson, Jeffrey, ed. and trans., Aristophanes, *Lysistrata* (Loeb Classical Library, 179, Cambridge MA, 2000).

Historical Manuscripts Commission.
11th Report, Appendix II.
Cowper.
Exeter.
Finch.
Hatfield.
House of Lords.

Hughes, Paul and James F. Larkin, *Tudor Royal Proclamations* (3 vols., New Haven, 1964–69).

Hull, Felix, ed., *A Calendar of the White and Black Books of the Cinque Ports, 1432–1955* (London, 1966).

Jackson, William, A., ed., *Records of the Stationers' Company 1602–1640* (London, 1957).

Jansson, Maija, ed., *Proceedings in Parliament 1614* (Philadelphia, 1988).

———. *Proceedings of the Long Parliament: House of Commons,* Volume IV (Rochester, 2003).

Jansson, Maija, and William B. Bidwell, eds., *Proceedings in Parliament 1625* (New Haven, 1987).

——. *Proceedings in Parliament 1626* (4 vols., New Haven, 1991–96).

Jesus, Fray Francisco de. *El hecho de los tratados matrimonio pretendidio porel principe de Gales con la serenissima infante de España Maria, yomado desde sus principios para demostración de la verdad, y ajustado con los papeles orignales desde consta por el maestro F. Franciso de Jesus, predicador de rey nuestro señor. Narrative of the Spanish marriage treaty.* Ed. S. R. Gardiner (Camden Society, old ser., 101, 1869).

Johnson, Robert C., Maija Jansson Cole, Mary Frear Keeler, and William B. Bidwell, eds., *Commons Debates 1628 and Lords Proceedings 1628* (6 vols., 1977–83).

Jonson, Ben, *Epicoene* (London, 1620).

——. *Workes* (London, 1616).

Jones, R. A., and G. B. Harrison, eds., *De Maisse: A Journal of All that was Accomplished by Monsieur de Maisse, Ambassador in England from King Henry IV to Queen Elizabeth Anno Domini 1597* (London, 1931).

Journals of the House of Commons (17 vols., London, 1742).

Journals of the House of Lords (19 vols., London, 1767).

Knighton, C. S., ed., *Acts of the Dean and Chapter of Westminster, 1543–1609* (Westminster Abbey Record ser., 2, Woodbridge, 1999).

Kyle, Chris R., ed., *Parliament, Politics and Elections, 1604–1648* (Camden Society, 5th ser., 17, 2001).

Larkin, James F., ed., *Stuart Royal Proclamations,* Volume II, *Royal Proclamations of King Charles I 1625–1646* (Oxford, 1983).

Larkin, James F., and Paul Hughes, eds., *Stuart Royal Proclamations: Royal Proclamations of King James I* (Oxford, 1973).

Latham, R., and W. Matthews, eds., *The Dairy of Samuel Pepys* (11 vols., London, 1970–83).

Les Voyages de Monsieur de Moncoys (4 vols., Paris, 1695).

Letters and Papers, Foreign and Domestic, Henry VIII (21 vols., London, 1862–1932).

Lyly, John *Campaspe, palyed before the Queenes maiestie on newyeares day at night, by her Maiesties children, and the children of Paules* (London, 1584).

——. *Midas Plaied before the Queenes Maiestie upon Twelfe day at night, by the Children of Paules* (London, 1592).

Manning, C. R., 'News-Letters from Sir Edmund Moundeford, Knt., M.P., to Framlingham Gawdy, Esq., 1627–1633', *Norfolk Archaeology* (V, 1859).

Manuscripts of the House of Lords.

Matthew, Sir Toby, *A collection of letters, made by Sr Tobie Mathews Kt. With a character of the most excellent lady, Lucy, Countesse of Carleile: by the same author. To which are added many letters of his own, to severall persons of honour, who were contemporary with him* (London, 1660).

McClure, N. E., ed., *The Letters of John Chamberlain* (2 vols., Philadelphia, 1939).

Mennes, Sir John, James Smith, Thomas Park, and Edward Du Bois, *Facetiae: Musarum Deliciae . . . and Wit Restor'd* (2 vols., London, 1817).

Nash, Thomas, *The Terrors of the Night* (London, 1594).

Notestein, Wallace, and Frances Helen Relf, eds., *Commons Debates for 1629* (Minneapolis, 1921).

Notestein, Wallace, Frances Helen Relf, and Hartley Simpson, eds., *Commons Debates 1621* (7 vols., New Haven, 1935).

Prayers and thankesgiving . . . from the most traiterous and bloody intended massacre by gunpowder (London, 1606).

Ransome, David R., ed., 'The Parliamentary Papers of Nicholas Ferrar, 1624,' *Camden Miscellany XXXIII* (Camden, 5th ser., 7, 1996).

Roberts, G., ed., *Diary of Walter Yonge esq., Justice of the Peace and MP for Honiton . . . 1604–1628* (Camden Society, old ser., 41, 1848).

Rous, Francis, *A Religious and Worthy Speech spoken by Mr Rous in Parliament* (London, 1641).

Rudyerd, Sir Benjamin, *Le Prince d'Amour* (London, 1660).

Scott, Thomas, *Vox Populi. Or, Newes from Spayne* (London, 1620).

Simpson, E. M., and G. R. Potter, eds., *The Sermons of John Donne* (10 vols., Berkeley 1962).

Sims, Catherine Strateman, ed., 'The Speaker of the House of Commons: An Early Seventeenth Century Tractate,' *American Historical Review* (45, 1, 1939), pp. 90–95.

Snow, Vernon F., ed., *Parliament in Elizabethan England: John Hooker's Order and Usage* (New Haven, 1977).

Spalding, Ruth, ed., *The Diary of Bulstrode Whitelocke 1605–1675* (Records of Social and Economic History, n.s. XIII, Oxford, 1990).

Spedding, James, R. L. Ellis, and D. D. Heath, eds., *The Works of Francis Bacon* (14 vols., London, 1857–74).

Strassler, Robert B., ed., *The Landmark Thucydidies* (New York, 1996).

Taylor, John, *Superbiae Flagellum, or, The Whip of Pride* (London, 1621).

———. *Taylors Goose* (London, 1621).

The Deserved Downfall of a Corrupted Conscience (London, 1621).

The New Tydings out of Italie, George Vessler, to be sold by Petrus Keerius dwelling in Calvert Street (Amsterdam, 1620).

The Proceeding of the parliament being this day related to the King . . . (London, 1628).

Thompson, Christopher, ed., *Sir Nathaniel Rich's Diary of Proceedings in the House of Commons in 1624* (Orsett, Essex, 1985).

———. *The Holles Account of Proceedings in the House of Commons in 1624* (Orsett, Essex, 1985).

Tyrwhitt, Thomas, ed., *Proceedings and Debates in the House of Commons in 1620 and 1621 by Edward Nicholas* (2 vols., Oxford, 1766).

Willson, David Harris, ed., *The Parliamentary Diary of Robert Bowyer 1606–1607* (New York, 1971).

Wither, George, *Wither's motto* (London, 1621).

SECONDARY LITERATURE.

Adams, Simon, 'Captain Thomas Gainsford, the "Vox Spiritus" and the *Vox Populi*,' *Bulletin of the Institute of Historical Research* (49, 1976), pp. 141–44.

Archer, Ian, 'The London Lobbies in the Sixteenth Century,' *Historical Journal* (31, 1988), pp. 17–44.

Arnold, Oliver, 'Absorption and Representation: Mapping England in the Early Modern House of Commons,' in Andrew Gordon and Bernhard Klein, eds., *Literature, Mapping and the Politics of Space in Early Modern Britain* (Cambridge, 2001), pp. 15–34.

——. *The Third Citizen: Shakespeare's Theater of the Early Modern House of Commons* (Baltimore, 2007).

Ashton, Robert, 'Jacobean Free Trade Again,' *Past and Present* (43, 1969), pp. 151–57.

——. 'The Parliamentary Agitation for Free Trade in the Opening Years of James I,' *Past and Present* (38, 1967), pp. 40–55.

Ball, J. N., 'Sir John Eliot in Parliament, 1624–1629,' in Kevin Sharpe, ed., *Faction and Parliament: Essays on Early Stuart History* (Oxford, 1978), pp. 173–208.

——. 'Sir John Eliot at the 1625 Parliament,' *Bulletin of the Institute of Historical Research* (28, 1955), pp. 113–27.

Barron, Caroline, 'London and Parliament in the Lancastrian Period,' *Parliamentary History* (9, 1990), pp. 343–67.

Basu, Sammy, '"A Little Discourse *Pro & Con*": Levelling Laughter and Its Puritan Criticism.' *International Review of Social History* (suppl., 15, 2007), pp. 95–113.

Beal, Peter, *In Praise of Scribes: Manuscripts and Their Makers in Seventeenth-century England* (Oxford, 1998).

Beale, J. H., *A Bibliography of Early English Lawbooks* (Cambridge, MA, 1926).

Bellany, Alastair, 'Libels in Action: Ritual, Subversion and the English Literary Underground,' in Tim Harris, ed., *The Politics of the Excluded, c.1500–1850* (Basingstoke, 2001), pp. 99–124.

——. 'Railing Rhymes Revisited: Libels, Scandals and Early Stuart Politics,' *History Compass* (5, 4, 2007), pp. 1136–79.

——. '"Raylinge Rymes and Vaunting Verse": Libellous Politics in Early Stuart England,' in Kevin Sharpe and Peter Lake, eds., *Culture and Politics in Early Stuart England* (London, 1994), pp. 285–310, 367–71.

——. 'The Embarrassment of Libels: Perceptions and Representations of Verse Libeling in Early Stuart England,' in Peter Lake and Steven Pincus, eds., *The Politics of the Public Sphere in Early Modern England* (Manchester, 2007), pp. 144–67.

——. *The Politics of Court Scandal in Early Modern England* (Cambridge, 2002).

Bindoff, S. T., ed., *The House of Commons 1509–1558* (3 vols., London, 1982).

Blair, Claude, 'The Armourers' Bill of 1581: The Making of Arms and Armour in Sixteenth-Century London,' *Journal of the Arms and Armour Society* (12, 1, 1986), pp. 20–61.

Blomefield, Francis, *Topographical History of Norfolk* (5 vols., Fersfield, 1739–75).

Bond, Maurice F., 'The Clerks of the Parliaments, 1509–1953,' *English Historical Review* (73, 1, 1958), pp. 78–85.

Campbell, Thomas P., *Henry VIII and the Art of Majesty: Tapestries at the Tudor Court* (New Haven, 2007).

Cockayne, Emily, *Hubbub: Filth, Noise and Stench in England, 1600–1770* (New Haven, 2007).

Cogswell, Thomas, 'John Felton, Popular Political Culture, and the Assassination of the Duke of Buckingham,' *Historical Journal* (49, 2, 2006), pp. 357–85.

———. *The Blessed Revolution: English Politics and the Coming of War, 1621–1624* (Cambridge, 1989).

———. 'The People's Love: The Duke of Buckingham and Popularity,' in Thomas Cogswell, Richard Cust, and Peter Lake, eds., *Politics, Religion and Popularity in Early Stuart Britain: Essays in Honour of Conrad Russell* (Cambridge, 2002), pp. 211–34.

———. 'The Politics of Propaganda: Charles I and the People in the 1620s,' *Journal of British Studies* (29, 3, 1990), pp. 187–215.

———. 'Thomas Middleton and the Court, 1624: *A Game at Chess* in Context,' *Huntington Library Quarterly* (47, 1984), pp. 273–88.

———. 'Underground Verse and the Transformation of Early Stuart Political Culture,' *HLQ* (60, 1997), pp. 303–26.

Cogswell, Thomas, and Peter Lake, 'Buckingham Does the Globe: Henry VIII and the Politics of Popularity in the 1620s,' *Shakespeare Quarterly* (60, 3, 2009), pp. 253–78.

Colclough, David, *Freedom of Speech in Early Stuart England* (Cambridge, 2005).

———. '"The Muses Recreation": John Hoskyns and the Manuscript Culture of the Seventeenth Century,' *Huntington Library Quarterly* (61, 2000), pp. 360–400.

Craig, John, 'Psalms, Groans and Dogwhippers: The Soundscape of Worship in the English Parish Church, 1547–1642,' in Will Coster and Andrew Spicer, eds., *Sacred Space in Early Modern Europe* (Cambridge, 2005), pp. 104–23.

Cressy, David, *England on Edge: Crisis and Revolution 1640–1642* (Oxford, 2006).

Croft, Pauline, 'Capital Life: Members of Parliament outside the House,' in Thomas Cogswell, Richard Cust, and Peter Lake, eds., *Politics, Religion and Popularity in Early Stuart Britain* (Cambridge, 2002), pp. 65–83.

———. 'Free Trade and the House of Commons, 1605–6,' *Economic History Review* (2nd ser., 28, 1, 1975), pp. 17–27.

———. 'Libels, Popular Literacy and Public Opinion in Early Modern England,' *Historical Research* (68, 1995), pp. 268–85.

———. 'Parliamentary Preparations, September 1605: Robert Cecil, Earl of Salisbury on Free Trade and Monopolies,' *Parliamentary History* (6, 1987), pp. 127–32.

———. 'Parliament, Purveyance and the City of London, 1559–1608,' *Parliamentary History* (4, 1985), pp. 9–34.

――. 'The Reputation of Robert Cecil: Libels, Political Opinion and Popular Awareness in the Early Seventeenth Century,' *Transactions of the Royal Historical Society* (6th ser., 1, 1991), pp. 43–69.

Cromartie, A. D. T., 'The Printing of Parliamentary Speeches November 1640–July 1642,' *Historical Journal* (33, 1, 1990), pp. 23–44.

Cust, Richard, 'Charles I and Popularity,' in Thomas Cogswell, Richard Cust, and Peter Lake, eds., *Politics, Religion and Popularity in Early Stuart Britain: Essays in Honour of Conrad Russell* (Cambridge, 2002), pp. 235–58.

――. 'News and Politics in Early Seventeenth Century England,' *Past and Present* (112, 1986), pp. 60–90.

――. '"Patriots" and "Popular" Spirits: Narratives of Conflict in Early Stuart Politics,' in Nicholas Tyacke, ed., *The English Revolution C.1590–1720: Politics, Religion and Communities* (Manchester: Manchester University Press, 2007), pp. 43–61.

――. *The Forced Loan and English Politics, 1626–1628* (Oxford, 1987).

――. 'The "Public Man" in Late Tudor and Early Stuart England,' in Peter Lake and Steven Pincus, eds., *The Politics of the Public Sphere in Early Modern England* (Manchester, 2007), pp. 116–43.

Dahl, Folke, *A Bibliography of English Corantos and Periodical Newsbooks* (Boston, 1977).

Davies, Matthew, 'Lobbying Parliament: The London Companies in the Fifteenth Century,' *Parliamentary History* (23, 2004), pp. 136–48.

Dean, David M., 'Image and Ritual in the Tudor Parliaments,' in Dale Hoak, ed., *Tudor Political Culture* (Cambridge, 1995), pp. 243–71.

――. *Law-Making and Society in Late Elizabethan England* (Cambridge, 1996).

――. 'Locality and Parliament: The Legislative Activities of Devon MPs,' in Todd Gray, Margery Rowe, and Audrey Erskine, eds., *Tudor and Stuart Devon: The Common Estate and Government* (Exeter, 1992), pp. 139–62.

――. 'London Lobbies and Parliament: The Case of the Brewers and Coopers in the Parliament of 1593,' *Parliamentary History* (8, 1989), pp. 341–65.

――. 'Parliament, Privy Council, and Local Politics in Elizabethan England: The Yarmouth-Lowestoft Fishing Dispute,' *Albion* (22, 1990), pp. 39–64.

――. 'Pressure Groups and Lobbies in the Elizabethan and Early Jacobean Parliaments,' *Parliaments, Estates and Representation* (11, 1991), pp. 139–52.

――. 'Public or Private? London, Leather and Legislation in Elizabethan England,' *Historical Journal* (31, 1988), pp. 525–48.

Elton, G. R., *The Parliament of England 1559–1581* (Cambridge, 1986).

――. 'The Sessional Printing of Statutes, 1484–1547,' in E. W. Ives, R. J. Knecht, and J. J. Scarisbrick, eds., *Wealth and Power in Tudor England: Essays Presented to S. T. Bindoff* (London, 1978), pp. 68–86.

――. 'Tudor Government, the Points of Contact, 1: Parliament,' *Transactions of the Royal Historical Society* (5th ser., 24, 1974), pp. 183–200.

Fletcher, Anthony, *The Outbreak of the English Civil War* (1981).

Forster, J., *Sir John Eliot: A Biography* (2 vols., London, 1864).

Foster, Elizabeth Read, 'Printing and the Petition of Right,' *Journal of British Studies* (14, 1, 1974), pp. 21–45.

——. 'Printing the Petition of Right,' *Huntington Library Quarterly* (38, 1974), pp. 81–83.

——. 'Staging a Parliament in Early Stuart England,' in Peter Clark, Alan G. G. Smith, and Nicholas Tyacke, eds., *The English Commonwealth 1547–1640* (Leicester, 1979), pp. 129–46, 239–48.

——. *The House of Lords, 1603–1649* (Chapel Hill, 1983).

——. 'The Painful Labour of Mr Elsyng,' *Transactions of the American Philosophical Society* (new ser., 62, 8, 1972).

——. 'The Procedure of the House of Commons against Patents and Monopolies, 1621–1624,' in W. A. Aiken and B. D. Henning, eds., *Conflict in Stuart England: Essays in Honour of Wallace Notestein* (London, 1960), pp. 57–85.

Frank, Joseph, *The Beginnings of the English Newspaper, 1620–1660* (Cambridge, MA).

Fraser, Ian H. C., 'The Agitation in the Commons, 2 March 1629, and the Interrogation of the Leaders of the Anti-Court Group,' *Bulletin of the Institute of Historical Research* (30, 1957), pp. 86–95.

Frearson, Michael, 'The Distribution and Readership of London Corantos in the 1620s,' in Robin Myers and Michael Harris, eds., *Serials and Their Readers* (Winchester, 1993), pp. 1–25.

French, J. Milton, 'George Wither in Prison,' *Proceedings of the Modern Language Association* (45, 4, 1930), pp. 959–66.

Gaskell, Philip, *A New Introduction to Bibliography* (Oxford, 1972).

Graves, Michael A. R., 'Elizabethan Men of Business Reconsidered,' in S. M. Jack and B. A. Masters, eds., *Protestants, Property, Puritans: Godly People Revisited* (*Parergon*, XIV, 1996), pp. 111–27.

——. 'The Management of the Elizabethan House of Commons: The Council's Men-of-Business,' *Parliamentary History* (2, 1983), pp. 11–38.

——. 'Managing Elizabethan Parliaments,' in David M. Dean and Norman L. Jones, eds., *The Parliaments of Elizabethan England* (Oxford, 1990).

——. *Thomas Norton: The Parliament Man* (Oxford, 1994).

——. 'Thomas Norton the Parliament Man: An Elizabethan MP, 1559–1581,' *Historical Journal* (23, 1980), pp. 17–35.

——. *The Tudor Parliaments: Crown, Lords and Commons, 1485–1603* (Harlow, 1985).

Green, Edwin, 'The Vintners' Lobby, 1552–1568,' *Guildhall Studies in London History* (1, 2, 1974), pp. 47–58.

Greg, W. W., ed., *A Companion to Arber* (Oxford, 1967).

Gurr, Andrew, *Playgoing in Shakespeare's London* (Cambridge, 1987).

Halasz, Alexandra, *The Marketplace of Print: Pamphlets and the Public Sphere in Early Modern England* (Cambridge, 1997).

Hammer, Paul E. J., 'The Smiling Crocodile: The Earl of Essex and Late-Elizabethan Popularity,' in Peter Lake and Steven Pincus, eds., *The Politics of the Public Sphere in Early Modern England* (Manchester, 2007), pp. 95–115.

Hart, James S., *Justice upon Petition: The House of Lords and the Reformation of Justice 1621–1675* (London, 1991).

Hasler, P. W., ed., *The House of Commons 1558–1603* (3 vols., London, 1981).

Hawkyard, Alasdair, 'From Painted Chamber to St. Stephen's Chapel: The Meeting Places of the House of Commons at Westminster until 1603,' in Clyve Jones and Sean Kelsey, eds., *Housing Parliament: Dublin, Edinburgh and Westminster, Parliamentary History* (Edinburgh, 2002), pp. 62–84.

Hawkyard, Alasdair, and Maria Hayward, 'The Dressing and Trimming of the Parliament Chamber, 1509–1558,' *Parliamentary History* (29, 2, 2010), pp. 229–37.

Heinze, Rudolph W., 'Proclamations and Parliamentary Protest, 1539–1610,' in Delloyd J. Guth and John W. McKenna, eds., *Tudor Rule and Revolution* (Cambridge, 1982), pp. 237–59.

Henderson, Frances, 'Reading, and Writing, the Text of the Putney Debates,' in Michael Mendle, ed., *The Putney Debates of 1647: The Army, The Levellers and the English State* (Cambridge, 2001), pp. 36–50.

Henning, B. D., ed., *The House of Commons 1660–1690* (3 vols., London, 1983).

Hexter, J. H., 'Introduction,' in Hexter, ed., *Parliament and Liberty from the Reign of Elizabeth to the English Civil War* (Stanford, 1992), pp. 1–19.

——. 'Parliament under the Lens,' *British Studies Monitor* (3, 1972–73), pp. 4–15.

——. 'Quoting the Commons, 1604–1642,' in DeLloyd J. Guth and John W. McKenna, eds., *Tudor Rule and Revolution* (Cambridge, 1992), pp. 369–91.

Hirst, Derek, *The Representative of the People: Voters and Voting under the Early Stuarts* (Cambridge, 1975).

History of Parliament Trust, unpublished draft biographies and constituency articles.

Howard-Hill, T. H., 'Political Interpretations of Middleton's *Game at Chess* (1624),' *Yearbook of English Studies* (21, 1991).

Hoyle, R. W., 'Petitioning as Popular Politics in Sixteenth-Century England,' *Historical Research* (75, 190, 2002), pp. 365–83.

Hulme, Harold, 'The Leadership of Sir John Eliot in the Parliament of 1626,' *Journal of Modern History* (4, 1932), pp. 361–86.

——. *The Life of Sir John Eliot, 1592–1632: Struggle for Parliamentary Freedom* (New York, 1957).

——. 'The Winning of Freedom of Speech by the House of Commons,' *American Historical Review* (61, 4, 1956), pp. 825–53.

Hunneyball, Paul, 'Prince Charles's Council as Electoral Agent 1620–1624,' *Parliamentary History* (23, 2004), pp. 316–35.

Hunt, Arnold, *The Art of Hearing: Preachers and the Audiences in Early Modern England* (Cambridge, 2010).

Jameson, J. F., 'The Origin of the Standing Committee in American Legislative Bodies,' *Political Science Quarterly* (9, 1894), pp. 246–67.

Jansson, Maija, 'Dues Paid,' *Parliamentary History* (15, 1996), pp. 215–20.

Jones, Norman L., *God and the Moneylenders* (Blackwells, 1989).

Keeler, M. F., 'The Emergence of Standing Committees for Privileges and Returns,' *Parliamentary History* (1, 1982), pp. 25–46.

Kishlansky, Mark, *Parliamentary Selection: Social and Political Choice in Early Modern England* (Cambridge, 1986).

Kleineke, Hannes, 'Lobbying and Access: The Canons of Windsor and the Matter of the Poor Knights in the Parliament of 1485,' *Parliamentary History* (25, 2, 2006), pp. 145–59

Kyle, Chris R., 'Attendance, Apathy and Order?: Parliamentary Committees in Early Stuart England,' in Kyle and Peacey, eds., *Parliament at Work: Parliamentary Committees, Political Power and Public Access in Early Modern England* (Woodbridge, 2002), pp. 43–58.

———. '"But a New Button to an Old Coat": The Enactment of the Statute of Monopolies, 21 James I cap. 3,' *Journal of Legal History* (19, 3, 1998), pp. 203–23.

———. 'From Broadside to Pamphlet: Print and Parliament in the Late 1620s,' *Parliamentary History* (26, 1, 2007), pp. 17–29.

———. 'Henry VIII, or *All is True*: Shakespeare's "Favorite" Play,' in Laurie Maguire, ed., *How to Do Things with Shakespeare* (Oxford, 2008), pp. 82–100.

———. '"It will be a Scandal to show what we have done with such a number": House of Commons Attendance Lists, 1606–1628,' in Kyle, ed., *Parliament, Politics and Elections, 1604–1648* (Camden Society, 5th ser., 17, Cambridge, 2001), pp. 179–235.

———. '*Lex Loquens*: Legislation in the Parliament of 1624' (Ph.D. diss., Auckland University, 1994).

———. 'Parliament and the Palace of Westminster: An Exploration of Public Space in the Early Seventeenth Century,' in Clyve Jones and Sean Kelsey, eds., *Housing Parliament: Dublin, Edinburgh and Westminster*, *Parliament History* (21, 2, 2002), pp. 85–98.

———. 'Parliament and the Politics of Carting in Early Stuart London,' *London Journal* (27, 2, 2002), pp. 1–11.

Kyle, Chris R., and Jason Peacey, eds., *Breaking News: Renaissance Journalism and the Birth of the Newspaper* (Folger Shakespeare Library, University of Washington Press, Seattle, 2008).

———. *Parliament at Work: Parliamentary Committees, Political Power and Public Access in Early Modern England* (Woodbridge, 2002).

Lake, Peter, 'Constitutional Consensus and Puritan Opposition in the 1620s: Thomas Scott and the Spanish Match,' *Historical Journal* (25, 1982), pp. 805–25.

———. 'The Politics of "Popularity" and the Public Sphere: The Monarchial Republic of Elizabeth I Defends Itself,' in Peter Lake and Steven Pincus, eds., *The Politics of the Public Sphere in Early Modern England* (Manchester, 2007), pp. 59–94.

Lambert, Sheila, 'Coranto Printing in England: The First Newsbooks,' *Journal of Newspaper and Periodical History* (8, 1992), pp. 1–33.

———. 'Procedure in the House of Commons during the Early Stuart period,' *English Historical Review* (95, 377, 1980), pp. 759–73.

———. 'The Beginning of Printing for the House of Commons, 1640–42,' *Library* (6th ser., 3, 1981), pp. 43–61.

———. 'The Clerks and Records of the House of Commons, 1600–1640,' *Bulletin of the Institute of Historical Research* (43, 1970), pp. 215–31.

Lehmberg, Stanford E., *The Reformation Parliament, 1529–1536* (Cambridge, 1970).

Lesser, Zachary, *Renaissance Drama and the Politics of Publication: Readings in the English Book Trade* (Cambridge, 2004).

Levy, Fritz, 'How Information Spread amongst the Gentry, 1550–1640,' *Journal of British Studies* (21, 1982), pp. 11–34.

Lindquist, Eric, 'Supplement: The Bills against Purveyors,' *Parliamentary History* (4, 1985), pp. 35–43.

———. 'The King, the People and the House of Commons: The Problem of Early Jacobean Purveyance,' *Historical Journal* (31, 3, 1988), pp. 549–70.

Love, Harold, *Scribal Publication in Seventeenth Century England* (Oxford, 1993).

Love, Harold, and Arthur Marotti, 'Manuscript Transmission and Circulation' in David Loewenstein and Janel Mueller, eds., *The Cambridge History of Early Modern Literature* (Cambridge, 2002), pp. 55–80.

Luckyj, Christina, *A Moving Rhetoricke: Gender and Silence in Early Modern England* (Manchester, 2002).

Mack, Peter, *Elizabethan Rhetoric: Theory and Practice* (Cambridge, 2002).

McRae, Andrew, *Literature, Satire and the Early Stuart State* (Cambridge, 2004).

Mendle, Michael, 'News and the Pamphlet Culture of Mid-Seventeenth Century England,' in Brendan Dooley and Sabrina Baron, eds., *The Politics of Information in Early Modern Europe* (London, 2001), pp. 57–79.

———, ed., *The Putney Debates of 1647: The Army, the Levellers, and the English State* (Cambridge, 2001).

Merritt, J. F., *The Social World of Early Modern Westminster* (Manchester, 2005).

Miller, Helen, 'London and Parliament in the Reign of Henry VIII,' *BIHR* (35, 1962), pp. 128–49.

Mitchell, Williams M., *The Rise of the Revolutionary Party in the English House of Commons 1603–1629* (New York, 1957).

Moir, Thomas L., *The Addled Parliament of 1614* (Oxford, 1958).

Morrill, John, 'Getting over D'Ewes,' *Parliamentary History* (15, 1996), pp. 221–30.

———. 'Paying One's D'Ewes,' *Parliamentary History* (14, 1995), pp. 179–86.

———. 'Reconstructing the History of Early Stuart Parliaments,' *Archives* (21, 1994), pp. 67–72.

Neale, J. E., *Elizabeth I and Her Parliaments, 1559–1581* (London, 1953).
——. *Elizabeth I and Her Parliaments,* Volume II, *1584–1601* (London, reprint 1969).
——. 'The Commons Privilege of Free Speech in Parliament,' in R. W. Seton-Watson, ed., *Tudor Studies Presented to . . . Albert Frederick Pollard* (London, 1924), pp. 257–86.
——. 'The Commons' Journal of the Tudor Period,' *Transactions of the Royal Historical Society* (4th ser., 3, 1920), pp. 136–70.
——. *The Elizabethan House of Commons* (London, 1949).
Notestein, Wallace, *The House of Commons 1604–1610* (New Haven, 1971).
——. *The Winning of the Initiative by the House of Commons* (London, 1924).
O'Callaghan, Michelle, 'Literary Commonwealths: A 1614 Print Community, *The Shepheards Pipe* and *The Shepherds Hunting,*' *Seventeenth Century* (13, 2, 1998), pp. 103–23.
——. '"Now thou may'st speak freely": Entering the Public Sphere in 1614,' in Stephen Clucas and Rosalind Davies, eds., *The Crisis of 1614 and the Addled Parliament* (Aldershot, 2003), pp. 63–79.
——. 'Performing Politics: The Circulation of the Parliament Fart,' *Huntington Library Quarterly* (69, 1, 2006), pp. 121–38.
——. *The English Wits: Literature and Sociability in Early Modern England* (Cambridge, 2007).
——. *The 'shepheards nation': Jacobean Spenserians and Early Stuart Political Culture* (Oxford, 2000).
——. '"Talking Politics": Tyranny, Parliament, and Christopher Brooke's *The Ghost of Richard the Third* (1614), *Historical Journal* (41, 1, 1998), pp. 97–120.
Orlin, Lena Cowen, 'Temporary Lives in London Lodgings,' in Deborah Harkness and Jean Howard, eds., *The Places and Spaces of Early Modern London, Huntington Library Quarterly* (71, 1, 2008), pp. 219–42.
Oxford Dictionary of National Biography, ed. H. C. G. Matthew and Brian Harrison (60 vols., Oxford, 2004).
Patterson, Annabel, *The Long Parliament of Charles II* (New Haven, 2008).
Peacey, Jason, *Politicians and Pamphleteers: Propaganda during the English Civil Wars and Interregnum* (Aldershot, 2004).
Peck, Linda Levy, *Northampton, Patronage and Policy at the Court of James I* (London, 1982).
Pierce, Helen, *Unseemly Pictures: Graphic Satire and Politics in Early Modern England* (New Haven, 2008).
Plomer, H. R., *A Dictionary of the Booksellers and Printers Who Were at Work in England, Scotland and Ireland from 1641–1667* (London, 1907).
Powell, William, *John Pory, 1572–1636: The Life and Letters of a Man of Many Parts* (Chapel Hill, 1977).
Prestwich, Menna, *Cranfield: Politics and Profits under the Early Stuarts* (Oxford, 1966).

Randall, David, 'Joseph Mead, Novellante: News, Sociability and Credibility in Early Stuart England,' *Journal of British Studies* (45, 2, 2006), pp. 293–312.

Rawcliffe, Carole, 'Parliament and the Settlement of Disputes by Arbitration in the Later Middle Ages,' *Parliamentary History* (9, 1990), pp. 316–42.

Raymond, Joad, 'Describing Popularity in Early Modern England,' *Huntington Library Quarterly* (67, 1, 2004), pp. 101–29.

———. *Pamphlets and Pamphleteering in Early Modern Britain* (Cambridge, 2003).

———. *The Invention of the Newspaper* (Oxford, 1996).

Reeve, John, 'The Arguments in King's Bench in 1629 concerning the Imprisonment of John Selden and Other Members of the House of Commons,' *Journal of British Studies* (25, 3, 1986), pp. 264–87.

Reeve, L. J., *Charles I and the Road to Personal Rule* (Cambridge, 1989).

———. 'The Legal Status of the Petition of Right,' *Historical Journal* (29, 2, 1986), pp. 257–77.

Ruigh, Robert E., *The Parliament of 1624: Politics and Foreign Policy* (Cambridge, MA, 1971).

Russell, Conrad, *Parliaments and English Politics 1621–1629* (Oxford, 1979).

———. *The Addled Parliament of 1614: The Limits of Revision* (The Stenton Lectures, Reading, 1991).

———. *The Causes of the English Civil War: The Ford Lectures delivered at the University of Oxford, 1987–1988* (Oxford, 1990).

———. *The Fall of the British Monarchies* (Oxford, 1991).

———. *Unrevolutionary England 1603–1642* (London, 1990).

Saul, A., 'The Herring Industry at Great Yarmouth,' *Norfolk Archaeology* (38, 1981), pp. 33–43.

Scott, David, *Politics and War in the Three Stuart Kingdoms, 1637–1642* (Basingstoke, 2003).

Shaaber, Matthias A., *Some Forerunners of the Newspaper in England, 1476–1622* (Philadelphia, 1929).

Shapiro, I. A., 'The Mermaid Club,' *Modern Language Review* (45, 1, 1950), pp. 6–17.

Sharpe, Kevin, 'Crown, Parliament and Locality: Government and Communication in Early Stuart England,' *English Historical Review* (101, 1986), pp. 321–50.

———. *The Personal Rule of Charles I* (New Haven, 1992).

———, ed., *Faction and Parliament: Essays on Early Stuart History* (Oxford, 1978).

Sherman, William H., *John Dee: The Politics of Reading and Writing in the English Renaissance* (Amherst, 1995).

Siebert, Frederick Seaton, *Freedom of the Press in England 1476–1776: The Rise and Decline of Government Control* (Urbana, 1965).

Skerpan, Elizabeth, *The Rhetoric of Politics in the English Revolution* (Columbia, MO, 1992).

Skinner, Quentin, 'Why Does Laughter Matter to Philosophy?' The Passmore Lecture, Australian National University, December, 2000.

Smith, Bruce R., *The Acoustic World of Early Modern England* (Chicago, 1999).

Smith, David L., *The Stuart Parliaments, 1603–1689* (London, 1999).

Stallybrass, Peter, Roger Chartier, J. Franklin Mowery, and Heather Wolfe, 'Hamlet's Tables and the Technologies of Writing in Renaissance England,' *Shakespeare Quarterly* (55, 2004), pp. 379–419.

Thomas, Keith, *Religion and the Decline of Magic* (London, 1971).

———. 'The Place of Laughter in Tudor and Stuart England,' *Times Literary Supplement* (21 January 1977), pp. 77–81.

Thompson, Christopher, *The Debate on Freedom of Speech in the House of Commons in February 1621* (Orsett, 1985).

Thrush, Andrew, 'The House of Lords' Record Repository and the Clerk of the Parliaments' House: A Tudor Achievement,' *Parliamentary History* (21, 3, 2002), pp. 367–73.

Tilley, Maurice, *Elizabethan Proverb Lore in Lyly's Euphues and in Pettie's Petite Pallace with Parallels from Shakespeare* (New York, 1926).

Tite, Colin G. C., *Impeachment and Parliamentary Judicature in Early Stuart England* (London, 1974).

———. *The Manuscript Library of Sir Robert Cotton* (London, 1994).

Tittler, Robert, 'Elizabethan Towns and the "Points of Contact,"' *Parliamentary History* (8, 2, 1989), pp. 275–88.

———. 'The English Fishing Industry in the Sixteenth Century, the Case of Great Yarmouth,' *Albion* (9, 1977), pp. 40–60.

Watt, Tessa, *Cheap Print and Popular Piety* (Cambridge, 1991).

Whitt, P. B., 'New Light on Sir William Cornwallis,' *Review of English Studies* (8, 30, 1932), pp. 155–69.

Willson, David Harris, *The Privy Councillors in the House of Commons, 1604–1629* (New York, 1971).

Yerby, George, *People and Parliament: Representative Rights and the English Revolution* (Basingstoke, 2008).

Zaller, Robert, *The Discourse of Legitimacy in Early Modern England* (Stanford, 2007).

———. *The Parliament of 1621: A Study in Constitutional Conflict* (Berkeley, 1971).

Zaret, David, *Origins of Democratic Culture: Printing, Petitions and the Public Sphere in Early-Modern England* (Princeton, 2000).

Index